Against Extinction

Against Extinction

The Story of Conservation

William M Adams

FAUNA & FLORA
International
Conserving wildlife since 1903

London • Sterling, VA

First published by Earthscan in the UK and USA in 2004

ISBN: 1-84407-056-5 paperback
       1-84407-055-7 hardback

Typesetting by MapSet Ltd, Gateshead, UK
Printed and bound in the UK by Creative Print and Design Wales
Cover design by Susanne Harris
Cover photo and interior photos by Juan Pablo Moreiras. Copyright © Juan Pablo
Moreiras/Fauna & Flora International

For a full list of publications please contact:

Earthscan
8–12 Camden High Street
London, NW1 0JH, UK
Tel: +44 (0)20 7387 8558
Fax: +44 (0)20 7387 8998
Email: earthinfo@earthscan.co.uk
Web: **www.earthscan.co.uk**

22883 Quicksilver Drive, Sterling, VA 20166-2012, USA

Earthscan publishes in association with WWF-UK and the International Institute for
Environment and Development

A catalogue record for this book is available from the British Library

Library of Congress Cataloging-in-Publication Data

Adams, W.M. (William Mark), 1955-.
    Against extinction : the story of conservation / William M Adams.
        p. cm.
    Includes bibliographical references and index.
    ISBN 1-84407-056-5 (cloth) – ISBN 1-84407-055-7 (pbk.)
    I. Nature conservation–History. I. Title.

QH75.A346 2004
333.72–dc22

                                                                                2004021888

This book is printed on elemental chlorine-free paper

Contents

Foreword

Earl of Cranbrook, President, Fauna & Flora International

The United Kingdom, to its detriment, has lacked a Teddy Roosevelt. Among our 20th century Prime Ministers, none has shown himself or herself to be a 'conservationist' in Bill Adams' sense of holding a passion for living things, based on personal engagement, and a desire to solve the self-evident crisis in nature and wildlife management. Indeed, as Lord Bellwin remarked at Second Reading (*Hansard*, 16 December 1980, col 983), until the Wildlife and Countryside Act of 1981, nature conservation was hardly seen to be the business of the national government.

Roosevelt was inspired by the losses of big game and wild habitat in the frontier lands of his own country. In Britain it was not the excesses of hunters at home that sparked concern, but the destruction on the frontiers of the rapidly expanding empire, notably in Africa. The proposal to abolish a game reserve in Sudan sparked the perceived crisis. This brought together a self-declared 'group of gentlemen of wide experience of the outposts of the Empire and a common enthusiasm for the preservation from destruction of many of its fauna', to form a new Society for the Preservation of the Wild Fauna of the Empire (SPWFE), formally launched a century ago, on 11 December 1903. Led by Edward North Buxton, these gentlemen successfully lobbied the Governor of Sudan, Lord Cromer, and the proposal was dropped.

In the pages of this fascinating book, Bill Adams charts the history of conservation through the 20th century. Winding through the narrative, at every stage, is the story of SPWFE and its transformation to Fauna & Flora International (FFI), a shift from conservation for the sake of hunting to conservation for the sake of species.

At first SPWFE was, in Bill Adams' words, 'a pressure group within the elite of a colonizing power'. These men were themselves recreational hunters for sport and trophies. Their objective was to ensure the designation and safeguarding of protected areas, notable reserves or sanctuaries, as the first essential for the preservation of those species that they favoured (typically, large ungulates). They were out of sympathy with the excessive killing undertaken by

European settlers, especially commercial hunters, who were perceived as 'those whose sporting instincts are undeveloped or perhaps stunted'. As social equals, they sought to influence colonial governors and members of the home government, and often succeeded. Although self-interest may have been a motivation, those pioneers were right in principle: the problem of extinction is still a burning issue that conservationists need to bring to the world's attention today.

There was no need, in the early days, to seek a huge membership. A year after its foundation, the society had attracted 70 ordinary members (and 30 honorary members, including President Theodore Roosevelt, the famous Lord Kitchener of Khartoum and Alfred Lyttleton, Secretary of State for the Colonies). After the First World War, it dropped the 'Wild' from its title, becoming simply SPFE, but did not materially alter its objective of preserving the fauna of the British Empire, through influencing key officials, encouraging the designation of protected areas and enforcement of game laws. By 1927, membership was 270, and by 1930, 760. After the Second World War, as events unrolled and perceptions of conservation were modified, the name was changed to the Fauna Preservation Society (FPS), and later (by an imaginative leap that recognized the huge threats to plants) to the Fauna and Flora Preservation Society (FFPS). The final name change, to Fauna & Flora International, has emphasized the role of the society and its objectives on a world scale.

Successive chapters of the book enlarge on the key themes of conservation priorities and emerging conservation perceptions during the 100 years since SPWFE was founded. Our attention is drawn to the dominating role of protected areas in conservation strategy, covering game reserves, national parks, wilderness areas and designated wildlife conservation sites. At first, the objective was to exclude people. As pointed out, this was often to the disadvantage of the local, land-based communities. The concept of exclusion was at times inhuman, leaving the deprived little option but to violate the protective regulations – becoming 'poachers' on their own land.

At English Nature, from the 1990s, we recognized that a conservation strategy based exclusively on site protection – the vaunted Sites of Special Scientific Interest (SSSIs) – was insufficient. In line with this thinking, the concept of biological networks or habitat corridors has emerged in the closing decades of the 20th century. A major example, involving FFI since 1998, is the 20,000 hectare Golden Stream Corridor Preserve in Belize. It is also now recognized as good practice to bring in the local communities, rather than exclude them. In this instance, FFI's Flower Valley in South Africa is an exciting venture – a commercial operation for the marketing of wild *fynbos* flowers and support for micro-enterprise projects based on flower products.

A second key theme in conservation has been species protection. This was, of course, the objective of the early Private Member legislation in the United Kingdom, with the plumage Acts of the 19th century. In the 20th century, a key advance in marshalling non-governmental energy and skills was the formation of the International Union for the Protection of Nature in 1948 (since 1956 renamed the International Union for the Conservation of Nature and Natural Resources – IUCN). Initially stationed in Brussels, this organization brought together national representatives and non-governmental organizations. It operated through a small number of Commissions, of which the Survival Service Commission (SSC) covered endangered species. Under the chairmanship of Harold Coolidge, the SSC became active in the field in 1954 with the appointment of Lee M Talbot as Staff Ecologist. FPS was closely involved, and Talbot's theme-setting *Look at Threatened Species* was published in May 1960 as a special issue of Oryx – 5(4/5). SSC went on to publish the series of *Red Data Books*, starting in 1962. These have now been supplanted by the Red List Programme, which, Bill Adams reminds his readers, now contains 18,000 species, and is web-accessible.

FPS remained closely involved with SSC, with a succession of chairmen and other officers serving both organizations, including Lieutenant Colonel C L Boyle, Sir Peter Scott and Richard Fitter. Peter Scott was also closely involved, with Julian Huxley and Max Nicholson, in a further key initiative in 1961 setting up the World Wildlife Fund (WWF) originally intended to be a fundraiser for the work of IUCN. Although WWF (now World Wide Fund for Nature) had grown to be a huge organization, with many independent national member bodies, FPS continued to find an individual role in raising funds for specific species-related conservation objectives, often in partnership with WWF or similar organizations, including the People's Trust for Endangered Species. Bill Adams lists Operation Blackbuck and 'Save the lion marmoset' in 1972, the scimitar-horned oryx in Niger in 1980 and Operation Tortoise in 1985. The Oryx 100% Fund was an initiative that attracted donors with the promise that the full value of their gift would be passed to the conservation objective.

The idea of extinction, so final and permanent, is still a powerhouse of conservation concern. Bill Adams quotes 'veteran conservation polemicist' Norman Myers from 1986, and Edward Wilson from 1992, suggesting that in the 20th century human activity has raised the extinction rate between 1000 and 10,000 times the 'background' geological rate – not a happy conclusion. The role of trade can be critical, and the operation of the Convention on International Trade in Endangered Species (CITES) has been a good example of scientific and governmental cooperation, although not without its problems, as Bill Adams shows. Extinction occurs at sea, as well as on land: the story of the drastic decline, but subsequent recovery, of sea otters is both alarming and reassuring; the collapse of cod fisheries and the plight of whales are less comfortable examples.

Since 1992, and the Convention on Biological Diversity, the new paradigm has been sustainability. This term is deployed in so many contexts that it has almost lost all meaning. Its users risk deluding themselves that natural resources, living or inanimate, can be tapped unendingly without change or deterioration. In this sense, since the emergence of modern man, the world has been modified continuously by human activity. Archaeology shows that exploitation has been continual, and often irreversible.

Where do we stand now? Bill Adams offers some aphorisms, emerging from his historical review. 'The 20th century saw conservation's creation, but nature's decline.' 'Conservation needs new thinking about what nature is.' 'Conservationists need to take a deep breath, and admit that nature is a social construction.' 'Natural science is just one of several ways of understanding nature.' 'The future of conservation will turn on the extent to which a strong individual connection to nature and natural processes is maintained for the world's people in the 21st century.'

These are matters for the ensuing debate, which will continue into the 21st century. Before embarking on the road ahead, it is useful to look back along the route we have taken. I have lived through two-thirds of the 20th century, and been active as a conservation-oriented biologist for almost half of it. I welcome Bill Adams' full and careful referencing of sources – including websites from that huge compendium of information that now exists, out there, somewhere, in the limitless and uncontrolled digitized environment, freely accessible. This is the new, virtual world library. My own bookshelves, more mundanely, carry the run of *Oryx* from 1960, through the 1970s when I was a Council member, to this day. What heroic names are found there among the Presidents, Vice Presidents, Chairmen, Secretaries, Editors and Council members? They achieved great things, and deserve to be celebrated. It is important to recognize that FFI, throughout its history, has played and continues to play an important part in the development and application of conservation. I recommend this history as a true and thoughtful guide to the people, key events and changing perspectives of conservation through the 20th century.

Preface

If conservationists have a consistent and shared sense of time, it is one that is oddly broken-up. In my experience their awareness of time falls into three discrete categories. The first might be called, with apologies to Charles Lyell, 'deep time'. I mean by this, time measured on the geological timescale of millions of years. This scale of time makes humans as a species seem rather trivial *arrivistes* in the long, teeming prehistory of life forms: a steady evolutionary game of planetary proportions in which *Homo sapiens* appears as a late, sudden and rather destructive disruptive force, whose effects Agent Smith, in the film *The Matrix*, rather nicely captures when he describes humans as a virus on Earth. Conservationists do this idea of time very well. They understand, through books like Edward Wilson's *The Diversity of Life*,[1] the astonishing diversity generated by evolution in the wafer-thin living skin of the Earth. They also respond in both an intellectual and emotional way to the enormity of the extinction spasm of the last few centuries in the light of previous episodes of destruction through the depth of geological time.

The second scale at which conservationists understand time is their own experience. Those who love nature tend to explain conservation to themselves in terms of things they have actually experienced. Most conservationists can trace their passion for living things to particular places and times, when they engaged with other species or with landscapes, when what is often called 'the wild' reached into the mundane and urban world and touched them. Conservationists remember childhood engagements with nature, and note how they have been marked by them.[2] They revisit places they knew long ago, and find them changed, sometimes beyond all recognition: lost under tarmac and concrete, devoid of former biodiversity, robbed of their charm. They see a trajectory of change, and all too often it is one of degradation. Scratch a conservationist, and beneath every upbeat line about success stories, there is usually a depressingly downbeat assessment of the retreat of nature over their lifetimes.

The third scale at which conservationists think of time is in the immediate present. It seems that conservation problems are always urgent; everything is a crisis. In books and films, and in the minds of conservationists, nature often faces catastrophe, usually at human hands. Something always needs to be done, and done at once.

Whatever sense of time conservationists have, I would suggest that they rarely have a good sense of history. They think they know what needs to be done, but in thinking things through, they tend to jump from deep time to their own lives' experience, and then again to the immediate challenge of today without much pause for thought. Often they have little understanding of the way in which problems have come about, or how their predecessors understood similar problems and tried to tackle them. Conservationists often know very little of their own history.

This book decribes the story of conservation in the 20th century. The idea of writing it was conceived several years before the Millennium, but it only became a live project in the summer of 2002. The trigger then was the centenary of the establishment of Fauna & Flora International (FFI), founded as the Society for the Preservation of the Wild Fauna of the Empire (SPWFE) in 1903. FFI's Director, Mark Rose, was, in 2002, finalizing plans for the celebration of its 100th birthday. The writing of this book became a contribution to that anniversary, a reflection on the achievements and challenges of conservation over the last 100 years. The book is not the history of one organization, although FFI and its predecessors provide a strong backbone from which the ribs of the book are suspended.

I have told the story as I know it, warts and all. The resulting tale may not be entirely as today's conservationists would necessarily wish it to be. Some may be dismayed that I have not tried to use the past to inspire a kind of call to arms, for action to protect biodiversity today. The past contains much for today's defenders of living diversity to be proud of, but not everything looks well in the 20–20 hindsight of history. I have, at relevant points, tried to take careful account of the arguments of conservation's many critics. I have tried to tell the story of conservation from the inside, to explain why people did what they did, and why they believed it mattered. It must be said that I am by no means an impartial observer. I have served on the boards of several conservation organizations, but I have also carried out research on the impacts of conservation policy on rural people, and I am painfully aware of the challenge of global poverty.

As will become clear, I do not see 'people' and 'nature' as opposed. Indeed, I do not believe that they are ultimately separable.[3] Can people live with nature? Of course: there is no question about that. We can do nothing else – live or die, we are part of nature. The questions to be asked are about the terms of the relationship we have with the biosphere – the ways we engage with other species. Conservation debates are not really arguments about nature, but rather about ourselves and the way we choose to live. They are moral debates, about the way we cope with our own demands of each other and the biosphere.

Cambridge, July 2003

Acknowledgements

Many people have helped me in writing this book. It could not have been begun without Mark Rose, Director of Fauna & Flora International (FFI), who first discussed the idea with me, and found the resources to make it happen. It would not have been possible without financial support from Dr Lisbet Rausing, and would not have been completed but for David Prendergast's wonderful enthusiasm, good humour and careful, tireless research. At FFI I owe a great debt to Mark Rose, Mark Day, Jon Hutton and Chris Loades for all their support through the short but intense life of the project, and to the members of staff and Council whose gentle enquiries (and challengingly sceptical body language) have at different times been a comfort and spur for action. I am grateful to Jonathan Sinclair Wilson, Rob West and Akan Leander of Earthscan for calm good humour in the face of cascading deadlines.

I would like to thank Juan Moreiras of FFI who took the photographs on the cover of the book and between chapters, and Emily Adams, whose drawing appears at the end of each chapter.

I have learned a great deal from the research of many colleagues and students at Cambridge, particularly Caroline Cowan, Lee Risby, Malcolm Starkey and Lucy Welford, who have given me more things to read than I can remember. I enormously appreciate the help of those who found time to read and comment on drafts of the book, including Dan Brockington, Mark Day, Richard Fitter, Francine Hughes, Jon Hutton, David Prendergast, Mark Rose, Bhaskar Vira and Liz Watson. Those errors that remain, despite their diligence and energy, are my own.

I am grateful to all of those who have suffered through my preoccupation and poor time management while the book was being written, particularly, as ever, to Franc, Emily and Tom, without whom life would have few good times.

List of Acronyms and Abbreviations

*, † *indicate the same organization, with dates given for name changes*

APE	Action Programme for the Environment
AWF	African Wildlife Foundation
AWLF	African Wildlife Leadership Foundation
CABS	Center for Applied Biodiversity Science
CAMPFIRE	Communal Areas Management Programme for Indigenous Resources (Zimbabwe)
CBD	Convention on Biological Diversity
CI	Conservation International
CITES	Convention on Trade in Endangered Species
COBRA	Conservation of Biodiverse Areas
CPRE	Council for the Preservation of Rural England (now Campaign for the Protection of Rural England)
DHKD	Dogal Hayati Koruma Dernegi
DRC	Democratic Republic of Congo
DTC	Development through Conservation (Uganda)
ECOSOC	Economic and Social Council (UN)
EIA	Environmental Impact Assessment
EIA	Environmental Investigation Agency
FAO	Food and Agriculture Organization (UN)
FFI	Fauna & Flora International* (from 1992)
FFPS	Fauna and Flora Preservation Society* (from 1980)
FoE	Friends of the Earth
FPS	Fauna Preservation Society* (from 1950)
GEF	Global Environmental Facility
GIS	geographic information systems
ICBP	International Council for Bird Preservation (previously International Committee for Bird Preservation, now BirdLife International)
ICDPs	integrated conservation and development projects
IFAW	International Fund for Animal Welfare
IGCP	International Gorilla Conservation Programme
IOPN	International Office for the Protection of Nature
IUCN	International Union for Conservation of Nature and Natural Resources† (the World Conservation Union) (from 1956)

IUPN	International Union for the Preservation of Nature† (pre 1956)
IWC	International Whaling Commission
LIRDP	Lwangwa Integrated Resource Development Project
MAB	Man and the Biosphere
NCC	Nature Conservancy Council
NEPA	National Environmental Policy Act (US)
NERC	Natural Environment Research Council
NGO	non-governmental organization
PTES	People's Trust for Endangered Species
RSPB	Royal Society for the Protection of Birds
SCOPE	Scientific Committee for Problems of the Environment
SPFE	Society for the Preservation of the Fauna of the Empire* (from 1919)
SPNR	Society for the Promotion of Nature Reserves
SPWFE	Society for the Preservation of the Wild Fauna of the Empire* (pre 1919)
SSC	Species Survival Commission
TRAFFIC	Trade Records Analysis of Flora and Fauna in Commerce
UNCED	United Nations Conference on Environment and Development
UNEP	United Nations Environment Programme
UNESCO	United Nations Educational, Scientific and Cultural Organization
UNSCCUR	United Nations Scientific Conference on the Conservation and Utilization of Resources (Lake Success Conference)
USAID	United States Agency for International Development
WCS	World Conservation Strategy
WWF	World Wildlife Fund (now World Wide Fund for Nature)

Chapter 1

The Challenge of Nature

BRINGING BACK THE WILD

It is just over a century since the scientific discovery of the mountain gorilla. The anniversary of this event, on 17 October 2002, passed almost unnoticed.[1] The animal was found by Captain Oscar von Beringe, travelling for the German colonial authorities in the mountains that now lie on the border between Rwanda and Uganda. His party had climbed onto the broad col between the two volcanoes of Gahinga and Sabinyo, and were high in the giant heather forests when they observed the gorillas. With the zealous concern for specimens that was characteristic of the time, they shot at them, killing two. The bodies were lost into the deep canyon below, but after five hours of labour they dragged one out again, and in due course dispatched it for the attention of taxonomists in Berlin.[2] It was named a separate subspecies in its colonial pursuer's honour, *Gorilla gorilla berengei*.

The mountain gorilla had led a charmed life. The lowland gorilla had been discovered by scientists in 1847, and the land around the Virunga volcanoes, between what has become Rwanda, Uganda and the Democratic Republic of Congo had been penetrated by many of the famous European expeditions of the late 19th century. Speke, Grant, Livingstone, Stanley, Stuhlman and Emin Pasha had all got within sight of them. The first of the Virunga volcanoes was climbed in 1898, and the border surveyed in that year and the next.

Several travellers reported rumours of gorillas in the hills before von Beringe got his rifle to them. It is, of course, a fiction worthy of those postilions of empire that his was the first sighting people ever had of mountain gorillas. This was the moment when Western science noted them down, locking them into its classificatory scheme and giving them an identity in the cabinet of natural history. Local people knew them already – had known them in some way for millennia, that blink of evolutionary time during which humans and other apes diverged.

Mountain gorillas are the kind of species whose significance for humans is fairly universally agreed. They are large and dramatic animals, quite obviously very closely related to people. They are also extremely rare, with something less than 700 estimated to survive in the wild. Gorillas share about 97.7 per cent of their genes with humans, slightly less than the bonobo or chimpanzee, slightly more than the orang-utan. Jared Diamond suggests that, were taxonomists less hidebound and anthropocentric, we would include them with chimpanzees in our genus, Homo: *Homo gorilla berengei*.[3]

That thought, with all it implies about the relations with great apes, was certainly far from the vision of von Beringe's colonial successors, although they too were in no doubt that the mountain gorilla was an extremely important animal. Unfortunately, its value could only be realized if it was dead or captured, brought back to Europe and North America and put on public display. At least 54 mountain gorillas were shot (as specimens) or captured (for zoos) in the first quarter of a century of science's knowledge of them. Their hunters had inherited the 19th century's taste for the systematic and objective compilation of facts about nature, of the urge to assemble different types and species and preserve and display them.[4] Like the eccentric Charles Waterton, who excelled in the art of taxidermy, which could bring dead specimens to permanent life, the proper place to experience the diversity of living species was the museum. Nature seemed inexhaustable.

Typical of these early hunters was the American Carl Akeley. In 1921 he shot five mountain gorillas on an expedition to the Virungas on behalf of the American Museum of Natural History in New York. This was a long-standing project, for he had originally obtained funds to hunt them in 1910, but was forced to abandon his plans after being injured by an elephant on Mount Kenya while hunting them for the museum.[5] Gorillas fascinated Akeley – he found the gorilla 'a much more interesting quarry than lions, elephants, or any other African game, for it was still comparatively unknown'.[6] Moreover, there was a cachet of being first – as his widow commented in 1928, 'not many others had shot gorillas'.

The ultimate destination of Carl Akeley's gorillas was as an exhibit of a gorilla 'family', in a diorama in the museum's African Hall. Donna Haraway has provided an unsettling reading of Carl Akeley's diorama.[7] The display features a silverback beating his chest ('the giant of Karisimbi'), a younger male, a mother eating and an infant, set against a painted panoramic backdrop of the Virunga volcanoes. The stuffed skins of the gorillas are presented as a 'natural' organic family, surrounded by photographically detailed representations of nature, 'a lush Eden crafted out of detailed reconstructions of leaves, insects and soils'. They are fixed as representations of the wild, as primal apes in the wild forests of Africa, and held up to the gaze of civilized white New Yorkers. The display hides all the physical activities that made it possible – the killing of the family, the stripping and preservation of the skins, their transportation to the United States and their petrification within the reconstructed artifice of the museum.

Today, in a Western culture long familiar with moving film and the instant availability of colour reproduction, the merits of the museum presentation of the gorilla seem highly questionable. The idea of a living collection in a zoo is more acceptable. It was already current (Burbridge captured eight infants in the Virungas between 1922 and 1925, in the process shooting a male[8]). However, through the 20th century, zoos changed. They moved slowly away from being mere spectacles for the presentation of specimens, essentially living versions of Akeley's gorilla family, the animation of their inmates making up for the replacement of his artistic backdrop with prison-like cages. They claimed a new role, presenting themselves as nature's saviours, through captive breeding of rare species in '*ex-situ*' conservation. Specimens were presented in enclosures that began to resemble Akeley's diorama, as part of a continuum of nature, a temporarily domesticated fragment of the wild.

Zoos, like museums, are designed to present animals in ways that allow humans to see and understand them in particular ways. Thus for example, Adelaide Zoo, in common with many others, was modernized in the 1960s and 1970s, with new moated enclosures to give a better experience to visitors and animals, and the development of the educational as compared to the entertainment or recreational dimensions of the zoo's work.[9] In the 1980s, postage-stamp philosophy gave way to a desire to present fewer animals in ways that related to their 'natural' ecosystems. Menagerie-style cages were replaced with naturalistic displays, and captive breeding programmes (in the Adelaide Zoo's case of Przewalski's horse and red panda) were established. Kay Anderson points out the oddness of this – how freedom came to justify captivity, 'wildness' to legitimize domestication. The zoo's 'World of Primates' places animals and visitors in a seemingly natural environment, a 'pristine jungle'. The educational message of habitat loss and the threat of extinction is presented with vision and energy. This artificial world of 'unspoilt' nature is a stage on which captive primates appear 'as monuments to their own disappearance in nature'.[10]

FROM GUNS TO PARKS

The heyday of conservation enthusiasm for zoos and captive breeding has passed. At the start of the 21st century, views about their contribution to conservation are more equivocal than they were. The Convention on Biological Diversity (CBD), signed at the United Nations Conference on Environment and Development (UNCED) held in Rio de Janeiro in 1992 (and popularly known as the Rio conference), noted the importance of '*ex-situ* measures', although it also pointed out that these were best implemented in the country of origin and not overseas.[11] The preamble to the CBD cited the fundamental requirement for the conservation of biological diversity as the *in-situ* conservation of ecosystems and natural habitats, and the maintenance and recovery of viable populations of species in their natural surroundings.

This is not surprising. The dominant 'big idea' of conservation throughout the 20th century has been the establishment of protected areas: nature reserves, game reserves, sanctuaries and national parks – the names vary, as has the way people think protected areas should be managed, but the principle has changed very little. The British conservationist Edward North Buxton (of whom more later), wrote of Africa in 1902 'the maintenance of reserves, or sanctuaries, is the first essential for the preservation of various species'.[12] The website for the Fifth World Parks Congress (in Durban in September 2003) described protected areas as 'a cornerstone of global conservation efforts', arguing that 'whether it be as reservoirs of biological diversity, sources of clean air and water, buffers from storms, sinks for carbon or places to escape and reconnect with nature, protected areas are vitally important to our individual and collective futures'.[13] Enthusiasm for protected areas spanned the whole 20th century as an enduring and central concern of conservation.

Mountain gorillas have been important icons for the national parks movement, as for so many other dimensions of conservation. Dian Fossey began work on gorillas in the Parc National des Volcans in Rwanda in 1970. Her book, *Gorillas in the Mist*, was published in 1983, just two years before her death. This, and more particularly Sigourny Weaver's representation of her in the Hollywood biopic of the same name just three years later, brought the plight of the mountain gorilla to international attention.[14] The Rwandan Parc National des Volcans is one of three national parks abutting each other across three national boundaries, including Uganda (Mgahinga Gorilla National Park) and Democratic Republic of Congo (DRC) (Parc National des Virunga in the DRC). The survival of the gorillas (and the endurance of park staff) through the genocide and civil wars of central Africa, with guerrillas in the forests and millions of refugees encamped nearby, has been a remarkable tale of human endeavour. Much of the credit must go to the work of the national parks' administrations in each country, supported by the International Gorilla Conservation Programme (IGCP), set up in 1991 by the African Wildlife Foundation (AWF), FFI and the World Wildlife Fund.[15] If evidence is needed of the importance of protected areas, the gorilla parks seem to provide it.

Mountain gorillas, however, also have a special place in the history of protected areas, for the first African national park, the Parc National Albert, was declared to protect them. There are various stories about who first suggested the idea of a national park in the Virungas to protect the mountain gorilla. Carl Akeley, who shot the gorilla family in 1921, may have had a hand in it.[16] Richard Fitter reports a meeting around a campfire in Yellowstone National Park in 1919, where King Albert of the Belgians had his ear bent by three conservation enthusiasts, Lee Merriam Talbot, Fairfield Osborn of the New York Zoological Society and Victor van Straelen of Belgium. Six years later, in 1925 the Parc National Albert was declared by royal decree in the Belgian Congo. In the subsequent decades, three further parks were declared in the Belgian Congo, including the Parc National des Volcans in what has become Rwanda.[17] This was an important symbolic achievement for the cause of conservation in Africa – indeed outside the world's industrial heartlands – for decades to come.

Carl Akeley believed that the national park was of the greatest importance: 'no other project of so moderate a size would render such valuable and lasting service to humanity and science as would the Parc National Albert'.[18] He believed 'that the disappearance of the African fauna was to be deplored and resisted by lovers of wild life, even as they realized its inevitability'.[19] Its most obvious value was its 'exceptional variety of flora and fauna', and 'extraordinary geological and geographical interest'. More oddly, to modern ears, Carl Akeley also believed that if the national park were kept inviolate, it would also provide 'an almost unique opportunity to save some of the primitive African pygmies, a race now threatened with extinction'.[20]

Gorillas apparently had a particular fascination for Carl Akeley. He returned to the Virungas with a second expedition in 1926, hoping 'to stimulate interest in upholding and furthering the cause of conservation of all the fauna and flora of the region'. He never made it home: he died after just three days in the mountains, and lies buried in the Virungas. He left his widow Mary and colleague J M Derscheidt to carry out the first field studies of mountain gorillas, and provide some kind of knowledge base for the new national park. Above all, the purpose of this park was to be scientific. The idea sold to the Belgian king was that national parks could not only protect landscapes and animals, but serve science. Mary Akeley wrote in 1929 that 'the promotion of Science is the definite and final goal, not only for today, but also for the benefit of future generations'.[21] From 1929 the Parc National Albert was run by an autonomous scientific institution, from 1934 named the Institut des Parcs Nationaux du Congo Belge, under Victor van Straelen.[22] Mary Akeley suggested that the Parc National Albert, with the Kruger National Park created from previous game reserves in South Africa, could be seen as forming the first links in a 'chain of nature sanctuaries'. In time this could be extended over Africa, binding together 'international interest in the protection of the most desirable, important and valuable regions for scientific research'.[23]

The Parc National Albert was extended in 1929 and again in 1935, to cover 0.8 million hectares.[24] Enthusiasm for protected areas was markedly less in neighbouring territories. In December 1928 the Belgian Ambassador in London, Baron Cartier de Marchienne, proposed the vote of thanks to Mary Akeley for her lecture to the SPFE. He pointed out sharply that, while the Belgian park protected most of the mountains, there was a 'wedge' in the British territory of Uganda that was the only home to mountain gorillas in British territory, and urged that this should be made a 'natural preserve of fauna and flora'.[25] This took a long time. A small game sanctuary (under 3500 hectares in extent) was created on the Ugandan slopes of the volcanoes in 1930, and a forest reserve nine years later. There was interest in the gorillas, especially from the German owner of a small lodge in the nearest town, but little effective protection until the 1980s, when a German non-governmental organization (NGO) paid for a warden. The Mgahinga Gorilla National Park was actually only declared in 1991, long after Ugandan independence.[26]

THE PROBLEM OF NATURALNESS

There are still gorillas on the slopes of Mount Sabinyo, where Carl Akeley found them. They wander across the national borders of the three adjacent national parks with rather greater freedom than the park rangers who seek to protect them. From time to time, particularly on the Rwandan side, they are still shot or trapped, although no longer in the name of Western science. After a decade of relative peace, eight gorillas were killed in 1995, although the courage and energy of Rwandan, Congolese and Ugandan national park staff have kept deaths to a remarkably low level, despite the civil wars and disruption of the last ten years. One reason for their success is that gorillas have become rather more valuable alive than dead. The trick is that tourists will pay considerable sums of money, in hard currency, to see gorillas. This money opens up all sorts of opportunities for conservation, potentially meeting some of the costs of managing the parks, and the needs of local people. Gorilla tourism is widely seen as one of the success stories of conservation, a glimmer of hope in an otherwise grim tale of threat, loss and destruction.[27]

Gorilla tourism began in the Parc National des Volcans in Rwanda in 1979 and was subsequently taken up in Zaire in 1985 and Uganda in 1993. Before tourists can hope to see wild gorillas without disturbing them, gorilla groups have to be habituated to human presence. This is something pioneered first for research purposes. People track groups of animals, slowly getting them used to the non-violent presence of humans, and eventually to the clumsy and stumbling presence of groups of tourists, with their inevitable noisy and potentially disturbing equipment (gorillas particularly hate flashguns, requiring visitors to remember how to de-program modern cameras). By the Millennium year, ten groups of gorillas had been habituated for tourist visits (four in Rwanda, three in DRC and three in Uganda), approximately a tenth of the global population. This is not an activity without risks for the gorillas. Habituation is stressful and disturbing, and there is a risk that habituated groups, who have lost their fear of humans, will be vulnerable to poachers. Furthermore, gorillas are highly susceptible to human diseases contracted from contact with tourists and game guards.[28]

In Uganda, gorillas are confined to two areas of forest tucked away in the most southwestern corner of the country, at Bwindi Impenetrable National Park and Mgahinga Gorilla National Park. Bwindi is large, and contains most of Uganda's gorillas and (despite a guerilla attack in 1999) is the destination of most tourists.[29] Mgahinga is tiny, a sliver of land high on the slopes of the mountains on the border. These parks are two of the few remaining pieces of mountain forest in Uganda. They are now surrounded by farmland, managed at incredible intensity on the steep slopes, all cleared from the forest in the current century.

The first view you get of Mgahinga is from the road that switchbacks over the hills from Kabale. When I travelled it in the 1990s, it had a well-graded dirt surface, although passage was considerably enlivened by the vast petrol trucks en route for the DRC. We hit the last brow about an hour before sunset, and the three volcanoes of Mgahinga lay glowing against the backlit sky to the west. From closer to, above the town of Kisoro, on a road almost blocked with people walking back from market, the mountains had disappeared, their summits obscured by cloud. The upper part of the park consists of the slopes and peaks of the mountains, the strange giant groundsels of the high alpine zone, and the tree heather and montane forests of the steep slopes of the mountain. Below this lie the bamboo forests into which the gorillas wander on their visits from Rwanda and the DRC.

Descriptions of the parks emphasize these vegetation types, linking the forest to the wider biogeographic unit of the Albertine rift forests, one of the most biodiverse and least extensive ecosystems in Africa. It is thought that the parks served as a refuge for forest species in the period of deep aridity about 15,000 years ago. The richness of their flora and fauna reflect the depth of time over which biodiversity has evolved. The parks are seen as important both for their rare and endemic species (primates of course, but also birds and butterflies and other taxa) but also because they provide what commentators describe as 'rare local examples of relatively natural ecosystems'.[30] The Management Plan for Bwindi states bluntly that the forest is 'a climax ecosystem', implying a stable final stage of succession. The forest is described as 'natural', although it goes on to note past and present human activity on 90 per cent of it.[31] Those activities include pitsawing of timber, human-set fires, gold prospecting, collection of honey and various plants, hunting and cultivation.

The boundary of Bwindi today is abrupt, with forest on one side and farmland on the other. The division between the two runs straight across the landscape, up and down hills almost too steep to walk. When I was there, a small piece of land had recently been de-gazetted (that is, legally removed from the park) – a bare, muddy hillside scattered with stumps and the scars of fires. At Mgahinga, the boundary is equally sharp, marked not only by concrete survey pillars, but also by a long wall of brown lava blocks. On one side of this wall are the neat mounds of sweet potatoes and beans, carefully mulched and weeded. On the other side lies a jungle of scrub and long grass.

There is an interesting story about this boundary. When Mgahinga was created in 1991, its lower boundary approximately followed that of the original forest reserve and game sanctuary, created before the Second World War. Local demand for farmland was such that the forest reserve had been reduced in size by a third in 1951, and the area was cleared and settled. The new settlement, cultivation and grazing were, however, strictly illegal under the regulations establishing the game reserve.[32] To make things even more complicated, in 1964 the game reserve had been extended by the inclusion of 1380 hectares of new land below the original boundary, all of which had long been settled and cultivated. This new boundary had never been demarcated, and its residents or users were not evicted, as the game reserve regulations in fact required. Given that there was already a great deal of pressure on land, this was – in humanitarian (and political) terms – entirely proper, but it made a nonsense of the conservation designation.

These reserves were classic 'paper parks', there in the official government list, but invisible on the ground. Moreover, a blind eye had been turned to agricultural encroachment inside even the reduced boundary of the forest reserve, and grazing and cutting were extensive through much of the lower forest on the mountains. Indeed, some of this use of the forest reserve was perfectly legal, for the 1954 Forest Act allowed local people to harvest timber, firewood, bamboo, fibrous and medicinal plants, fruit, seeds, grass, bushmeat, honey and drinking water for domestic use. There was a formal system of licences for cutting bamboos used for making houses and granaries.[33]

When the new national park was declared in 1991, all agriculture, settlement and forest product use became illegal, and in the rather quaint language of Ugandan conservation, the people suddenly became 'encroachers'. However, very large numbers of people benefit economically from some of the land within the park. Surveys have shown that over 1700 people in fact lived within the park area, with a further 680 cultivating there. Many of these residents had been in the park a long time: over half claimed to have been born there, and some had been present before the gorilla sanctuary was created in 1930. Almost three quarters of landholders claimed to have inherited land, presumably from pre-existing residents, suggesting long-established land rights. This 'natural' place was, in the very recent past, very much humanized.[34]

COMMUNITY AND CONSERVATION

When you go to Mgahinga, you drive up a steep and profoundly potholed road through densely occupied land. Schools, houses and farms are wedged tightly along the edge of the track, and people are everywhere. When you get to the park gate, the road simply stops, amidst a small community campground with a few small huts for accommodation and space for overlanders' trucks. There is a bar across the road, and a fine carved sign with a gorilla and the park's name. Beyond that is a sea of grass and scrub. To either side of the road stretches the lava-block wall, running right along the southern boundary of the park. This is both symbolic and practical.

Symbolically, it separates the wild nature of the forest from the tamed and domesticated landscape of farmers' fields. It partitions the landscape between nature and people – in the tradition of protected areas, it keeps nature in and people out. Its practical purpose is the reverse of this: it stops animals raiding local people's fields. The wall (approximately 9 kilometres long) was built by local people, with funding from the CARE Uganda 'Development through Conservation' (DTC) Project at Bwindi and Mgahinga, to stop wild buffalo getting into the fields at night from the abandoned farmland inside the park.

The wall formed part of a diverse 'community conservation' programme at Mgahinga.[35] CARE, for example, undertook agricultural development work, tree planting and agroforestry, and developed water supply schemes to bring water from swamps high in the park to local communities. A number of parallel projects were also developed, notably the establishment of a trust fund (the Mgahinga Bwindi Impenetrable Forest Conservation Trust) with capital of US$4 million from the GEF (the Global Environmental Facility) to fund community projects.

These projects were an explicit response to the problems of local communities, arising both from their poverty and the existence of the park. The programme reflected an important shift in global conservation thinking, towards local communities.[36] They reflected, too, problems on the ground around Mgahinga. There was quite an outcry about the injustice of the new boundary of the park, both from local people and their political leaders, and also (allegedly) from more shadowy absentee landlords. The foreign donors supporting the idea of the new Ugandan parks offered to help, and funds were provided by USAID (the United States Agency for International Development) (their delightfully named 'APE' programme – 'Action Programme for the Environment') to provide some US$15,000 for farmers to allow them to resettle. In return, all farmers and residents agreed to leave the park.

Of course, this compensation did not end local grievances. In village meetings in 1998, I heard people claim that some had received too little compensation money, or none at all, that payments had ceased prematurely, or that those who carried out the exercise were not fair because they gave to some and not to others. Everybody thought the compensation was inadequate, quite insufficient to allow replacement land to be acquired. When I was there in 1998, farmland was said to be changing hands for US$1900 per acre, whereas average payments to farmers had been about US$30, ranging from US$1200 to US$6. This is not surprising, since the payments were not intended to be 'compensation' as such, they were simply designed to meet some of the more immediate hardships associated with the eviction process.

The other source of revenue to offset hardship and deflect resentment in local people at Mgahinga is the fees paid by tourists to view gorillas. Arguably, this offers the possibility of sustained wealth generation derived directly from wildlife. There is one group of habituated gorillas at Mgahinga, although they frequently depart to Rwanda or DRC for extended periods. Only six people can visit them per day, for which privilege they each pay US$250. When gorilla tracking began at Mgahinga, in 1993, political instability had drastically reduced the potential for tourism in Rwanda and DRC. Uganda was able to benefit from its recently established stability, and soaked up the strong demand of tour companies for gorilla tracking destinations. The number of tourists in the 1990s has been variously estimated at between 1100 and 1500 per year, bringing in between US$60,000 and US$190,000. There are many claims on that money, not least the costs of conservation itself, at Mgahinga and elsewhere, and the Ugandan government has changed its mind on the allocation of the revenue several times. Nonetheless, the Uganda Wildlife Authority remains committed to sharing a proportion of this revenue. In October 1997, US$6667 was handed over, and committed to the construction of classrooms in local schools.[37]

HYBRID NATURE

Whatever the success of the community conservation work at Mgahinga Gorilla National Park in defusing tensions and offsetting resentments, its intention is clear – to ensure that the park survives. The park boundary separates wild and domesticated, forest and field. And yet this distinction is not as sharp as it might appear. One evening when I was staying at Mgahinga, I walked with a game guard along the path inside the boundary of the park, Kalashnikov and binoculars both slung ready for use. To my right were sweet potatoes, to my left a wild ocean of grass, with extensive clumps of young trees. Further away was a hard line of the edge of the evergreen forest. The ground was horribly uneven, furrowed with the mounds of abandoned fields, impossible to see below the blanketing grass. It was a picture of contrast between nature and culture, wild and tame. Here was nature re-establishing itself, recovering from human management.

On closer inspection, however, this illusion began to fragment. The clumps of young trees were not outliers of the forest, but eucalyptus, an exotic tree from Australasia. They had been planted when the land was farmed, to produce fuelwood. They were now naturalized, and not only growing energetically but regenerating rapidly. The forest that regenerates in this area will be dominated by exotic species. For now it is prime habitat for buffalo rather than gorillas, hence the need for the restraining wall.

Nature within the national park is not pure and untouched by human hands, but a hybrid. It is natural, but also human-made. The reclaimed fields show this most clearly, but the human influence has been extensive throughout the park. When it was declared, the park was traversed by 12 heavily used paths (over the ridge to Rwanda), vines and wood were cut and honey barrels set out in most suitable areas. On my walk, the quiet evening was broken by the shouts of men deep in the woods, and the clunk of an axe: there were soldiers camped locally and they needed fuelwood. Well-marked paths crossed the wall and led off into the grassland. People were still entering the park, using its resources, despite the prohibition. Recognizing the cultural and economic needs of local people, the Uganda Wildlife Authority has begun to allow some resource collection by local people within the park. Neighbouring farmers have been escorted in and allowed to dig up bamboo rhizomes to plant on their farms to provide building materials and bean poles, and there are plans to allow recognized local healers to collect medicinal herbs. Honey keepers have been allowed to set barrels in a 'multiple-use zone', stretching half a kilometre inside the park boundary.[38]

THE CHALLENGE OF CONSERVATION

Nature in the national parks at Mgahinga and Bwindi is not free of human influence, even in the deep forests. Gorillas, like other animals, are not something remote from humanity, only to be appreciated through some narrowly defined set of rules, be they those of the 19th century hunter or the 21st century tourist. People and nature interact, even across the wall bounding a national park. Buffalo come out to raid fields, as do many other species (sometimes, at Bwindi, even gorillas). People go in, legally and illegally. Sometimes they bring about major changes (even disasters – for example killing gorillas). Sometimes there is little to mark their passing, barring a few lopped vines or the sound of expensive camera motor drives and the smell of deodorant.

Carl Akeley and the mountain gorillas for whom he felt such deep (if initially oddly expressed) fascination therefore span the whole 20th century history of conservation. What began with hunting ended for Carl Akeley a few decades later in a very familiar science-based conservation agenda. This persisted through the end of the colonial period and decolonization, through Idi Amin's Uganda, civil and international war in Congo, Uganda and Zaire, and eventually through the genocide in Rwanda. By the time the Mgahinga Gorilla National Park was declared, in 1991, a vast international conservation community had been created, with numerous international organizations, and the plight of the gorilla, and that of countless other charismatic species, had become a commonplace issue. The medium of television especially had brought extinction and the threat of humans to other species into living rooms and to the consciousness of an increasingly affluent middle class across the industrialized world. On the ground, the simplistic idea of creating 'sanctuaries' for nature and keeping people out had given way to the new ideology of community conservation. Having fought for much of the 20th century to keep people out of protected areas, by its end, conservationists were struggling to work out how to bring people and nature back together.

Baron Cartier de Marchienne foresaw the development of conservation when he concluded his remarks about Mary Akeley's 1928 lecture. He spoke for a considerable band of colonial conservationists in saying 'we lovers of nature – of birds, trees and flowers – we ought to band together'. This is the heart of the story of conservation through the 20th century. What was this 'nature' that de Marchienne loved? And why did he and so many of his successors love it so, when the forces of change and progress in the 20th century seemed so universally bent on its destruction?

These are the questions addressed by this book. Conservation faces vast challenges, and some interesting questions. It is poised between the 19th century, which saw the rise of conservation as a global movement, and the 21st, when the future of biological diversity on Earth will be determined. At such a moment, the shape of conservation policy is of huge importance. Yet we bring to debates about that policy a significant amount of intellectual and emotional baggage from the past. What can we learn from the last century of conservation to carry forwards to the future?

OUTLINE OF THE BOOK

This book tells the story of conservation through the 20th century. It is a complex tale, and one that increases in complexity as the century advances. At the outset it is relatively simple to understand what was being urged in the name of conservation and by whom, and to get some kind of a handle on why they held their beliefs and concerns. But then, at the start of the 20th century, the circle of conservationists was small, a patrician elite network, almost all of them men, who used their influence to try to hold back their more rapacious or short-sighted colleagues, the captains of industry, commerce and colonial governance. By the end of the 20th century, conservation was an integral part of debates of enormous scope, about sustainability, development, poverty and human rights. These were the focus of a battery of international meetings, and governmental and non-governmental organizations of all kinds.

Three things need to be said about the way this book is organized. First, the story does not follow a single chronological channel, but at times explores various byways. In places it has to leap ahead in time to explain what became of particular activities or concerns. In others it hangs resolutely back, to explore exactly what was imagined or created at particular places or times.

Second, the story that is told is one that has a particular geography. Africa, the United States, and the United Kingdom all feature strongly, and the story moves between them and elsewhere in trying to explain what took place. In part it reflects the importance of certain places for the development of the international conservation movement, particularly the continent of Africa. In part it also reflects my particular knowledge (and, doubtless, biases) as an author.

This is inevitably a partial account – certainly not an encyclopaedic one – and very much an individual view. I am neither a historian, nor the scientist that most professional conservationists seem to be, but a geographer. Moreover, I have not spent the last few decades working in some remote national park, or managing a community wildlife project, but in a British university. It is unlikely that the same geographical emphasis would have commended itself to a writer from Asia or Latin America. The story would have been the same: the illustrations and landmarks in places (not all places) somewhat different.

The third thing that needs to be said about the book is that it is not only geographically specific, but culturally so. This is a story of a particular phenomenon, the rise in ideas about conservation that took root in Western industrialized countries around the turn of the 19th and 20th centuries, and went on to become something shared internationally, borne like a computer virus on the software and hardware of the international organizations that flowered after the Second World War. This is the story of Western conservation, as postcolonial writers would term it, although it is now as rooted as economics, canned drinks or human rights in every modern state across the world. There are many other traditions of human relations with other living things, 'sacred ecologies', to steal the title of a recent book by Fikret Berkes.[39] There are many sacred groves, many examples of indigenous environmental management, just as there are, as Chapter 2 will point out, many roots of conservation thinking that pre-date the 20th century. The story here is dominated by Europeans and North Americans from a position that has traditionally been blind to subaltern voices, and which is distant from today's global periphery. There are other ways to view this story, and other important stories to write, about indigenous ideas of nature and ways that people have organized themselves to relate to the living world. I hope that I have been fair to my sources, and that those who would tell the story differently will be stimulated to do so, and not offended that I have told what I knew.

This, therefore, is a story about ideas that grew and flourished in northwest Europe and North America, and among people of European extraction overseas, particularly for the first half of the century in the colonized world. One of the most important changes to arise from the 20th century was the gradual evolution of ideas about conservation, from something that indeed reflected the views of colonial white men, to something that could embrace a diversity of ideas of proper relations between humans and other species. By the end of the century, a fairly standard model of conservation had been established worldwide. It is interesting to speculate on the extent to which its pioneers would have recognized it, or applauded its aims.

Chapter 2 begins the story at the end of the 19th century, tracing the origins of conservation concern in North America, Europe and colonial Africa. It describes the roots of ideas about conservation among big game hunters, alarmed at the extent to which large animals could be shot in open country. In particular, the chapter describes the foundation of the Society for the Preservation of the Wild Fauna of the Empire (SPWFE), and outlines its early work, sliding conservation ideas deftly into the cogitations of the Colonial Office in London, and corresponding prodigiously with authorities in Africa. The chapter ends by pointing out that while conservationists are no longer universally former shooters of wildlife, the links between hunting and conservation have run deep through the century, and that the notion of 'safari' – a holiday watching (or shooting) big game – has been a potent source of inspiration for conservationists in Africa and elsewhere.

Chapter 3, in a sense, tells the story of conservation through the length of the 20th century, focusing on the rise of the international movement. It takes the narrative on from the pre-Second World War world of London and its amateur scientists and penitent big game hunters. It traces the growth of international action for conservation, leading eventually to the establishment of the organization that became the International Union for the Conservation of Nature (IUCN). It then moves forwards, to discuss the massive growth in support for conservation and in international conservation organizations in the 1960s, and to discuss how the traditional concerns of wildlife preservationists related to the wider phenomenon of environmentalism.

The book then offers a series of thematic discussions of the major strategies used by conservationists. Chapters 4 and 5 discuss protected areas – the foundation of conservation strategies for most of the century. Chapter 4 discusses the rise of the national parks movement in the United States, and of national parks and wildlife conservation in the United Kingdom, before discussing how these ideas were disseminated across the world (first through the colonial world before and after the Second World War) the way these initiatives developed through the period of decolonization, and the development of an international regime of protected areas. Chapter 5 then discusses some of the ideas behind the growth of protected areas – the seductive but problematic idea of wilderness, the issue of poaching and the problem of conservation as something that has to 'defend' nature against attack, particularly from the poor. It discusses the way ideas about protected areas changed from the 1980s to treat people as partners with conservation, the attempt to develop community-based conservation, and the idea that parks were for people, not against them.

Chapter 6 looks at the other main approach used by conservationists in the 20th century, the focus on protecting particular species. Despite the mantra of biodiversity, most conservationists, for most of the 20th century, worked hardest for certain species, especially charismatic large mammals (and to a lesser extent birds). The chapter describes the work of the IUCN Species Survival Commission, and its *Red Data Books*, and the numerous operations in the 1960s and 1970s to save particular species, such as rhinoceros or Arabian oryx. It describes the attempt to build species-orientated projects *in situ*, for example to protect the mountain gorilla. Lastly, it discusses captive breeding, and the importance of wild species to ordinary people, as flagships of conservation projects, and as symbols that can inspire people to care for nature.

The irony of the 20th century for conservationists is the fundamental clash between conservation and development. It was development (urbanization, industrialization, technological advances of the modern rational state) that delivered the freedom from want that could make conservation a mass movement. Yet that same development drove the destruction of nature. Discussions of both protected areas and species conservation eventually run up against the idea of sustainable development, the idea that development and environment could be reconciled. Chapter 7 describes the human impact on nature at the global scale, and the rise of debates about conflicts between conservation and development. It does so first in the context of colonial Africa, where conservationists agonized about the incompatibility of agriculture and wildlife, and fought for many decades to stop the slaughter of game to protect people and cattle from sleeping sickness. It moves from these particular issues to explore the rise of the concept of sustainable development in the 1970s and 1980s. It explores the dilemmas of the environmental impacts of development in the case of dams, and brings the debate up to date with discussion of the Rio and Johannesburg Summits and the Convention on Biological Diversity.

One issue above all emerges from the debate about conservation and development: can species and ecosystems be harvested sustainably? Can people refrain from using their technological capacity to over-exploit species, and hold back their economic urge to do so? This is the subject of Chapter 8. It takes the story right back to the start of the 20th century, when the founders of conservation lamented the exhaustion of elephant populations because of an uncontrolled trade in ivory, and when the impacts of industrial fishing and whaling were first recognized. The chapter discusses the various ways in which these concerns have been expressed, from birds' feathers through whaling to spotted cat furs, and the resort to international agreement to try to regulate trade. The chapter ends with an account of the debate about the significance of the Convention on International Trade in Endangered Species for conservation.

At the end of the 20th century, conservation faced many challenges. Chapter 9 discusses some of them. It starts with the rise of corporatism within conservation, and the phenomenal growth in the size and power of conservation organizations, then moves on to the 'back to the barriers' movement, whose adherents question the efficacy of community-based conservation, and community-based natural resource management. The chapter ends with a consideration of the argument that market-based conservation needs to be taken seriously if people are to find the incentives they need to support conservation in the face of human need. Chapter 10 concludes the book, drawing some reflections on the past for the century ahead.

A number of words and phrases used in this book deserve some explanation. I have used the word 'conservationist' to refer to all of those who, through the 20th century, have worked for conservation as they have seen it. I recognize the distinctive use of conservation to refer to doctrines of rational resource use, and also to distinguish between passive 'preservationist' protection and active 'conservation' management. However, these usages do not have universal currency, and I believe that, although an ugly word, the title 'conservationist' can include all those about whom I have written. Where it is appropriate, I have also called people 'preservationists', and their work preservation. This was the common usage up to the 1950s, certainly outside the United States. It is not intended to be perjorative, or to imply that preservation is an unworthy cause. As will be clear, I believe that in a sense it is the desirability of preserving living diversity that best characterizes conservation through the 20th century.

I have used the words 'nature', 'wild life' (or the more modern 'wildlife') interchangeably, to fit with the usage of the period and people I am describing. Similarly, the now widely obsolete word 'game' is used: early conservationists tried to preserve things they liked to shoot. They thought this was a good idea, and often packaged wider preservationist concerns under this heading.

I use 'Western' and sometimes 'Northern' as shorthand for 'developed' or 'industrialized' countries. I am not automatically implying criticism by doing so, although I am well aware of the arguments of postcolonial theorists. I use the phrases 'developing' and 'Third World' to refer to those countries that are poorer and less industrially and economically developed, and the word 'development' in its conventional sense. This is a deeply problematic concept, and in using it I do not imply that 'development' is always, for everybody, an unmitigated good thing.

Where I have paraphrased the words of past writers, I have mostly used the words they have used without correcting for modern gender or ethnic usages (for example the unconscious generic 'he', or the term 'native'). I have tried to minimize the use of inverted commas as a way of implying my doubts as an author about this language: the effect is mannered, knowing and disruptive to the reader. This does not apply where I have felt free to express myself as I would choose today. If any of this usage offends, I can only apologize.

Several organizations have changed their names through the 20th century. I have everywhere tried to use the names relevant to the period concerned. Of particular note are the name changes in what is now Fauna & Flora International. This was founded as the Society for the Preservation of the Wild Fauna of the Empire (SPWFE). It dropped the word 'wild' from their title after the First World War, and became the Fauna Preservation Society (FPS) in 1950. They added 'Flora' to their title in 1980 (becoming the Fauna and Flora Preservation Society – FFPS), and became Fauna & Flora International (FFI) in 1992. I have tried to use the names in full at least the first time they are referred to in each chapter. The Society's journal followed its name, until 1950, when the name *Oryx* was adopted.[40]

The other organization whose name has most potential to confuse the reader is the International Union for Conservation of Nature and Natural Resources (the World Conservation Union). I have generally referred to this by its familiar acronym IUCN. Prior to taking this name in 1956, it was called the International Union for the Preservation of Nature (IUPN). The story in this book is complex, and, as the century wears on, increasingly so. It is easy to become mired in the jungle of acronyms and organizations, meetings and projects. I have tried to provide a clear guide, without writing in too densely academic a style.[41] It should be noted that the book is primarily based on secondary sources.

Much has changed in the last century. In 1903, Britain was the world's foremost colonial power, and conservation was the visionary obsession of an elite group of big game hunters. A century on, and the British Empire is long consigned to history, but conservation has become a global movement, something that every government in the world has found space for alongside its other concerns. The aim of this book is to describe that change – the process by which conservation moved from a minority to a common concern.

The story of conservation neither started nor ended with the 20th century, but it was central to it. In terms of human consumption, this 100-year period saw an unprecedented challenge to the biosphere, and levels of habitat transformation, a demand for wild products and pollution at a level that beggars belief. Edward Wilson provides a powerful description of the biosphere, that 'stupendously complex layer of living creatures whose activities are locked together in precise but tenuous global cycles of energy and transformed organic matter'. It holds the world we inhabit 'in a unique shimmering disequilibrium'.[42] When we move, all 6 billion of us, with our cars and bicycles, aeroplanes and aerosols, pets and garden furniture, and our endless hunger and poverty, the biosphere flexes. The challenge for conservation in the 21st century is to deal with the unprecedented scale of these human impacts on the biosphere.

The constant in conservation's endless battles of the 20th century was the problem of the loss of living diversity. As Edward Wilson points out, the challenge that conservationists face is to 'to let no species knowingly die'.[43] The common concern in a changing century of conservation is this: the stand against extinction. Although much changed in conservation thinking in practice through the 20th century, much did not. Human demands on nature rose progressively, and squeezed the biosphere hard and ignorantly. That is the bad news. We also began to understand what we were doing and conservationists began to organize themselves, to stand out against extinction in particular cases. By the end of the century we had begun to see the wide picture, to protest that there had to be another way to live. That is rather better news. It is the story of this book.

Chapter 2

Good Hunting

Your true sportsman is always a real lover of nature. He kills, it is true, but only in sweet reasonableness and moderation, for food if necessary, but mainly for trophies. Wholesale and unnecessary slaughter is abhorrent to him; and he always has an eye to the preservation of the stock, and so leaves severely alone all immature, and particularly all female of-their-kind-producing wild animals, except, of course, of the carnivora (Henry Seton-Karr, 1908).[1]

EMPTY PLAINS

The quagga looks a strange animal to modern eyes. It is resembles a zebra of sorts, but it is mostly brown on the back and not white, with the familiar black stripes only on its neck and shoulders. It is indeed a zebra – or rather it was, for the quagga has been extinct for over 100 years. In the early 19th century they lived in the wild on the plains of the Karoo and southern Free State of South Africa. The last animal died in the wild sometime in the 1870s, and the last captive specimen, a mare, died at the Artis Magistra Zoo in Amsterdam on 12 August 1883.

The quagga is something of an enigma. The name, taken from local African languages, came to be used generally for zebras in Afrikaans. Its passing in the wild was unobserved, lost in the clutter of zebras and hunters' reports on the open southern African frontier. For a long time it was not clear if the quagga was a distinct species or not. Now scientists see it as a subspecies of the widely distributed plains zebra, graced by its own Latin trinomial *Equus quagga quagga*.[2] What is certain, is that once extinct, the quagga acquired a new importance, and by the end of the 19th century museum collectors were vying with each other to obtain the few preserved specimens. Walter Rothschild obtained one for his museum at Tring in 1889, a female killed long before, its skeleton originally mounted in Amsterdam in the 1850s.[3] This is one of just 23 mounted specimens in museums around the world (all but one in Europe). With a few paintings, this is all that remains of the quagga to tell us what it looked like.

Perhaps because of the gutteral distinctiveness of its name, the quagga has come to resonate with conservationists in the century or so since its demise. It is one of a small number of commonly-known animals to have been driven to extinction by European hunters. It shares with the dodo of Mauritius, the related solitaire of Reunion, the Steller's sea cow of the northern Pacific, the great auk of the northern Atlantic, and the passenger pigeon of North America an almost mythic status. The dodo was discovered by Europeans in 1507 and was extinct by 1693.[4] The solitaire was discovered in 1625, and was extinct by 1746. Steller's sea cow, a 7-metre long dugong, was hunted to extinction as an accidental impact of the sea otter fur trade by 1768. The flightless great auk was also eaten to extinction, although the last known adults were killed for European collectors on Eldey, off Iceland, in 1844. The passenger pigeon was shot in vast numbers through the 19th century, and was extinct in the wild by 1900, the last captive bird dying in Cincinnati Zoo in 1914.[5] These are among conservation's iconic species, held up for veneration and as a visual reminder of past sin. Their names trigger a familiar morality tale, of human greed and irresponsibility. As one commentator described, in 1907, the demise of the American bison, 'it took but a few years to exterminate the vast masses of the American bison which used to darken the prairie and were counted one of the wonders of the new World'.[6]

The quagga was not alone in bearing the impact of hunters' guns in the Cape. The first Dutch settlers in 1652 found the Cape alive with grazing animals, but by the start of the 19th century the great migratory herds were gone. Game was a great free resource, a bounty for the settler and an economic subsidy for European colonization. The frontier was open, and shooting unregulated. Boer trekkers and farmers hunted for sport and for meat, and as they drove the agricultural frontier northwards, game disappeared before it.[7] Another antelope, the blaubok, had disappeared by 1798, almost before Europe's naturalist collectors had registered its existence.

Through the 19th century, hunters reached further and further north, and the trade in ivory, horns, skins and ostrich plumes grew. The quagga was killed for meat and for its leather, but more particularly because it ate grass, and in the dry and drought-prone Karoo, settlers saw it as a competitor for their sheep and a threat to the merino wool industry. John MacKenzie comments that neither humans nor game were permitted to compete with intensive sheep farming.[8] Hunting was regarded as a fundamental right for settlers, and an important form of socialization for young Boer men.[9] As intensive settlement spread, hunters had to move further north, travelling on long expeditions in slack seasons.

From the 1830s a new kind of hunting developed. Visitors, many of them en route for military or civil service in India, organized expeditions far up-country to shoot. They killed prodigiously, and wrote best-selling books about their exploits. They combined two Victorian enthusiasms, for natural history and for shooting as sport.[10] Their trophies began to grace walls in illustrious Victorian houses, and their specimens the collections of public and private museums. The sale of ivory and other products provided a valuable subsidy for their expeditions, and sometimes substantial profits. Men such as William Harris and Roualeyn Cumming penetrated north to the Limpopo and beyond. Their accounts of their exploits reported plains teeming with game, a paradise for the hunter. Their guns were simple smooth-bore devices, and their larger quarry had to be shot repeatedly before they succumbed, but their tally of kills was prodigious and their trophies legion. Their books, such as Harris's *The Wild Sports of Southern Africa* (1839) and Cumming's *Five Years of a Hunter's Life in the Far Interior of Africa* (1850) became best-sellers.[11] Their bloodthirsty accounts of killing were an integral part of their appeal to the hunting-obsessed Victorian elite.

By the time William Baldwin added his *African Hunting and Adventure from Natal to the Zambezi* to the canon (in 1863), the impacts of all this blood enterprise were becoming clear.[12] He completed seven hunting journeys, each reaching further into the hinterland; the last covered 2000 miles. He shot, and he employed Africans to hunt for him as he pursued the shrinking herds to an ever more distant hunting frontier. By the 1860s, both he and the African rulers from whom he sought permission to hunt were becoming aware of a shortage of game. By that time, high-velocity breech-loading rifles had come into use, and the killing of game had become much easier. Over much of what has become South Africa, game was shot out, and the once crowded plains were denuded. Within a century, the hunting frontier had stretched beyond reach. By the end of the 19th century, there were only two tiny populations of elephants south of the Limpopo, in the Addo bush near Port Elizabeth, and the Zitzikanna forest near Mossel Bay.[13] Accounts of hunting began to move beyond the celebration of plenty and destruction, to speculate openly on the destruction. Books like H A Bryden's *Gun and Camera in Southern Africa*[14] warned of the imminent destruction of game. The age of preservation had arrived.

IMPERIAL CONSERVATION

In a sense it had long been there. The first game legislation in the Cape was introduced by the Dutch in 1657, with a law in 1684 that distinguished between protected animals (like hippopotamus) and vermin (like lions). A close relative of the quagga, the Cape mountain zebra, nearly shared its fate. Hunting of this species was officially banned in 1742, but without much effect (Jonathan Kingdon notes that by the 1950s, the population was reduced to eleven animals on a single farm; the present world population of 700 is descended from seven animals).[15]

The impacts of settlers and hunters on wildlife in South Africa were not unusual. John MacKenzie cautions against the idea that European imperialism triggered some kind of environmental apocalypse, but locally its impact could be near disastrous.[16] In Australia and New Zealand, and in North and South America, colonists established little replicas of Europe on foreign shores. European settlers cut forest and tilled soil, shot, trapped and poisoned any organism that threatened the new ecological imperialism.[17] They set bounties on any species that walked, flew, swam, or crawled, and could be construed a pest.[18] Indigenous people were treated with little more respect. Many of those who survived the onslaught of European diseases were removed from valuable lands, some even hunted to extinction. New-found lands were emptied and cleared for economic production. Only in places like lowland tropical Africa, did this cruel ecological enchantment fail to have its effect; here disease kept European colonization and even exploration at bay until the 19th century.

These impacts were not entirely lost on colonial observers. The destruction of forests and endemic species on islands was particularly obvious (including of course the solitaire and dodo of the Mascarene islands from the 1760s). In time there emerged more general concerns, for example about the impacts of deforestation on climate.[19] Forest protection began to be institutionalized in British Caribbean territories in the 18th century, but it was in India that formal environmentalist forestry developed on a large scale. By the mid-19th century, forests had become an important dimension of imperial policy in India, driven by concerns about timber shortage, soil erosion and fear of disastrous climatic change: Gregory Barton says that 'fear of catastrophe haunted empire foresters'. In response, a formal, scientific forestry regime was developed: by 1890 there were 130,000 square kilometres of forest reserves and 52,000 square kilometres of protected forest in India, and a small army of government functionaries to look after it.[20] The model for Kipling's Mowgli in *The Jungle Book* was a forest service employee.[21]

There were successive attempts to legislate to protect wildlife in southern Africa through the 19th century. These began with the Game Law Proclamation of July 1822, which reintroduced the idea of vermin, as well as closed seasons and, for some species (initially including elephants), a licence fee. It also, however, granted rights in game to private landowners, and allowed travellers to hunt for food. Legislation to preserve open areas close to Cape Town was passed in 1846, and an act for the preservation of forests in 1859. A colonial botanist was appointed to the Cape Colony in 1858. By about 1880, a pattern of conservation (derived from a mix of Indian and Cape Colony philosophies) was established in southern Africa.[22] The real preservationist enterprise began with the passage of the Act for the Better Preservation of Game, in 1886. This awarded special protection to a number of species, including the quagga (which was in fact already extinct in the wild). In truth, by then, there was little game left in the Cape Colony to shoot, but the provisions of this act were replicated in the Transkei, and other areas, including Natal, in the 1880s and 1890s.[23]

This was a time when preservation and conservation initiatives were springing up all over the world. In the United States, the Yellowstone National Park was established in 1872, and the Sierra Club in 1892.[24] National Parks were also established in the 1880s and 1890s in the British Dominions of Canada, South Australia and New Zealand.[25] In Europe, International Ornithological Congresses were held in Vienna in 1884 and Budapest in 1895, leading eventually to a treaty being signed in 1902 to protect bird species 'useful in agriculture'.[26] The early years of the 20th century saw the foundation, in 1909, of the Swiss League for the Protection of Nature (primarily to raise funds for a National Park, achieved in 1914), and of the Swedish Society for the Protection of Nature.

Concern about the loss of game in southern Africa found a ready echo in East Africa, much more recently brought under imperial control. The ivory trade through the East African coastal ports was huge, driven in part by consumer demand in Europe and the United States for the accoutrements of a gentleman's smoking room and drawing room, billiard balls and piano keys.[27] Soldiers, traders and administrators hunted for ivory to pay their way out to and back from East Africa in the closing years of the 19th century, just as they had in the south – indeed, men such as Arthur Neumann came north because the hunting had not yet been exhausted. However, observers reported the same process of a moving frontier of game destruction. In particular, Joseph Thomson's account of the Royal Geographical Society's expedition to East and Central Africa in 1878–1880 reported that ivory traders were pushing further and further into remote areas away from the coast.[28] They employed Africans to obtain ivory, spreading firearms deep into the hinterland. Thomson predicted the demise of the elephant and of the ivory trade, reporting that in 14 months around the Great Lakes he saw not a single elephant, a shocking contrast to the ubiquitous herds found by David Livingstone 20 years before. In retrospect, it was clear that Thomson was wrong to report the elephant's imminent demise, his conviction reflecting primarily the lack of data on places such as Uganda, Sudan and northern Kenya. However, the assault of unregulated hunting was undoubtedly considerable, and expanding. The notion that it could not be sustained struck a chord in both Africa and London.

Disease also shattered the illusion of limitless game. Rinderpest arrived on the tail of colonial penetration into northeast Africa from the Indian subcontinent in the 1880s. It swept across the plains of East Africa, and then southwards. It destroyed the livelihoods of pastoral people such as the Maasai, who were also suffering epidemics of smallpox, drought and internecine strife that followed the collapse of systems of social reciprocity.[29] Rinderpest also drastically reduced populations of wild ungulates (for example buffalo, eland and wildebeest), with long-term impacts on ecology.[30] In what became Kenya and northern Tanganyika, the loss of livestock and the crash in wild herbivore populations allowed scrub and tsetse fly to expand. Maasai social organization collapsed, and insurgent European colonists could imagine a land scantly unoccupied, and its people warlike and turbulent cattle raiders. The loss of game had severe impacts on the provisioning of settlers and troops, for example in the bloody suppression of the Ndebele rebellion of 1896–7 in what became Rhodesia.[31]

Regulations for the preservation of game began to be passed in a number of African colonies at the end of the 19th century, for example in Kenya in 1898, 1899 and 1900, and by the British South Africa Company in Rhodesia in 1898. The problem of hunting was well established within the mental architecture of colonial responsibility. British legislation developed the southern African approach of issuing regulations about what could be shot, and by whom, on close seasons and licences. By the turn of the century, game preservation regulations had already been enacted in British Central Africa, British East Africa and Uganda, and (by the India Office) in Somaliland and various other African territories. Reserves had been set aside in Sudan, Kenya, Uganda, British Central Africa (a small reserve in what is now Malawi, at Elephant Marsh, sadly even at that time without elephants) and Somaliland. British colonial territories had established schedules of protected species (typically including the giraffe, eland and buffalo), and larger and slow-breeding species whose breeding females and young should be preserved (for example rhinoceros, hippopotamus and greater kudu). In addition, licences set a limit on the numbers of each species that could be killed, and demanded a list of what had been killed when the licence expired. There had also been some progress with the establishment of game reserves. In Kenya, the Ukamba Game Reserve was created in 1899.

The main reason for this sudden activity was interest from the British government in London. In 1896 Lord Salisbury (both Prime Minister and Foreign Secretary) wrote a circular to the Commissioners of the East African Protectorate and Uganda requesting information on game regulations. In the words of the *Saturday Review*, ten years later, he 'suddenly awoke to the fact that a grand national possession was being ruthlessly squandered, the great game of the empire'.[32] Salisbury also circulated regulations recently formulated by Hermann von Wissman in German East Africa, which established reserves, on the Rufiji and west of Mount Kilimanjaro. Britain's colonial governors in Africa did not favour the idea of reserves as a means to achieve preservation, but the idea was to take firm hold.

Wissman proposed a conference on game preservation, and eventually one took place, in 1900, under the auspices of the British Foreign Office. This was dominated by Germany and Britain, but included also the other African colonial powers (France, Portugal, Spain, Italy and the Belgian Congo). The resulting Convention for the Preservation of Animals, Birds and Fish in Africa sought to strengthen and standardize game laws across colonial Africa. Signatories agreed to establish a select list of species in danger of extinction that should be protected from all hunting (as should immature animals and breeding females) to limit the sale of elephant tusks of less than 11 pounds, and to establish 'adequate reserves and protect them from encroachment'.[33] Few parties ratified the Convention, but the principle that colonial authorities should regulate hunting and set aside reserves was established.[34]

EXTINCTION

What was emerging in debates about game in southern and East Africa was a concentration of concern about extinction. This was to become the great theme of 20th century conservation. Graeme Caughley and Anne Gunn suggest that population decline is one of two fundamental paradigms of conservation biology (the other being the persistence of small populations of species).[35] They suggest that much of the work of contemporary conservation biology can be understood as detecting, diagnosing and reversing population decline.

In the popular imagination, the quagga has been joined by a succession of other charismatic species threatened with extinction as popular subjects of conservation's openly emotional appeal.[36] The chinchilla, the Seychelles magpie-robin, the woodhen of Lord Howe Island, have all won a place in conservation's list of *causes célèbres*. Some icons are unlikely, such as the thylacine (or Tasmanian tiger), which after years of persecution received protection in 1936, six years after the last wild animal was shot, and barely two months before the last zoo specimen (in Hobart's Beaumaris Zoo) died of neglect.[37] On the other hand, the cuddly giant panda, selected and drawn by Peter Scott as the symbol of the World Wildlife Fund in 1961, perfectly captured this slightly mawkish public sentimentality about extinction.[38] There has often been both an anger and a desperation about it. My childhood hero, Gerald Durrell, explained in the introduction to his exotic account of the animal collecting expedition to West Africa from which he eventually founded Jersey Zoo, that 'to me the extirpation of an animal species is a criminal offence, in the same way as the destruction of anything we cannot recreate or replace, such as a Rembrandt or the Acropolis'.[39]

The idea of extinction is still a powerhouse of conservation concern, but, since the 1990s, emotional responses are frequently locked within a more coolly constructed rationalistic argument, built around the concept of biodiversity. This vogue word, currently so dominant in the things conservationists (and their opponents) say, was only coined in the 1980s. It hit public prominence in the proceedings of a conference of the US National Academy of Sciences and Smithsonian Institution in 1986, edited by Edward Wilson and Frances Peter in

1988.[40] The purpose of that meeting was to reflect on the 'intricate tapestry of interwoven lifeforms' that we call the biosphere, and the way human activity was altering and destroying it.[41] A man called Walter G Rosen coined the beguilingly simple word biodiversity, seeming to make simple the complexity of what was under threat.

The concept of biodiversity was at the core of Edward Wilson's *The Diversity of Life*,[42] and given global authority by its use as the foundational concept in the Convention on Biological Diversity (CBD) in 1992. The text of that convention defined biodiversity as 'the variability among living organisms', including terrestrial, marine and other aquatic ecosystems and the ecological complexes of which they are part; the term includes diversity within species, between species and diversity of ecosystems.[43]

Biodiversity is a clever word for the multitude of living things, and links between things, that late 20th century industrial society threatened. And in the language of biodiversity, extinction was what they faced, if the conservationists failed to get things right. At the 1986 US National Forum, veteran conservation polemicist Norman Myers opened his paper saying 'there is strong evidence that we are into the opening stages of an extinction spasm'.[44] Four years later, Edward Wilson suggested that in the 20th century, human activity has raised background rates of extinction to between 1000 and 10,000 times the geological 'background' rate of one species per million species per year: the sixth great episode of extinction in the history of the earth.[45]

Of course, the measurement of extinction rates is problematic, since, as a friend of mine likes to explain in lectures, 'you have to be absolutely sure that you know the identity of absolutely the last individual of a species, and you have to watch it die'. There are few taxonomists in the rainforest, and many species (most of them beetles, of which the world enjoys the widest diversity) must pass uncounted. The Secretariat of the CBD estimated in 2001 that some 300–350 species of vertebrate and 400 invertebrate animals (plus an indeterminate number of plants) had become extinct in the last four centuries of the second millennium of the common era.[46] Conservation biologists, however, warn that such numbers provide a poor guide to current human impacts.[47] Much effort goes into computing the dreary statistics of rarity and extinction. The IUCN-World Conservation Union Species Survival Commission has a Red List (formerly *Red Data Book*) programme that defines no less than eight categories of near-extinction.[48] Of the two groups assessed comprehensively, 12 per cent of birds and 24 per cent of mammals are judged threatened (defined as critically endangered, endangered or vulnerable). Research suggests that future extinction rates may be ten times current rates.[49]

The number of species becoming extinct matters, but not to my argument here. Indeed, even contrarians such as Bjorn Lomborg, the 'sceptical environmentalist', accept that something untoward is going on.[50] The significance of environmentalist concern about enhanced rates of extinction in the 20th century is the parallel knowledge that the creation of diversity has come, in Wilson's words, so 'hard and slow', through billions of years of evolution. The modern fauna and flora consist of 'survivors that somehow managed to dodge and weave through all the radiations and extinctions of modern history'.[51] Behind the science-speak, Wilson's conservationist passion is unmistakable – 'Earth has at last acquired a force that can break the crucible of evolution'.[52]

PRESSURE FOR PRESERVATION

Those who bemoaned the loss of the quagga and the emptying of the southern African plains did not think on such a scale, or with so clear and scientifically inspired a vision, but their concern about extinction, and the urgent need for conservation, was remarkably similar. One such was an Essex man called Edward North Buxton. He was a wealthy City of London business owner, of dogged East Anglian Quaker stock. His grandfather was Sir Thomas Fowell Buxton, who had taken over the anti-slavery movement when Wilberforce died. Buxton was a hunter and, in the words of his obituary, 'an ardent preserver of game'. He inherited the Victorian gentleman's visceral awareness of managing covert and park for shooting. He knew quite well that hunting 'must not be done in such a way as to endanger the existence or seriously diminish the stock of game'.[53] He had also hunted in Africa, travelling there twice, to British East Africa and Somaliland.[54] His gun and camera had been deployed in what he described as 'two of the best game districts remaining in Africa', (the 'Kenia-Kilimanjaro plateau', and the Sudan).[55] His experiences, set out in his 1902 book *Two African Trips*, led him to become a formidable campaigner for the preservation of big game in Tropical Africa. He cited experience in America and South Africa that showed 'how rapidly the teeming millions born of the soil may be shot out'.[56]

Buxton already had a proven track record in the embryonic British conservation movement. He was a leading figure in the Commons Preservation Society, founded in 1865 to fight the enclosure of areas such as Hampstead Heath and Wimbledon Common.[57] Conservation had emerged in Britain in the 19th century from an amalgam of the natural history movement, concerns for animal welfare, and reaction to the prodigious growth of towns and the effects of uncontrolled industrialization. In 1865, legislation was passed to protect seabirds on their nesting cliffs, and the Society for the Protection of Birds was founded in 1893, a year before the National Trust for Places of Historic Interest and Natural Beauty.[58]

Buxton and his cousin had caused controversy in the 1860s by supporting local commoners taken to court for exercising their ancient rights to cut wood in Epping Forest, where they lived. Most landowners wished to extinguish these rights, in order to enclose and develop the forest, as had been done in nearby Hainault Forest. Eventually, in Buxton's words 'a truer and juster view of the needs and rights of the public began to prevail', and the land was vested in the Corporation of the City of London under the Epping Forest Act of 1878.[59] Buxton acted as a Verderer of the forest for much of the next half century, and remained committed to conservation in Britain throughout his life.[60]

In 1903, Buxton led the creation of the Society for the Preservation of the Wild Fauna of the Empire (SPWFE) to exert influence on the British Colonial Office for game preservation. The SPWFE was the first conservation organization with a global focus, albeit one confined to the vast smears of imperial pink on maps of the British Empire. It was also the embodiment of Buxton's views on game preservation in Africa, and the stimulus for its creation lay in Buxton's own travels in Africa. The authorities in the Sudan had recently created a vast game reserve between the White and Blue Niles and the Sobat River. In 1903 they had changed their mind, and proposed to open this up to hunting, one part for the use of government officials and the other for the recreation of non-official visitors. A new reserve further south was proposed to replace it, much further south on the Zeraf River, in the Sudd wetlands. Buxton regarded this as a disaster, and he decided to pull some strings.

Buxton called a series of meetings with friends and associates at his house, and they decided to gather powerful signatories for a letter to Lord Cromer, then Governor-General of the Sudan. This was duly written, and signed by a panoply of aristocratic or political figures, including the Duke and Duchess of Bedford, Sir Edward Grey, Lord Avebury, the Marquis of Hamilton, and the Earl of Rosebery, Sydney Buxton (Edward North Buxton's brother), and Sir Henry Seton-Karr; businessmen such as brewery owner Samuel H Whitbread; scientists and naturalists including Oldfield Thomas, Ray Lankester, P L Sclater and Richard Lydekker. There were also colonial administrators such as Sir Harry Johnston, and famous hunters and writers about Africa, notably Frederick Courtney Selous.

The letter was polite, but firm. It took no issue with the idea that white colonial officers and visitors should hunt for recreation, but pointed out that the new reserve was too far from Khartoum. Game close to the capital, without a sanctuary, would be quickly shot out. The new reserve on the other hand, was so remote that it could not be supervised, and anyway would be flooded for half the year and empty of game.

The willingness of leading figures to sign this letter suggested a considerable depth of interest in game preservation in far-flung corners of empire: Buxton was by no means the only gentleman in London who had travelled, marvelled and shot in Africa. On 30 July 1903, a meeting of the letter's signatories was held in the House of Commons to discuss the creation of a permanent society to promote game preservation. In early December a note was circulated celebrating the success of the petition and announcing the first meeting of a small association, 'for the purpose of collecting information as to the number of wild animals killed each year, the gradual disappearance of species &c, and to take steps as far as possible to check this destruction'.[61] The society would gather and propagate information amongst its members about 'game reserves, game laws, the amount of game killed, the gradual disappearance of species, etc. throughout Africa'. In 1908, Henry Seton-Karr summed up what the Society was for: 'where opportunity presents itself, we who know something of what may be going on in outlying regions wish to lose no chance of advocating, in season and out of season, and at the risk of becoming nuisances, all reasonable and effective game preservation'.

It was the Society's belief that game preservation could best be done 'by Imperial Government action in the case of Crown Colonies and Protectorates; by a healthy and active public opinion working through Colonial Governments in the case of self-governing Colonies'.[62] It was the society's self-allotted task to stimulate both the official and the public mind, and they did so with energy. It worked within the elite political and business world of London, particularly using its influence in Parliament. It arranged for questions to be asked in the Houses of Commons and Lords, and it wrote directly to authorities in Africa. One of their first acts was to write to question British South Africa Company policy of allowing its railway construction workers to kill game for meat, pointing to the lessons to be learned from the extermination of the American bison and the Union Pacific railway. They followed up by meeting the directors of the company (including Earl Grey, who at that time was vice-chairman) to be reassured that the company would not allow game regulations to be broken, and would contact native commissioners to identify the best places for game sanctuaries.

Above all, however, the society worked on the British government. Between the years 1905 and 1909, the SPWFE had three meetings with different Secretaries of State for the Colonies. Their first concern was the need for game reserves. In 1902, Buxton had criticized the areas selected for the first reserves, 'not always chosen with sufficient knowledge or regard to the surrounding conditions and the need of the game'.[63] He also criticized the way they were run, and particularly that colonial officers were allowed to shoot in them. He felt that 'a sanctuary where people are allowed to shoot is a contradiction in terms', and that the purpose of the reserves as 'sanctuaries' was being undermined by lax controls on the activities of government officers themselves.[64] In the Kenia Reserve, for example, officers had interpreted the regulations to mean they had free access to the whole of the reserve. Such abuse was more pronounced in the Sudan, where the game reserve was regarded as an 'officers' reserve'. Buxton points out a little peevishly that vast areas of the Sudan (Darfur, Kordofan and land south of the Sobat for example) were declared closed to hunting by travellers, but open to officers and civil servants. Such practices led to abuse – as he noted, 'game may disappear before the official uniform as well as the unprivileged traveller'.[65]

At the first meeting with the Secretary of State, in 1905, Lyttelton undertook to send dispatches to the African protectorates about game reserves, of appropriate size and location. He also promised to press upon the administrators of self-governing colonies (such as Rhodesia) both the commercial value of game and the aesthetic importance of beautiful places. The dispatches that resulted from these enquiries were published as a series of Blue Books between 1906 and 1913.[66] In response the society detailed their recommendations for preservation policy.

Looking back on the SPWFE's foundation in 1907, Samuel Whitbread commented 'its first year saw it in the shape of a modest and unpretentious group of gentlemen of wide experience of the outposts of Empire, and a common enthusiasm for the preservation from wanton destruction of many of its fauna'. By 1906 it was 'fairly launched upon the stream of public affairs as a going concern'.[67] Lords Curzon, Minto, Grey, Cromer and Milner, and Mr Alfred Littleton MP 'attest the fact that our great administrators are alive to the Imperial obligation of guarding from wanton destruction the marvellous varieties of life which are still to be found within the circumference of His Majesty's Dominions beyond the seas'.[68]

PROPER HUNTING

There is no doubt that the driving force for wildlife conservation at the start of the 20th century in both Africa and India were the European hunters. The ideas, and the activities, of preservation grew in part from the European tradition of aristocratic hunting, with beasts reserved for the King and his lords, in descending order of priority. Areas of land, forests and parks were set aside as reserves for formalized elite hunting, and woe betide any ordinary mortal caught hunting beasts for the pot. In the Victorian period, the shooting, for pheasants, grouse and red deer, and the chasing of foxes with packs of dogs, became vital rituals of the landowning class, a mark of social achievement and the markers of a shared culture. Whole landscapes in the United Kingdom were reworked for the practices of hunting, most brazenly in the Scottish clearances.[69] The hardy backwoods hunter was a staple of boy's fiction, from Rider Haggard's Allan Quatermain to John Buchan's Peter Pienaar.[70]

Historians such as John MacKenzie have demonstrated how hunting in Africa and India was tied in by connections of class and wealth to this British Victorian world. It was the same people, and the same enthusiasms at work. In India, the British took over and adapted elite Mughal hunting practices, especially tiger shooting from elephant back and the use of beaters. They added to them their favourite sports such as pig sticking and fox hunting. Robert Baden-Powell, founder of the Boy Scouts, was an enthusiastic pig-sticker; he also, with Earl Grey, joined the first meeting of the foxhounds in Salisbury, Rhodesia, in 1896, just after the suppression of the Ndebele rebellion.[71] In 1845, Sir Thomas Peyton kept a pack of foxhounds at the hill station of Ootacamund ('Ooty') in the Nilgiri hills in India, and in 1869 there was a regular pack. By the end of the century an area of about 80 square kilometres of grass and woodland was specifically reserved for hunting jackal, and the Ooty hunt met twice a week between May and September. A contemporary commented 'the hill jackal is an animal of wonderful speed and bottom. I should consider him the superior of the pampered foxes of the English counties'.[72]

European hunters abroad took with them a long tradition of opposition to subsistence hunting. This was generally seen to be haphazard, inefficient, wasteful and cruel. In Africa it was something that colonial observers thought distracted rural people from gainful employment in cash crop production or wage labour. It was widely proscribed by formal law, and the problem of poaching became an increasingly important issue in conservation as the 20th century progressed. The significance of poaching is discussed later in this book in Chapter 5, and the wider issue of commercial hunting in Chapter 8.

The problem of excessive and/or unsporting hunting by European hunters was initially more important in the development of conservation ideas. It was something that many hunters themselves worried about, and it led them both to start to regulate themselves, and (perhaps more surprisingly) to support regulation by the colonial state. In the Nilgiri hills in India, for example, the Nilgiri Game Association was established in 1877 to police hunters in the hills. They campaigned for the Nilgiri Game and Fish Preservation Act 1879, which imposed a closed season and a licence fee for shooting. Apart from local Indians, there were three groups who did not comply with the new game regulations: – British planters (who claimed that sambhur and spotted deer were pests destroying their plantations); army personnel of Wellington cantonment (whose disregard for local society was amply demonstrated by practices such as the theft of pedigree dogs); and visitors from the plains 'bent on slaughter', who had no stake in Nilgiri society.[73] Under the act, shooting could be done only for trophies, not for food. It stopped local Indians holding guns, registered native shikaris and banned the sale of game meat to British residents of Ooty.

By the end of the 19th century, elite hunters in America had come to share the same preservationist ideas. Hunting expeditions were fashionable among the new industrial elite, particularly as the western frontier was declared 'closed' in 1890.[74] From the 1860s, wealthy young men had begun to frequent the Adirondacks to engage in the masculine pastimes of shooting and fishing. Their approach was an odd combination of British upper-class tradition and an attempt to recreate the American frontier experience, albeit often as a thin veneer over tourist luxury. What was the fairest, the most manly and the most interesting way to hunt? The ideas of these 'sports' were far removed from those of local people who had long hunted for food.[75] The palaeontologist George Bird Grinnell took over as editor of the weekly *Forest and Stream in 1880*, and began to argue for action to counter the disappearance of game and habitat. He proposed that hunters should pay fees to support game wardens and game laws, a revolutionary concept, cutting across the traditionally untrammelled hunters' world.[76]

One man epitomizes the engagement of wealthy east coast Americans in game conservation, Theodore Roosevelt. He first visited the Adirondacks in

1871, and hunted in the Maine Woods in 1878 following the death of his father. He had been a sickly child, but became a symbol of and fierce advocate for a manly outdoor life. He first visited the west in 1884, hunting buffalo in Dakota Territory. He returned to New York the owner of two ranches, and the following year wrote the hugely successful *Hunting Trips of a Ranchman*. He shot duck and rode to foxes in the east, but it was in the west that his heart lay. He returned repeatedly to hunt in Dakota and elsewhere in the west, shooting elk, bear and even a few residual buffalo for sport, and hunting cougar and coyote not only for pleasure but also as a form of vermin control.

Roosevelt adored the whole adventure of hunting, felt keen delight in finding and killing game, and broader pleasure in wilderness. He extolled the virtues of the wild landscape and the hard rancher's life. It was a world that he recognized was passing. He wrote 'the broad and boundless prairies have already been bounded and will soon be made narrow. It is scarcely a figure of speech to say that the tide of white settlement during the last few years has risen over the West like a flood; and the cattlemen are but the spray from the crest of the wave, thrown far in advance, but soon to be overtaken.[77] This sense of loss was brought into focus by the disappearance of game from the prairies. On a hunting trip in the Little Missouri River, Dakota in 1887, Roosevelt was deeply disturbed to find the plains empty of game, beavers trapped out of the streams, the buffalo hunted out, the grassland overgrazed. On his return in December 1887, he invited a dozen like-minded men to dinner at his house in Manhattan, notably George Bird Grinnell. He floated the idea of an amateur association, named after two childhood American heroes, Daniel Boone and Davy Crockett. The first formal meeting of the Boone and Crockett Club took place in January 1888, with Roosevelt as president. They set up a committee to promote a national zoo, and another to push the Secretary of the Interior to enlarge Yellowstone National Park, created in 1872 but under assault from logging, tourism, railway construction and hunting.[78] A bill was pushed through the New York State legislature to create the New York Zoological Society in 1895; the Bronx Zoo was opened in 1899.[79] In 1905, the Society's President, William Hornaday, led, as its first campaign, a programme of reintroduction of the Zoo's captive American bison to government lands in the west.[80]

Roosevelt did not forswear hunting – far from it. He last shot American bison in 1889, noting (apparently without irony) that 'I felt the most exultant pride as I handled and examined him, for I had procured a trophy such as can fall henceforth to few hunters indeed'.[81] To men such as Roosevelt (and hunters and conservationists at this time were almost all men), it was not hunting itself, but unreasonable volumes of killing that were at fault for depleting game. The same argument inspired the hunting members of the Society for the Preservation of the Wild Fauna of the Empire. In the United States in 1921, William Hornaday wrote that 'the great mass of worth-while sportsmen are true protectors and conservators, who sincerely desire the perpetuation of game and hunting sport, and the conservation of the rights of posterity therein'.[82] US regulations were good, and 'the more ignorant and vicious the gunner', the more he feared the 'long arm and the strong hand of the federal government'. However, there was a 'really savage element in the army of destruction' that was 'just as brutal, savage and relentless as it ever was in the worst days of the past. The real game hog is just as hoggish as ever'.[83]

Edward North Buxton believed the disappearance of 'game' from Africa (by which he meant almost all large mammals, especially antelope, but including carnivores, elephant, rhinoceros and hippopotamus) was the result of 'reckless shooting' and bloodthirstiness (shooting of excessive numbers of animals).[84] In 1908, an editorial in the *Saturday Review* had attributed the decreases in game in Africa to big-game hunters and to rich and irresponsible young Englishmen excitedly amassing large game bags.[85] In an article in the SPWFE's journal, Sir Henry Seton-Karr was at pains to quash the notion that the society itself consisted of 'penitent butchers'.[86] He and his like were ignorantly thought to be 'men who, having in earlier days taken their fill of big-game slaughter and the delights of the chase in wild, outlying parts of the earth, now, being smitten with remorse, and having reached a less strenuous term of life, think to condone our earlier bloodthirstiness by advocating the preservation of what we formerly chased and killed'.[87] It was not so.

Seton-Karr expressed himself confident that 'British sportsmen, as a class, have done nothing in any wild country to reduce or wipe out any kind of wild big game'. Their 'so-called depredations' (he regarded this term as a misnomer) had been 'more than compensated for by the natural reproduction and increase of the wild game'. His argument was that real sportsmen had nothing to be penitent about, since their demands were modest, although he admitted that 'amateur ivory hunters and certain sportsmen-naturalists in search of specimens' were not altogether clear of guilt. The former had been tempted to kill 'more than a fair proportion' of elephants in Central Africa for their ivory, while certain 'sportsmen-naturalists', in their desire for zoological specimens, had committed 'greater depredations on African big game than the reasonable humane sportsman can approve of'. The problem was not with the reasonable hunter – but rather that some big game hunters needed education in true sportsmanship. Even in 1902, licences set a limit on the numbers of each species that could be killed, and demanded a list of what had been killed when the licence expired. Buxton dismissed objections to these regulations with revealing ferocity: 'the legitimate sportsman has no reason to fear it, and the mere butcher should be gibeted (*sic*)'.[88]

The chief problem with European hunting in Africa was therefore portrayed as a failure of 'true sportsmanship', especially the killing of excessive numbers of animals, where 'an otherwise sane man runs amuck'.[89] There were also problems with 'those whose sporting instincts are undeveloped or perhaps stunted',[90] or 'sportsmen, some of them very young, who get bitten by the 'buck fever', and who fire away far more shots than they need'.[91]

European settlers, of course, were very often fiercely energetic killers of game. In their attempt to fit game preservation into the legislative agenda of colonial governments, early conservationists found themselves out of sympathy with the way settlers hunted. When they first arrived in Kenya, settlers were in many cases looked on by colonial officials as people 'whose sole object was to slaughter game and break laws'.[92] Colonial officials themselves hunted (Lord Cromer, for example, saw it as 'perfectly justifiable' that British civil and military officials in the Sudan should be allowed 'certain privileges in the matter of sport' in 'part return for the excellent and very arduous services' they rendered[93]). On the other hand, James Stevenson-Hamilton argued that this created quite the wrong effect in terms of the wider public acceptance of conservation (that is by settlers). There should be no exceptions allowing 'privileged persons' to shoot, because this would 'arouse discontent among the less favoured portion of the population', and 'is pretty sure to work havoc with the scheme'.[94]

Lord Hindlip (himself a prominent Kenyan settler) argued in the SPWFE's journal in 1905 that making exceptions in this way had the effect of angering settlers and alienating them from the cause of game preservation.[95] The game licence did not allow the settler to kill as much as an official who paid the same £10 fee, and the settler could not shoot more than the specified number of animals even 'to protect his crops or homestead against the depredations of wild animals, large or small'. Lord Hindlip also protested about the 'extraordinary latitude' that allowed officials to hunt in the southern or Masailand Reserve.[96] Eventually, to test the law, Lord Delamere (informally the leader of the settler interest, and like his flamboyant friend Ewart Scott Grogan a member of the Shikar Club and a tireless hunter) killed one zebra more than his licence. He was fined by the magistrate, but the law was changed, allowing a settler to kill game on his own land, and kill Royal game damaging his property.[97]

To early conservationists, settlers did not share the ideals (or indeed in many cases the moneyed leisure) of the traditional sportsman. Sir Henry Seton-Karr noted 'it is a curious fact that the men who, one would think, are, or should be, mainly interested in game preservation, the men who are indigenous to a country or have gone there to settle, and to whom the maintenance of its natural wealth of wild animal life for sport, for food, for revenue and gain is all-important – these are the very men who have invariably been most apt to diminish or destroy it'.[98]

Sir Charles Eliot, author of *East African Protectorate* (described in the SPWFE Journal as writing 'as one outside the fraternity of sportsmen; indeed he regards the act of destroying an antelope as 'devilish'[99]), did not think that settlers could be made to observe schedules of game because of the damage animals did in gardens and plantations.[100] Perhaps for this reason, in 1909, the Society reported 'a serious recrudescence of the agitation among British East African settlers for absolute freedom to make a profit by the destruction of game and the sale of hides'.[101] Eliot's successor, Sir J Hayes Sadler, agreed with him. He wrote to Lord Crewe in 1908 that the time had come to remove restrictions on settlers' hunting that cut across 'the assistance the settlers have a right to expect from the State in securing immunity to their estates from the depredations of wild animals'.[102]

Whatever the ideal benefits of game as a source of 'sport, for food, for revenue and gain', colonists were reluctant to share the landscape they had taken and settled. In 1909 a motion was proposed to the Colonists' Association in Kenya that 'in the interests of the farming community', restrictions on killing game in settled districts should be removed'.[103] The South African model, so painful to the SPWFE and its friends in London, was here applauded. Zebra and wildebeest were no longer rare (as when the Ordinance was passed in 1900), and they 'carried disease all over the country'. Game should be 'got rid of' and not at the settlers' expense: it 'ought to be made worth the while of settlers to kill them' by selling skins, horns and bones. This was exactly what the conservationists wished to avoid. The arguments were identical to those that had prevailed in South Africa: one correspondent wrote 'I am of the opinion that under modern conditions, given trade in horns and skins, the fauna of the high open plateaux here would be completely extirpated within five years'.[104]

The early conservationists of the SPWFE believed that, treated aright, settlers could be won over to conservation, and could in the process become true sportsmen: 'treat the settler fairly as regards game, and the good ones will preserve it; and I hope the authorities will be down on anyone who slaughters or wantonly kills beyond his limit'.[105] The problem was 'those who fancy that their livelihood has been interfered with'.[106] For decades, African game departments had to contend with the view that game laws are 'a nuisance invented by a bureaucratic government, and as hampering shooting'.[107] Settlers were not 'as a class as antagonistic to the preservation of game'. This did them a great injustice, and was 'not advisable in the interest of the game itself'.[108]

Both would-be sporting settler hunters and conservationists could agree on one thing (apart from the problem of African hunting discussed in Chapter 5), that much excessive hunting by settlers in East Africa was due to settlers from South Africa, referred to as 'Boers'. They shot too much, they sometimes killed cruelly, and they killed for subsistence: all highly undesirable traits. A correspondent in 1902 said that in southern Kenya 'certain Germans send their men into English territory to drive zebra into their traps'.[109] In 1905, Lord Hindlip reported that small parties of four to five Boers were hunting in the southern game reserve of Kenya from their settlement in German territory.[110] In 1907 S H Whitbread MP reported that 'marauding bands of Boers' had crossed the frontier to poach in the southern reserve.[111] Sir J Hayes Sadler wrote to the Earl of Crewe in October 1908 that there was a need for an early decision on licensing and game reserve boundaries because of 'the influx of Boers, whose proclivities in the matter of game are well known'.[112] Sir Clement Hill wrote to the Secretary of State for the Colonies in 1909: 'they shoot with very great freedom very large quantities of game which they do not require', and 'care should be taken that the Boers are kept in order in that respect'.[113]

It was in the interests of the real sportsman, and particularly resident officers of colonial administrations, that the game should be 'played fair'. It was 'bloodthirstiness', and not 'honest sport', which was responsible for the depletion of so many 'game fields'. The arrival of the railway and other forms of communication were a serious threat to Kenyan game, because they improved access for hunters. The decimation of the dense herds of game on the South African veldt showed what might happen, where 'a paradise of varied life, which is now irretrievably lost through the carelessness and wastefulness of white men'.[114]

Give the prevalence of hunters among its ranks, it is interesting to note the SPWFE's determination to draw a line between its work and that of purely hunting organizations. The idea of an international sporting club was current by the 1850s, although the Shikar Club was only founded in 1908. Two of its founders were active in the SPWFE (P B Van der Byl and F C Selous), and there was substantial cross-membership between the Societies (for example Sir Alfred Pease, Abel Chapman and Sir Henry Seton-Karr). Indeed, the question of merging the two societies was discussed by the SPWFE in 1908, but dismissed because 'the objects of the two societies were dissimilar'.[115] The close contacts were maintained, however, and Lord Lonsdale of the Shikar Club approached the SPFE about a possible alliance again in 1925, although the same conclusion was reached.[116] By that time the society was far more concerned with the creation of national parks as inviolable sanctuaries for game than about the niceties of sportsmanship, but hunting was still important to a number of leading members of the society. In 1909 the society's journal published a letter from William Hornaday listing 'Fifteen Cardinal Principles' that 'apply everywhere to the pursuit and the preservation of large game'. They had been adopted by the Camp Fire Club of America, the Lewis and Clark Club of Pittsburgh, and the North American Fish and Game Protective Association, and were being presented 'to sportsmen of our kind throughout the world'.[117] Lord Onslow, the SPFE's President, said in 1928 'I do not think anybody believes that this Society will interfere in any way with reasonable and legitimate sport ... we count on all big game sportsmen for their help'.[118] In 1928 the shooting editor of the *Field* agreed to give prominence to the Society's work.[119]

By the 1930s, the moral discourse of the sporting code of big game hunters was clear. The brute fact of the sportsman's kill was deemed acceptable because of the manner of the hunt (on foot, traversing hard country and facing the wild animal at close range), and the expert cleanness of the killing shot. The opposition to native hunting (discussed in Chapter 5) was expressed in (and to an extent stemmed from) a sense that the methods used showed an unacceptable lack of concern at the animals' suffering. In 1936, Dr A H B Kirkman of the University of London Animal Welfare Society proposed that a resolution be sent to the Secretary of State for the Colonies about West Africa, deploring the 'uninterrupted persecution of the fauna by barbarous native methods and the danger of extermination of many of Africa's game animals'.[120] However, the idea on which arguments for game conservation were based, of safeguarding animals for shooting, was itself potentially repugnant. By the 1930s, such 'idealists' were expressing their concerns. Indeed, in their efforts to increase membership, the SPFE was itself extending its appeal to the 'many in this country to whom cruelty and senseless slaughter are abhorrent.[121] To the sportsmen of the SPFE, sport hunting was neither cruel or senseless: C W Hobley dismissed the squeamishness of idealists 'until nature lovers are prepared to subscribe the amount required for its [wildlife's] protection their plaints carried inadequate weight'.[122]

SHOOTING AS AN ARGUMENT FOR CONSERVATION

The chief problem for conservation's advocates at the start of the 20th century was one only too familiar 100 years later: conservation cost money. When Theodore Roosevelt became Governor of New York in 1898, he set about establishing policies for forests and wildlife that reflected the ideals of the Boone and Crockett Club, strengthening and reforming the management of the Adirondacks and the Catskill mountains. When he became US President in 1901, he did the same on a national scale, passing the Reclamation Act of 1902 to establish the Bureau of Reclamation, creating the United States Forest Service in 1905, and establishing the National Conservation Commission in 1908, headed by his guru Gifford Pinchot.[123]

In the United Kingdom, the SPWFE urged the Secretary of State for the Colonies towards greater efforts on conservation. When he met their first deputation in 1905, the Colonial Secretary made clear that there was to be no money from the Imperial Exchequer for conservation. However, he made protestations of sympathy, and followed them up by the practical step of becoming an Honorary Member of the Society. Lord Elgin, who succeeded him, likewise promised 'sympathy, consideration and assistance', but no money.[124]

The issue of funding for game reserves and protection was urgent. Buxton's view was that game preservation was important even if it cost money – in 1902 he urged that 'all necessary sacrifices' should be made to preserve game 'while there is yet time'. Game should be viewed as 'a precious inheritance of the empire, something to be guarded like a unique picture, 'something which may easily be lost, but which cannot be replaced'.[125] Buxton preferred to present a business case for preservation, arguing that a share of the revenues from hunting licences could help pay for effective game protection by well-qualified staff. He argued that reserves could even create a profit and that hunting also provides an outlet for the energies of young officers, isolated in the field.[126]

To conservationists, game preservation seemed not only a thoroughly worthy thing for the colonial state to invest in, but a prudent one too. In presenting their case to the Colonial Secretary in 1905, the SPWFE contrasted the expenditure of 6 million pounds on the Uganda railway in the sanguine hope of economic return to the need for modest expenditure on game reserves: 'is not the preservation of animal life of which nature has been so lavish in these regions, also an imperial object? Is nothing due to this inheritance of the Empire?'.[127] The return from game hunting was considerable, far more than the sum spent on preserving it.[128] In 1906 Rhys Williams argued that State preserves 'would not only tend to protect animals from wholesale destruction, but would, if properly managed, bring in large and constantly increasing sums to the Protectorate exchequer'.[129] To win that income, early action was needed, before herds became rare as in Transvaal or the United States.

The Colonial Secretary asked whether they proposed that the 'Imperial interest' meant that they believed that these costs should be borne 'from home' (by Britain itself)?[130] Buxton replied that they should, that conservation formed part of the responsibility of empire, arguing 'the nation has 'pegged out claims', and must bear charges'. Seton-Karr agreed, suggesting that a reserve in South Africa should be 'an imperial claim', and not paid from local pockets.[131] In asking the Secretary of State for the Colonies to seek to have influence on the Chartered Company in Rhodesia ('conspicuous by its absence' in the Blue Book) in its destruction of game, Rhys Williams said 'we regard this as an imperial question, and we ask the Colonial Office to claim a voice in it, and not allow this sort of thing, at least without reference home, and a case being proved for such strong steps'.[132]

Again, Henry Seton-Karr concurred. Wild animals (and particularly the larger big game) not only made the Empire attractive to sportsmen, naturalists and travellers, but contributed to its material wealth and revenue. He argued that the fauna of British East Africa were 'an asset of large pecuniary value', estimating that the direct revenue from licences at between £8000 and £10,000 a year, while the indirect annual revenue from the visits of sportsmen was over £20,000. These figures were not to be despised in 'a young and sparsely populated portion of the Empire'.[133]

Others were more cautious – the *Saturday Review* quoted Lord Curzon's view that preservation should not be seen as a matter of financial gain and loss. He preferred that 'more patriotic' view that it should be done 'as a duty to the empire and to posterity'. The newspaper doubted if the nation could make money out of reserves, and it should make up its mind 'to spend more than it makes'. It noted that the Americans responded to the near-extinction of species like the bison by spending freely on what remained, and it expressed it shameful that Britain should lag behind America, Germany and even Norway.[134]

The SPWFE's 1906 deputation to the Secretary of State quoted estimates from F J Jackson of the game department that £2344 was needed to protect the fauna of British East Africa. The issue was followed up later in the year by the MP Samuel H Whitbread in questions to Winston Churchill, then Under Secretary of State for the Colonies in the House of Commons. It was eventually announced, in 1908, that the budget for the game staff in British East Africa had been raised by the Colonial Office from £300 to the £2300 per year asked for by the SPWFE deputation. By this point, the society noted in an editorial that it was urgently needed due to a dramatic increase in the 'white development' of East Africa (as reflected in the increase in the net railway receipts from £2639 in 1904–5 to £76,150 in 1906–7).[135] The man appointed as chief of this new game staff was SPWFE member (and member of the Society's deputation to the Colonial Office) Colonel J H Patterson, author of the book *Man Eaters of Tsavo*.[136]

ON SAFARI

Whatever the economic importance of hunting in Africa, there is no doubt of its social significance. Critically, African big game began to exert a powerful appeal to wealthy men from the United States as well as Europe. Theodore Roosevelt was the first of this new breed of 'Safari' hunters. At the end of his Presidency in 1908, he set off on a year-long hunting safari to East Africa with his son Kermit. Interestingly, his decision to go there rather than the wilds of Alaska was due to a White House dinner conversation with Carl Akeley, with whom he later ended up hunting elephant on Mount Kenya.[137] His trip was planned with help from old friends Edward North Buxton and Frederick Selous, the latter travelling with him to Mombasa from Naples. He reached Kenya in April 1909, and travelled inland across the southern reserve, sitting on a special seat on the cowcatcher of the train. They travelled the plains and forests of Kenya and then Uganda, feted by settler society and government officials, collecting specimens for the Smithsonian Museum, and material for a series of lucrative articles for *Scribner's Magazine*.[138] They shot everything they could find, from bongo to white rhinoceros; Kermit took photographs.[139]

Where Roosevelt led, many others followed.[140] It was a specialized business before the First World War, but by the 1920s, the safari had become a fad for the rich in both Europe and America. The roll-call of the great and glamorous included the Duke and Duchess of York (the future George VI and Queen Elizabeth) on their honeymoon in 1924–5, George Eastman (1926 and 1928), the Prince of Wales (1928 and 1930) and Ernest Hemingway (1934).[141] The safari became the symbol of glamour, and the hunter no longer had to aspire to Roosevelt's style of 'manliness'. The latter-day hunters were still willing to be coopted for conservation: the Prince of Wales for example became Patron of the Society for the Protection of the Fauna of the Empire in April 1929.

Changing times brought new technologies to bear on the hunt that were in many ways more transforming than the sporting rifle. By the 1930s, safaris were powered by the motor car and not a string of porters: George Eastman travelled with three cars and a mechanic. Permanent camps became possible, and safaris could be completed in much shorter periods of time – a brief holiday, not a lifetime's expedition. Poor shots found it easy to hunt from vehicles, although this was soon dubbed unsporting and destructive, and banned. In 1929 the Society noted its 'deep concern' that 'big game has been shot from motor cars' (particularly lions in Serengeti in Tanganyika[142]), and urged Colonies and

Dependencies to check this practice.[143] The matter was discussed in The Times, and the Government of Tanganyika took action promptly. At a discussion in the House of Lords on 21 November 1929, Lord Allenby spoke on game preservation, and Lord Passfield's reply was sympathetic, particularly on stopping the 'monstrous habit' of shooting game from motor cars'.[144] The practice persisted in northern Rhodesia, particularly among prospectors.[145]

In 1928, the Society noted 'with concern and regret' that an English party had left for Africa equipped to shoot wild animals from the air'.[146] In 1931, SPFE complained about game being harassed from the air in East Africa.[147] To each generation of conservationists, new technologies seemed to threaten wildlife populations. A meeting of the SPFE at London Zoo in 1930 was told the familiar story that 'the fate of the wild game is hanging in the balance in many places' owing to modern methods of precision shooting and transport: it was 'the ease with which game can be destroyed which is threatening its existence'.[148]

Machines transformed the journey to Africa, too: the Prince of Wales arrived for his safari in 1930 by aeroplane, while the air ace Beryl Markham was spotting tuskers for Bror von Blixen in the dense bush behind Mombasa.[149] With the mass market came a new cadre of tour leaders, the 'white hunters', professionals whose forerunners included Leslie Tarlton who had guided Roosevelt at the start of the century, and who was still going in the 1930s. The ideals of sportsmanship remained important, being rehearsed to justify successive generations of elite hunter-conservationists. When King George VI became Patron of the SPFE, the society recalled the Duke and Duchess of York's shooting safari in East Africa. They had wished to make 'a representative collection of African heads' but proved themselves 'sportsmen of the best type'. Their camp was simple ('no ice machines and no aeroplanes'), and they worked hard for their shot, and shot well.[150]

With Eastman, and especially his second safari with Martin and Osa Johnston, photography became both a medium of record and also advertisement. Like Hemingway, whose stories *The Short Happy Life of Francis Macomber* and *The Snows of Kilimanjaro* became widely known and reprinted, African hunting became part of the wider world of global consumer culture.[151] Walt Disney's *Bambi* was made in 1942, and the culture of hunting in the United States was overlain with a new humanitarian view of nature. In East Africa, the gun gave way to the camera as the primary means of obtaining trophies, and the hunting safari merged into safari tourism. As early as 1905 a german hunter's practice of catching lions in traps was dismissed by the SPWFE as 'contrary to our code', but his flashlight photos 'opened a new line for photographers of wildlife'.[152]

The idea that hunting could raise money for conservation did not however die out. Big game hunting continued, and in the 1980s it began once again to become central to the way conservationists thought about their task. It was expressed in a form that Theodore Roosevelt would have thoroughly approved of, the harvesting of wild animals to create an economic return, both for private landowners (on game ranches or conservancies in southern Africa), and for communities of smallholders (for example in Zimbabwe's CAMPFIRE Programme).[153] In an atmosphere of Reaganomics, the romanticism of *Bambi* and *The Lion King* were out. Echoes of Gifford Pinchot's Conservation Movement, and the 'wise use' of nature as a resource was back in. Wildlife had to 'pay its way', and how better than through the bankable enthusiasm of the First World hunter for a shot at the great game animals of Africa? This story too is taken up later in this book, in Chapter 8.

Before turning to discuss recent ideas about hunting and conservation, it is necessary to set out the story of the evolution of ideas about conservation itself, and the main strategies of conservation's proponents. This is the task of the next chapter, which describes the development of the international conservation movement through the 19th century.

Chapter 3

The Global Conservation Regime

Today, in human society, we can perhaps hope to survive in all our prized diversity provided we can achieve an ultimate loyalty to our single, beautiful and vulnerable earth (Barbara Ward and René Dubos).[1]

THE NEED FOR INTERNATIONAL ACTION

In June 1992, the Convention on Biological Diversity (CBD) was signed in Rio de Janeiro by 156 states (and the European Community), at the massive United Nations Conference on Environment and Development (UNCED).[2] IUCN had been planning a treaty on the conservation of natural resources since 1984, and UNEP (United Nations Environment Programme) set up an expert working group in 1987 to consider an umbrella convention. In 1991 this group became the Intergovernmental Negotiating Committee for a Convention on

Biological Diversity, and began work on the text of a treaty for Rio. They added many elements into the relatively straightforward recipe envisaged by IUCN, particularly issues of trade (the new trade regime under the World Trade Organization would come into force in 1994), and biotechnology. Nonetheless, in the guise of biodiversity, the old concerns of conservationists were there, at the centre of a treaty that was signed by a galaxy of world leaders. By August 2001, the convention had 181 contracting parties. The United Nations declared 22 May as 'International Day for Biodiversity'.[3] Conservation had gone global.

The idea of conservation as a global problem was not new. It was precisely their belief that the processes at work driving extinction in Africa were the same as those in the United States that exercised the early conservationists of the Society for the Preservation of the Wild Fauna of the Empire (SPWFE). The fellowship of sporting conservationists of that era was global, because of globe-trotting by hunters and conservationists. In 1924, the society was said to have been founded by 'men whom have had opportunities of studying wild game in many parts of the world; many are sportsmen of the best type, and others are trained as naturalists'.[4] It was a global view, although through imperial blinkers. The Earl of Onslow commented in his inaugural address as President in 1928 that the aims of the society were: 'to preserve wild life throughout the British Empire'.[5] An editorial in the Journal put its purpose even more plainly 'to ensure than no more species of wild animals shall be exterminated within the British Empire'.[6]

One view of international action, from the days of the 1900 conference on game preservation in Africa onwards (see Chapter 2), was on collaboration between sovereign states through treaties – exactly the strategy followed in the 1992 Convention at Rio, and at various points in between (notably CITES (Convention on Trade in Endangered Species), see Chapter 8).[7] An alternative was the idea of a truly international organization to promote collaboration in conservation. This chapter discusses the development of the international institutional structure of conservation, and the main organizations that were created through the 20th century. It also describes the way ideas about conservation and about wildlife evolved, particularly the rise of popular environmentalism in industrialized countries from the 1960s.

There were infant conservation organizations at the very start of the 20th century in a range of European countries and Australia, and of course in the United States.[8] As so often, it was the ornithologists who led the way with the idea of international collaboration. The idea of an International Convention for the Protection of Birds was proposed by the Swiss in 1872, and in 1902 an International Convention for the Preservation of Useful Birds was signed by 12 European countries.[9] In 1916, the Migratory Birds Treaty was signed by the United States, Great Britain and later Mexico and other countries, and in 1922, the American Gilbert Pearson, president of the Audubon Association, convened an International Conference for the Protection of Birds at which the International Committee for Bird Protection (ICPB) was launched, with Britain,

France, the Netherlands and the United States as members. It met for the first time in 1928, and in various guises (the latest of which is BirdLife International), this organization has survived ever since.[10]

The idea of an international conservation body with a broader remit was proposed at an International Congress for the Protection of Nature in Paris in 1909.[11] Paul Sarasin, of the Ligue Suisse pour la Protection de la Nature, approached a range of industrialized countries (including Argentina, Japan and the United States) about creating an international nature conservation body. In 1913, delegates from 17 countries signed an Act of Foundation of a Consultative Commission for the International Protection of Nature in Berne, and this was formally constituted in 1914 by 14 countries. The work unravelled during the First World War, and the Swiss government declined Sarasin's suggestion of an approach to the League of Nations. An International Congress for the Protection of Nature in Paris in June in 1923 urged that the Commission be reconvened, but to no avail.

However, the congress did promote international dialogue – the SPFE identified a series of sister organizations (the French Commission Permanente pour la Protection de la Fauna Coloniale in Paris, the Nederlandsche Commissie voor Internationale Natuurbescherming Vereenining tot Behoud van Natuurmonumenten in Nederland, and the Cercle Zoologioque Congolais).[12] And in this spirit of coordination, the Dutch conservationist Pieter van Tienhoven stimulated the creation of Dutch, French and Belgian Committees for the Protection of Nature, and made contact with William Hornaday of the New York Zoological Society, and with conservationists in the United Kingdom.[13] At the General Assembly of the International Union of the Biological Sciences in 1928 a francophone Office International de Documentation et de Corrélation pour la Protection de la Nature was created. This was consolidated into the International Office for the Protection of Nature (IOPN) in 1934.[14]

Domestically, conservation movements were growing in a number of countries between the wars. In the United Kingdom, the national parks movement gathered pace, and with it calls from the British Ecological Society and the Royal Society for the Protection of Birds (RSPB) for government commitment to nature conservation. A series of government committees considered such matters.[15] In the United States, the Isaak Walton League, the National Wildlife Federation, the More Game Birds Foundation and the Wilderness Society were all founded, and F D Roosevelt convened the North American Wildlife Conference in 1936, holding the first national Wildlife Week in 1938.[16] Academically, the science of wildlife management was also being established, associated particularly with the work of Aldo Leopold, whose achievements included the establishment of the Gila Wilderness Area, and publication of *Game Management* in 1933, and the posthumous classic *Sand County Almanac*.[17] The Boone and Crockett Club set up the American Committee for International Wildlife Protection in 1930. This committee assisted the IOPN financially, and also itself promoted nature protection and carried out research, particularly during the Second World War, when the work of the IOPN (based in Amsterdam) was severely disrupted.

EMPIRE PRESERVATION

After the First World War, the SPWFE reformed, meeting in February 1919 at the House of Commons under the Chairmanship of their founder, E N Buxton. It dropped the word 'wild' from its title, becoming the Society for the Preservation of the Fauna of the Empire (SPFE), usually referred to as 'the Fauna Society'.[18] It established an Executive Committee in 1920, separating the professional work of the society from its general meetings.[19] When the Earl of Onslow took over as President in 1926, he presided over larger and more socially illustrious meetings, often with lantern slide lectures, or films.[20] The Prince of Wales agreed to become Patron in 1929,[21] just before his safari in East Africa.

As the pace of colonial development quickened, the society began to feel its lack of resources. In the 1920s, for example, it frequently bemoaned its restricted circumstances.[22] In 1927 it produced only one issue of its journal instead of two; it held a ball at the Royal Opera House in 1932 to raise funds, attended by the Prince of Wales.[23] It began actively to recruit members as supporters, rather than simply those with particular knowledge of conservation, or influence that might help them achieve their aims. Onslow himself wrote letters to prospective members, and the Society grew, from 380 members in 1927 to 760 by 1930.[24] In 1928, 5000 copies of a pamphlet 'The passing of Wild Life' were printed, both to get the conservation message out, and to make the society better known.[25]

Despite its limited resources, worry about money led to a visit by the Society's Secretary (C W Hobley) to the eastern United States in 1930 to arouse interest in its work. He was promised substantial support from the Boone and Crockett Club (including Madison Grant, Fairfield Osborn and Kermit Roosevelt) 'to promote efforts with which American conservationists are in sympathy', and from the Wild Life Protection Society of America (through Dr Hornaday). This help had to be matched by funds from the United Kingdom, and the Society urged its members 'not to fail us in this respect'.[26] The money was to be kept as a 'special fund', for projects.

The society sought to maintain its patrician role, advising the Colonial Office on the development of wildlife policy across great tracts of Africa, Asia and the Caribbean. They had some success in India. In 1929, the Earl of Onslow noted that the society enjoyed the sympathy of the India Office, and had done so for a long time.[27] The society made good use of its contacts, not least in the person of Onslow himself, who had written to Lord Irwin. He replied that initiatives for preservation could not be driven from the centre, but from the provinces; he wrote to Provincial Governments, and anticipated a sympathetic attitude. The big difference between India and Africa in terms of specialized measures to deliver conservation was the vast area of preserved forests, and the entrenched bureaucratic power of the forest department.[28] Irwin observed that much wildlife existed within the 105,000 square miles of reserved forests, where staff rendered the protection of game 'practicable'.[29]

However, by this time there were limits to what the society could achieve by operating levers in London through debates in the House of Lords and deputations to the Colonial Office. The latter in particular became less warmly received, and less effective, as the complexity and sheer volume of government affairs in the East African colonies grew. Interestingly, it is this period in the society's history that has attracted the opprobrium of historians. Roderick Neumann in particular uses the Earl of Onslow as the of focus his critique of the aristocratic hunter-preservationists of the SPFE.[30] He links Onslow's tenure as President of the society to his upbringing in Clandon Park, Eton and Oxford, his penchant for foxhunting and shooting, and his tenure of a great landed estate through the major period of aristocratic decline. However, John MacKenzie is right to place the society's period of greatest influence to the earlier decades of the century. By the 1920s, the impact of the society (and the networks of interests that Neumann describes) had in fact begun to be diluted.[31]

The society tried to establish new ways of influencing game policy. In a move that foreshadowed IUCN's Arusha Conference 30 years later, in 1930 they proposed a conference of game wardens for the East African Dependencies, with representatives of the society, the Joint East African Board and the Secretary of State to discuss 'general policy' for game preservation. The Secretary of State dismissed the idea, pointing out that the game wardens were the servants of their several governments, who had responsibility for policy. He also made it clear that conservation could not take pride of place in policy: 'actually, no species of wild animal in East Africa was in danger of being wholly exterminated, so that the matter could not be said to be an extremely urgent one'.[32] The Secretary of State did establish a Commission to consider wild life conservation in the Federated Malay States in 1930,[33] but overall the society's power to influence the official ear in London was waning, while its limited resources made other strategies problematic. In 1933, for example, the Executive Committee noted that serious efforts to influence opinion in India would be far beyond present resources.[34] The society responded by building its contacts with the new cadre of professional conservationists on the ground. Between the wars, the society's London office became the chosen meeting place of game wardens at home on leave.[35]

BEYOND EMPIRE

The United States was poised to take over the leadership of the international conservation movement at the end of the Second World War.[36] A wide range of societies existed, including the American Museum of Natural History, the Boone and Crockett Club, the Conservation Foundation, Ducks Unlimited, the Isaak Walton League, the National Audubon Society, the National Wildlife Federation, the New York Zoological Society, the Sierra Club, the Smithsonian Institution and the Wilderness Society.[37] A Convention on Nature Protection and Wild Life Preservation in the Western Hemisphere had been signed in 1942.[38] The Conservation Foundation was established in 1948 (by the New York Zoological Society) and the Nature Conservancy in 1951.

An important element of the American approach was the tradition of conservation as rational resource use. An international conference on conservation had actually been proposed under Theodore Roosevelt early in the century, but when he died it was promptly axed by President Taft (who indeed also undid many of Roosevelt's conservation innovations). Subsequently, Gifford Pinchot tried to interest successive US Presidents in the idea of such a meeting, eventually winning a favourable ear from F D Roosevelt in 1944.[39] However, the State Department was unenthusiastic, seeing the matter more than covered in the newly-established United Nations organizations (particularly ECOSOC, the Economic and Social Council, and the FAO (Food and Agriculture Organisation)), and the World Bank. The initiative was lost with the second Roosevelt's death in April 1945.

Moves towards an international organization in the post-war period were therefore initially still led from Europe, and focused on wildlife conservation rather than resource use. They were renewed through both the IOPN and the ICBP, and the Ligue Suisse pour la Protection de la Nature. Julian Huxley, chairman of the British government committee on wildlife conservation, visited the Swiss National Park in 1945, and arranged a visit for a larger British delegation the following year.[40] Charles Bernard and Johann Büttikofer, of the Ligue Suisse, organized a meeting around them at Basel that proposed a new organization. The proposal was taken up by the newly established UNESCO (the United Nations Educational, Scientific and Cultural Organization) by Julian Huxley, its first Director and a man with wide experience of wildlife biology, eugenics, conservation and Africa.[41] He persuaded the UNESCO General Conference in Mexico in 1947 to include conservation within their remit, on the basis that the enjoyment of nature was cultural, and its conservation depended on science.[42]

A follow-up to the Basel meeting was held in Brunnen in 1947, at which 24 countries were represented, although not all had powers to vote (the UK representatives, including an observer from the SPWFE, for example, did not). The United Kingdom and the United States favoured an organization under the aegis of the United Nations, while others preferred swift independent action. In the end, a draft constitution for a Provisional International Union for the Protection of Nature (IUPN) was agreed, and UNESCO was requested to pass this on to all governments for comment. UNESCO agreed to convene a congress to adopt the constitution, held at Fontainebleau in October 1948.

There were representatives from 23 governments (invited by UNESCO) and 107 private, national and international organizations (invited by the Ligue Suisse), plus seven international organizations.[43] A new constitution, drafted by the British Foreign Office was tabled, amended by UNESCO and the US delegation and signed. IUPN resulted in being a hybrid blend of governmental and non-governmental organizations. A later Director General, Martin Holdgate, has lovingly (if exasperatedly) chronicled the way the intricate personal and international political machinations of its birth marked the growing organization.[44] Its purposes were to promote the preservation of wildlife and the natural environment, public knowledge of the issues, education, research and legislation. UNESCO granted financial support a month later. Despite perpetual constraints of funding, the IUPN survived and grew.

GLOBAL NATURE CONSERVATION

The immediate horizon for IUPN was the United Nations Scientific Conference on the Conservation and Utilisation of Resources (UNSCCUR) at Lake Success in New York State. This derived from an American proposal (shades of Pinchot's proposed post-war conference on resource conservation), and was attended by over 500 delegates from 49 countries.[45] It discussed wildlife as one among many natural resources. It was concurrent with a somewhat smaller IUPN meeting, an 'International Technical Conference on the Protection of Nature', attended by representatives from 32 countries and seven international organizations. This also discussed natural resources, but there was a major emphasis on the achievement of conservation through international cooperation to promote ecological research (including concerns about sleeping sickness control, exotic species introductions and the plight of the large mammals of Africa and Asia). A World Convention on Nature Protection and the problems of trans-boundary national parks were also discussed.[46]

In IUPN, conservationists in industrialized countries had created a new arena within which to air their concerns, and a new network for influence. The organization prospered, in 1956 changing its name to the International Union for Conservation of Nature and Natural Resources (IUCN) the name reflecting the strong influence of US ideas about resources as opposed to simply wildlife conservation. In this new world order, the power of the colonial old boys' network of the SPFE dwindled, while that of others, notably US-based organizations, waxed strong. However, the continued influence of British-based conservationists, and especially the SPFE, should not be underestimated. In his book *Penitent Butchers*, Richard Fitter (who was frequently an eye-witness) recounts the influence of people such as Max Nicholson in the conferences of the 1940s that established the organizations of the international conservation community.[47] Nicholson, and the British contingent as a whole, thought the establishment of IUPN premature, and the link to the UN unhelpful.[48] The

SPFE Journal commented that 'in the elaboration of the mechanics of conservation we may lose sight of the intended product, and, through having too many persons or organizations busy respectively with their own machines, much well-intended effort will be wasted'.[49] The Secretary of the SPFE led the British delegation (representing 21 organizations) at Brunnen.[50]

The foundation of IUPN epitomizes the changing of the guard in conservation. The United States had begun to reveal itself as the most significant force in international conservation, not least in Africa. In extending their interests in this way, they ran up against European colonial sensibilities, and the traditional European heartland of decision-making about conservation. Thus in 1949 Richard Pough, Curator of the Department of Conservation and Use of Natural Resources, sent an article entitled 'S.O.S. for African Wild Life' to the SPFE, asking how Americans could help African conservation.[51] The SPFE noted that while the conservation of African fauna was a matter for the whole world, it was a delicate matter to impress this upon those controlling the destiny of the fauna without 'apparent presumption and the risk of rebuff'.[52] An obvious route for influence was of course the IUPN, but the SPFE preferred the British governments (central and colonial) to take an enlightened view without outside prompting. With wonderful condescension, the SPFE suggested that the most useful thing for Americans would be to visit Africa in their tens of thousands asking to be shown the fauna, thus convincing local governments of the money to be made from keeping animals in their natural states, and to make funds available for research into problems such as fly-borne and infectious diseases.

The IUPN drew heavily on British expertise, but it was a vigorously independent organization. The SPFE was rather rueful about its growing independence, describing it as 'a flourishing rather audacious child determined to dispense as best may be with the fostering care of the nursery and the schoolroom'.[53] Conservation had indeed outgrown the metaphorical domestic geography of upper class British childhood. Time, political tide and poverty were against the colonial old guard. Much of the energy, vision and money put into conservation across the world was going to come from either the United States, or from the UN organizations.

Within the United Kingdom, however, the SPFE continued to be influential, and to urge conservation on British colonial planners, although in British colonies themselves their urgings were muffled by the complex concerns of emerging governments, particularly those of indigenous self-government. At home, following the Second World War, they honed their image, and continued to court high society. The King was still their Patron, and in 1946 the SPFE President, the Duke of Devonshire, invited Princess Elizabeth and Princess Margaret to attend an SPFE meeting to hear the veteran Stevenson-Hamilton speak about Kruger National Park, ahead of their trip to South Africa the following year.[54] When King George VI died in 1952, the new Queen agreed to take over as the society's Patron.

In 1950, the society changed its name to the 'Fauna Preservation Society' (FPS), and its journal to *Oryx*.[55] The society shook off the language of colonialism, defining its purpose as simply 'to safeguard wild animals from extermination', by interesting the public in the preservation of wild animals in their natural conditions, by promoting the establishment of national parks and reserves and the enactment and enforcement of laws for the protection of wild animals, and by establishing relations with other societies having similar interests throughout the world.[56] In 1953, the society celebrated its 50th anniversary relatively quietly, with a joint meeting with the RSPB at Church House Westminster on 24 October. Six hundred people attended, and FPS films were shown, one about 'wild animals of the Indian jungle', the other about foxes and badgers.[57] This was a society with a more modest imagination than heretofore.

DECOLONIZATION AND CONSERVATION

International conservation concern was dominated, as it had been pre-war, by Africa. Africa, like so much of Asia, was now becoming independent, and new (and relatively inexperienced) governments were taking over. The process of political decolonization was sometimes remarkably abrupt. In retrospect it is the durability of conservation ideas and procedures that stands out.[58] However in the 1950s and 1960s, conservationists feared the implications of independence for wildlife. The issue of African hunting (more usually referred to as poaching) had been of growing importance for some decades. Ideas about this problem are discussed in Chapter 5. Now, to conservationists, the poachers were to become the gamekeepers.

One response to the change was the creation of national parks, discussed in Chapter 4. Another was the foundation of new non-governmental conservation organizations. In Kenya and Tanganyika, Wild Life Societies were formed in 1956, to establish a counterpart outside government to promote conservation. They merged in 1961 to form the East African Wildlife Society, drawing together wildlife enthusiasts in Kenya, Tanzania and Uganda. They promoted efforts for the protection of rare species, working particularly with the growing tourist industry, both building links between business and government conservation, and engaging tourists themselves.[59]

Most new conservation initiatives aimed at countries approaching independence originated from outside. Many were American, and not European. In the late 1950s, the New York Zoological Society began a series of wildlife surveys and projects in Asia (Burma and Malaya), and in Africa (Kenya, Tanganyika, Uganda, Ethiopia and Sudan). In 1959 it supported George Schaller's research on mountain gorillas in Rwanda and Congo, and in 1966 the society established its Institute of Research in Animal Behaviour, sponsoring work by George Schaller in Serengeti, Thomas Strusaker in Uganda on primates in Uganda and Roger Payne on whales.[60]

Africa was the centrepiece of US international conservation concern in the 1950s and 1960s. In 1957 the Fulbright Commission began a programme to send scholars to look at biological problems in parks in Uganda. In 1961 Judge Russell E Train, of the Washington Safari Club's conservation committee, formed the African Wildlife Leadership Foundation (AWLF) specifically to build a new cadre of conservation leaders among Africans. In 1962, their first project was to give US$25,000 to start the College of African Wildlife Management at Mweka in Tanganyika, close to the Serengeti 'to train Africans to take responsible positions in game and national parks departments, so that the Africanization of these services will result in continued and increased conservation of Africa's wild life'.[61] In 1963, they sent four African students to study wildlife management conservation in American colleges, and built a conservation education centre in Nairobi National Park.[62] In 1965 the first cohort of graduates left Mweka, and the UN Special Fund gave almost half a million dollars over five years to develop the college. In the same year, the American Conservation Association sent an emergency grant of 10,000 dollars to the Congo to support the staffing of the national parks. Such substantial investments in African conservation dwarfed the efforts of the post-war FPS and other ex-colonial institutions.

The Serengeti National Park in Tanzania epitomized international conservation's uncertainty about independent Africa. The great grasslands of what has become referred to as the Serengeti-Mara ecosystem had been picked out from the earliest years of the century for their enormous herds of migratory herbivores.[63] Serengeti National Park had been proposed in 1937, and was designated in 1948. Seven years later, conservationists in the United States and the United Kingdom learned that the Tanganyikan government was planning to reduce its area to exclude the Ngorogoro Highlands and central plains. The young ecologist Lee Talbot was dispatched by Hal Coolidge (Chair of the Species Survival Commission) to investigate.[64] Talbot confirmed the rumour, and wrote a paper to the Colonial Secretary urging a thorough study. The FPS put up the funds for this, duly undertaken by the eminent British plant ecologist W H Pearsall.[65] This experience, combined with Julian Huxley's conclusions from a long tour with UNESCO in 1960, suggested a need to present conservation in a new way for an independent Africa.

This had also been the theme of a meeting held at Bukavu in the Belgian Congo in 1953. The Third International Conference for the Protection of the Fauna and Flora in Africa argued for a broader approach to conservation than simply species preservation, addressing resource conservation in general.[66] The problem, as Huxley saw it, was one of competition between different land uses, a competition in which wildlife tended to lose out. Moreover, he noted widespread resentment against the whole paraphernalia of national parks and game reserves on the part of ordinary Africans, as 'European inventions and relics of 'colonialism' which occupy land coveted by Africans'.[67] Huxley proposed a joint conference between IUCN and the Commission for Technical

Cooperation in Africa south of the Sahara (CCTA) for October 1961. At the Warsaw General Assembly in 1960, IUCN duly set up the 'African Special Project', to be chaired by Barton Worthington.[68]

The overall aim of the 'African Special Project' was 'to inform public opinion in Africa through African leaders of the need for nature conservation based on ecological knowledge', that is to influence the new generation of political leaders in independent Africa.[69] It had three phases. The first was a tour by the IUCN Secretary General to 16 African countries in West and East Africa (half the costs of which were paid by the FPS).[70] The second phase was a conference ('The Pan African Symposium on the Conservation of Nature and Natural Resources in Modern African States') sponsored by IUCN, CCTA, FAO and UNESCO at Arusha in Tanganyika, in September 1961. The FPS dipped further into its meagre resources to sponsor 12 young African scientists as delegates to this, and also sent ex-colonial conservation stalwart Captain Pitman with Lord Willingdon (FPS President) as delegates, and the public relations officer John Hillaby as observer.

The conference took place on the eve of Tanganyika's independence. The Prime Minister, Julius Nyerere, presented a keynote statement, the 'Arusha Declaration on Conservation'. This duly stated that 'the survival of our wildlife is a matter of grave concern to all of us in Africa'. It also, however, stressed that wildlife was a potentially important economic resource: 'These wild creatures amid the wild places they inhabit are not only important as a source of wonder and inspiration but are an integral part of our natural resources and of our future livelihood and well-being'.[71] The final resolutions of the conference stated 'the earnest desire of modern African states to continue and actively expand the efforts already made in the field of wildlife management', and that they 'recognize their responsibilities and the rightful place of wildlife management in land use planning'.[72] Phase Three of the Africa Special Project involved the establishment of a team in IUCN (with FAO support) to advise African governments on conservation policies and their integration into general conservation programmes.

The conservation presented at Arusha was not at all the game preservation of old, but a new and more utilitarian concern for wildlife as a resource. It was noted that ecosystems needed managing ('nowadays habitat cannot just be left to nature'),[73] and that both plant and animal populations yield a surplus that can be harvested, yielding either money or meat – or both. Conservation was also not something that could be neutral or above politics – 'the prime preoccupation of the conservationist is with the maintenance of the habitat and everything it represents, but governments are most concerned with people, or to put it another way, the politician is the most important factor in land-use planning'.[74] The Fauna Preservation Society's re-named journal, *Oryx*, noted with characteristic paternalism that several African states (including Congo, Sudan and Dahomey) had made 'satisfactory declarations of policy'. They believed that the 'earnest desire' of the 'modern African states' represented was 'to continue and actively expand the efforts already made in the field of wildlife management'. These countries 'recognized their responsibilities' and the rightful place of wildlife management in land use planning.[75]

IUCN followed up the African Special Project with missions to 17 African countries. However, although Africa was important, it was not unique in its problems. Conferences to try to reproduce the spirit of Arusha were also held around the world, in Bangkok in 1965 and at San Carlos de Bariloche in Argentina in 1968.[76]

THE NEW PROFESSIONALS

IUCN provided an international organization for conservation that did the job of coordinating thinking and planning very well by linking national governmental and non-governmental organizations. But there were limits to what could be achieved by coordination and exhortation, particularly in terms of resources. IUCN offered no mechanism for individuals to become directly involved as supporters, especially not for them to provide funds. In 1961, Max Nicholson proposed a new initiative, an International Wildlife Trust. This idea had surfaced in 1960, following a mission to Africa by Julian Huxley for UNESCO, reported in a series of articles in the *Observer*. Huxley raised it with Nicholson, who had already discussed it with Peter Scott.[77] A trust registered in Switzerland was proposed, with a supporters club for wealthy donors, a series of national appeals (each sending two-thirds of their revenue to the organization internationally) and an operations section to set priorities for conservation and allocate funds. From the first, the new organization was crafted to make the best use of public relations and consciousness-raising expertise. Peter Scott designed the famous panda symbol as a logo, capturing the public enthusiasm for the arrival of Chi-Chi the panda at London Zoo. The World Wildlife Fund (WWF) was launched in London on 11 September 1961, with national appeals launched in the United Kingdom (with HRH The Duke of Edinburgh as President) and the United States in December, and the Netherlands, Austria and Germany over the next two years.[78]

The launch of WWF was a new departure organizationally, but not in terms of ideology. It scaled up the intensity with which the existing preservationist agenda was presented, in a form that was little changed. The *Daily Mirror* ran a special issue in October 1961, with a black rhinoceros and its calf on the cover, and the banner headline 'DOOMED – to disappear from the face of the earth due to Man's FOLLY, GREED and NEGLECT'.[79] Buxton could not have put it better himself. The public response was immediate, £60,000 being donated within a week of publication.

This impassioned presentation of the conservation message reflected the 'Morges Manifesto' which preceded WWF's foundation. This was signed by a number of leading European conservationists, including Peter Scott, Charles

Bernard, Julian Huxley, Max Nicholson and Barton Worthington. It lamented the destruction of wildlife and urged that 'although the eleventh hour has struck, it is not yet too late', pointing out that 'skilful and admirable men, and admirable organizations, are struggling to save the world's wildlife'. What they needed above all was money 'to carry out mercy missions and meet conservation emergencies by acquiring land where wildlife treasures are threatened, and in many other ways'.[80]

At its launch, WWF issued a 'World Wildlife Charter', which committed its signatories to seven steps:[81]

- to prevent any further extinction of wildlife;
- to make sure that room shall be left for wildlife;
- to protect all wildlife from unintentional or wanton cruelty;
- to encourage children to develop a love and understanding of wildlife;
- to make certain that all those whose work has an impact on nature should recognize their responsibility to wildlife;
- to arrange to help those nations in need of it in order to preserve their wildlife;
- to work together to save the world's wildlife.

The message was one that was to become utterly familiar through the rest of the 20th century. It mixed the need for urgent and decisive action with the need for long-term 'hearts and minds' campaigns, particularly among the young. It used the language of 'saving' wildlife, urged the moral agenda of responsibility (excoriating human folly, greed and neglect), and it made an explicit humanitarian appeal against 'wanton cruelty'. It was an appeal that fell on ready ears in industrialized countries, for nature was no longer the preserve of an elite of scientists, hunters and government administrators and political figures.

Since the 1960s, action for conservation has involved two types of partners. The vast majority of the expenditure, and the heavy burdens of reconciling different political and economic interests, has been the responsibility of government. It is governments that have passed legislation to protect species, established protected areas and paid for staff to run them. They have not always done this well, and there is, in most countries, a yawning gap between the amount of money that is needed for conservation and the amount that governments have to spend, but actions of this kind remain firmly in their court.[82] Alongside them, and sometimes on their back, have been their partners in promoting conservation, non-governmental organizations (NGOs). These are noisy, visionary, and perpetually appealing to their supporters for money. They are also extremely powerful, for their grip on international thinking about conservation and their ability to influence governments and international organizations.

The pattern of influence of conservation NGOs was established by the 1960s. The classic organization is the WWF itself. WWF's national appeals began to yield significant sums of money early in its life. In its first three years, WWF raised and donated almost US$1.9 million to conservation projects. Some early grants were substantial, for example to the Charles Darwin Foundation for the Galápagos Islands (founded in 1959, with Victor van Straelen as its first Chairman),[83] to IUCN and ICBP. Others were small, for example the provision of a road grader and rotary mower for Kenya's Masai Mara Game Reserve, and a travel grant for E P Gee to survey Indian wild ass in the Rann of Kutch.[84] In 1962, WWF purchased a farm in Tanzania to allow the creation of what was to become Arusha National Park, and in 1969 purchased a section of the Guadalquivir Delta marshes and allow establishment of the Coto Doñana National Park.[85]

In 1970, WWF International , under its President HRH Prince Bernhard of the Netherlands, set up a US$10 million trust fund, known as *The 1001: A Nature Trust*, to provide an endowment for core activities.[86] WWF ran a series of major campaigns, including Project Tiger with the Indian government (in 1973),[87] the Tropical Rainforest Campaign (1975),[88] the Marine Campaign 'The Seas Must Live' (1976),[89] and the 'Save the Rhino' Campaign.[90] It has also led other initiatives such as debt-for-nature swaps (brokering agreements whereby debts to First World institutions are cancelled in return for local expenditure on conservation).[91] By 1981, WWF had 1 million supporters worldwide, and was becoming increasingly successful in fundraising, for example through wheezes such as the Conservation Stamp Collection.[92] By 2003, WWF had 5 million supporters distributed throughout five continents in over 28 national organizations. Since 1985, WWF has invested over US$1165 million in more than 11,000 projects in 130 countries.[93]

As an international organization, WWF suited the new mutually-dependent post-empire world. Its slick publicity and simple structure avoided all the painful multilateralism of IUCN, among other things allowing it to take a more circumspect line on the idea of the conservation of nature as a natural resource (see Chapter 7). For WWF and its supporters, the message of the panda was quite clear: here was an organization dedicated to saving nature, personified by Peter Scott's cuddly logo.[94] I can remember WWF 'bring and buy' sales in suburban London in the 1960s, and the clarity with which WWF seemed (for me at least) to focus much more general environmentalist concerns at a time before broader environmental organizations were established to harness them.[95] As for their elitist forbears in the SPWFE, conservation for WWF supporters was unashamedly emotional and romantic (while being also, from the first, thoroughly hard-headed in terms of organization).

However, the the existence of the new organization had considerable implications for the established players, especially the Fauna Preservation Society (FPS). At first, its expertise won it a role advising WWF on the allocation of money to conservation projects. The FPS President, Lord Willingdon, was also made a Trustee of the British National Appeal. Arguably, WWF had the potential to be a global version of the old imperial SPFE, and in 1964, a merger between WWF and the FPS was explicitly considered. The idea was that FPS would gain from the much larger membership and funding base of WWF, while WWF would gain from the scientific and administrative experience of the FPS, and (perhaps most importantly) from its influential members.[96] The merger never happened, but the idea continued to be mooted, particularly after 1965 when Peter Scott (who was a central figure in WWF internationally) took over as Chairman of FPS's Council.[97] The earning powers of the two organizations were massively different. In 1970, European Conservation Year, the WWF British National Appeal sought to raise £1 million, the FPS more modestly obtained donations of almost £2000 to set up the 'Oryx 100 per cent Fund'. On its 70th anniversary in 1973, the FPS noted the grave threats to wildlife, from poachers and sportsmen, habitat destruction, deforestation and wetland drainage. The message was familiar, but the society's ability to lead in responding to the challenge was much reduced.[98]

WWF also had interesting, sometimes difficult, relations with IUCN. In 1971, in fact, there were plans to merge IUCN and WWF, with the new trust funds underpinning IUCN's work, but the idea lapsed.[99] WWF was never simply a device for raising money for IUCN, however much some conservationists at the time imagined it should be.[100] At the same time, WWF was always more than one among the galaxy of organizations represented in IUCN. Nonetheless, as WWF developed its own conservation programme, IUCN suffered continuous shortages of funds, and the need for closer coordination seemed very strong. In 1979 both organizations moved from the village of Morges to ugly but effective modern office buildings in Gland, between Geneva and Lausanne, to maintain their intimate but rivalrous family relationship.

Behind the politics, WWF and IUCN, backed by a growing number of international NGOs, were thrashing out the boundaries of a new world system of conservation. The rush of former colonies to independence had been weathered, and while the problems facing conservationists were acute, they were increasingly understood as outworkings of processes that had a global scope. Despite the Africa Special Project, Africa was not special, at least as far as its problems went. Hunting, habitat loss, and above all overpopulation were the threats to wildlife across the world. That threat extended not only to animals, the traditional target of conservation concern, but to plants. The Fauna Preservation Society reflected this trend in 1980, when it changed its name to Fauna and Flora Preservation Society, commenting 'in the modern world, it is increasingly unrealistic to suppose that fauna can be protected or conserved and flora ignored. Any habitat is an interwoven amalgam of plants and animals, neither of which can survive without the other, and increasingly wildlife conservation is seen to mean conservation of habitat and whole ecosystems, not just species'.[101] Moreover, not only were the problems global, but so too were the ideas and attitudes conservation-minded people took to them. There was a growing worldwide orthodoxy about the environment and its conservation.

BROADCAST NATURE

Hobley noted in 1924 that 'a love of wild life has sprung up in civilised man'.[102] His definition of a civilized 'man' was probably quite narrow, and eight decades later this sensibility is still far from universal. Nonetheless, thanks to the efforts of the myriad of conservation organizations, it is something that today many of the world's 6.5 billion people, and certainly almost all those in the industrialized world, would be aware of. Bumper stickers might say 'save the elephants' or, reflecting an alternative worldview, 'save the world shoot a greenie', but they reflect a common awareness of the significance of environmental concern. Many people, especially in industrialized countries, love nature. Why?

Conservation organizations have been indefatigable publicists for their cause. From the 19th century onwards, conservationists have turned to the written word to get their message across, many of the most famous names being those who have captured the public attention most successfully, from Fairfield Osborn to Edward Wilson or John Terborgh.[103] The collections of animals in zoos, and the exhibits in museums, have also been important. The New York Zoological Society began the world's first formal zoo education programme in 1929, and men like Peter Chalmers-Mitchell saw education of the public as a key justification for new development such as the creation of the Zoological Society of London's rural park at Whipsnade.[104]

One form of communication has, however had a disproportionate influence on ideas about wildlife and its conservation, and that is film and latterly television. The cinema has not always been regarded kindly by conservationists. Early film-makers saw wild animals, and particularly the capture and killing of wild animals, as a source of melodramatic action sequences, and took the callousness of wild animal circus shows for granted. In 1923 William Hornaday persuaded the SPFE to use its influence with the Colonial Office to stop a proposed animal filming expedition in British East Africa by a Mr Snow, and ban its leader from British territory.[105] In return, the SPFE asked Hornaday to tighten up regulations for approving animal collecting expeditions from the United States. Armand Denis, in the 1960s a leading television wildlife film-maker, reported with distaste the methods used to create melodramatic scenes for the film *Wild Cargo* in the late 1920s.[106] During this period, the Shikar Club condemned films that showed unsporting hunting practices, such as hunting from motor cars and the filming of wounded and dying animals. These gave a false impression of how real hunters behaved: in contrast, Major Radclyffe-Dugmore's film, *The Wonderland of Big-Game*, showed shooting in an 'artistic' and responsible light.[107]

The possibilities of mass communication media were quickly picked up by conservationists. Captain Ritchie, Chief Game Warden in Kenya, saw the radio as a means to promote 'sound public opinion' about game in Kenya among officials, soldiers and settlers, who otherwise had little love of game except from a killing point of view'. He also urged a programme of lectures at 'top Public

Schools'.[108] C W Hobley suggested that the use by skilled lecturers of the excellent nature films being produced would 'mould the outlook of the youth of Empire'.[109] From the late 1920s, under Lord Onslow, the SPFE transformed its London meetings from small cabals of experts to larger public affairs. Lantern slides and films were basic to this strategy, but it was moving film that made the greatest impact. Mary Akeley was due to show a film of the Parc National Albert to the SPFE in London in 1928 (although in the end she showed slides), and Mr W A Wetherall exhibited a film of 'African game in its natural surroundings' at a meeting in November 1929.[110] In March 1930 they showed a film by Colonel Patterson of an expedition to East Africa guided by Hon Denys Finch-Hatton (at the time guide to the Prince of Wales' safari). Onslow noted that 'Mr Patterson was a sportsman as well as a photographer, and although ... he has shot a few trophies, he had devoted much of his time to photography'.[111] In 1938, the society's speaker Colonel J L Sleeman was said to have 'given up the rifle for the camera, which was more difficult'.[112]

The beastly behaviour of film makers was something that needed control, however, both because it was itself cruel, and because it blackened the name of sport hunters. In the 1930s, film-makers were seen to need control in their treatment of 'big game', and the creation of melodramatic 'jungle' films.[113] In 1938, C W Hobley suggested that the new sport of nature photography as a whole needed a code of behaviour, which should prohibit the staging of incidents requiring cruelty or undue compulsion, fake combats between animals or with people, and stampedes.[114] The need for censorship was publicized in an article in the *Field*.[115] Films of the death of animals, or, as in contemporary cases, the death of those hunting them, were not acceptable on film. Such scenes challenged the civilized code of sportsmanship: 'brazen boastfulness of feats of prowess do not go with the make up of the true sportsman'. C W Hobley argued that 'cruelty to animals is repugnant to the Anglo-Saxon race, and it would be a grievous sin if, for purposes of greed, a policy of reviving any primeval bloodthirsty instinct be pursued'.[116] The Society interviewed the Film Censor, and joined with the Zoological Society of London and the Trustees of the British Museum to advise the British Board of Film Censors in order to prevent such scenes being shown.[117] In 1934, Major F E Austen was appointed to the newly-created British Film Institute.

By the end of the Second World War, wildlife film had moved on. Armand Denis filmed *Savage Splendour* and *Below the Sahara*, both pandering to audiences' wish for excitement, but concentrating on filming animals in their natural environment. Excitement came from the filming of quasi-scientific attempts to capture animals (lassoing rhinos for example in 1948, over a decade before this technique became part of standard wildlife capture and release techniques), and from filming local people hunting (including the hunting of gorillas in Congo).[118] In 1951, the FPS began to build up a library of wildlife films, Walt Disney lending his new 'True Life Adventure' series'.[119] These films were loaned not only within the United Kingdom but internationally – a letter from Thailand in 1958 noted that films had been shown at 20 places, often several times, to a combined audience of 31,000 people (including an audience of 2300 at the University of Agriculture). In 1963, National Nature Week in the United Kingdom featured special films by the Rank Organisation and the BBC, and extensive coverage by BBC and independent television as well as the printed press. In 1970 the FPS made a two-hour colour film *The Last of the Wild* as a contribution to the European Conservation Year, and held monthly showings of wildlife films at the New Gallery Cinema on Regent Street in London. By that time, conservation had entered the film mainstream, with the film of Joy Adamson's book about Elsa the lioness and her husband George (employed by the Game Department in the North of Kenya), *Born Free*, produced in 1966, starring Virginia McKenna and Bill Travers.[120]

From the 1950s, television came to be the chief medium for the presentation of wildlife and conservation on film. For Armand Denis, television generated an 'inconceivable' swing of public opinion, saying 'our television programmes are propaganda for a world I know now can be saved'.[121] A young David Attenborough produced a short series called *The Pattern of Animals* featuring Julian Huxley speaking about animals from London Zoo, live in the studio. Then, in 1954, Attenborough went to Sierra Leone on the first of the ground-breaking *Zoo Quest* series. Charles Lagus filmed Jack Lester of London Zoo catching animals (using the unprecedented 'bootlace' 16mm film), and this film was combined with live studio presentation of the same animals on their return. It was an instant success, and was followed by other expeditions to British Guiana, Indonesia, New Guinea, Paraguay and Madagascar'.[122]

In the United Kingdom, studio-based programmes such as *Look* and *Out of Doors* demonstrated the appeal of more local natural history subjects.[123] The BBC established the Natural History Film Unit in Bristol in 1957, following collaboration between the producer Desmond Hawkins and Sir Peter Scott.[124] It has maintained an enviable record of technical innovation and high impact, with programmes such as *Wildlife on One* (begun in 1977) and *Natural World* (1983) having found mass audiences for biological science and conservation. Many series have enjoyed worldwide success, notably David Attenborough's epic series *Life on Earth*, with its unforgettable footage of Attenborough with Dian Fossey's mountain gorillas. This was the first of a sequence of globally viewed series, including *The Living Planet, The Private Life of Plants, Life in the Freezer, Life of Birds* and *Life of Mammals*.

NATURE LOVERS: THE GROWTH OF POPULAR ENVIRONMENTALISM

The principles and concerns of the new ideology of environmentalism were growing rapidly within industrialized countries. A new movement arose in North America and Western Europe in the 1960s and 1970s, on the strength of the realization of environmental issues of global significance. This environmentalism had many dimensions, especially the concerns about industrial pollution and the depletion and exhaustion of natural resources that led to the United Nations Conference on the Human Environment in Stockholm, and in the process to the coining of the term 'sustainable development' (see Chapter 6). However, a core element within it was a concern for nature in the sense of wildlife. The existence of such concern in countries like the United Kingdom, the United States, Switzerland and the Netherlands in the early 20th century have been described in Chapter 2. They grew considerably as the century wore on.

In the United Kingdom, membership of established wildlife conservation societies like the RSPB grew between the two world wars, and new ones were founded, notably the first of many county wildlife trusts in Norfolk in 1926. In 1943 the RSPB began a youth branch, the Junior Bird Recorders' Club.[125] In the 1940s and 1950s new wildlife trusts were founded in Lincolnshire, Yorkshire, West Wales, Leicestershire and Cambridgeshire. By 1957 they were discussing federation under the SPNR.[126] By 1964 there were 36 trusts, and new bodies were created to coordinate non-governmental conservation organizations, such as the Council for Nature, formed in 1958. Within four years, 292 groups had affiliated.[127] The Council for Nature promoted National Nature Week in May 1963, with wildlife postage stamps, 46,000 visitors to the *Observer* Wildlife Exhibition in London and activities across the country. Its role was taken over for a later era by Wildlife Link in 1980, created to lobby Parliament and put pressure on the government conservation organization (the Nature Conservancy Council) during the passage of the Wildlife and Countryside Act 1981.[128]

By that time, conservation had become a mass movement in the United Kingdom. The Wildlife Trusts' combined membership grew from 3000 in 1960 to 100,000 in 1975. It had doubled by the late 1980s, and by 2002 doubled again to over 400,000.[129] The RSPB's membership was 10,000 in 1960, but half a million in 1980, and (including the Junior Bird Recorders' Club, now known as the Young Ornithologists' Club) over a million by 2002.[130] By the start of the new millennium, membership of the Wildlife and Wetlands Trust and the Woodland Trust had risen above 100,000. The National Trust had more than 3 million members.[131]

This growth in enthusiasm for conservation was not wholly parochial. The Worldwide Fund for Nature UK (WWF-UK) grew from 60,000 to 227,000 members between 1981 and 1993. Nor was it narrowly concerned with wildlife: Friends of the Earth (FoE), founded in 1971, had 230,000 members by 1993; Greenpeace (founded in 1977 in the United Kingdom) had over 400,000 by the same date. Membership of the Ramblers Association doubled during the 1980s, and that of the Council for the Protection of Rural England rose from 30,000 in 1985 to 460,000 in 1993.[132] It is not possible to add the memberships of these organizations together to arrive at a figure for the number of people in a country like the United Kingdom who are active supporters of conservation, for many people are members of more than one organization. However, most observers suggest that up to 4 million people may be signed-up members of a conservation organization, perhaps as many as one in twelve people. This dwarfs the number of those who are members of all political parties put together.

PARTNERS FOR CONSERVATION

The massive growth in First World environmentalism does not have a direct counterpart in the Third World. There is a strong environmental movement in a number of countries outside the Europe–North American axis, and within some (such as India) it is large and vigorous. However, it is very different: it has been described as an 'environmentalism of the poor'.[133] The Indian historian Ramachandra Guha typifies the environmentalist surge of the 1960s and 1970s as 'the ecology of affluence', the protest at the impacts of technology and industrialization by a generation that had benefited from those very advances in terms of securing economic security and health. By contrast, Third World environmentalism included struggles of asset-poor people against the rich, landless rural dwellers against the state or large landowners, of those displaced by dams against the state security apparatus, of homeless urban people against city corporations and private landlords, of those exposed to pollution against the corporations that generate it.[134]

Struggles of this sort certainly characterize mass environmentalism in countries such as India (for example campaigns against the Narmada River dams, or against Union Carbide following the Bhopal disaster) or Nigeria (for example the Ogoni dispute in the Niger Delta).[135] It is also true that these disputes differ in their causes and in the way they are articulated from those that are familiar in industrialized countries: these are protests about the environmental conditions necessary for immediate household survival, not about the importance of the biodiversity or even the moral rights of old growth forests. The binary distinction between the two forms of environmentalism can be overdone, nonetheless most observers accept the need for a broader analysis of global environmentalism than conventional studies of the United States or the United Kingdom in the last 30 years can offer.

The 'environmental revolution' that powered wildlife conservation onto the radar screens of politicians in the closing decades of the 20th century in the United States and Europe is not, or not yet, a global phenomenon.[136] This is quite a challenge for a global conservation movement whose entire logic is built on a concern for nature at the global scale. The colonial SPFE could speak about imperial responsibility in urging conservation action, and the need to maintain wildlife within the Empire. In the last four decades, conservationists have stressed the moral responsibility of humankind as a whole, and the challenge of stopping global processes of extinction. The SPFE shared in this new global perspective, stating in 1945 'human interests include things spiritual as well as things material, and the present generation has not the right to deprive generations to come of natural treasures which, once destroyed, can never be restored'.[137] The standardized global conservation ideology of the last third of the 20th century is one that reflects thinking that is only widely popular within Western countries. It has been disseminated through media that are owned and produced in the West, and which reflects dominant Western values – and that effectively means the values of city people, most of whom are well educated.

The ideologies that dominate media coverage of the environment in the West can be very different from those in the South. Indeed, the very idea that there is something called 'nature' or 'the environment' as a category that is logically separate from humanity is itself a product of centuries of post-enlightenment thinking. It seems self-evident to almost all Western conservationists – certainly all conservation scientists – but it is not universal. Even in a country like India, where there is a large sophisticated middle class urban audience, 'environmental' news has a frame of reference that is very different from that in, say, the United Kingdom or the United States.[138]

The main strategy for conservation organizations rooted in Northern industrial countries and thinking has been to work through partners in the South. National conservation organizations with aims very like those in the West do exist in developing countries, although they tend to be quite small, and to have memberships drawn primarily from the elite. There are also typically a wide range of locally-based grassroots organizations, sometimes with a single-issue focus, sometimes more broadly based. Sometimes Northern NGOs will found partners in the South with whom they can work.

Two examples of the 'partnership' model for conservation will show something of how it works. A classic model is provided by the work of BirdLife International.[139] BirdLife, founded in 1928 as the International Committee for Bird Protection, describes itself as 'a global partnership of non-governmental organizations'. BirdLife Partners are all independent, membership-based, grassroots, national NGOs governed by a democratic body. They represent BirdLife in a unique area or country, and implement BirdLife's Strategy and Regional Programmes. Every four years a 'global partnership' meeting is held to adopt strategies, programmes and policies and elect a Global Council and regional committees. The qualifications necessary to become a BirdLife Partner are considerable. They need to have a clear bird conservation programme, an ethic which fits well with that of BirdLife, and willingness and capacity to commit to the Mission, Vision, Strategy and Regional Programme of BirdLife. They need to be financially self-sufficient and with qualified staff to run their affairs, to have the experience and capacity to work on the documentation and conservation of species, sites and habitats, and to promote interest in birds, conservation and the environment through public campaigning and education. The combined capacity of the organization, steered by its Secretariat in Cambridge, is considerable, with more than 4000 staff working for conservation, over 2,500,000 members worldwide and over 2 million children involved in their work every year. The partnership's organizations manage or own over 1 million hectares of land.

Fauna & Flora International has a less tightly structured approach to partnership, and works with a broad spectrum of local NGOs and communities. In the Philippines, for example, it has a partnership with the Cebu Biodiversity Conservation Foundation and the Government of the Philippines to promote the conservation of forest fragments. This is supported by the UK Government Darwin Initiative, the Global Environment Facility, UNDP and the Bristol, Clifton and West of England Zoological Society.[140] Cebu is rich in endemic species, and subject to rapid deforestation. Only a few small and isolated forest patches are left. These are not only a critical site for species conservation, but also of great importance as a source of native plants for use in future forest restoration programmes. Existing reforestation initiatives in Cebu use exotic species of negligible or negative biodiversity value and unknown long-term impacts on the environment. These have little cultural value and allow few non-timber forest products. FFI has supported local conservation activities in Cebu since 1991, developing funding proposals; completing research and survey work; training local forest wardens to protect forest fragments; assisting with the locally initiated establishment of the Cebu Biodiversity Conservation Foundation; producing a preliminary management plan for the Tabunan area; undertaking preliminary GIS mapping and analysis of forest fragments throughout Cebu; and promoting conservation on the islands among national and international stakeholders.

Sometimes collaborations take more novel forms, for example in Kyrgyzstan FFI works in the Kyrgyzstan Community and Business Forum (CBF). This seeks to increase understanding between businesses and local communities, with the goal of delivering sustainable social and environmental benefits. The project was established, with funding from the European Bank for Reconstruction and Development and International Finance Corporation, in response to an accident near the Kumtor gold mine that released cyanide into a local river, endangering both human health and local biodiversity. It addressed the need to validate environmental monitoring processes at the mine, and the breakdown in communication between the mining company and adjoining communities. The forum developed through a series of consultations with local stakeholders to identify priorities, and involves the use of workshops, newsletters, the establishment of resource centres, mine site visits, reinterpretation of technical documents and training programmes. There is also a small grants programme to provide opportunities for local communities, which has supported a range of projects including a beach clean-up and the development of a rug-making business.[141] The forum has had some success in improving dialogue and understanding between different stakeholder groups, increasing the credibility of information, providing a voice for local communities, and promoting discussion of the wider issues of the relationship between business, the environment and sustainable development.

Partnerships of this kind are a double-edged sword for Third World environmental organizations. They typically lack resources, both core funds to run themselves, and operating funds to undertake any practical conservation programme. There are rarely major sources of finance available within Third World countries that they can draw on, as First World NGOs do. Furthermore, they mostly lack the resources and the expertise to apply successfully for funds available internationally, for example from First World government aid programmes, or international organizations like the Global Environmental Facility (GEF). To these relatively small and impoverished potential 'partners', international conservation organizations offer an astonishing cornucopia of resources. At the same time, local organizations tend inevitably to be driven by the agendas of their larger, richer and better connected cousins from the industrialized world. Although cash-strapped themselves, the modest resources of First World NGOs represent considerable riches to their Third World partners. The rhetoric of partnership can hide a highly dependent relationship. This issue is taken up again in Chapter 9.

The international conservation movement changed a great deal during the 20th century. What began as a concern of a small number of influential people, ended as something much larger and much more popular. Its global reach was different, both more complete (because more truly international) and less complete (because it had lost its privileged opportunity to speak in the ear of colonial government). In the 1990s, the largest conservation organizations became more corporate in their structure, and raised substantial sums from businesses. Some had remarkable success in building relations with corporate donors, such as Conservation International (CI), set up in 1987.[142]

This very success inevitably affected the ability of conservationists to engage effectively at local level, despite their efforts to do so by working with partners. At the Rio Conference in 1992, the largest Northern environmental NGOs were criticized for their remoteness and corporate style, their willingness to speak for grassroots organizations without actually helping them to find their own voice.[143] The accusation that in the 1990s wildlife conservation organizations were the new 'Nature Lords', wielding power from remote corporate headquarters over the heads of developing world governments and against the wishes of rural people, had enough truth in it to be uncomfortable.[144]

The implications of conservation's 'corporate turn' are discussed in Chapter 9. First, it is necessary to explore what conservationists have done, or tried to do, and to assess its impacts. In Chapter 4 the story turns first to the most important theme of 20th century conservation – the establishment of protected areas.

Chapter 4

Nature in Its Place

Nature is safe in parks, or so it is presumed (John Terborgh).[1]

But when, fifty years from now, a lion walks into the red dawn and roars resoundingly, it will mean something to people and quicken their hearts whether they are bolshevists or democrats, or whether they speak English, German, Russian or Swahili. They will stand in quiet awe as, for the first time in their lives, they watch twenty thousand zebras wander across the endless plains (Bernhard Grzimek).[2]

RESERVES FOR WILDLIFE

If pressed to identify places that best represented both the potential of conservation, and the need for it, many would point to the plains of the

Serengeti–Mara ecosystem in northwest Tanzania and southern Kenya. This area has been extensively researched, and endlessly filmed.[3] It is the focus of countless tourist safaris, whether to Kenya's Maasai Mara Game Reserve, or Tanzania's Serengeti National Park. These are the archetypical short grass plains of East Africa, where seasonal cycle of the rains fuel a vast ecological engine of grass growth, a moving carpet of green that draws wild and domestic stock across the landscape to feed. Teeming herds of wildebeest, zebra and Thomson's gazelle migrate across the plains, as Walt Disney's cartoonists characterized so skilfully in *The Lion King*.

Serengeti was made a game reserve in 1908. The National Parks Ordinance that established the Serengeti National Park under an independent Board of Trustees was passed in 1948, although the boundary (disputed immediately by those Maasai, Sukuma, Ndorobo people who lived within it) was only set in 1951.[4] The National Park Ordinance allowed those Maasai already within the park to remain, but the hope was to gradually reduce the number of residents by encouraging them to go elsewhere. Within ten years of its translation to its new status, conservationists believed Serengeti was in trouble. In 1948, the Society for the Preservation of the Fauna of the Empire (SPFE) in London was already noting problems of understaffing, disorganization and unclear policy. The SPFE now worried about proposals for a 'game free area scheme' (noting 'perhaps shooting is carried out on the old principle of killing them to save their lives!'[5]). Locally, land rights were being vigorously pursued by Maasai and others and (in the light of the Mau Mau Emergency running full flood in nearby Kenya) alarming colonial officials.

In 1955, the Government of Tanganyika published a White Paper proposing partition of the Serengeti National Park, removing the central plains (where livestock grazers were concentrated), and isolating the western plains and the Ngorogoro Highlands. There was an instant hostile reaction from the SPFE and the Wildlife Societies of Kenya and Tanzania. By March 1956 this had spread to the United States. And as described in Chapter 3, Lee Talbot (Staff Ecologist with IUCN) led a mission to Serengeti and then came to London to lobby the Colonial Secretary on behalf of the American Wild Life Management Committee, the American Committee for International Wild Life Protection and the (US) Nature Conservancy. He emphasized the international repercussions across Africa if Serengeti were broken up. In June, the SPFE called on the Minister of State for the Colonies to carry out an ecological assessment and an independent enquiry, and with the IUCN General Assembly about to open in Edinburgh, they got their way: it was announced at Edinburgh that the Tanganyikan Government would establish an independent Commission on Serengeti.[6]

The SPFE sent out Professor W H Pearsall from University College London (former student of Arthur Tansley, and leading British botanist, a particular expert on salt marshes) to report on the ecology of the Serengeti and the impacts of the proposals.[7] The Committee of Enquiry proposed to extend the western part of the park to provide dry-season water supplies and meet the Maasai Mara Reserve in Kenya, but to excise the whole of the Crater Highlands in the East to create a special 'Conservation Unit' where human presence (and Maasai grazing) would be tolerated, while the rest of the park was cleared. A White Paper in 1958 established new boundaries broadly on these lines, but the status (and funding) of the 'special conservation area' remained problematic, although helped from 1959 by grants from the Colonial Development and Welfare Fund and the Nuffield Foundation (for research).[8]

In the midst of this, in 1957, the Director the Frankfurt Zoo, Bernhard Grzimek, flew out to Serengeti with his mercurial son Michael to undertake aerial surveys of plains animals, and in the process to publicize the importance of Serengeti, and the threat posed by the new boundary revisions. To this end, for two years, they made films, darted animals and followed migrating herds from the air. Michael was killed in 1959, when their plane was in collision with a griffon vulture over the Salei plains, but his father's moving book about their work, *Serengeti Shall Not Die*, was a best-seller. He wrote:

> *Large cities continue to proliferate. In the coming decades and centuries, men will not travel to view marvels of engineering, but they will leave the dusty towns in order to behold the last places on earth where God's creatures are peacefully living. Countries which have preserved such places will be envied by other nations and visited by streams of tourists. There is a difference between wild animals living a natural life and famous buildings. Palaces can be rebuilt if they are destroyed in wartime, but once the wild animals of the Serengeti are exterminated no power on earth can bring them back.*

Grzimek's appeal precisely captures the conservationist vision for the protection of particular places. His appeal for Serengeti was particular to a moment in time, but the concern for places where nature stands for the whole 20th century. It was a vision that transcended place, being carried along elite networks of like-minded people between America and Europe, and from these across colonial empires to the world. The nature reserve or national park was a constant point in the minds and writings of conservationists. Thus in Britain, Sir Edwin Ray Lankester, formerly professor of Biology at University College London and Oxford, and Director of the Natural History Museum, wrote a letter to *Nature* in 1914 urging 'all worshippers of uncontaminated nature' to work to promote the establishment of nature reserves in Britain. It was, he said, proposed to secure 'the right to preserve from destruction in this country as much and as many as possible of the invaluable surviving haunts of nature'.[9] Lankester was announcing the establishment of the SPNR, but he was also drawing attention to what was to become the defining strategy for conservation in the 20th century, the nature reserve or protected area.

In Britain, the idea that in order to protect nature you had to protect the land on which it stood had been growing for a while. The notion that nature was precious and humanity destructive, led in time to the view that nature needed to be separated from the rest of the landscape and protected against the things people did there. In the United Kingdom, the Commons, Open Spaces and Footpaths Preservation Society (founded in 1865) played an important role in protecting land from development for public amenity, however they could not own and manage that land. The creation of the National Trust for Places of Historic Interest and Natural Beauty in 1894 (drawing in its constitution on the Trustees of Public Reservations in Massachusetts, itself founded in 1891) made such landholding possible. By 1913, the National Trust owned 13 areas of land important for their wildlife, however they lacked the resources to do more; moreover their remit did not extend to Scotland.[10] Four men, led by Charles Rothschild (entomologist banker and brother of Lionel Rothschild, the creator of the private natural history museum at Tring) determined that more should be done. In 1912 they established the Society for the Promotion of Nature Reserves (SPNR), to survey the country for potential nature reserves, and to stimulate support for their preservation.[11] This they did, although the idea of nature reserves remained outside the mainstream of the nature preservation movement in Britain (which was primarily concerned with issues such as bird-catching, egg-collecting and cruelty to animals) until the 1940s.[12] Calls for government support for nature reserves in Britain were to continue to fall on deaf ears until the end of the Second World War.

Outside the United Kingdom, in the British Empire, the idea of reserves for wild life was more easily realized, at least on paper, because of the scope of the arbitrary power of colonial governance. Sir Charles Eliot, writing in 1902 of the East Africa Protectorate, suggested that the future of game preservation depended 'on game reserves in which nothing at all can be shot rather than on prohibitions to shoot particular animals'.[13] The Society for the Preservation of the Wild Fauna of the Empire (SPWFE) had considerable success in lobbying the Colonial Office to persuade the governors of British African colonies to establish game reserves. In 'semi-wild' country (which East Africa was in the early decades of this century, in a political if not an ecological sense) the game reserve was widely seen as the best solution to the preservation of game. The illusion was that there was plenty of room for both settled and developed land and reserves. In 1905, P L Sclater commented that the East African Protectorate covered 'an undeveloped, and it appears, sparsely peopled land, especially in its north-eastern parts'.[14] Here, in areas large enough for annual migrations of changes of pasture, the killing of game could be absolutely prohibited and traffic regulated.[15] Conservationists recommended that game reserves should be located in remote areas, on land without 'settlers or natives' on it (or passing through it). They saw railways as a particular menace, for hunting was all too easy along transport lines. They suggested different licences (and different fees) for those hunting within 10 miles of the railway line and those braving more remote areas.[16] They urged that railways should be directed away from game reserves, and wherever reserves existed, railways next to them should be opposed.[17]

However, while it might be easy to set up game reserves by bureaucratic *fiat*, it was far from easy to ensure that the land and game within them remained protected. African game reserves proved fragile vessels for the conservationists' hopes, particularly in the face of the willingness of colonial governments to de-gazette reserves as other claims on the land emerged. It was, of course, such a re-working of reserve boundaries in the Sudan that had given rise to the establishment of the SPWFE in the first place in 1903 (see Chapter 2), and the adjustment of game reserve boundaries continued to be a problem. In 1908, the area of the Northern Game Reserve (Jubaland Reserve) in Kenya was reduced by about half, cutting out the old Sugota Reserve (north of lake Baringo), and drawing back the eastern boundary. It was also agreed to remove a strip of land from the Southern (Ukamba) Game Reserve because it abounded with *sanseveria* fibre and was required for the development of that industry.[18] In 1909 Buxton found himself retracing familiar ground with a new Colonial Secretary, urging that if it was necessary to limit or alter the area of game reserves, it should be 'a matter of public knowledge and discussion'.[19] Though some reserves might be needlessly large, such changes needed to be carefully planned and discussed. New land added on in replacement would be unlikely to have the same scientific value as the lost land, because smaller animals living in virgin untouched land tend to be destroyed when the land is cultivated.[20] Issues such as the granting of concessions in the Kenyan Southern Game Reserve should be 'referred home'. The society argued (successfully) that local administrators should not be allowed to revise game reserve boundaries (even if they replaced them with other areas), unless such a decision were countenanced by the Colonial Office itself.

Not everybody had confidence in the reservation as a means of preserving big game. F Gillet argued 'that they will more than stave off the evil day, when most species have become extinct, I do not for one moment believe'.[21] However, those urging preservation on the Colonial Office rightly saw the clash of interests over land as the critical test of colonial vision and resolve. As Buxton explained to Lord Elgin in 1906, it was precisely when other land uses became attractive that the value of a game reserve was revealed – it was when nature came into contact with 'civilization' that the game was apt to be killed out, and when the settler of the future would most appreciate the precaution of maintaining the reserve where it is of most use'.[22]

The problem for the conservationists was that they were not the only voice urging action on the Colonial Office. White settlers had a powerful influence, and public opinion among white settlers in Africa was mostly hostile to wildlife. Game was all very well as a subsidy for the annexation and settlement of farms, but once the immediate benefits of cheap meat and saleable hides and horns were no longer needed, game animals were fairly swiftly re-classified as crop pests, whatever their shape or intrinsic attractions. In 1909, for example, Sir Harry Johnston noted that settlers in Jamaica had shot out parrots (for attacking fruit), while on the East African plains, zebra and other game were regarded as competitors with cattle, and dangerous reservoirs of disease.[23] In 1908, Sir

Henry Seton-Karr laid the blame on settlers for diminishing game populations in Africa (he also blamed natives – but this issue will be taken up in the next chapter).[24] Clearly, game was a nuisance close to agricultural settlements, either of European or natives, and would not be tolerated.[25]

It was important that game for reserves should be kept off settlers' farms. Ostrich farmers on the edge of the Kapiti and Athi plains, exercised at the losses to lions, and the spread of ticks from zebra and kongoni, favoured fencing the Southern Reserve. On the other hand fencing the reserve would be costly, and would prevent farmers entering it to obtain ostrich eggs. Sir Alfred Pease suggested providing fencing posts and wire at cost price to farmers. 'This plan would be best for the settler, cheapest to the Government, and would preserve the Game Reserve as the unique and wonderful place it is'.[26] The revision of game reserve boundaries continued to be an issue. In 1924, for example, the society heard that six farms were to be alienated from the Kenyan Southern Reserve, land important to the reserve but 'quite useless for farming'.[27]

In addition to the vocal claims of European settlers, there was little truck from government architects of colonial development with the idea of setting aside land for game reserves if it might have any other more lucrative use, for example if it held minerals. Frederick Selous pointed out to the Colonial Secretary in 1905 that, in Rhodesia at least, white men simply would not allow land to be reserved for wildlife when mineral exploration was a possibility – and if they did find payable reefs in a reserve 'probably the Game Reserve would be no longer maintained'.[28] The only solution was that potential game reserves should be very thoroughly surveyed before declaration (particularly for minerals), to ensure that the area was not more suited for other purposes.[29] Under the British colonial dispensation in Africa at least, game reserves had to be on otherwise economically useless land.

Thus to colonial planners, reserves should not be established near railways or navigable rivers, even if they were cheaper to manage there, because such land were the most valuable for settlement, and the inevitable outcry from settlers would be 'Give us back our land and make your reserve elsewhere',[30] backed by the railway and public opinion. James Stevenson-Hamilton, a tireless campaigner for conservation against the claims and predation of settlers in South Africa, pointed out that antagonism to game reserves could arise simply because settlers resented the mere fact that they are forbidden a stretch of country; perversely they would immediately pronounce it to be 'the very best in the whole country for settlement'.[31] In fact, although the objections of settlers to reserves were commonly specious, they could easily lead astray people who had 'no actual personal knowledge of conditions obtaining on the spot'. The Colonial Office should listen to the advice of conservationists in London and Africa, and think about their duty to posterity, not attend to the shrill and short-sighted clamour of settlers.

In response to threats from settler demands, colonial conservationists often chose emotional language to express their conviction that reserves should be maintained and not carved up or parcelled out to settlers as the process of development proceeded. Stevenson-Hamilton expressed the hope 'all sportsmen and lovers of Nature will continue to stand firmly together in strenuously opposing all reactionary policy regarding that rich heritage of wildlife which is still ours to do what we will with'.[32] In urging that lands should not be given to settlers or others within the Southern Reserve in Kenya, and in regret that land north of the railway had 'tacitly been allowed to drop out of the reserve',[33] Buxton argued that game reserves should be considered 'sacred'.

DIVIDING THE LAND

In the British Empire, the needs of non-Europeans for land were not as clearly articulated as those of settlers. However, indigenous grievances and interests found a voice, and an ear of some sort in government. In Africa, conflicts between wildlife and African farmers also began to receive attention, and the potential of game reserves to reduce this conflict became an important issue. At first concern arose from the desires of colonial governments to maximize the productivity of farm households, particularly those from which they wished to draw labour for mines or European agriculture. Latterly, particularly from the 1940s, the needs of rural Africans for economic development opportunities and medical and health services, became important. In settler-dominated colonies such as Kenya or Zimbabwe, the needs of settlers and Africans became a complex three-cornered running skirmish between colonial office, governor (and eventually, in many colonies, African legislatures) and settlers. In this turmoil, conservationists tried to find a path between all sides to promote what they saw as the interests of wildlife. Thus in 1946 the SPFE noted the problem of the protection of native crops from animals in Nysasland, and agreed that the protection of wildlife should be compatible with human interests. In 1952 Peter Freeman MP asked a question in the House of Commons about the impacts of a bounty system to eradicate crop-raiding monkeys in Gambia on rare species. He subsequently wrote to the Secretary of State for the Colonies, enclosing a letter from the FPS, but received a strong reply criticizing the plausibility of alternative suggestions and saying the campaign must continue because of the paramount importance of agricultural crops.[34]

African farmers complained as vociferously as settlers at the depredations of protected wild animals, although they lacked the same capacity to make themselves heard. Sir Alfred Sharpe, the Commissioner in British Central Africa, wrote in 1903 'constant complaints are being made by natives regarding the depredations of hippopotami, which since their stricter preservation, have likewise increased. As they enter the native grain gardens along the banks of the rivers by night, they in a very short time ruin a whole crop'.[35] The problem was more general than this, however. Buffalo and particularly elephant were also serious crop raiders, and here it was less easy to classify them as vermin, for they were central to the hunting roots of game conservationists. Interestingly, in some places, administrators were identifying the game regulations themselves as the cause of the problem. In 1908, Hesketh Bell, Governor of Uganda, reported that 'the native population is suffering severely, both in life and property, from the attacks of the wild animals that are protected by our game laws'.[36] In particular, buffalo had multiplied greatly, and were 'a serious danger to the people'. Eighty-seven people had been killed by buffalo or elephant in the Kingdom of Toro in the last three years, yet natives were forbidden to kill them save in self-defence. In 1933, Captain Pitman noted the 'havoc wrought by game' in northern Rhodesia, where the elephants 'swarmed' in the crop season.[37]

Colonel Hayes Sadler was concerned that the game regulations set the balance between people and nature in the wrong place: 'whilst preserving the elephant, we have also to think of the people. Latterly, and as a practical result of protection, many complaints have been received of damage done to *shambas* and cultivation by elephants, plantations being destroyed, and, in several instances, habitations and villages being deserted'.[38] In Uganda, crop raiding elephants in 1908 were dealt with by allowing elephants actually found doing damage to plantations to be killed, while a few licences were issued to the Chiefs, allowing them to shoot two elephants each under the Game Regulations on payment of the prescribed fee.[39] Hayes Sadler thought that the hippoptamus should be destroyed 'wherever it is found', believing that 'there is not the slightest fear of its extinction, but it should be driven to seek its habitat away from the haunts of man, where it is a most decided nuisance.[40]

It was not easy to see how to keep people and animals apart when African cultivators not only lived in small scattered communities, but practised shifting cultivation. Colonial observers, by and large, deplored shifting cultivation wherever it occurred. This was the considered view of administrators and (when finally appointed, particularly after the Second World War) technical experts on agriculture and pastoralism. In Northeastern Rhodesia, for example, the British South Africa Company banned *chitemene* (shifting cultivation) in 1906, and although they had to remove the ban three years later in the face of local starvation and poverty, official opposition endured.[41] Wildlife conservationists were no exception to this orthodoxy about the feckless and destructive pattern of indigenous African agriculture. T H Henfrey described it as 'a policy fraught with many evils', including the destruction of tribal homogeneity, increased problems of administration and providing medical relief, and deforestation. It also made it impossible to protect African farmers' crops.[42]

Europeans tended to settle land so closely that game was driven away, both by shooting for meat, and through disturbance. Patterns of land use in European settled areas therefore naturally separated people and animals, and game reserves fitted the new landscape. They kept people and animals apart, essentially making 'nature' a land use like agriculture. Those animals remaining were regarded as pests, and the solution conventionally adopted to deal with them was to allow crop-protection hunting on European farms (accepting that this would mean that game would be shot out). The preservation challenge was meanwhile met by establishing game reserves on suitable (that is not valuable) land.[43] In this way, the 'development' of the settler economy was allowed, and yet species could be preserved 'for all time'. Moreover, there was shooting at hand for the sportsman: the Earl of Onslow extended this argument about the separation of people and wildlife, suggesting a third zone, uncultivated land where shooting might be allowed 'and considerable revenue' derived from licenses'.[44]

Could this approach be extended to Africans, allowing them to carry guns and to hunt animals that attacked their farms? Some administrators favoured allowing natives to hunt: Hesketh Bell, urged that buffalo be removed from the schedule of protected animals, although he doubted that even with this inducement, natives would voluntarily attack these formidable animals.[45] Others worried about security if natives were allowed to bear arms, particularly precision weapons. To the Governor of Nyasaland, 'the practical possibilities of any such action are so grave that I hesitate to contemplate such a measure'.[46] Laws against the importation and possession of arms and ammunition by Africans effectively prevented the substantial slaughter of game (although, of course, they promoted just those practices such as use of pits that sportsmen deplored for their cruelty).[47] The idea of natives hunting with guns was anathema to most conservationists, because it would lead to the extinction of all game. T H Henfrey wrote 'pray God [it] will never be allowed'.[48] When the Colonial Secretary proposed throwing open the Lake Chad Reserve in 1921 'on account of the great damage done by the game in general, and elephants in particular, to native crops',[49] the SPFE argued that allowing natives half of the proceeds of the ivory killed in the area was 'a very dangerous precedent and liable to abuse'.[50]

The issue of hunting, or 'poaching' as it was almost universally described by conservationists, is discussed in Chapter 5. It is important to note here that most conservationists appear to have shared the common colonial conviction that Africans were reluctant and lazy farmers, and argued that allowing hunting would lead to the end of African agriculture, presumably because they would find hunting less effort.[51] As late as 1953, there was a discussion in the House of Lords (involving Lord Willingdon, President of the Fauna Preservation Society), worrying about the use of firearms by natives to kill wild animals in Northern Rhodesia. The government replied that most of the recorded 47,366 guns were muzzle loaders and used only for ceremonial purposes. The FPS's correspondents disagreed.

The alternative to allowing Africans to shoot game animals was to make them behave like European farmers, living in specified areas utilized more intensively. Hobley and others argued that if African cultivation were more concentrated it would be easier to defend farms against the inroads of wild animals.[52] What was needed was a new system of native land tenure that gave a definite right to land either on an individual or tribal basis. This was prescient, for it foreshadowed the enthusiasms of the aid donors in independent Africa three decades later for land apportionment and privatization in the name of agricultural efficiency.[53] Land should be divided up, with sufficient given to tribes to allow for cultivation and grazing, with allowance for expansion. After this 'no more land should be available except by purchase'.[54] This would 'eliminate the pernicious habit of wandering about the countryside',[55] promote tribal spirit, facilitate administration and provision of medical services, improve crop production and save forests. In this way, with game and people safely partitioned in the landscape (and, of course, Europeans and Africans also partitioned), game preservation could be compatible with 'ever-increasing settlement and agricultural development' in Tanganyika. This was a model for inter-species as well as inter-race apartheid.

THE IDEA OF NATIONAL PARKS

In both territory annexed by Europeans and that farmed or grazed by local people, the game reserve came to be the centrepiece of colonial conservation, their establishment its great success. However, the great limitation of game reserves was their impermanence, for in many areas they were no more than a temporary palliative to the problem of loss of wildlife. They worked, but only while development pressure were slight: push them and their boundaries moved, to accommodate settlers' demands, or became permeable, to admit despoiling natives into the sanctuary. Game reserves ought not to have anybody in them; but many of them did. When push came to shove, colonial governments were only too willing to adjust game reserve boundaries. They would not lock up large areas of land if a more profitable use for it became apparent. The idea of protected areas was one that conservationists hung on to, but they needed something more permanent, a new idea with which to challenge colonial governments. The model they chose was the idea of a national park, first developed in the United States at Yellowstone in 1872.

The idea of national parks matched the long-standing belief of colonial conservationists in a higher purpose for conservation. In the 1906 delegation, Lord Curzon argued to the Earl of Elgin that game preservation should not be undertaken for sport (although he stressed emolliently 'I hope I may regard myself as a keen sportsman') nor to supply specimens for zoos and museums, nor for the financial benefits from hunting, but 'as a duty to nature and the world'.[56] Reserves 'ought to exist not for the gratification of the sportsman, but for the preservation of interesting types of animal life'.[57] Peter Chalmers-Mitchell said in 1931 'the living animals and plants of the world are an inheritance', and 'it is one of the most fundamental duties of modern civilized beings to preserve that heritage from the past and hand it on in a more stable condition to our successors'.[58] The national park was the only way to do that: as H G Maurice wrote in 1938, 'neither commerce nor sport, nor that soulless process we call development, should be prosecuted up to the point of exterminating a species. And so we come to the conclusion: let there be sanctuaries'.[59]

The main attraction of national parks in the colonial context was their permanence as such sanctuaries. They offered the possibility of securing land for game that was proof against the whims of Governors and the demands of development. In 1930 the SPFE Executive Committee argued that game preservation needed to be carried 'a great deal further than before', conservation needed something more than a game reserve, 'to stabilize the reserves and make actual sanctuaries or National Parks'.[60]

The SPWFE drew attention to the merits of the US model repeatedly. In 1905, its journal noted 'we may occasionally derive useful lessons from the experience of other nations. The Yellowstone National Park in the United States, was the forerunner of true Game Reserves, of which the American nation and its President may well be proud'.[61] The 'success' of Yellowstone was referred to repeatedly in the first delegation to the Colonial office in 1905: 'perhaps I may mention, for the sake of illustrating this point, that outside the Empire, in America, they are spending enormous sums on their Reserve'.[62] In 1906 Rhys Williams wrote to the Secretary of State for the Colonies pointing out that the people of the United States had given up a large area for Yellowstone Park, and that 'we maintain that it is the duty and the interest of Great Britain to follow this example in East Africa'.[63] By 1921 William Hornaday could argue, with some justification, that the United States and Canada had 'the best system of laws for game and general wildlife protection that can be found anywhere'.[64]

The creation of national parks in the United States is an oft-told story. Alfred Runte argues that no institution is more symbolic of American conservation than the national parks – and it is also probably a fact that no institution has been more influential across the world.[65] The Yosemite Valley in California was in many ways the forerunner, made a state park in 1864, and a national park in 1890. The first national park proper however was Yellowstone in Wyoming (1872). The idea of a national park had been first voiced by the great painter of the West (and its indigenous peoples), George Catlin, in 1832. He proposed 'A *nation's park*, containing man and beast, in all the wild and freshness of their nature's beauty'.[66] The 'beast' in this case was undoubtedly the bison, whose rapid demise Catlin and many others deplored.[67] He was also perhaps responding to criticism of the despoliation of America's natural bounty and beauty that was prevalent at the time, particularly from arrogant Europeans. The degradation of the Niagara Falls, which he painted many times, was already obvious.

Catlin expressed a widely-held sense that the destiny of the United States was epitomized in some way by its magnificent landscapes. Alfred Runte argues that nature was marshalled as a proof of national greatness from the moment of American independence. The new nation might lack sophistication and great ancient art, but its great natural riches supplied valuable cultural bottom. The American West could help define and epitomize the greatness of late 19th century America: indeed it could be argued that a failure to conserve the natural wonders of the west would demonstrate that the youthful democracy and industrial power lacked precisely those civilized impulses to which the eastern elite wanted to lay claim. However, despite the scale and diversity of landscapes in the east, it was hard to find the distinctiveness that could be the basis of cultural identity, particularly in the face of European scepticism and rapid American development. By the 1860s, even the Niagara Falls had become 'a natural wonder that failed to astonish', because of water abstraction for industry and sprawling development.[68] The conquest of the west, however, revealed landscapes of an unheralded magnificence, and the discovery of the Yosemite Valley and the Sierra redwoods in 1851 and 1852 revealed wonders of a new order. Such landscapes bore very comparison with the natural wonders of Europe (surely no valley in Switzerland could match the symmetry of Yosemite?), and the proposal to create a state park was widely supported across the United States when Abraham Lincoln signed the Yosemite Bill in 1864. The park was small, enclosing just the Yosemite valley and the Mariposa 'big trees', and its purpose was cultural, to protect the remarkable wonders of the scenery.

The same concerns drove the creation of the Yellowstone National Park, in a region that was slowly opened up to Europeans from the 1860s. Reports suggested that the geysers, lakes and waterfalls of Yellowstone stood comparison with anything in Europe – even its architectural heritage; Yellowstone's rock pillars were an extravagant natural architecture, a geyser evoking 'a natural Coliseum'.[69] In the 1870s, Yellowstone became the talk of the popular press back east. However, the wonders were not only a potential source of national pride but (very quickly) the focus of commercial exploitation. The fencing of the geysers for private gain (as had happened at Niagara) would be a failure of cultural imagination, and the campaign to make Yellowstone a park like Yosemite grew. After sustained lobbying, the Yellowstone Park Act was passed in March 1872.[70]

The American experiment with national parks was soon emulated in Canada (Banff National Park, 1887), Australia (Royal National Park, 1879, Belair National Park, 1891, and Lamington National Park, 1915) and New Zealand (Tongarivo, 1894).[71] Successors to Yellowstone and Yosemite within the United States, however, came slowly, still driven by what Alfred Runte calls 'monumentalism'. National parks were important because of the magnificence of their scenery, but equally important was that they were not needed for anything else. Parks did not at first prevent other forms of economic activity, and they actively promoted tourist development. The Sierra Club, founded in 1892, became a fierce advocate of restrictions on the commercial excesses of tourism in the 'wilderness', as well as the depredations of sheep ranchers, timber and mineral claims, and hunting. The parks were only loosely protected. Yellowstone's first Superintendent had a full-time job as a bank examiner, and did not visit the park for years at a stretch. His successor spent the winters in Michigan.[72] Under President Theodore Roosevelt's doctrine of 'conservationism', meaning rational resource exploitation, national parks took a lowly place compared to water, timber and minerals. The area of national forests grew hugely, while the area of national parks remained very limited, the minimum necessary to allow the public access to their monumental features. The loss of the Hetch Hetchy Valley in Yosemite to a reservoir in 1913 to serve urban San Francisco was symbolic of the power balance (or to conservationists imbalance) between use and preservation. The National Parks Service was only established in 1916, setting up a Federal bureaucracy to taken over management of national parks and monuments from the Department of the Interior.[73]

Nonetheless, despite their shortcomings, the idea of the early US National Parks acted as a beacon to conservationists elsewhere, particularly in Europe, an object lesson in what could be achieved with vision, determination and a modicum of government resources. They bequeathed three institutions in particular to their successors at home and abroad. First, they were created on the illusory premise that these lands were wholly natural, unmanaged by human hands. Second, they established a militaristic approach to management. Third, they brought a close relationship with the development of tourism.

The American belief in the lack of human presence in remote and natural-seeming areas has been widely translated into other contexts, sometimes with highly damaging effects. The Yellowstone landscape (like the open meadows of Yosemite) is full of Indian cultural sites, and early tourists were shocked to encounter Indian bands. However, the historical engagement of those indigenous peoples with the land, and their ecological impact on the landscape, were soon lost to white American memory. Their heritage was extirpated from maps, whose newly-minted place names featured the park's 'natural' wonders. To the Europeans from the east who 'discovered' and 'explored' these landscapes, it was their very wildness and apparent *lack* of human presence that made them seem so valuable. The effacement of the indigenous people in America's national parks was, of course, possible because Indians were also removed physically from the landscape. The creation of Yellowstone took place in the context of the US Army's suppression of Indians across the west, and alongside the creation of small, scattered reservations for Indian people. As Karl Jacoby notes, 'whether or not the tourists who later came to the park realized it (and most of course did not), Yellowstone's seeming wilderness was the product of a prior, state-organized process of re-arranging the countryside, in which native peoples and nature were slotted into distinct categories and separated from one another'.[74] The problematic heritage of the concept of wilderness, and the issue of evictions from national parks, are discussed further in the next chapter.

The second heritage of the American national parks, that of military-style control, arose simply because of the people who managed them. The first penetration of the Yosemite Valley was military, and it was cleared in 1852 by the army, who executed five Indians believed to have attacked prospectors, and scattered the remainder.[75] Yellowstone was also the context for military manoeuvres associated with the so-called 'Sioux Wars' of 1876–7, of which the engagement at Little Big Horn is the best known.[76] Finally, after years of ineffectual civil administration, the management of Yellowstone was handed over to the US Army in 1886, when troops from Fort Custer Montana under Captain Moses Harris marched in as a military garrison. John Muir and the Sierra Club both rejoiced to see firm management at last. The army was to stay 32 years.[77] Its influence was to last much longer – when the Park Service took control of Yellowstone in 1918, it copied military uniforms for its own, and it hired former soldiers in service in the park as its rangers. Smokey the Bear had a strong military heritage.[78]

The primacy of tourism (and indeed its awkward relationship with the idea of wilderness) also dates from the very beginning of the US national parks. Tourists began to arrive in the Yosemite Valley in 1855, and by 1857 a primitive hotel was accepting guests opposite Yosemite Falls. By 1864, when the Yosemite Park Act was passed, development was already advanced.[79] By 1890, when Yosemite became a national park (along with General Grant and Sequoia National Parks), the potential for over-exploitation by tourism was one of many problems that was highlighted by John Muir, and championed by the Sierra Club. It led, in due course, to the creation of a larger national park at Yosemite in 1890, but while this helped direct and control the development of the tourist industry, it by no means ended it. Park and wilderness advocates chose to promote tourism in parks in the hope of showing their value, both in terms of economic returns and wider public support. Scenery was a potential national asset, a point quickly taken by business interests, particularly the railways.

Following the first National Parks Conference at Yellowstone in 1911, the railroads began to lead the way in marketing the scenery of the west. Glacier National Park, established in 1910, soon featured vast Swiss-style tourist lodges, built by the Great Northern Railway. Over the border in Canada, the small reserve around the Banff Hot Springs established in 1885 (only 26 square kilometres) was extended to almost 700 square kilometres 'as a public park, a pleasure ground for the benefit, advantage and enjoyment of the people of Canada' in 1887.[80] Further parks had been established nearby, Glacier (in the Selkirk Mountains) and Yoho in 1886, Waterton Lakes in 1895 and Jasper in 1907. The Dominion Forest Reserves and Parks Act 1911 standardized the management of these parks under a Commissioner. The early National Parks in Canada grew out of wider policy for the development of natural resources, reflecting a doctrine of 'usefulness' closely akin to that in the United States.[81] Banff National Park was 'trapped, prospected, mined, cut-over and burned in the same manner as most of Western Canada and the United States in pioneer days'.[82] The mountain parks became vehicles for economic development, and in the case of the Canadian Pacific Railway (CPR), a strategy for business survival.[83] The CPR created luxurious mountain tourist resorts (Banff Springs

Hotel and Chateau Lake Louise are still extant, thriving exercises in Gothic extravagance), and brought over Swiss mountain guides to create safe routes in new mountains, and lead tourists up them from the rail head.[84] In Glacier National Park in the United States, waitresses were dressed in Swiss costume for greater verisimilitude. The 'See America First' campaign continued the tradition of urging the merits of America's natural monuments over Europe's weary cultural heritage.[85]

However, it was the motor car that transformed tourism in North American national parks, and with it increasingly exacted drastic change in the parks themselves. By 1916 more people had entered Yosemite by car than by rail, and by 1918 the ratio was seven to one.[86] A third of a million people visited Canadian national parks in 1926 (38 per cent from the United States), the majority by car. Ominously, the Canadian National Railway had laid out a golf course in Jasper National Park, and mosquito control was in progress.[87] Camping by car (or 'sagebrushing') became hugely popular in the 1920s and 1930s, and there was a relentless rise in the number of cars and visitors in national parks. By the 1950s only 1 or 2 per cent of visitors reached US national parks by public transport. The huge programmes of road construction, like the creation of hotel resorts and formal campgrounds and the laying on of entertainments for tourists (for example Yosemite's dubious 'Indian Days'), had become the target of conservationist complaint, led of course by the Sierra Club.[88]

It is obvious, of course, that in industrialized countries the motor car and the tarmac road became the dominant forces driving economic and land use change. The impact of the affordable motor car, epitomized by Henry Ford's Model T (introduced in 1908, first built on a production line at the Highland Park Factory in 1912, and still in production in 1927) was socially progressive, at least until the 1960s.[89] It was also, increasingly, destructive of nature and natural beauty. National Parks featured pioneering techniques of 'parkway' design in creating new roads, but while the genius of designers such as Frederick Law Olmstead allowed the creation of 'artful wilderness' of great aesthetic appeal and superficial naturalness, the extent of the engineering of landscapes were significant intrusions into 'wild' nature, and in some instances highly damaging to species and habitats.[90] Mass tourism was the raison d'être of the US national parks for much of the 20th century (at least until the Wilderness Act of 1964), but it re-worked landscapes in often fundamental ways.[91]

The infant International Union for the Protection of Nature (IUPN) discussed tourism and conservation at its third technical meeting, in 1953. The possibility of the partnership was obvious: 'man travels, enjoys nature, begins to understand it and determines that it should not be destroyed. That is what ought to happen, and sometimes it does'.[92] Yet it often did not – conservationists faced the paradox that visitors, 'in their carelessness and ignorance, even by their mere numbers endanger the very existence of the parks and nature reserves'. They did this first in the United States, but by the 1950s the problem was recognized everywhere: in 1957 the Chief Game Warden of Southern Rhodesia observed that 'demand for more facilities, more comforts, more accommodation and so forth become increasingly insistent until they, themselves become the primary function and nature conservation may sink into complete oblivion. Commercialisation rules the day'.[93]

THE NATIONAL PARK SPIRIT

The North American model was the main driving force internationally in what C W Hobley referred to in 1924 as 'the National Park spirit'. In Europe it was a similar rise of mass concern for nature (particularly in the mountains) in Italy that gave rise to the creation of the Gran Paradiso National Park in 1922, and Abruzzi in 1923.[94] Hobley urged in 1924 that in those countries of the British Empire where European colonization 'had progressed far enough', reserves should be given the status of national parks.[95] Canada, for example, had 19 parks that were also game reservations, covering in total 24,000 square kilometres. He noted that the policy was to make these accessible to people of the country and international visitors by the construction of roads and lodges in beauty spots. He believed that this model had much to offer African, Indian and Asian colonial territories. At the Jubilee Meeting of the Bombay Natural History Society in 1933, a speaker gushed that India's wildlife compared in its beauty and marvellous variety with that of any country in the world. Its fauna and flora were a magnificent asset, and a potential source of pride which would be generally appreciated by its people if they were led to know of it.[96]

The pre-eminent example of progress towards such parks outside Europe, the British Dominions and the United States, was the Kruger National Park in the Transvaal in South Africa. For the conservationists in the SPFE, the Sabi Game Reserve had been the type-example of the conflicts between settlers and game since the start of the century (Chapter 2). James Stevenson-Hamilton on the ground, backed by the SPFE in London, had campaigned for years to secure the upgrading of the Singwitsi and Sabi Game Reserves (later the Transvaal Game Reserve) to a national park. They were opposed by various forces, most consistently by Boer farmers fearing the tsetse that the game might harbour, and desirous of freedom to hunt for meat and hides.[97]

Stevenson-Hamilton left South Africa in 1914, and when he returned after the First World War he was depressed by the deterioration in the management of the game reserves.[98] However, the various calls for the nationalization of the game reserves were finally heeded by government. The Transvaal Land Owners Association accepted the notion of giving up farms within the reserves for land elsewhere, and at a conference in 1921 the Native Affairs Department agreed new boundaries on the west side of the Sabi Game Reserve. In 1922, Prime Minister Jan Smuts announced his intention to create a National Park and Game Reserve in the next parliamentary session. Stevenson-Hamilton suggested that 'future generations of South Africans will have cause to bless the prescience of the government in creating a 'great national faunal sanctuary'.[99]

In the event, the government changed, and it took until 1926 to establish the park. However, by that time, the inevitability of the park had brought white Voortrekker politicians strongly behind the project, which became (somewhat ironically given the consistency of Afrikaans-speaking white opposition in earlier decades) publicly presented as the fulfilment of the dream of Nationalist politician Paul Kruger. Proponents of the national park positioned conservation cleverly within the complex national politics of the 1920s. Most popular accounts suggest (wrongly) that it was Kruger's pet project.[100] Kruger was an avid hunter and a connoisseur of biltong, but the myth of Kruger as conservationist allowed conservation to be enfolded within the Afrikaaner cultural tradition, and as National Party politicians manipulated the Voortrekker past to gain the support of 'poor whites', the park became identified with Afrikaaner ideals. Deneys Reitz, Minister of Lands from 1921 to 1924, argued that it was a national duty to preserve the park 'just as the Voortrekkers saw it'. Conservation (and especially the Kruger National Park) became something that united classes within Afrikaaner society in the 1920s.

The Kruger National Park, in time, became a magnet for urban white tourists, just like those in the United States.[101] It was placed under a Board of Trustees, answering to the Minister of Lands. Stevenson-Hamilton, who had previously been employed by Natal Province, at first declined to be appointed as warden, to answer to a Board and work within a government he expected to be hostile to English-speaking civil servants. He returned to the United Kingdom to work with the SPFE and the Zoological Society, but he hated London and came back in 1927, and ran the park (and duelled with the Board) until 1946. Tourism began slowly, with an income from tourists of only three pounds in 1927, although this rose to £850 in 1929, and in 1930 there were 900 cars and 500 kilometres of new roads within the park.[102] South African Railways ran facilities for visitors, providing transport, publicity and catering, while the Board provided rest camps, guides and guards. Tourists arrived in ever-increasing numbers, and in the 1930s there were huts and tented accommodation for over 700 people.

As Warden, Stevenson-Hamilton disapproved of luxurious facilities and entertainment, and tried to maintain a 'wilderness' experience for visitors. In 1928, he described Kruger as 'a sanctuary for human foes of every kind of wildlife without exception'.[103] The park was managed by nine Europeans and 100 native police, and administration cost £7000 per year, with an income of £1000 from gate fees, fines for poaching and (strangely) fees from African squatters.[104] After Stevenson-Hamilton's retirement, the age of roughing it passed, and camps became more comfortable, with electricity and improved washing and cooking facilities. By 1954 Kruger was 'bulging with people', its 3000 places all filled. The Park took over all visitor facilities (catering, trading and garage services), and the park became 'the abode of big business, managed with the visitor in mind'.[105]

In the heyday of apartheid, Kruger National Park became an enduring symbol of Afrikaaner nationalism, a place of recreation and spiritual restoration for urban white South Africans, where they could affirm their God-given role as the rightful guardians of a land carved from the wilderness. James Stevenson-Hamilton saw Kruger National Park as a display of 'unspoiled nature', to give the public 'some notion of how the country appeared before the white man came to it'.[106] The myth of Paul Kruger the conservationist, and the idea that conservation was somehow an integral part of Afrikaaner identity, were especially politically useful in the post Second World War years, when the policy of apartheid caused South Africa's political isolation. The success of the national park ideal in South Africa was therefore not only a core element of self-belief for white conservationists in Africa, it was extremely useful to the government of South Africa in international political battles.

NATURE AND PARKS IN THE UNITED KINGDOM

As a London-based society, the interest of the Society for the Preservation of the Fauna of the Empire (SPFE) in the late 1920s in the idea of national parks in Africa is interesting, because parks were also being discussed at the time in the United Kingdom. The idea was not new to the British scene. The sparsely-inhabited lands of Ireland and Scotland, cleared by emigration to the New World, were particularly attractive to early proponents of British national parks.[107] In 1909 Charles Stewart advocated the creation of a national park in the west of Scotland, on the islands of Jura and Rum. He suggested that the government should provide funds to buy the deer forests, and in return would reap revenues from sport shooting, fishing and forestry, while also protecting against developers and providing recreation for tourists and naturalists.[108] In the same year, 1909, the SPWFE Journal carried an article by Sir Harry Johnston suggesting that Achill Island, in County Mayo on the west coast of Ireland would make an ideal national park.[109]

In the eyes of leading members of the SPFE, national parks were best understood as glorified shooting estates. The Earl of Onslow likened national parks in South Africa, the Belgian Congo and Switzerland to Scottish deer forests, where wise owners establish sanctuaries where deer could breed unmolested, and 'come on' for shooting 'in a sportsmanlike and reasonable manner'.[110] He remarked that the protection afforded by the Swiss National Park (founded in 1914) for example, was allowing chamois populations to recover.[111] Onslow saw national parks, game reserves and strict game reserves as 'reservoirs' whose 'overflow' of game would keep surrounding areas stocked.[112] He was not alone in this vision: C W Hobley saw game reserves and national parks as 'natural reservoirs where the mammalian fauna and avi-fauna will be available for study, and for the supply of specimens to renew the collections in the museums of Empire for all time'.[113]

In the context of the parks in Africa and Switzerland, Onslow noted in 1928 that there were suggestions to do 'something of the same kind' in England, and he put the question of national parks down for discussion in Parliament in 1929.[114] The SPFE was broadly in sympathy with the movement for national parks in Britain, but only in as much as they promoted wildlife conservation.[115] They proposed that parks should be chosen and administered 'to provide sanctuaries for the avifauna and such indigenous mammals as can reasonably be expected to have a permanent habitat therein'.[116] The proper way to protect animals and plants was 'to have preserves and sanctuaries in places specially adapted and from which the public would, at necessary time, be excluded'. The need for public recreation was a different issue, and while the SPFE was in favour of national parks 'for the amusement and recreation of the public', it feared that these would have limited value for the protection of animals and plants.[117]

However, it was not shooting but access to the countryside that was the critical issue in Britain. Lord Bledisloe, Parliamentary Secretary to the Ministry of Agriculture, visited Yellowstone, Banff and Jasper National Parks in 1925, and reported that not only did they provide a sanctuary for wild plants and animals, but 'a most perfect holiday resort for persons of all classes engaged normally in strenuous work'.[118] This was the idea that drove the demand for national parks (and eventually, like the tail of a populist comet, wildlife conservation) in the United Kingdom, the need for places for industrial workers to find health and outdoor recreation.

Demand for access to the countryside had risen steadily since the end of the 19th century, a cultural change equivalent to that described in Chapter 3 when environmental and wildlife organizations began to grow from the 1960s. The Federation of Rambling Clubs, established in 1905, had 40,000 members by 1931. The Youth Hostels Association (YHA) was established in 1930, the Ramblers Association in 1935. The YHA had almost 300 hostels and over 83,000 members by the outbreak of the Second World War.[119] However, rural land in Britain was almost all privately owned, and landowners were opposed to the idea of allowing urban workers access to it. In 1894 James Bryce placed a Bill before Parliament to allow the public to walk over mountains and open moorland for recreation, artistic or scientific purposes. It failed, as did repeated attempts to get such a Bill passed in the face of fierce opposition from landowners who feared damage to their grouse shooting (in 1908, and three times in the late 1920s and early 1930s). In April 1932, a Manchester man, Benny Rothman, led a mass trespass of 500 people on to moorland on Kinder Scout in the Peak District, owned by the Duke of Devonshire. They were opposed by the Duke's keepers, and with four others, Benny Rothman was arrested and jailed for four months at Derby assizes.[120] The Access to the Mountains Act was finally passed in 1939.[121]

The idea of national parks provided a less universal approach to the need for public access to the countryside. In 1928, Lord Bledisloe wrote to the Prime

Minister suggesting that the Forest of Dean (on the borders of south Wales in Gloucestershire) be turned into a national park, offering part of his own estate in the area as a contribution. In 1929, following an approach from the newly-formed Council for the Preservation of Rural England (CPRE) and its Welsh and Scottish cousins, the Prime Minister, J Ramsay MacDonald, set up a committee under Christopher Addison to investigate the question of national parks for Britain. This reported in 1931, noting among other things the impossibility of parks in the US style (with massive tourist development) or on the US scale (for lack of vast areas of government land). The Addison Committee also pointed out the soon-familiar tension between preservation and access.

Wildlife or nature conservationists (for example the RSPB and the British Ecological Society) urged the need for strictly protected reserves within larger national parks, or for a system of national nature reserves separate from national parks. These organizations, with others like the Linnean Society and the Zoological Society of London, were members with the SPFE of the British Correlating Committee for the Protection of Nature in the 1930s, under the chairmanship of Sir Peter Chalmers-Mitchell. They noted the two possible meanings of national parks, firstly to provide opportunities for people to enjoy a holiday in the open air and observe wildlife, and secondly 'to preserve unaltered, as far as possible, the animals and plants of the district'. The Correlating Committee was determined to press the need for the latter, independently of the recreational aspect of national parks.[122] The SPFE kept close watch on British debates about the need for nature reserves as well as recreational national parks through the 1930s.[123]

Although the CPRE and other organizations established a Standing Committee on National Parks in 1934, to maintain pressure on government to do something, the 1930s were a disappointment of park advocates. In part this was because of the parlous state of the national economy, so slowly recovering from the Great Depression of 1929. Some also argued that the Town and Country Planning Act of 1932 made parks unnecessary because it allowed local authorities to conclude planning schemes with private landowners to control development (as on the English South Downs). Arguably, areas like the New Forest, a Royal Forest protected under an Act of Parliament, in some sense already acted as national parks, with public access over wide areas.[124] Park advocates pushed their case, arguing that parks could promote employment (for example proposing a park in the Vale of Neath in south Wales in 1934). The only achievements were innovations by the Forestry Commission, establishing the National Forest Park in Galloway in 1936, and others subsequently in the Forest of Dean (1939) and Snowdonia (1940).

In the event, the outbreak of the Second World War cut across the government's piecemeal moves towards national parks, and the issue was swept up into the new concern for post-war reconstruction planning. The provision of parks now became an integral element within a strategy to create a 'land fit for heroes', under Sir John Reith. The early 1940s saw a succession of government committees consider all aspects of rural land use, nature conservation and national parks. By 1949 they had thrashed out the shape of post-war land use planning, the responsibilities of the local authorities, and roles for a government nature conservation agency (created as the Nature Conservancy in 1949) and a National Parks Commission. National parks were to be declared nationally by this commission, but managed by committees of their constituent County Councils, under the existing Town and Country Planning Act 1947. Land in national parks remained privately owned.[125] National parks could be protected for the nation, but the powers of the National Parks Commission to defend them were slight. Moreover, despite a recommendation for an independent National Parks Commission in Scotland, the 1949 Act made no provisions for national parks in Scotland, or indeed Northern Ireland.

The first British National Parks were created in 1951, all in hill areas of long-proven recreational importance, the Peak District, Dartmoor, the Lake District and Snowdonia. Between 1951 and 1957, the National Parks Commission designated ten national parks in England and Wales, and added to this other similar conservation designations of private land in Areas of Outstanding Natural Beauty and Heritage Coasts.[126] In 1968 a new organization was created to reflect a wider agenda for the whole countryside in the Countryside Commission. In 1989, the first new national park in over 40 years was created in the Norfolk Broads: an area of human-made wetlands mentioned in the war-time lists of potential parks.[127] Scotland had to wait a long half century for national parks, under the National Parks Scotland Act 2000, although much had been achieved by the Countryside Commission for Scotland in the meantime with a different concept, the National Scenic Area.[128] The first Scottish national park, Loch Lomond and the Trossachs (one of those listed by the Ritchie Committee in 1949) was finally opened in July 2002. The Cairngorms national park was declared a few months later.

British national parks did not meet the original interest of nature conservationists in strict nature reserves. However, the National Parks and Access to the Countryside Act 1949 created a unique double-barrelled system for conservation in the United Kingdom. Calls from nature conservationists for national nature reserves fared well in the various committees that met in the 1940s.[129] These reserves were the 'sanctuaries' favoured by Onslow, the SPFE, and the British Correlating Committee – 'a scheme of sanctuaries selected on an ecological basis', to protect typical fauna and flora from post-war government schemes to increase the productive capacity of rural land in Britain.[130] In 1945 Arthur Tansley, author, plant physiologist, Freudian and conservationist, called for a 'National Nature Reserve Authority' that would give 'explicit recognition of public obligation to take responsibility for the conservation of wildlife – the formal placing of wildlife under formal State protection'.[131] The government's Wild Life Conservation Committees established the importance of wildlife conservation as a national interest, proposing national nature reserves in addition to further reserves within the proposed national parks. Unlike the parks themselves, such small reserves seemed to pose little threat to the interests of private landowners or the emerging powers of local government planners. The Wildlife Conservation Special Committee for England and Wales, originally chaired by Julian Huxley, also cleverly argued that national nature reserves could contribute to the advancement of science as well as protect wildlife for public benefit. They argued that nature reserves should be selected, acquired and managed by a single Biological Service with research and advisory functions.[132] In due course, the Nature Conservancy was made responsible to a new committee of the Privy Council rather than to the Minister of Town and Country Planning.

The British government's Nature Conservancy began to establish National Nature Reserves (NNRs) on land purchased, leased or held under an agreement with landowners and Sites of Special Scientific Interest (SSSIs).[133] By 1962 there were over 1700 SSSIs, by 1990 about 5500, covering 17,000 square kilometres.[134] However, the Nature Conservancy had enemies in Whitehall, and among landowners (particularly in Scotland) who resented its powers to designate private land. It never acquired the power and strength that those who conceived it had hoped. In 1965 it was placed within the newly-created government Natural Environment Research Council (NERC), but the arrangement was not satisfactory, and in 1973 it was recreated as the Nature Conservancy Council (NCC), losing its scientific research functions.[135] The NCC survived until 1991, when new legislation, responding to renewed opposition from Scottish landowners and communities to conservation apparently imposed from England, broke it up.[136] The NCC's role was taken on by English Nature in England, and new combined agencies for wildlife and countryside in Scotland and Wales, the Countryside Council for Wales and Scottish Natural Heritage.

PARKS FOR THE COLONIES

The national parks in the United States, the Dominions (Canada, Australia, New Zealand and above all Kruger in South Africa) all adhered to a broadly similar model, and it was this, quite unlike the approach in the United Kingdom itself, that commended itself to colonial conservationists. National parks in the US mould had a number of important advantages. First, they demanded much greater and more permanent commitment from governments: their borders could not be so easily pruned away, and their governing boards might act as strong defenders against outside demands. Second, they would have to be properly funded, for any failure in this regard would reflect badly on national reputation. Third, they would be declared in the interests of the whole country, and at a stroke escape the lurking suspicion that conservation was, in some way, a secret service to elite hunters. Fourth, national parks on the US or Kruger model could generate income from tourism – they could themselves be a driver for development, an especially neat outcome. By 1938, colonies had grown to see the game reserve as 'a nice thing to have, for it attracts visitors who spend money' (and did so in areas generally unsuitable for anything else).[137] National parks would make that benefit much more substantial and readily generated. Such economic benefits, for regeneration or development, were particularly relevant at a time of drastic economic recession, as in the late 1920s and 1930s. As Peter Chalmers Mitchell pointed out, it would cost little to raise the status of reserves to national parks.[138]

In 1926, the year of the successful establishment of Kruger, and influenced by its chief advocate, James Stevenson-Hamilton, who had agreed temporarily to be Secretary of the society, the SPFE met the High Commissioner for Southern Rhodesia in London to suggest the creation of a national park (to be called the Selous National Park).[139] Two years later, the SPFE approached the Colonial Office to propose the creation of parks in East Africa on the lines of that at Kruger. Their letter was forwarded to the Governors.[140] However, the very permanence of national parks – which attracted the SPFE – made the Colonial Office wary. In the House of Lords on 21 November 1929, the Secretary of State for the Colonies stated that game reserves (whose boundaries could be modified when necessary) should be maintained in preference to a system of national parks, in which land would be permanently set aside for the use of game.[141] At his meeting with the SPFE in March 1930, the Secretary of State expressed general support for their suggestions, but re-affirmed this position, and also dismissed the joint conference of the Game Wardens of the East African territories that the SPFE proposed. The SPFE retired, baffled as to how to push forwards their conservation agenda.

By the start of the 1930s, the SPFE could point to government reserves and sanctuaries all over the world. In Europe, they were to be found in Denmark, Germany, Austria, France, Switzerland, Spain, the Netherlands, Norway, Sweden, Poland, Czechoslovakia, and the Soviet Union (although not, yet, in Britain). Further afield there were reserves in Mexico, Argentina and Brazil, throughout the British Empire (Canada, New Zealand, Australia, Ceylon, British India, the Federated Malay States and territories in Africa) and the Netherlands Indies (Java, Sumatra), as well as, of course, the United States.[142] In these countries there were 'large tracts almost empty of resident population', with vegetation 'almost undisturbed by the ravages of man', that harboured many species of animals. Here the SPFE believed that true national parks should be created, protected against the sportsman, the settler and the prospector, dedicated for all time, independently of the protection afforded to individual species within it (that is whether they were considered pests elsewhere or not). Here, too, should be motor roads and rest camps, conveniences for tourists and naturalists, overseen by a staff of wardens, keepers and specialists in fauna and flora.[143]

In 1930 the SPFE asked Major Richard Hingston (who had previously led the Oxford University expedition to British Guiana[144]) to make a tour of the

East African colonies to report on the need for national parks. This was classic boosterism, his fact finding as much an exercise in consciousness-raising. He held discussions with Governors, game wardens and 'other interested persons'. On his return, he wrote a report that was widely distributed, and undertook a series of lectures, notably to the Royal Geographical Society in London.[145] His view of the challenge facing conservation was bluntly articulated, and was a direct expression of the concerns of the Society over the previous 30 years. 'It is as certain as night follows day that unless vigorous and adequate precautions be taken several of the largest mammals of Africa will within the next two or three decades become totally extinct. Should that occur then assuredly we will have abused a trust and future generations will judge us accordingly'.[146]

Hingston's view of the causes of the decline in African wildlife were utterly conventional. He first stated that 'the whole African fauna is steadily failing before the forces of destruction brought to bear against it', an assault that was near catastrophic for certain species such as the gorilla, nyala and Grevy's zebra, whose numbers had 'shrunk to minute number and are on the verge of disappearance'.[147] He reviewed the usual suspects, the demands of trade, the activities of sportsmen, the menace of disease (or more specifically the measures taken against one disease, sleeping sickness), the spread of settler farming (he noted 'in Africa cultivation is incompatible with wildlife'[148]), and native hunting. He saw the last as the most serious (see Chapter 5), but all threats pointed in the same direction – 'so long as man and animals live together there will always be trouble'.[149] His solution was simple, to separate people and wildlife 'permanently and completely'.[150] Game reserves were too fickle a defence against the demands of settlers, the hunting of Africans and the arbitrary whim of government. Their boundaries were too fluid, too liable to change. It was 'the belief of all who desire the perpetuation of the fauna' that what was needed was stability and permanence (indeed in Hingston's word the 'rigidity') of national parks.[151]

Hingston set out what was needed. National parks should contain 'all possible types of animal life', and should be 'well-stocked' (that is with growing populations). They needed to be of 'adequate size', sufficient to cope with the migration of plains game (such as the wildebeests of Kenya and Tanzania) and provide food all year. National parks should not contain land whose development is 'essential to the territory' and no minerals of economic value. They should contain 'the fewest human inhabitants possible'.[152] They should, on the other hand contain 'natural features of scenic and geographical interest', they should be accessible, and they should be healthy, for visitors.

Hingston proposed a specific list of national parks in East Africa. These were South-Central Africa National Park on the borders of Nyasaland and Northern Rhodesia, Nyala National Park (the Mkuzi Reserve in Zululand), Selous National Park and Kilimanjaro National Park in Tanganyika, Serengeti National Park ('the most important sanctuary in East Africa' according to Hingston[153]) overlapping both Tanganyika and Kenya, the Kenya National Park (effectively the Northern Game Reserve East of Lake Rudolf) and Bongo

National Park (in the Aberdare Mountains) in Kenya, and the Bunyoro-Gulu and Gorilla National Parks in Uganda.

Hingston's report was forwarded to Colonial Office, but the SPFE waited with impatience through March 1932 for something to be done.[154] There seems to have been considerable resistance to the idea of national parks within the permanent staff of the Colonial Office at this time.[155] The SPFE was not idle, however, sending a further mission to West Africa (A H W Haywood, formerly of the West African Field Force, in November 1931).[156] It also turned its attention to the international stage, and the International Congress for the Protection of Nature held in Paris in July 1931. Fourteen countries were represented, 13 from Europe plus a non-governmental delegation from the United States. Lord Onslow, President of the SPFE, there (with Captain K Caldwell and C W Hobley of the SPFE) as the British government's representative, presented a personal message from the British Prime Minister, Ramsay MacDonald. This recognized the grave losses suffered by fauna and flora across the world, and noted that 'international action is required to supplement the effects of individual governments'.[157] The hand (and pen) of Onslow and the SPFE is not hard to see at work here. Onslow was instructed to express the British government's sympathy with the idea of revising the 1900 Convention for the Preservation of Animals, Birds and Fish in Africa, which was now obsolete, and also to note that 'close and sympathetic consideration' was being given to the recommendations for national sanctuaries by Hingston and the SPFE (although 'until fully seized of the views of local administrations', they would not commit themselves to any specific actions).[158] Onslow, however, went further, suggesting that the British government might be sympathetic to a recommendation for a further conference, to draw up a new version of the 1900 Convention.

The 1931 conference agreed a series of resolutions, addressing everything from animal trade to the need to curb excessive numbers of travellers to sensitive sanctuaries. Critically, Onslow was able to use it to persuade the British government to take up the question of a new convention.[159] After discussion between the Foreign Office and Colonial Office, it was decided to confine efforts to Africa in the first instance. A preparatory committee was therefore set up under the Economic Advisory Council in October 1932 to plan a conference to draw up a convention to secure the preservation of the fauna and flora of Africa. Naturally, the Earl of Onslow was in the chair.[160] The loss of species was of scientific, aesthetic and material importance, affecting the world at large, and future generations. The committee believed that African fauna and flora could become 'a rich source of pleasure and a valuable educative influence in the lives of large numbers of people'. And while the value of unique and irreplaceable wild animals and flowers was not simply material, when properly understood, the policy of protection would be seen to have advantages even in the material sphere. Modern travel was widening the range of the ordinary tourist, and the committee believed that tourists from Europe would come in some numbers to national parks in East Africa (on the model of Kruger) to see and photograph wild animals.[161]

The Preparatory Committee's ultimate vision was that each government should create within its African territories national parks 'similar in general character to the Kruger National Park in the Union of South Africa, whose story, vicissitudes, successes and administration were carefully analysed'.[162] The committee also proposed discussion of smaller reserves (like those in the Netherlands East Indies), and suggested that the Conference should discuss hunting (particularly the threat to wildlife of 'destruction at the hands of the native hunter'), the export of trophies, and the ethics of hunting from aeroplanes and motor cars.[163]

The conference was held in October and November 1933 at the House of Lords, with government representatives from Great Britain, France, Belgium, Italy, Portugal, Spain, Egypt, Anglo-Egyptian Sudan, and South Africa, with observers from the United States, the Netherlands and India.[164] Many of the delegates were old friends of the SPFE, and the conference accepted the draft convention prepared by Onslow's committee as a basis for discussion. The agreed text, a 'Convention Relative to the Preservation of Fauna and Flora in their Natural State' focused and clarified thinking about protected areas. Signatories were committed to exploring the possibility of establishing both national parks (where visitors would be allowed subject to overriding requirements, surrounded by buffer zones where hunting would be possible) and strict nature reserves (a French proposal, meaning places where absolutely no human activity at all was to be allowed). The convention also established annexes listing species to be completely protected from all killing or capturing (17 mammals, three birds and one plant), and others requiring a licence.

The Convention came into force on 14 January 1936, and the agreed follow-up to review progress was held in May 1938. Meanwhile, in India, a National Parks Bill was passed by the United Provinces of India in 1934 following lobbying from the United Provinces Game Preservation Society, and a conference on the preservation of wildlife was held in Delhi in January 1935, a direct outcome of Indian representation at the 1933 conference.[165] The United Provinces Game Preservation Society had been established in 1932; its secretary was Jim Corbett, famous as a hunter, and latterly as the author of the best-selling *Man-Eaters of Kumaon*.[166] In the Netherlands Indies, wildlife legislation was overhauled in 1931 and 1932, and 17 wildlife sanctuaries were established, in Sumatra, Java, Kalimantan, Bali, Lombok and the islands of the Komodo group.[167]

The SPFE was focusing considerable attention on Asia at this time. They sent Sir Thomas Comyn Platt to Malaya in 1935 to speed up the government's response to the Wild Life Commission.[168] As a result of his report, Captain A T A Ritchie was seconded from Kenya to reorganize the game department, Comyn Platt returning to Malaya, and visiting Ceylon and Cyprus, in 1936 to follow up his report.[169] However, the looming threat of war cast a shadow over such initiatives. It had been hoped to combine the follow-up to the 1933 meeting with a second conference to consider the question of the protection of fauna and flora in South-western Asia and Australasia. The British Government issued invitations in November 1939, but plans were cut short by the outbreak of the Second World War.[170]

DECOLONIZATION AND NATIONAL PARKS

When the Second World War was over, the idea of national parks was resurrected, and took root with vigour. By then, the principle of national parks had been accepted in Britain, and at that time too, all things American were the height of fashion. There was a remarkable renaissance of interest in national parks internationally. In Canada there for example, the National Parks Act was passed in 1930, and new parks were created in Nova Scotia (1936), Prince Edward Island (1937), Fundy (1948) and Terra Nova in Newfoundland (1957).[171] In Malaysia, E O Shebbeare noted in 1940 the potential to make the King George V National Park in Malaya more accessible to visitors in motor cars (important 'from a box office point of view'), on the model of Kruger, and thus a self-supporting national asset rather than a burden.[172] It is interesting to note that by 1945 there were almost 11 million hectares of state reserves in the USSR.[173]

In Africa there were several national parks in existence at the end of the war, Kruger in South Africa and the Parc National Albert, Kagera and Garamba in the Belgian Congo (created in 1929). Others were soon added. The first of the new crop were in Kenya, most beloved of the UK and US based conservationists of earlier decades. It was not until 1938 that the Kenyan government responded to the 1933 Convention, setting up a committee to make recommendations for national parks. This committee reported in 1942 and 1945, recommending the establishment of Tsavo as well as two mountain national parks and a number of national reserves. The National Parks Ordinance was gazetted in 1945, and Trustees were appointed for Nairobi National Park in 1946, the park springing up, remarkably, right on the edge of the growing city of Nairobi, at the northern margin of the famous Athi Plains.[174] Nairobi was followed in 1948 by Tsavo, 'an area of almost discarded heterogeneous bush', as the Director of the Kenya National Parks described it. Other parks, at Marsabit and the Aberdares were planned.[175]

The vast and poorly-known Tsavo was soon threatened in 1954 by plans to build a dam to provide water to Mombasa, raising the water level in the Mzima Pools in Tsavo West, with their famous hippos. In the face of public outcry in the press, and a question in the House of Commons by SPFE council member, Colonel Clarke MP, the Kenyan government commissioned a new study, and decided to draw the water above the head of the relevant spring, thus saving the habitat. The SPFE claimed this as a triumph for national parks as 'the decision has not only established the fact that the general public have rights and interests in national parks, but has confirmed the principle that a national park is not an area to be at one moment set aside for complete protection, and at the next endangered by claims for the use of its natural resources'.[176]

It was much the same story elsewhere. In Tanganyika, the Serengeti National Park was finally established in 1948, and was soon followed by Arusha, Tarangire and many others, in an astonishing commitment of land to conservation purposes. In Uganda, a National Parks Committee was set up in 1948, and a National Parks Act was passed in 1952.[177] Murchison Falls and Queen Elizabeth National Parks were created in 1952, the new queen coming to open the park named after her in May 1954. The royal imprimatur, long established by her forbears, was secure, and national parks were firmly on the elite agenda in the British Commonwealth.[178]

Despite the acceptance of conservation by (in the words of one advocate in India) 'almost all civilized countries', decolonization was a worrying prospect for the advocates of national parks in a number of countries.[179] In 1948, the SPFE rather plaintively noted its hopes that the 'new regime' in India would be interested in continuing conservation in the Bengal Rhino Sanctuary. In 1950 the Second IUPN General Assembly noted questions over the fate of the 'exemplary nature protection service' of the Dutch colonial authorities in independent Indonesia.[180] Fears were particularly great in the Belgian Congo, where conservation had been so strictly enforced for so long, and where functioning (and fiercely protected) national parks had existed since 1926.[181] In 1949, the SPFE noted its unease about the future of what had previously been thought of as 'an impregnable sanctuary for wild life', while in 1952 Victor Van Straelen made clear his unhappiness with the recent developments in the Congo to the Marquess of Willingdon (SPFE President), who was on a tour of the United States at the invitation of the US National Parks Association of the United States, when they met over lunch with Fairfield Osborne in New York.

Van Straelen was a central figure in the movement for protected areas. He had been intimately involved in the creation of the Parc National Albert; he had been on the Board of IUCN since Fontainbleau and was a founder-member of the Commission on National Parks. He was Director of the Musée Royale d'Histoire Naturelle of Belgium, and President of the Institut des Parcs Nationaux du Congo Belge, which ran the Parc National Albert.[182] His links with the FPS were long standing and close. In 1955, Willingdon was appointed by the King of the Belgians as a member of the Institut, while Van Straelen was made a Vice President of the FPS. In 1960, independence was declared in Congo, followed by the virtual collapse of governance and the extremely hasty withdrawal of the Belgian presence, and soon civil war. The national parks survived, but not without a struggle. Their survival owed much to Van Straelen's personal prestige with park staff.[183] The threats were very real in the Congo following the outbreak of civil war in 1960, as in the other Belgian possessions of Rwanda and Burundi (in 1962, the Conservator of the Kagera National Park was murdered in his home).

In 1960, Bernhard Grzimek urged the need for a new example for newly independent nations: 'we should convince them that wild animals are part of the beauty and wealth of their country and of all mankind, as much as the Acropolis, the Louvre and St. Paul's Cathedral'.[184] This is not so different a vision to the one early American promoters of national parks set out, the use of nature's magnificence as a source of national pride. Such pride could only be awakened through education. In 1958 Hal Coolidge spoke in Brussels on the problem of the ignorance of people of all levels about national parks (he focused in particular of course on the Belgian Congo). He advocated education and propaganda aimed at Africans living near the boundaries of national parks. Ronnie Bere, the second Director of Uganda National Parks, saw that if national parks were for posterity, then the attitudes of ordinary Africans would determine their future. General public acceptance was vital, for 'without public confidence our Parks are doomed', and education of all kinds was an urgent task.[185]

Such education began post haste in many colonial territories as independence loomed. In Southern Rhodesia, the Natural Resources Board undertook a conservation education campaign in 1961, with poster and slogan competitions for schools, and the distribution of 10,000 copies of a poster urging children to 'Conserve wild life, don't destroy' and 40,000 copies of a wildlife colouring book for primary schools, sponsored by Brooke Bond and Coca Cola.[186] In Northern Rhodesia, the Game Preservation and Hunting Association constructed a permanent camp in the Kafue National Park to provide educational holidays for schoolchildren.[187]

Despite conservationist fears, national parks survived independence, and in many countries conservation prosepered under the new regimes. The language and sentiments of the Arusha Declaration (see Chapter 3) were widely echoed by independent governments. In several countries, newly-elected Presidents took a personal interest in conservation, whether as part of a more general assumption of the trappings and interests of the former European elite from which they took over, or because conservation fitted the odd and sometimes turbulent political economy of newly independent states. In Nyasaland, for example, preconceived ideas about likely African attitudes to wildlife were overturned when President Banda took a personal interest. Conservationists rejoiced that the Lengwe Game Reserve, where the rare nyala was rediscovered by the new Department of Forestry and Game in 1963, had received investment following the President's personal intervention.[188] In retrospect it is clear that while conservation was something Malawi under Hastings Banda did very well, this was at least in part because it fitted a wider ideology of authority and control. In Zambia, too, President Kenneth Kaunda was superficially at least an ardent conservationist, although the political economy of illegal hunting created strong and complex counter-currents in conservation policy through the decades following independence.[189]

Sir Dawda Jawara, President of Gambia (one of the last British colonies, reaching independence in 1977), actually included a pledge about conservation in his speech at the independence day celebrations. He said 'it is a sobering reflection that, in a relatively short period of our history, most of our larger wildlife species have disappeared together with much of the original forest cover. The survival of the wildlife still remaining with us and the setting aside of protected natural habitats for them is the concern of all of us. It would be tragic if this priceless natural heritage, the produce of millions of years of evolution, should be further endangered or lost for want of proper concern. This concern is a duty we owe to ourselves, to our great African heritage and to the world'.[190] Many similarities exist between these sentiments and what Lord Curzon had said so many years earlier in a delegation to the Colonial Office, about the duty of conservation.[191] The Fauna Preservation Society wrote to congratulate him.

While conservationists certainly pushed for national parks with particular energy as independence loomed after the Second World War because they feared what new governments would do with the flexible conservation regimes in force, national parks continued to be declared by independent governments in considerable numbers. This does not simply reflect the power of the international conservation regime, of its ideology, or its international pressure groups (see Chapter 3). It reflects also the fact that wildlife could be made a symbol of the power and strength of African society and polities, and play a role in fostering national identity.

The ideological significance of nature and national parks can of course be complex. One example of this is Rhodesia, where a Department of National Parks was established in 1949. The Wankie National Park (now Hwange) was created in 1951 out of a former game reserve, and others were progressively added, including Victoria Falls, Matusadona on the southern shores of lake Kariba, Mana Pools on the lower Zambezi, and Gonorezhou in the southeast low veld, abutting the borders of Mozambique and South Africa. As in South Africa, the large white middle class, the draconian land laws and the strong internal security system favoured formal conservation in the years preceding Zimbabwean independence in 1981.

The complex ideological significance of apparently straightforward conservation action is well demonstrated by the Matopos National Park in Zimbabwe, whose history is described in *Voices from the Rocks* by Terence Ranger. The Matopos Hills have been regarded as important both in colonial Rhodesia, in independent Rhodesia, and in Zimbabwe.[192] Land was first set aside in the Matopos in the name of conservation in 1926, both for its intrinsic values of landscape and because it was the site of Cecil Rhodes' grave. Colonial conservationists recognized that the hills had been occupied in the distant past by hunter-gatherers, who had left cave paintings behind. However, they did not recognize the extent or legitimacy of contemporary agricultural activity, and more or less completely eradicated its traces when they declared the National Park. They also proscribed the ritual use of the hills, which were the centre for a spirit important to the Ndebele people.

However, people continued to use the park, even after that use had been declared illegal. In response, in 1962, the park was divided into two, and part was depopulated by force to create a 'wilderness area'. This could only be entered by tourists and officials travelling on foot or on horseback. Within it, rare wildlife species (such as rhinoceros) were introduced or re-introduced. Thus the 'Rhodes Matopos National Park' became a wilderness, its wildlife conservation value enhanced and guaranteed. Furthermore, it became effectively a white Rhodesian shrine, sacred to the memory of Cecil Rhodes, and demonstrating the determination of white Rhodesians to maintain their possession of land and political power. Perhaps for this reason, the hills became important to the black revolutionaries who fought for majority rule – the spirit cult a major rallying point for protest, and the hills a bitterly fought-over terrain of guerrilla warfare.

Some of the colonial overtones were removed by independence, while other 'voices from the rocks' were more clearly articulated. However, even though they had fought in an independence war that might have been expected to lead to the return of expropriated land, people evicted from the park were not allowed to return to their homes. The Matopos National Park remained as 'wilderness', the economic importance of its wildlife and landscape for tourists overriding the former history of human occupation and management. The human-made history of the Matopos Hills has effectively been expunged from official memory, even if it survives among local people.

THE CONSERVATION ESTATE

The establishment of the IUCN created a new forum for the promotion of national parks across the globe. At the Athens General Assembly in 1958, a Provisional Committee on National Parks was established under Hal Coolidge , with eight of its eleven members from the Third World (five from Africa, three from Asia).[193] This grew into the IUCN Commission on National Parks in 1960 (now the World Commission on Protected Areas[194]). In 1959, the 27th Session of the UN Economic and Social Council held in Mexico (following debate at the IUCN General Assembly in Athens the year before), recognized 'National Parks and Equivalent Reserves' as important in the wise use of natural resources, and led to the compilation of a 'World List of National Parks and Equivalent Reserves', eventually adopted by the United Nations General Assembly at its 16th Session in December 1962 on economic development and nature conservation.[195]

Publication of the list of national parks and protected areas (which ran to over 300 pages) demanded standardization of increasingly diverse practices of governments around the world. If this was to be a list of what was protected, it had to establish standards of protection. Yet there were very different ideas about what protection meant, indeed about what was worth protecting. At one extreme was the US-style national park, carved out of vast national government landholding and often styled as a wilderness, while subject to extensive development for tourism, including private business concessions. At the other extreme, perhaps, lay the British National Parks, almost all privately owned, effectively special planning zones where patterns of built development could be steered by local council committees.

Behind these models were serious questions of what conservation was for, and how it should be done. Were protected areas places for some kind of 'strict' protection of nature, or for human enjoyment? Were they places where nature was supposed to be pristine, or was it acceptable to cut, burn, shoot and trap to tune the balance of nature, or simply for scientific research? Was it only their natural species and ecosystems that were valuable, or also their landscapes? Could they include cultural features, indeed cultural landscapes, where people and nature intertwined to created patterns of land use and ecology? Above all, what was the proper role of people in protected areas, especially national parks? Were government rangers allowed to walk their hallowed grounds? scientists? tourists? If all these were acceptable, by what right could local people be excluded, particularly if they had been long-duration residents of the protected area, holding it as their home before the conservationists arrived to 'discover' it. Such issues have been debated at length over the decades at a series of international conferences organized by the World Commission on Protected Areas. The first World Conference on National Parks was held in Seattle in 1962, and intended to 'achieve a more effective international understanding and encouragement of the national parks movement'. Subsequent World Parks Congresses have been at Yellowstone and Grand Teton in 1972, Bali in 1982, Caracas in 1992, and Durban in 2003.

The World Commission on Protected Areas defines its role as 'promoting the establishment and effective management of a worldwide representative network of terrestrial and marine protected areas'. The IUCN definition of protected areas, and its classification, has evolved in detail, particularly to give more space to cultural dimensions of conservation, although not in spirit. It defines a protected area as 'an area of land and/or sea especially dedicated to the protection and maintenance of biological diversity, and of natural and associated cultural resources, and managed through legal or other effective means'.

IUCN recognizes a number of different categories of protected areas.[196] At one extreme are category I areas, which include Strict Nature Reserves (managed mainly for science) and Wilderness Areas (land retaining its natural character and influence, without permanent or significant habitation, which is protected and managed so as to preserve its natural condition). Mainstream National Parks are classified as category II protected areas, areas of land or sea, designated to protect the ecological integrity of one or more ecosystems for present and future generations, to exclude exploitation or occupation inimical to the purposes of designation of the area and to provide a foundation for 'spiritual, scientific, educational, recreational and visitor opportunities' (all of which must be environmentally and culturally compatible).

Category III areas are Natural Monuments or Landmarks (specific natural or natural/cultural features of outstanding or unique value for their inherent rarity, representative or aesthetic qualities or cultural significance). Category IV comprises Habitat and Species Management Areas (areas subject to active management intervention to maintain habitats or to meet the requirements of specific species). Protected areas in category V (Protected Landscapes or Seascapes) are areas where the interaction of people and nature over time has produced a distinct character with significant aesthetic, ecological or cultural value, and often with high biological diversity. Here the safeguarding of the integrity of this traditional interaction is vital to the protection, maintenance and evolution of such an area. Lastly, Managed Resources Protected Areas (category VI) contain predominantly unmodified natural systems that are managed to maintain a sustainable flow of natural products and services to meet community needs while ensuring long-term protection and maintenance of biological diversity.

The area officially 'protected' in one or more of the IUCN categories has grown, decade on decade at a near exponential rate. The decade of the 1970s saw the area protected globally more or less double.[197] The idea of national parks was no longer restricted to industrialized countries and the more exotic bastions of the colonial world, but became truly global. It did so through the same channels as conservation itself spread, through IUCN and United Nations agencies, through the work of the new international conservation organizations discussed in Chapter 3, and through the established networks of influence and expertise. Thus in 1974, the FPS was asked by Dr David Harrison (newly elected FPS council member) and Major Michael Gallagher to help their plans to start a reserve in Oman and help develop the idea of national parks in the Arab world. It jumped at the chance, contacted the Omani authorities, secured permission for the necessary survey and agreed to sponsor a scientific expedition to be carried out in 1975.[198] National parks spread in the 1980s in Latin America, and in countries such as the USSR: by 1991 17 national parks protected 3.65 million hectares across Russia.[199]

The area of protected areas in the UN list rose from about 2.4 million square kilometres in 1962 to 8.8 million in 1982, 12.3 million in 1992 and 18.8 million square kilometres in 2003. In numbers, they rose from 9200 in 1962 to 102,000 in 2003. By any standards, this is an astonishing rate of growth, evidence enough of the abiding concern of 20th century conservation. Many countries have very substantial areas of protected land. Some of these are wealthy (Europe has 23,000 protected areas, for example). Others are relatively poor, such as Central America, with 14.5 million square kilometres. Even very poor countries like Bangaldesh or Ethiopia boast a substantial system of protected areas (97,000 hectares in Bangladesh in 1996, 0.7 per cent of their land area, and a massive 6 million hectares in Ethiopia, 5 per cent of its land area.[200]

Rich or poor, by the end of the 20th century, all countries had created protected areas of some kind. They had become a universal phenomenon, the most obvious expression of the global reach of the nature conservation movement. This very success, however, brought problems in its train. Who were the parks for? What about those people evicted to make way for nature? What were the real costs and benefits of national parks? These questions are the subject of the next chapter.

Chapter 5

Poachers to Partners

Conservation will either contribute to solving the problems of the rural poor who live day to day with wild animals, or those animals will disappear (J S Adams and T O McShane)[1].

SAVING THE WILD

In 2003 Conservation International published a book called *Wilderness: Earth's Last Wild Places*, the work of 200 researchers under their Center for Applied Biodiversity Science. The book was lavishly illustrated, including nearly 500 images of 'untamed lands and rare glimpses of the people who inhabit them with the most current scientific analyses of their endangered ecosystems'.[2] To qualify as 'wilderness', the areas had to have 70 per cent or more of their original vegetation, cover at least 10,000 square kilometers, and have fewer than five people per square kilometre. Using these criteria, they identified 37 'wilderness areas' around the globe, representing tropical rain forests, wetlands, deserts, and arctic tundra. They included the forests of Amazonia, the Congo basin and the North American Pacific northwest, the deserts of the Sahara, Arabia, Australia, large chunks of tundra and boreal forest. The book described the biological diversity of each wilderness area, and explained the threats to each and the conservation measures in place. Most of the terrestrial globe, the densely populated bulk of the world, was blank.

The book also, intriguingly, described 'the human cultures unique to each area'.[3] This is worth a moment's pause. The idea of a coffee-table book presenting an analysis of 'nature under threat' is not of itself remarkable. The analysis from which the map of 'the last of the wild' derives is a valuable attempt to map the human footprint on earth (in terms of population density, land transformation, transport routes and power consumption), although such attempts to measure the human footprint have been made before.[4] The 'wild' areas selected are those where the measures of human impact adopted suggest there has been least modification of ecosystems, ecosystem process and biodiversity. They are places where the range of conservation activities might be put in place to preserve what is there through establishing protected areas. What is interesting is the ease with which the word 'wilderness' suggests itself to the publicists of Conservation International to describe these areas. It is a particularly strange way to describe places where people live, even in small numbers.

WILDERNESS AND CULTURAL IMAGINATION

The idea that places little transformed by cities, roads and other features of industrial and urban development are 'wilderness' is in fact commonplace in conservation thinking and writing, but it is nonetheless odd for that. It is in many ways a particularly American idea, although it is one that has spread and been adopted around the world. It underpinned the concept of the national park that was developed in the United States in the late 19th century, and which was such a powerful cultural export (see Chapter 2).

In Europe, the traditional meanings of 'wilderness' date from the time when people feared nature – feared its teeth and claws, and the blind impartiality of mountain, forest and storm that took and killed people as they wrested a bare living from the face of the earth. This is the wilderness of European folklore, of dark forests and wolves in woodcutters' cottages, of elves and trolls and highwaymen. The wild was the un-tame, lying beyond the tended fields and managed woods, where lawless men roamed and danger lay, when anyone benighted or set upon would not find help. Wilderness and wildness were not then virtues, but symbols of barrenness, of lack of harvest, of lack of care. Wars made wilderness, peace made the fruited plain.[5] Men like Daniel Defoe, travelling rural Britain in the 18th century, or William Cobbett in the 19th, spoke of 'wastes', land too wild and rough to be brought under the plough. Land beyond the reach of the hand of agricultural improvement was worthless – worse than that, it was an affront to improvement, and should be taken in hand (ironically, of course, where they have survived un-developed, these very places have become among Britain's best wildlife sites, greatly valued by a very different generation).[6]

It was only with the Romantic movement that the brutishness of wild places became re-interpreted as mystery, and the savagery of nature became a source of wonder and moral instruction. In the English gentleman's country park, cleared of untidy peasant cottages and landscaped to fit an aesthetic of pastoral beauty by Capability Brown or Humphrey Repton, nature was portrayed in genteel form, and the naked capitalism that created the wealth that sustained it was hidden away.[7] Then, to a generation insulated by wealth from the rigours of subsistence, the wild itself began to become an object of wonder and aesthetic appreciation. To the Romantic eye, epitomized by William Wordsworth's presentation of the Lake District, the raw mountain crag, roaring waterfall and plunging chasm were deemed sublime things of wonder and beauty.[8] By the latter part of the 19th century, in both Europe and eastern North America, the nature that remained was seen as something to be treasured, and the inroads upon it of industry and urban squalor to be deplored.

At the same time, outside the mountains of areas such as the Lake District and the Alps, nature in Europe was still seen in pastoral mode. People were important elements within 'natural' landscapes, creating as well as destroying the patterns of nature. When the science of ecology was in its infancy in the late 19th century, studies of British vegetation emphasized the influence of human actions in natural processes. Arthur Tansley, who in 1935 defined the concept of the ecosystem, always understood that vegetation was human-influenced, 'anthropogenic' as he put it. His *Types of British Vegetation*, and the list of potential nature reserves that he helped prepare for the Society for the Promotion of Nature Reserves in the First World War, did not seek to distinguish between 'wild' and 'made' landscapes. Conservation was about protecting diversity, and 'unnaturalness' meant the loss of that diversity to plough, pollution or housing estate.[9]

Colonial observers took these complex ideologies of nature to newly colonized worlds. They saw the landscapes of America and Australia and in due course Africa as open, under-used and largely un-settled. They seemed to lack effective human occupation, because they lacked visible improvement. In legal terms they were defined as *terra nullius*, land without value or property status. In Australia, for example, the importance of aboriginal people's use of fire in creating and maintaining open landscapes was not understood until well into the 20th century, and neither this nor the deep and complex cultural meanings of land were accepted until recent decades. The Australian outback was considered as wilderness in the original European sense, to be settled and civilized by European farmers and their introduced livestock and technologies. Aboriginal people were pushed aside, or actively persecuted, and their impact on the land ignored. Ironically, those landscapes that survived the onslaught of European settlers and their introduced livestock and wild species were later re-read according to the new romantic meanings of wilderness, and the rising tide of environmentalist thinking in the later 20th century, as wild places of great natural value.[10]

The story was similar in North America.[11] As European colonists eventually found more than their initial uncertain coastal foothold, acquiring crops and techniques that suited the land (in part from those who lived and worked the lands they occupied), they headed west, into the inhabited 'wilderness'. As they moved across the face of the continent, indigenous Indian populations shrank before the onslaught of European disease, and latterly were fiercely suppressed, removed from valuable lands into reservations. They were also airbrushed from history, for the story America told about itself was one of a frontier carved in the wilderness.

Vast areas of land in the American West were annexed by the state, and held for the public good for the resources they contained, feedstock for the burgeoning industrial economy back east. When the great debates about conservation began in America at the end of the 19th century, they were between those who wanted to manage those lands and resources wisely to sustain their output and those who wanted to preserve their wildness for posterity, between the romantics like John Muir and the Sierra Club, and the rational pragmatists Gifford Pinchot and the Department of the Interior.[12] Interestingly, neither Muir nor Pinchot seriously considered the previous inhabitants of the 'wild West', a silence only conclusively broken by historians reflecting on the 500-year anniversary of the 'discovery' of the Americas in 1492.[13] By the end of the 19th century, Americans were worrying about the impacts of the closing of the western frontier on the doughty pioneer spirit that they believed defined the American national character. Early US conservationists who saw nature under threat, expressed their concern in terms of the very wilderness that had been so recently conquered. Far from being awful, as perhaps actual frontier settlers might have thought it, wilderness was now precious, a fount of wonder, a repository of value.

In colonial settler countries, wilderness became an important element in emergent national identities.[14] The existence in Australia or the United States of empty (indeed emptied) landscapes ripe for colonization by bold individuals was central to the way settler societies imagined themselves. The land of America, Australia and South Africa allowed their settler peoples to see themselves as different from those left behind in Europe precisely because of the distinctiveness and wildness of their landscapes of desert, mountain, bush, savanna and veld.[15] The frontier between wild and settled, sown and developed country was important for what it implied about national character, just as for what it offered in economic opportunity. Unfortunately, such thinking ignored indigenous people, and allowed no recognition that 'wild' landscapes were the fruit of their ideas and labour.

In the plains of East Africa, the first colonial governments encountered landscapes whose creators had recently suffered linked disasters of disease, famine and war.[16] Elsewhere, slaving and colonial annexation had disrupted economy, society and environment. Such landscapes (like those in North America) perhaps genuinely seemed empty and wild, in the manner of the garden of an abandoned house. Moreover, to an extent, African populations could be seen to fit such a 'wild' landscape, understood in a sense as 'natural' themselves, with their primitive use of technology and 'savage' customs.[17] The creation of national parks in Africa like Serengeti involved the application of an Anglo-American nature aesthetic which included such ideas.[18] Africa was imagined as some kind of 'wild' Eden, a garden to be bounded and protected from those who would defile it, such as the Maasai pastoralists whose stock grazed the Serengeti plains. It is characteristic, and revealing, for example, that H G Maurice, Secretary of the SPFE, entitled a paper on game reserves and national parks in 1938 'Man-made Edens', and James Stevenson-Hamilton's book about the creation of the Kruger National Park was entitled 'South African Eden', a place of 'unspoiled, wild nature'.[19] To the Director of Kenya's national parks in 1955, Africa was 'the last stronghold of wild nature', where there was some chance that a park could be established that was 'faunally complete'.[20]

To early colonial conservationists in Africa, as to those of Conservation International in the 21st century, Africans living 'traditionally' could be considered as an element of nature. Indeed, as we have seen, it was the impacts of European settlers and not African farmers and herders on wildlife that initially obsessed colonial conservationists. This perception of a 'natural' state in Africa lasted well after colonial states were established, white settlers had moved in, and African populations had begun to boom. In his autobiography, *Memories*, Julian Huxley rejoiced at his luck in seeing Africa in 1929, 'a continent which had hardly changed in the last five hundred years'.[21] A recent volume of memoirs of colonial game wardens is dedicated 'to a Pleistocene Africa, which we so enjoyed and sought to preserve, but which is gone. It was an impossible dream'.[22] It was in fact a profound illusion.

People have lived in and influenced the ecology of almost all habitable regions of earth. Even in places remote from centres of learning and commerce, people have organized active agricultural, pastoral, manufacturing and trading economies. Colonial authorities, the scientists who advise them, and the soldiers and settlers who fought to survive and recreate the familiar order of home by and large failed to recognize this. They were unobservant and uncaring about the ways people created and used nature, just as many conservationists are today.

Sometimes human influence is now slight, for example where land has been ravaged and more or less abandoned (as in the forests of the eastern United States, or the remote Scottish islands), or where current levels of technology and poverty restrict the impacts people and their economies can inflict (for example in remote rainforest areas). But in Australasia and countless islands across the world everywhere, species have been driven to extinction by human hunters and introduced animals and plants; everywhere the long fingers of capitalist market economies have reached and drawn societies into trade; and everywhere the insidious influence of industrial waste gases released to the atmosphere are felt.[23] Indeed, this ubiquitous human impact was the basis of Bill McKibben's claim that humans had brought about 'the end of nature'.[24] Humans have always been making and un-making patterns in nature: the critical thing about the 20th century was that the speed and scale of change became so fast that we forgot this, and instead came to believe that nature could exist in some pristine form. We came to call it, and the places to which it was confined, wilderness.

The trouble with wilderness, as William Cronon sets out in his essay of that title, is that it is not what it appears, for 'far from being the one place on earth that stands apart from humanity, it is quite profoundly a human creation'. In the United States in particular, but now globally, we use the concept of wilderness to put nature in a box: a place where nature is, and we are not. And yet when we gaze into wilderness expecting to see pristine un-affected nature, free from all human influence, what we see is a reflection of our ideas, our longings, our own attempt to separate the 'natural' from the 'human'. We also tend to see quite specific places (often remote and rugged places), which are quite carefully managed to keep them in a particular state. Very often we see national parks.[25]

Ideas of wilderness as something wonderful are culturally specific. A conservation ethic based on the standard Western transcendental and Romantic idea of wilderness, for example, might be quite meaningless to people of a different tradition and ethnicity.[26] In Kikuyu thought, for example, wilderness never meant an absence of people. The wild was a place engaged by a frontier of settlement, a place of some danger and of intensive human interaction. The un-settled forest was to be approached by people as a group and transformed through a social process of settlement. The closure of the Kikuyu frontier disrupted Kikuyu ideas of the wild. This was not a communal process, but was arbitrarily imposed by the Kenyan colonial state to provide land for white settlers and (ironically) to created reserves for wild nature. The American idea of wilderness led to the creation of parks, where society plays with transcendental ideas about nature in places separated from issues of human survival or economy. Kikuyu people were not only denied economic opportunities, but were also denied their understanding of what nature was, as wilderness was converted from social space to 'the domain of beasts, a tourist's pleasuring ground'.[27]

Conservationists have tended to imagine that ideas of wilderness are universal, and are bound to touch somewhere on indigenous ideas about nature. There is in fact no reason to expect this to be the case. Specific ideas about the value of wilderness, as about nature, are primarily the products of human culture. They vary, as people vary.[28] I am not denying here the possibility of a sociobiological argument about the evolutionary significance of a sense of the value of biological diversity. The best known of these is Edward Wilson's concept of biophilia, 'a sense of genetic unity, kinship, and deep history' that bonds human to their living environment, and acts as a survival mechanism for the human species.[29] I am simply trying to say that even if that is accepted, it is extremely dangerous to jump from such an argument to assumptions about the universal evolutionary importance of *particular* ideas about the right way to understand and respond to the values of nature. Even if biophilia were innate, a short geographical, anthropological or historical exploration would make quite clear that its expression through arguments about the need to protect 'the wild', or even 'biodiversity' are quite obviously culturally created.

MANAGING WILD NATURE

Ironically, even pre Second World War proponents of national parks saw 'wild' nature as something that needed management. In 1946, James Stevenson-Hamilton reflecting on his lifetime's experience at Kruger National Park, took what might be thought a rather modern laissez-faire view. He bemoaned the 'high-sounding schemes put forward for the supposed betterment of wildlife, proposing instead the principle that 'it is best to trust nature in all matters pertaining to wild life'.[30] On the other hand, while Sir Peter Chalmers-Mitchell told the British Association in 1931 that in national parks, 'no gun should be fired, no animal slaughtered or captured', he went on to note that such sanctuaries needed management by wardens or keepers. He saw them as part of a family of zoological institutions, extending from urban zoos (like his own London Zoo) through a zoological park in country area (like the Zoological Society of London's Whipsnade Zoo). Their wardens needed to intervene in nature – shooting was quite acceptable when it was done by authority of the warden, and 'for the direct advantage of the denizens of the sanctuaries' – to remove 'noxious individuals, the controlling of species that were increasing out of reason, and the extirpation of diseased or unhealthy animals'.[31] An interventionist approach also dominated American thinking about wildlife management, with a vigorous (and in retrospect shocking and foolish) policy of predator control in protected areas. Most famously, the conservationists' guru, Aldo Leopold, for years advocated predator control in the name of wilderness conservation.[32]

The close management of nature became a characteristic feature of conservation in Britain under the Nature Conservancy, and at the time of Chalmers-Mitchell's lecture the need for such management was just becoming clear to British ecologists concerned with the preservation of the living diversity of the British countryside. Subsequently, national nature reserves were subject to intensive regimes of cutting, flooding and burning both to recreate archaic land management practices that had created species-rich ecosystems, and to maintain species diversity.[33] The British Nature Conservancy had statutory responsibility for advising the Colonial Office until 1961, carried these ideas of active management abroad. There was considerable interchange in staff between it and African colonial services. In 1961, Barton Worthington, then Deputy Director General (Scientific) of the Nature Conservancy, toured eastern and southern Africa to report on their wildlife resources. Among his recommendations were the need for more scientific research and much more systematic planning of national park management: he believed that 'nature rarely if ever stands still' and that knowledge of such change could allow a measure of control.[34] National parks, like British nature reserves, needed management 'to maintain species in their maximum variety and in reasonable abundance', even if the tools available were few and crude (the rifle for reducing animal populations and fire for controlling vegetation).[35]

THE POACHER AT HOME

Whether 'wild' nature needs to be managed or not, those committed to the conservation of nature in the 20th century have always found the presence of people in supposedly 'wild' places an enormous conceptual and practical challenge. Although local people engaged in traditional pursuits were initially tolerated, as they began to encroach on land set aside for nature in reserves and national parks (see Chapter 4), they began to be seen as unnatural, threatening the balance of nature. They hunted or used resources in unacceptable ways for unacceptable reasons and had no measure of a reasonable level of consumption. The idea that protected areas could separate nature from the world of people made hunters into poachers, wood-cutters into law-breakers, and farmers into the enemies of conservation, from the forests of the Adirondacks to the savannas of East Africa.[36]

R W G Hingston represented a common view of sporting conservationists in the first half of the 20th century, when he told the Royal Geographical Society in 1931 that the decline of the African fauna should be blamed on 'the native hunter'. Such a person operated utterly outside the civilized code of sport hunting, caring nothing about species or trophies, or the sex of the animal he kills. Nor, crucially, did the native hunter 'hunt for the fun of the thing': they were not sporting at all.[37]

Hingston's comments reflected a long tradition among British and other European landowners of attempts to stop poaching. In medieval England, poaching was a capital offence, and even in Georgian England, the Black Act had condemned poachers of the landowner's game to transportation, or worse. The Victorian sporting estate had generated a complex and extensive hierarchy of employees devoted to protecting their master's game from the depredations of the landless and lawless poacher. At the same time, there was a certain romantic flavour to the enterprise of the lone poacher. Colonial attitudes were influenced somewhat by the affectionate romantic exasperation felt for poachers in Britain in the early 20th century. In the spirit of Robin Hood, the skilful lone poacher, outwitting the blundering forces of the law to put meat on the table, fitted a familiar and popular literary stereotype. Examples would include Richard Jefferies' lyrical book *The Amateur Poacher*, or in the way John Buchan portrayed his sporting gentlemen poaching salmon and stags from hapless neighbours in the fictional adventure *John Macnab*.[38] Poachers in colonial Africa were also sometimes regarded with paternalistic tolerance for their sad lack of perception of the damaging effects of their undisciplined ways.

Hingston reflects this tolerance of individual peasant subsistence hunting, writing 'when he hunts as an individual with his primitive weapons with the object of killing everything obtainable he probably does not cause any greater destruction than does the discriminating sportsman with his modern weapons'. However, poaching of African game was potentially far more serious that this: 'it is otherwise when natives hunt collectively. They then have the power to cause serious depletion through wholesale and indiscriminate methods employed'. There is no romance to such hunting: in Hingston's analysis (and it was a view that was widely held and carefully articulated) 'what the native wants is as many animals as possible for the purpose of either of meat or barter'.[39] That was not acceptable.

Conservationists in the early part of the century had been mixed in their view of the severity of the threat of local hunting. Edward North Buxton, for example, pointed out in 1902 that animals were the Africans 'birthright', and that 'from time immemorial the destruction caused by the indigenous inhabitants has not appreciably diminished the stock'.[40] In the SPFE delegation to the British Colonial Secretary three years later, he argued that it would not be easy or expedient to interfere with 'ancestral methods' such as pitfalls and traps that had been used 'for an indefinite period'. However, like Hingston, he urged that special care should be taken to prevent modern weapons getting into the hands of the natives',[41] and he castigated the French for importing rifles into Djibouti.

Other members of the SPFE delegation to see Lord Lyttelton, such as Colonel Delme Radcliffe, thought that even natives without guns should be prohibited from hunting because the effectiveness of their hunting techniques had already been improved by colonialism. Such commentators believed that some traditional balance between ill-armed and relatively unambitious indigenous hunters and abundant populations of their prey had been upset. Sir Henry Seton-Karr, a founder member of the SPWFE, laid the problem of diminishing game at the door of the 'depredations' of natives (along with their fellow ill-doers, unsporting settlers).[42] It was certainly obvious by the first decade of the 20th century that colonialism was triggering diverse economic and social change. Buxton observed that '*Pax Britannica*' had created new opportunities for killing game. There were Kamba hunters 'at every water hole' on the Athi Plains because the Maasai were not there to keep them away, and 'everything that walked was killed with poison arrows'. He suggested that 'as we allow the natives to kill game to a certain extent by preventing fighting among them, we should also prevent their trapping and killing on a large scale'.[43]

Whatever the official attitude, tolerance of native hunting in practice was severely limited. Sir Alfred Sharpe, acting commissioner of the Central African Protectorate after a number of adventurous shooting expeditions, wrote to the SPWFE in 1905 that 'there seems to have been a general tendency, while rigidly restricting Europeans from shooting big game, to leave the native free to slaughter all he wishes without let or hindrance'. There was much 'indiscriminate slaughter of small game' in nets and pitfalls, and if this was to be stopped, it would be necessary to 'check' the natives. Sharpe applauded steps 'to restrain the native hunter more or less', and urged that more should be done, following the success in the protectorate of British Central Africa – enforcing a native gun tax (such that whereas 12 years ago 'every native carried a gun', now not one in a thousand owned one), making natives subject to the same licences as Europeans ('in consequence very few take out licenses or shoot game'), and persuading District Magistrates to punish natives found guilty of shooting game without licences.[44] A correspondent from South Africa commented 'of course it is difficult to watch all the natives, but the constabulary have instructions to do all they can'.[45] In the slightly uneasy post-war and pre-independence years, Mervyn Cowie, Director of the Royal National Parks of Kenya, wrote 'the Judiciary must be convinced that the disastrous destruction of God's great beasts by ruthless poachers is a crime against the rights of posterity, deserving really effective punishment'.[46]

This concern to police hunting was by no means confined to Africa. In India, Lord Curzon reported 'progressive diminution', of animal life due to improvements in firearms, 'depredations of the natives' to protect crops or seek food (both he recognized as worthy reasons) and ('alas') for money by selling skins and hides.[47] The dominant sporting code from which so much conservation stemmed in the first three decades of the 20th century had little time for indigenous hunting, whether in the British Empire or indeed in North America. In his 15 point 'sportsman's platform', which he disseminated widely in 1909, William Hornaday wrote of the USA: 'An Indian or other native has no more right to kill game, or to subsist upon it all year round, than any white man in the same locality. The native has no God-given ownership of the game of any land, any more than its mineral resources; and he should be governed by the same laws as white men'.[48]

The need to stop hunting, particularly 'indiscriminate slaughter' by 'natives', was agreed by colonial conservationists. The idea of reserved or protected species had been common from the start of colonial hunting regulations, with many arguments about what should be on the list and what omitted. The 1933 London Conference on the Preservation of the Fauna and Flora of Africa urged signatories to the convention to establish a schedule of species that should not be hunted, killed or captured in their territories.[49] The real purpose of colonial regulation of hunting and poaching was of course 'to protect the natives against the results of their own reckless exploitation of their natural resources'.[50]

It seemed obvious to conservationists that the needs of wildlife should take precedence over those of local people in reserves, or places that deserved to be reserves. Thus the SPFE Deputation to the Colonial Office in March 1930 urged 'a close watch' on native hunting 'to prevent indiscriminate slaughter of game by natives'.[51] However, this argument carried decreasing weight with the Colonial Office. Individual Governors were often a great deal more sensitive to the needs of their charges. Sir Peter Chalmers-Mitchell commented 'Personally, I am inclined to think that Statesmen and Colonial Governments have often given perhaps an undue attention to the rights of natives compared with other matters'.[52] In 1928, the Society proposed (through the Colonial Office) that forest reserves in Nigeria should be made into reserves 'for the indigenous fauna', but this was rejected by the Governor because preservation would interfere with the hunting rights of the considerable number of people living in them.[53] At the end of his tenure as secretary of the SPFE, C W Hobley noted that in the Sudan and in some parts of West Africa, there was a school of thought which would recognize 'vested rights of natives to the Elephant'.[54]

As poaching became more extensively commercialized, and the use of cheap but arbitrary killing techniques such as wire snares became more widespread, the impact of poaching on species such as the rhinoceroses and elephant (for their horns and ivory) became an overwhelming conservation problem, and a headline issue for global conservation. The methods used by poachers were now not only highly effective, but obviously not directly 'traditional': there might be romance and a sense of fair play for some in the idea of an elephant hunter armed with a bow and arrows, but there was clearly none in a wire snare. Moreover, there was no doubt about the cruelty. Any lingering paternalistic benevolence in accounts of poaching became buried beneath a welter of humanitarian compassion for maimed animals. The emotional response of the anti-plumage campaigners of the late 19th and early 20th centuries was reawakened, still photographs and film powerfully available to express the cruelty, futility and destructiveness of the poachers' trade.[55]

NATURE'S FORTRESS

The fight against poachers and 'encroachers' in parks is a stock-in-trade of accounts of conservation in practice, whether in books by retired colonial Game Wardens, or the day to day stories of their successors today.[56] While hunting has been very widespread in many regions, the focus of the 'poaching menace' has always been the protected area, first the colonial game reserves, later the National Park. Here nature is most precious, its perfection most vulnerable to destruction. Here too, to be more prosaic, wildlife is concentrated, and valuable wildlife products (like ivory or horn) are temptingly there for the taking.

The classic approach to the management of protected areas is one of defence. Game reserves were only set up against opposition from settlers, and once established, continuous vigilance was needed to keep them intact. The attempt to secure their future as national parks faced conflicting demands for land for development from government planners. Even then, poaching, foremost of a range of problems, threatened their sustainability and security. Conservation has therefore been good at negative thinking for much of the 20th century – stopping people from doing things that harmed nature, and above all keeping people out of protected areas. The phrase now commonly used to describe such policy is 'fortress conservation'. This is generally used rather rudely, to draw attention both to the odd notion of 'wild' nature locked up behind human barriers, and the element of coercion in the way peoples' access to the nature within is regulated. The phrase reflects a common view among researchers (particularly historians and anthropologists) that wildlife conservation has imposed unacceptable costs on poor rural people in many parts of the world, and has done so with unacceptable procedures in terms of human rights.

Dan Brockington, for example, chose to title his book on the clearance of Parakuyo and Maasai pastoralists from the Mkomazi Game Reserve, Tanzania *Fortress Conservation*.[57] The front cover shows people sporting jewellery and champagne glasses at a wildlife fundraising party in London. He argues that the Mkomazi reserve and its wildlife primarily serves the interests of such people, and reflects their understanding of what the African bush ought to be like, and how wild animals and people should interact there. Mkomazi is understood by the European and North American conservationists who fund it, and who support the Tanzanian state's decision to establish and protect it, as part of 'wild' Africa. People – at least, local people and their livestock – are seen as a threat to the pristine state and diversity of the wild nature within the reserve. In 1988, the decision was taken to clear local people from the reserve. The eviction of pastoralists made Mkomazi 'wilderness' for the first time, because of the fears of conservation planners of the impacts of the people and their livestock on rangeland, and their fears of the unknown dimensions of future impacts.[58]

When the Mkomazi Game Reserve was created in 1951, there were just a few pastoralist families and about 5000 cattle, who were allowed to stay. By the mid-1980s, there were almost 100,000 cattle, and the reserve was integrated into the local and regional economy as a supplier of seasonal grazing resources. However, conservation planners believed the pastures were overstocked and threatened with permanent degradation. There were a number of unsuccessful attempts to remove stock and their owners in the 1970s and early 1980s, before the Department of Wildlife gained enough political clout to enforce their vision of a reserve free of local human use. Permits for residence and grazing were revoked in 1986, and by July 1988 the reserve had been cleared: those present and listed by name in the 1950s were last to go.[59]

The story is by no means unusual. In Tanzania, Roderick Neumann suggests that 40,000 people were relocated from the Selous Game Reserve, while about 1000 Maasai and 25,000 head of cattle were removed from Serengeti in 1959. The involuntary resettlement of people for protected areas has in fact taken place in every inhabited continent, with sometimes catastrophic social impacts. The issue is widely reported and researched.[60]

The methods conventionally used to impose natural conditions vary in form and intensity, but they typically involve the exclusion or removal of the influences of local people. I will pick one such case study of conventional national park thinking. I do so because, while the author was angry at the actions and ideas of conservationists, they are not inherently hostile to their aims. They do not commence from the premise that the desire to conserve nature must be destructive of human interests.

David Turton describes how the proposal to create a second national park in the Omo Valley in Ethiopia in 1978, and exclude the Mursi people who lived there, was based on a false view of the area as some kind of wilderness.[61] The Omo National Park had been established in 1966, following a mission from UNESCO led by Julian Huxley in 1963, and a study of potential parks by Leslie Brown and Ian Grimwood.[62] It was inaccessible, but it had potential as a tourist destination because of its rugged 'wilderness' character. They had proposed an extension to the east of the Omo River, and although management and maintenance of the original park had fallen into a poor state (and road access was nil), a Japanese park planning team investigated the area and in 1978 proposed a 'Greater Omo National Park'. A new area, effectively a second Mago National Park, was set aside, and a wardens' post established in the Mago valley (accessible by road from Addis Ababa) in 1979–1980. The report on the new park at the same time dismissed the extent to which Mursi people exploited the area, and identified them as a threat to conservation. It proposed exclusion and resettlement.

Foreign eyes saw the Omo Valley as a wilderness. Planners failed to understand the fact (quite obvious to the anthropologist David Turton) that the ecosystems of the parks were in fact anthropogenic – landscapes maintained by the Mursi economy of cattle keeping, rainfed cultivation, flood-retreat farming on Omo River, and hunting for ivory and skins for trade. In the 1980s the Mursi themselves did little damage to the wildlife resources of the park (although drought in the 1970s had forced them into the area in larger numbers causing human use of the park to intensify). However, the arguments about eviction were not made on the basis of detailed studies of human impacts on nature. The Mursi must be removed in case their presence excused the presence of other people, driven into the area by land hunger, or proposals to develop the region. Development of the national park as envisaged, involving eviction from key areas, would in Turton's view 'render the economy of the Mursi totally unviable'.[63] Fortunately for them, in the 1980s at least, the park was not tightly managed, and the Mursi economy limped on, game guards just one more hazard to be negotiated. However, the latest destructive power of the idea of a park as a means of preserving the 'wild' by separating people and nature remained a real threat. Turton argues that such arguments for conservation, taking it for granted that conservation and development are opposed, are 'narrow, defeatist and fundamentally are pessimistic'.[64]

'Fortress' thinking typically involves a series of ideas about people and parks. First, that people (specifically 'native' people, or those making a living) are an unnatural presence in what is (or should be) a natural place. Second, such people threaten park ecosystems (for example through farming, burning or overgrazing). Third, such people threaten park species through hunting (usually referred to as poaching, for the simple reason that it is usually illegal by national statute). Once the idea of pristine nature as something separate from people is accepted, it is a small step to the idea that it needs to be protected from ordinary human activity, especially from direct use of land, water, plants or animals. This idea goes deep within the dominant modern model of conservation. It has made the extinction of occupancy rights and eviction or resettlement a common experience across the world, in both industrialized and developing countries.

The history of relations between people and protected area managers can be complex. Jane Carruthers describes how African 'squatters' were initially evicted from the Pongola Game Reserve in the 19th century, and its successor the Sabi Game Reserve from 1903. However, from 1905, their presence was tolerated, because they provided a source of labour and rent (although they remained a thorn in the side of the administration, resenting and resisting discipline and perpetually being suspected of poaching).[65] Then, as recently as 1969, 1500 Makuleke people were forcibly removed from Kruger National Park under the apartheid regime. Their land rights were only recognized following the end of apartheid, when the Makuleke laid claim to the land restitution commission for 250 square kilometres of land at the northern edge of Kruger, and their rights to this land were recognized. The eventual outcome of this case was an innovative agreement to restore the land subject to an agreement with South Africa National Parks that maintained management of the land and the development of wildlife-related tourist enterprises.[66] The success and long-term sustainability of this, and similar, solutions to past land expropriations for conservation remain to be seen.

Colonial willingness to evict Africans from game reserves and national parks reflected fairly normal practice at the time. Conservation was an integral element in a general colonial model of rational allocation of land to different purposes. In colonial Africa, there were also forced translocations in the name of sleeping sickness eradication and dam construction for hydro-electric power, and above all to clear land for agriculture (see Chapter 7). In countries like South Africa, Kenya or Rhodesia, such clearances took place from early in the colonial experience to make way for European settlers, but the lure of modern agriculture has continued to drive land expropriation for intensive schemes to grow crops such as wheat.[67] Sometimes these forced migrations were highly organized and peaceful, at other times coercive.[68] National parks were concerns of the state, and that is how many colonial states operated: arbitrarily, and if necessary backed up by force; indeed, many of today's less democratic governments still operate the same way.

However, the impacts of the creation of national parks are not confined to developing countries. There is an equivalent history in North America, Australia and Russia for example, where the 'Yellowstone model' has been followed, attempting to protect the 'pristine' quality of land by not allowing traditional land uses and permitting access for visitors under carefully controlled conditions.[69] The parallels between the creation of national parks as reserves for nature and native reservations for dispossessed Indian peoples in the American west have been remarked upon above. Karl Jacoby describes the impacts of the Grand Canyon Forest Reserve and (after 1919) the Grand Canyon National Park in Arizona on the Havasupai people. Their economy was transformed from one of subsistence hunting and farming to a dependence on wage labour for survival. Jacoby comments 'By the 1920s, the plateau lands above the Havasupais' reservation, which for the tribe had once been an intimate geography of family camping grounds, or hunting areas, and of places for gathering wild stuffs, had instead become a symbol of their diminished status as wage workers in a touristic "wilderness"'.[70]

Canada's policy until the 1970s was also to expropriate and move communities within national parks. Thus, in the 1960s, some 200 families were moved to create the Forillon National Park in Quebec, and 228 households (1200 people) to create Kouchibouguac National Park in New Brunswick. Controversy and violence attending the Kouchibouguac clearance led to a government inquiry, and in the face of mass protests over the creation of Gros Morne National Park, the government revised its policy, and communities were allowed stay (while being encouraged to move). Seven villages remained as enclaves within the park.[71] In 1988, the Canadian National Parks Act was amended to allow people to snare rabbits and cut firewood.

The debate about the impact of protected areas on local people is a diverse and sometimes acrimonious one. Its energy comes in part from the hostility between academic disciplines, since most of those criticizing the social impacts of parks were trained in the social sciences and humanities (economists, sociologists, historians, anthropologists, political scientists and human geographers), while most of those arguing that those impacts are either over-stated, mis-represented, or reasonable, were trained as natural scientists (mostly as biologists of some kind). There is a difference of academic culture, of language and theory, of research methodology, of cultural frame of reference, that makes informed debate across this disciplinary divide very difficult.

LIVING WITH PARKS

Many of those people who live adjacent to protected areas harbour significant grievances against park management authorities. Instances of direct injustice blend into those of ignorance, remote and formulaic styles of planning, lack of imagination and refusal to admit mistakes. Some of that injustice stems simply from the costs of being neighbour to a protected area. These costs can be considerable.[72]

The costs of conservation in protected areas include the obvious problems of eviction, the loss of homes, the asset value of land or resources and the stream of benefits that derive from them. They also include the opportunity to derive benefits in the future, through intensive use of land or resources (for example the economic benefits of converting forest to farmland). Locally, such opportunity costs can be very great. Around Mgahinga Gorilla National Park in Uganda for example, rural population densities are high and the people poor, with enormous pressure on agricultural land. Farming is intensive and diverse (beans, sorghum, maize, Irish and sweet potatoes and wheat), and the main source of household income. As discussed in Chapter 1, when the national park was created, in 1991, there were 272 households (over 1700 people) living within the park area, with a further 680 people cultivating there. All this settlement, agriculture and other forms of resource use became illegal. Seven years later, local people still spoke of the economic cost to their livelihood and income of the loss of productive agricultural land. The annual value of lost agricultural production was approximately US$0.85m, vastly greater than the compensation paid (US$15,000). Not surprisingly, the park's neighbours believed that the costs and benefits of park creation were not in balance.[73]

The establishment of protected areas also brings a cost to local people in terms of non-use values, for example religious and cultural values. Roderick Neumann, for example, describes the way in which members of the Meru Mbise clan cannot get access to a ritual site in the Mount Meru Crater in Arusha National Park in Tanzania (and contrasts the park administration's ideas of developing this as a 'cultural site' for visitors with local plans to build a church there). Land for Arusha National Park originally came from Meru people. The park was included on Hingston's list in 1931, and the tiny Ngurdoto Crater National Park (700 hectares) was declared in 1960 (being opened a year later, during the Arusha Conference, see Chapter 3).[74] This land was a former forest and game reserve, but Rod Neumann argues that Meru people still believed they had rights to it. The park was expanded during the 1960s through inclusion of further forest reserves, European farms purchased by the World Wildlife Fund, and farms nationalized by the state using funds from the African Wildlife Leadership Foundation.[75]

People living as neighbours of national parks, and other wildlife rich zones, often suffer problems of crop raiding wild animals. Elephants, buffalo, baboons, even extremely rare species such as gorillas, can be extremely destructive raiders of crops. The edge of a montane forest protected area can be a highly unattractive, exhausting, dangerous and uneconomic place to farm, and to subsistence farmers looking in at the forest, it is a bitter thing to see your hard work turned into some wild neighbour's next meal.[76] The labour demands of crop-protection are extremely heavy, and difficult for some households (for example single-parent households, those where someone is sick, or those without children); and, of course, children chasing monkeys are children who are not at school: crop-raiding cuts at the capacity of poor households to invest in the next generation of breadwinners. Furthermore, some wild animal neighbours can be extremely dangerous: it is obviously extremely hazardous as well as difficult to defend crops against elephants, or buffalo, while animals like tigers are quite liable to see people as possible prey.

The problems park neighbours experience from animals in protected areas can be compounded if they are harassed by park officials. Those on the boundary are most likely to be suspected (indeed, most likely to be guilty) of minor infringements of park boundaries (for example children allowing stock to graze across a boundary), or infringements of regulations (for example cutting fuelwood, or collecting medicinal plants). The rule book says that such infringements need to be stamped down on, and rangers walk a line between a Nelsonian blind eye (which prevents ostracism in the local community but risks serious damage to the wildlife of the protected area), and such fierce pursuit of every minor infringement that it amounts to persecution. It is very easy for the latter to grade into corrupt practice, with arbitrary arrest avoided only by paying protection money. Even though most national parks are typified by misplaced goodwill muffled by bureaucratic confusion rather than draconian law enforcement or even paramilitary violence, park neighbours typically have an uneasy relationship with protected area wardens and rangers, untrusting and, at least latently, hostile.[77]

All this means that while protected areas make enormous sense to the conservationist desperate to hold back the demands of people, they can be extremely unattractive to the people who actually have to share the landscape with them. If the protected area is located on land which those people used to hold as their own, their resentment and sense of injustice is redoubled. Under conventional protected area models, the protection of nature has often been bought at the cost of the livelihoods of poor people. In the words of Roderick Neumann, 'parks and protected areas are historically implicated in the conditions of poverty and underdevelopment that surround them'.[78]

PARKS FOR PEOPLE

Conservation planners have not been oblivious of the growing critique of conventional protected areas. From the 1950s onwards, very different sets of ideas about the relations between people and protected areas began to develop, emphasizing not the threat local people posed, but the need to foster mutually beneficial relations between protected areas and their neighbours. This new thinking is often broadly referred to as a narrative of 'community conservation' or as 'community-based conservation', and is often presented as a strict contrast to 'fortress conservation', or the 'fences and fines' approach to conservation, as if one displaced the other in some kind of ecological succession.[79] In practice, changes in ideas about people and parks have been much less clear-cut than this caricature would suggest. They have been more diverse and sometimes contested, and the new ideas have been highly variable in their uptake in different places.

A potent source of new ideas were UNESCO's 'Biosphere Reserves', developed under the 'Man and the Biosphere' (MAB) programme launched in 1971. Traditional wildlife conservation was important in the MAB programme, although its focus was broadly about what we would now call sustainability.[80] It was the fruit of the Biosphere Conference, originally a suggestion for an international meeting on endangered species suggested at the IUCN General Assembly in Nairobi in 1968, but developed into the broader 'biosphere' approach by ECOSOC (the UN Economic and Social Council), and UNESCO, in the light of experience with the International Biological Programme. The Biosphere Reserves (MAB Project 8) were to be zoned nature reserves, whose aim was to conserve 'natural areas and the genetic information they contain' in core zones, while allowing suitable human activities to continue in outer zones. Existing nature reserves could be reclassified (and sometimes extended) to fit the MAB framework as Biosphere Reserves. This initiative linked conventional wildlife conservation to the idea of the conservation of natural resources for human use and the sustainability debate (see Chapter 7).[81]

The principles of community-oriented park management were developed in the context of protected areas at successive World Congresses on National Parks and Protected Areas, particularly the Third in 1982 and Fourth in 1992.[82] At Bali in 1982, the conclusions of the congress addressed the role of protected areas in sustainable development, and the question of protected areas and traditional societies. The Caracas congress, in 1992, developed this approach. It took as its title 'parks for life', and the question of people and protected areas, and the creation of partnerships to support protected areas, was central to its discussions.[83] In his opening address, Sir Sridath Ramphal, President of IUCN, urged that ways be found to ensure that protected areas provide more benefits to local people. He said 'quite simply, if local people do not support protected areas, then protected areas cannot last'.[84]

These moves were in part a response to changes in the way developed countries regarded the rights of indigenous people. Legal cases in both Canada and Australia led to substantial shifts in the way land title was understood.[85] Most Canadian national parks were designated before the federal and provincial governments acknowledged the existence of aboriginal right and title.[86] They were located according to biophysically-defined 'natural areas', rather than either to minimize impacts on aboriginal people or to provide security for their living resources on which they depended. Attitudes began to shift in the 1970s, in response to rising aboriginal political awareness, and to the ground-breaking Berger inquiry into the Mackenzie Delta oil pipeline, and then the Inuvialuit Final Agreement in 1984. In 1972, the Canadian Parks Service introduced the idea of National Park Reserves, to be treated as national parks pending the completion of land claims. This opened up the possibility of joint management of parks, although experiences, for example in the Pacific Rim National Park

Reserve on Vancouver Island and GwaiiHaanas/South Moresby National Park Reserves have been mixed.[87]

IUCN passed the Zaire Resolution on the Protection of Traditional Ways of Life at its General Assembly in 1975, calling on governments not to displace people from protected areas, and to take specific account of the needs of indigenous populations.[88] In the same year, the UNESCO World Heritage Convention made specific provision for the conservation of areas of historical and cultural significance. In 1984, the World Bank published guidelines on indigenous people and development projects, proposing not to fund projects that caused their resettlement.[89] Following the Caracas Congress, IUCN published a policy on 'Indigenous and Traditional Peoples and Protected Areas'.[90] On paper at least, the need of local people, especially indigenous people, was firmly on the agenda. The issue of mobile and indigenous peoples, and the issue of 'community controlled' protected areas, were critical to the Fifth World Parks Congress in Durban in 2003.

This openness to community conservation has an interesting parallel in partnerships with private landowners. Thus, from 1979, the government of Canada was prevented from acquiring land compulsorily purchased from private landowners. More recent Canadian national parks such as Grasslands (in the western prairies) are being created piecemeal with purchases from willing sellers.[91] The same approach of creating is being used in the Agulhas Plain in South Africa. Biological diversity in the *fynbos* biome is high, and threatened by intensification of land use (especially the spread of vineyards, invasive alien trees and housing developments); land of high biodiversity is highly fragmented.[92] A new national park, based on a comprehensive regional biodiversity planning process, involves drawing together several tiers of government (South African National Parks, the Natal Parks Board and others), NGOs and private landowners (donating or selling land, or agreeing a conservation contract with the state).

The Greater Agulhas National Park is also drawing on partnerships with NGOs. In 1999, FFI purchased Flower Valley, 50 hectares of *fynbos* with a major donation from the Arcadia Fund, with support from the Conservation Foundation, the Countryside Restoration Trust and a concerned individual. Flower Valley is a working farm, one of the largest exporters of wild harvested *fynbos* flowers in the Cape. The commercial operation is now being managed by a private company Fynbos, for the Flower Valley Conservation Trust. The rate and pattern of wild flower harvest is based on scientific criteria. The farm is investing in invasive species clearance, and purchasing harvested wild flowers from local landowners and farmers. The Trust is developing certificated schemes for marketing wild *fynbos* flowers, supporting micro-enterprise activities based on *fynbos* products and creating an early learning centre and adult education facilities.[93]

South African National Parks has begun to experiment quite widely with contractual national parks, in which land is kept under conservation management through a contract with the state, usually as the basis for a wildlife-based business enterprise. This approach has also been extended to communal land, for example in agreements with the Makuleke people, evicted from Kruger National Park in the 1960s (mentioned above), and the Nama people in Richtersveld National Park in the Northern Cape.[94]

The concept of 'community' conservation more generally carries a considerable amount of romantic baggage. It draws on a long history of idealistic and simplistic Western ideas about the nature of communities in the colonial world, and political ideas in Europe about the essential nobility of the peasant life.[95] The idea that Third World villages comprise organic human communities has been important as a reference point for Western thinkers opposed to the rapid transformations of modernity and capitalism (technology, industrialization, urbanization, pollution) in the last 200 years. This was a potent element in the roots of environmentalism and conservation, particularly in the United Kingdom and United States. For many critics of development and economic and social change, 'tradition' has been imagined as in opposition to 'modernity'. The idea that 'small is beautiful', and that bloated Western consumer society had much to learn from simple rural people in its search for sustainability, was fundamental to environmental critiques of development in the 1980s and 1990s.[96] From this it was a short step to the idea that conservationists have a natural affinity with indigenous and rural people.[97] Both nature and 'traditional' lives and lifestyles are threatened by 'modern' development.[98] It is easy to assume that conservation will be supported by an intrinsically pro-conservation 'indigenous community'.

The community conservation narrative became important in the 1980s, a time of significant shifts in the dominant discourses of development, with a rejection of 'top down', 'technocratic' planning (because it was seen to have failed to deliver economic and social development), in favour of 'development from below', 'bottom up planning', and 'participatory' development. By the early 1990s, aid donors and development planners had committed themselves in attempts to adopt participatory approaches. The link that had been forged between conservation and development in ideas of sustainable development persuaded conservationists to do the same. Indeed, it created an opportunity for conservationists (and particularly international and domestic NGOs) to tap into new sources of funds in aid budgets, enabling them to link their activities to 'development'.

The idea of 'community-based' conservation represented a wholesale shift in the dominant thinking about conservation, one whose ramifications are still being worked through. Such shifts in policy are not unusual. Policy makers facing urgent problems tend to adopt sets of ideas that promise to work, so-called 'policy narratives'.[99] Once policy narratives are established, they tend to be very persistent, even when research starts to challenge their validity in particular situations. They are adopted by political leaders, researchers, and policy professionals, backed by accounts of 'success'. Even community leaders learn to express their needs in terms of widely-accepted narratives to attract investment. Policy narratives become culturally, institutionally, and politically embedded as they become entrenched in the thinking of politicians, policy makers, bureaucrats, donors, technical specialists and private consultants whose needs they serve.[100] In the context of conservation, the old idea that the best way to ensure conservation was to establish a protected area, and defend it rigorously against all comers, was such a policy narrative. The new ideas which grew in the 1980s about the need to build a very real concern for local communities into conservation practice comprised a counter-narrative, a similarly simplistic idea that served as a new blueprint for conservation policy.

The community-based conservation narrative contained two distinct elements. First, it allowed people living in and around protected areas, or those with property rights there (in land or living resources) or other claims on the land (for example spiritual claims), to use protected living resources: 'people and park' projects. Thus, in East Africa, experience at Amboseli National Park through the 1970s,[101] subsequently developed into the Wildlife Extension Project, experience from which in turn led to the establishment of the African Wildlife Foundation's Tsavo Community Conservation Project (launched in 1988), the Kenyan Wildlife Service Community Wildlife Programme and the USAID-funded COBRA project (Conservation of Biodiverse Areas), launched in 1991, and the African Wildlife Foundation's 'Neighbours as Partners' Programme.[102]

Park outreach projects typically involve one or more of the following: involvement of local people in park management and operations; in the provision of services to local communities (for example education, health care); in provision for traditional land uses (for example hunting and gathering, agriculture, religious practices, pastoralism); and provision that local people should be involved in park-related tourism.

The second element in the community-based conservation narrative links conservation objectives to local development needs through what have been called 'conservation-with-development projects' or 'integrated conservation and development projects' (ICDPs).[103] The need to take poverty and the development aspirations of communities around national parks seriously was recognized in the WWF's Wildlife and Human Needs Programme (launched in 1985). One example is CARE's 'Development Through Conservation' project, begun in Uganda in 1988 and which has worked extensively with communities around the gorilla parks (see Chapter 1).[104] ICDPs try to link conservation and sustainable development, and hence capture the huge upwelling of policy commitment arising from the Brundtland Report, the UN Conference on Environment and Development at Rio in 1992, and the World Summit on Sustainable Development in Johannesburg in 2002 (Chapter 7).

Underlying all these elements of the community-based conservation narrative is the moral argument that conservation goals should contribute to and not conflict with basic human needs. Thus 'fortress conservation' must be abandoned if it has adverse impacts on the living conditions of the rural poor, and conservation goals should be integrated with the development objective of meeting human needs. The World Conservation Strategy (published in 1980) sought to link conventional conservation concerns with those of development, using the notion of sustainable development, a concept later popularized by the Brundtland Report in 1987, and central to *Agenda 21* (see Chapter 7). From the perspective of sustainable development, the conservation of biodiversity and the challenge of meeting human needs must be integrated: community conservation provided a conceptual framework within which this could be made to happen in and around protected areas.[105]

Within community conservation approaches, Barrow and Murphree describe a continuum between 'park outreach' projects (based in protected area management authorities and involving a wide range of programmes with local communities) and 'community-based wildlife management projects' (or community-based natural resource management or CBNRM projects).[106] The latter are discussed further in Chapter 7. These comprise elements of what David Hulme and Marshall Murphree have described as 'the new conservation' of the 1990s. This changed the emphasis in conservation from state-centred to society-centred activity, particularly society at the local level, from a concern with preservation to sustainable development, where both conservation and development goals are achieved at the same time, and from a concern to protect nature from economic change to a concern to achieve conservation through economic interventions.[107] These ideas reflected the new development orthodoxy of the 1980s concerning the importance of the market as a driver of economic betterment, and the need to slim down costly and ineffective state bureaucracies. A reduced role for the state promised to allow 'communities' (villagers, private individuals, companies, groups of companies) a larger role in conservation.

One reason for the desire of conservation planners to 'reach out' from parks into surrounding landscapes and engage with their neighbours was the recognition that conservation goals can often not be achieved within the boundaries of protected areas alone, where these exist as islands within a developed landscape. Research in conservation biology and on the genetics of small populations showed the perils of small isolated blocks of habitats and isolated populations. Therefore, even if conservation 'fortresses' could be established, paid for and policed, they would not be enough. Recognition (for example in the Biosphere Reserves) that conservation needed to reach out of protected areas into the wider landscape to establish 'buffer zones', has grown into an awareness that conservation must be conceived at the landscape scale. Therefore, neighbouring communities (that is the people whose land mobile species graze and cross) are key stakeholders in conservation and needed to be recognized as such.

Some wildlife species (particularly predators) have home ranges of a scale that dwarf even the largest parks. They wander abroad, and if they are to survive, efforts for their conservation must extend beyond parks and into the lands around them. The conservation of grizzly bears in the Canadian Rockies cannot be isolated from the passion of real estate developers for homes, condominiums and golf courses on prime valley lands.[108] Much wildlife exists outside parks; indeed, in some countries (in Africa for example) most wildlife exists outside parks. David Western argues that land beyond parks is the best hope and biggest challenge for biological conservation for the 21st century.[109] Anthropogenic climate change is also likely to have serious implications for the capacity of existing protected areas to sustain their species diversity into the future. As climatic zones move, species will simply run out of habitat to follow suit.[110]

For these reasons, the connectivity of blocks of habitat across the landscape is becoming an increasingly important factor in protected area planning. Long-term maintenance of diversity demands regional biogeography and landscape pattern.[111] Of course, such an agenda could see conservation organizations riding roughshod over the interests of park neighbours. Indeed, there has been criticism on such grounds of proposals for trans-boundary parks in areas such as southern Africa, where conservationists have appeared to be more interested in extending their control than caring for the people affected.[112]

However, pushing conservation to the landscape scale does not have to be like that. One example is the Mesoamerican Biological Corridor, from Mexico to Panama in Central America. Fauna & Flora International is collaborating with the Central American Commission for Environment and Development and governmental, NGOs and university partners in a regional land use plan to create ecological corridors between protected areas. One initiative is the 20,000 hectare Golden Stream Corridor Preserve in Belize. This was purchased with money from FFI's Arcadia Fund in late 1998, to protect tracts of forest on the southern coast of Belize fragmented by timber extraction, citrus cultivation and shrimp farming.[113] The reserve safeguards the core area of the Port Honduras Marine Reserve into which the Golden Stream flows, and provides a link in the southeastern Belize section of the Mesoamerican Biological Corridor. A partnership has been created between local NGOs, local communities and the private sector to manage the area for sustainable tourism. The land, formerly part of a private estate, will in due course revert to local ownership.

Debate at the Fifth World Parks Congress in Durban in 2003 emphasized the importance of these issues of the linkages between protected areas and their surroundings, and their role in promoting the alleviation of poverty. Its theme was 'benefits beyond boundaries'. The promise of that phrase is alluring, the challenge of living up to it considerable. The Director of IUCN, Achim Steiner, wrote of protected areas:

> *In the past they have been seen as islands of protection in an ocean of destruction. We need to learn to look on them as the building blocks of biodiversity in an ocean of sustainable human development, with their benefits extending far beyond their physical boundaries.*[114]

One further innovation in national park planning deserves a mention here. By the end of the 20th century, the role of private parks was growing once more. There have always been private parks, from the days of medieval kings' hunting preserves. Many protected areas remain private, either in the hands of individuals or companies (for example the game ranches or Conservancies of southern Africa), or owned by NGOs. The Nature Conservancy, for example, protects 6 million hectares in United States and 41 million hectares outside (mainly in the Caribbean, Indonesia and Central America).[115]

However, traditionally, the establishment of national parks was, above all, an achievement of national governments. It represents, in a sense, a nationalization of private rights in land, a recognition that the benefits of nature should accrue to the people in general, rather than to private landowners. However, national tenure and responsibility has often only been achieved through private contributions. Thus in 1971 an opportunity arose to extend Nairobi National Park in Kenya by 40,000 hectares by getting people to buy it from the County Council at one pound per acre. Bernard Grzimek immediately bought 20,000 acres and the Fauna Preservation Society called upon their members to help support the initiative. The first farm in what came in 1962 to comprise Arusha National Park in Tanzania was purchased (from the European farmer who 'owned' it, native tenure having been annulled by land alienation during colonial rule) by the World Wildlife Fund, with extensive further purchases supported by the African Wildlife Leadership Fund.[116] Subsequently, in 1974 WWF raised half a million pounds for the Kenyan government to purchase the land surrounding Lake Nakuru to safeguard its huge flamingo population.

A prime example of such privately-funded national conservation is the Area de Conservación Guanacaste in Costa Rica. This covers 120 square kilometres (plus and 70 square kilometres of sea) containing about 230,000 species (65 per cent of the biodiversity of Costa Rica), and comprising a series of different national parks and other protected areas. The Guanacase project was the brainchild of Dr Dan Jansen of the University of Pennsylvania, who in the mid-1980s developed the idea of rebuilding the fragments of the remaining tropical forest by purchasing land around tiny and isolated protected areas to form a continuous block.[117]

In a variety of diverse forms, protected areas remained the core of conservation strategies at the end of the 20th century. However, they were by no means the only focus of conservation endeavour in the 20th century. Alongside the urge to protect nature in particular places has gone the desire to protect it in particular form: the conservation of species. This is the subject of the next chapter.

Chapter 6

Two by Two

The animals came in two by two, hurrah, hurrah!
The animals came in two by two,
The elephant and the kangaroo
And they all went into the ark
Just to get out of the rain (traditional).[1]

SOME ARE MORE EQUAL THAN OTHERS

Despite the mantra of the importance of all biodiversity, people have remarkably specific likes and dislikes when it comes to species. The polymath J B S Haldane (founder of population genetics, geneticist, Marxist and scientific author) famously replied to a question about what might be learned about God from a study of his works, 'an inordinate fondness for beetles'.[2] Haldane's humour was as usual in service to his science: over 360,000 species of beetles have been described by taxonomists, with probably several million more that have not yet received their attention.[3]

But beetles are not particularly popular. It is usually other species, particularly mammals, that dominate public concern about conservation. Sea otters, for example, are animals seemingly honed by evolution for a starring role in childrens' books, with a natural chubby cuteness normally the result of the efforts of the Walt Disney Corporation's animators. This is a view born of television and the luxury of the world free from physical want experienced by Western environmentalists in the late 20th century. In the 18th and 19th centuries sea otters were simply valuable furs waiting to be killed. They began to be hunted for their skins around the North Pacific in the 18th century. At that time there were 150,000 to 300,000 animals from northern Japan to the Alaskan Peninsula and down the North American coast to Baja California, with 16,000 to 20,000 in California. When Russian explorers under Vitus Bering discovered sea otters in 1741 the resulting demand for pelts in Russia, Europe, Japan and China brought them to the brink of extinction. The United States bought Alaska from Russia in 1867, and hunting pressure down to California rose. At its peak, 500 to 600 sea otters were taken weekly from San Francisco Bay alone.

Sea otters were finally given protection under the Fur Seal Treaty of 1911 (signed by the United States, Great Britain, Russia and Japan), by which time they were so scarce as to be effectively commercially extinct, with only 1–2000 animals across their entire range.[4] By the mid-1970s the Alaska population had recovered to between 110,000 and 160,000 animals, and despite the threat of oil pollution (notably from the *Exxon Valdez*), populations are increasing. In California, sea otters were widely assumed to be extinct until the early 1930s. In fact, a relict population survived in Bug Sur, and by the time the coast highway opened in 1938 it had grown to several hundred animals. By the mid-1970s, the population had grown to about 1800 animals. It then declined because of drowning in gill nets. Legislation to push nets offshore allowed recovery to about 2300 animals by 1995. Since then, numbers have declined again, although the reason is not understood.[5]

The demise of the sea otter is commonly used as an object lesson in conservation, and evidence for the significance of the loss of particular species for ecosystem change. The story goes as follows. Sea otters have a remarkable appetite for sea urchins, and sea urchins, in their turn for algae. On the exposed west coast of North America, the rolling waters of the Pacific are quelled by huge beds of kelp. Between their fronds a complex, diverse and characteristic community of life is maintained. Remove the sea otters (as fur hunters did with ruthless efficiency) and sea urchin populations boom, stripping the sea floor of vegetation, and removing the vast offshore kelp beds.[6] With the removal of the kelp, a whole marine ecosystem disappears, creating dismal and species-poor 'urchin barrens'. For the loss of the otter the kelp was lost; for the loss of the kelp, the crabs, fish and other species disappeared. Of course, it is more complex than that – sea urchin populations are affected by pollution, food availability, disease and many other factors, and the recovery of sea otter populations has not brought about automatic return of the biodiverse kelp bed ecosystems.

However, sea otters are held to be a classic example of what conservation biologists like to call a 'keystone species', whose existence seems to be essential to maintaining ecosystem structure. Keystone species have a disproportionate impact on ecosystems due to their size (like elephants) or their activities (like North American beavers).[7] In times past, many terrestrial ecosystems held mammals of more than 1 metric tonne in weight, so-called 'megaherbivores'.[8] In the late Pleistocene (about 11,500 years ago, when much of the northern latitudes of the Earth were ice-covered), there were numerous megaherbivores, including the giant ground sloths of the Americas and the marsupial Diprotodon of Australia.[9] Eight remain, (two elephants, four rhinoceroses, the hippopotamus and giraffe). The rest appear to have died out fairly rapidly as the world warmed after the last ice age, and organized human societies developed.

The ecological importance of large 'bulldozer herbivores' such as the elephant is obvious from even a cursory survey of areas where they occur at high density. In Hwange National Park in Western Zimbabwe, for example, large areas of open forest are coppiced by elephants pushing trees over to reach new growth, and some areas are left completely open. In Amboseli in Kenya, David Western showed that plant species diversity increased with elephant density up to a certain point, then declined as densities rose.[10] Elephants are fierce woodland managers, local extreme natural events that walk about. As such they obviously deserve close attention from ecological scientists. They also receive a disproportionate fraction of attention from conservationists. In part this reflects simply their ecological role, but it is more than this. For Norman Owen-Smith, the biology of what he rather nicely describes as 'these giants among our fellow inhabitants of this planet' have important implications for humans, who in biomass and structuring and destructive power have surpassed them and usurped their role.

Megaherbivores, large carnivores, primates and a rather small list of other species, most of which are mammals or birds, have provided the dominant focus of concern for conservation over the last century. Many conservationists are reluctant to think this through. Are all species equally important? This question is shocking and ridiculous to many conservationists. Arguing it in an idle moment at a recent conference, I greatly annoyed a friend, who quickly offered the classic rebuttal, referring to the concept of biodiversity, and the belief of many biologists that each and any species can be critically important in maintaining the structure and diversity of existing ecosystems.

However, my suggestion that in conservation, some species matter more than others, was not intended to imply that some species *ought* to be given greater importance than others in conservation, but that in my experience they often were. Conservationists are a strange bunch, and while everyone preaches the importance of all biodiversity, from tardigrade to tiger, conservationists repeatedly act as if it were the large, charismatic, attractive species that matter most.

Conservationists concentrate on particular species for a number of reasons.[11] First, species are the building blocks of ecosystem and biosphere, and their survival is essential to all wider conservation goals. Second, isolated populations of species represent one of the chief units on which natural selection operates. Third, there are relatively plentiful data available on species, making them natural choices for monitoring the success of conservation, as well as the only obvious currency within which to talk about biological diversity. Above all, species are understood by people, whereas concepts like genetic diversity or ecosystems remain fuzzy.

It is for this last reason that conservationists have often presented their work through particular species, as means to enlist public support. The World Wildlife Fund's selection of the giant panda as its symbol, like that of the Jersey Wildlife Preservation Trust of the dodo, was quite deliberate.[12] These species were intended to be symbolic of the threat of extinction and to awaken public sympathy for those species threatened with extinction. Species were used as the flagships for campaigns because they worked with the public. With a little imagination, a 'flagship' species could focus concern on what might otherwise be an amorphous problem. A good example is the forest conservation campaign launched by the Fauna Preservation Society (FPS) in 1989. Although this was explicitly habitat-based, the FPS built it round a flagship species – in this case the orang-utan. The campaign was named 'Red Alert'. It began with a survey of central Borneo's forests (funded by a donation from the Vincent Wildlife Trust) in 1989. Whatever the problem, for a while it seemed that conservation could find a species to represent it.[13]

The favour shown to particular species is nothing new. Animals were anthropomorphized by colonial observers in the 19th and 20th centuries, and hunters in particular almost universally accorded human traits both to their chosen prey (the noble antelope, the brave elephant), and to 'vermin'. Until very recently, nobody had a good word to say for the African wild dog (alternatively the spotted dog) or the hyena, any more than the cougar or the wolf. In January and February 1901, Theodore Roosevelt killed 14 cougars in Colorado, chasing them down with dogs and sometimes photographing them before shooting them. He said they looked like 'large, malevolent pussies'.[14] Roosevelt was in good company: as noted in Chapter 5, the legendary conservationist Aldo Leopold, founder of the discipline of game management, was for many years an indefatigable promoter of the control of carnivore predators of game.[15]

In colonial Africa, administrators also placed some wild animals beyond the pale. Crop raiders were cast as villains by most observers. Hippopotami, for example, were widely disliked early in the 20th century. In the Sudan, Lord Cromer reported to the Colonial Office that in the narrow rivers of the Bahr-el-Ghazal 'they swarm and are a positive pest', and suggested that they 'should be treated as vermin, and shot on sight'.[16] Col. Hayes Sadler wrote from the Uganda Protectorate protesting that hippos should be included in the list of the partly protected animals: 'this mischievous beast has more of original sin in its nature than it is generally given credit for, and has but little to show in return. Not content with making nightly raids on all cultivation within its reach along the shores of our lakes and banks of our rivers, it indulges in wanton attacks on boats and canoes, and is a real source of danger to life at the ferry at Jinja and in the narrow passages of the Nile'.[17]

Hunters had clear likes and dislikes, and so too did settlers. In Kenya the preservation of some species from hunting was much more acceptable than others. In the 1930s, London-based conservationists heard that public opinion about game shooting in Kenya was 'floppy' – people liked giraffe and impala, and would report anyone who shot them. However, anyone (that is any settler) shooting a rhinoceros was said to be popularly regarded as 'something of a hero'.[18]

RED FOR DANGER

Concern for species formed the centrepiece of the new international conservation movement after the Second World War. Of course, this reflected the long-standing interests of conservationists within the SPFE and outside, but it was American influence that was decisive, particularly the work of Hal Coolidge. In 1930, he had helped found the Boone and Crockett Club's American Committee for International Wildlife Preservation, which had in turn funded a series of studies of endangered species, Glover Allen's *Extinct and Vanishing Mammals of the Western Hemisphere* in 1942, and a companion volume on the Old World in 1945.[19] Coolidge was elected the first Vice-President of the IUPN at Fontainebleau in 1948 (see Chapter 3).[20]

The Fontainebleau meeting that established IUPN set out six areas of work: to safeguard species and habitats, to apply existing knowledge of conservation, to promote conservation education, to instigate international agreements for the protection of nature, to increase scientific knowledge relevant to conservation, and to disseminate information that will promote conservation.[21] All of these were engaged with energetically from the earliest stage, with the tiny IUPN Secretariat developing its role as catalyst of what Martin Holdgate calls the 'Green Web' of members. Of all these charges, the first stood out, the challenge 'to participate in safeguarding those parts of nature, habitats or species which are in danger of being destroyed'.[22]

At the Lake Success Conference, Hal Coolidge led the foundation of an organization to pursue the problem of endangered species, the Survival Service, with funding from UNESCO.[23] He copied the structure of the US National Academy of Sciences, drawing upon volunteer experts, working mostly by correspondence. By 1949 IUPN was starting to make approaches to newly independent governments about the status of particular rare species, for example Indonesia (orang-utan and Javan and Sumatran rhinoceros), Nepal and India (one-horned rhinoceros), as well as Algeria, Morocco, Belgium, the Netherlands, Switzerland, the United Kingdom, Italy and the military authorities in Germany. Some of these had limited success. As had become familiar to the SPFE in the colonial world as colonial governments gained in competence and freedom, enquiries were often greeted by 'polite rebuffs', or bureaucratic deflection.[24]

In 1954, the Survival Service became active in the field, when Hal Coolidge obtained a grant to appoint Lee Talbot as an ecologist-at-large.[25] He came to Europe to talk to IUPN and various experts (visiting the United Kingdom, Belgium, Holland, Germany, France and Denmark), then set off on a long tour through the Middle East and Asia (everywhere from Libya to Iraq, then on through Pakistan, Nepal and India, Thailand, Indonesia, Malaya, Burma, Cambodia, the Philippines and Japan). He gathered data on six species at the top of the IUCN's list (Sumatran, Indian and Javan rhinoceros, Indian lion, Arabian oryx and Syrian wild ass), and acted as what Hal Coolidge described as 'goodwill ambassador' across Asia, considering how the IUPN could work with governments and other bodies. He spoke to various heads of state, including Nehru in India; two months later Nehru declared the Gir Forest a national park.[26]

In 1956, the Survival Service became a permanent Commission of IUCN, chaired by Hal Coolidge.[27] In 1958 he handed over to Lieutenant Colonel C L Boyle, Secretary of the Fauna Preservation Society. The format was a great success, acting as a clearing-house for information on threats, as a network for the collection of advice and ideas, and as a platform for campaigns on particular species. 'Threatened species' proved a most effective shorthand for wider conservation problems, well-suited to raising public support both for specific species and for the wider ideas of conservationists.

At the centre of the SSC's work were the *Red Data Books* (more recently called *Red Lists*), a brainchild of Peter Scott. A list of threatened species was drawn up at Lake Success (14 mammals and 13 birds),[28] primarily as a means of concentrating the minds of those gathered on the task of halting extinction. This was not the first time that such a thing had been proposed. Major Austen had recommended in 1925 that the SPFE publish an annual list of species considered 'in danger of extinction', but Peter Chalmers-Mitchell (of London Zoo) spoke against the idea. He argued that it might 'arouse the cupidity of unscrupulous collectors catering for foreign zoological gardens or museums', and make the problem worse.[29] As a compromise, it was agreed that the list could be sent to local governments, so that at least the governing elite in British colonies (presumably beyond corruption by the base attractions of the wild animal trade) were informed.

The Survival Service Commission had no such scruples. They published a list of animals and plants threatened with extinction, supplemented by Lieutenant Colonel Boyle with a card file index. The *Red Data Book* was intended as a complete record of the status and conservation problems of all rare and endangered animal and plant species. Data for mammals were relatively easily collated, and there was information of some kind for birds, and a little for reptiles. Other taxa were much less well known, and information took longer to acquire and organize.[30]

The first of a series of Red Data Books were produced from 1962.[31] Initially about 50 copies of these were produced, in loose-leaf format, for WWF and IUCN staff. Later they were published. The first, for mammals, was produced in 1962, and by 1973 there were five (mammals, birds, amphibians and reptiles, fish, and flowering plants). By 1975, the mammals Red Data Book listed 150 endangered species, 79 vulnerable, 52 rare, 34 indeterminate and 6 out of danger species.[32] In 1979, the Survival Service Commission established the Species Conservation Monitoring Unit, to compile the Red Data Books as well as collect data on wildlife trade and to work on threatened plants.[33]

The SSC (since 1980 the Species Survival Commission) is still active, a network of more than 8000 people in a wide variety of partner organizations, and its Red Lists are the foundation of most evaluations of the conservation status of plant and animal species.[34] In 1994 a scientifically rigorous approach was developed to determine risks of extinction that were applicable to all species and subspecies. The IUCN Red List Programme now seeks not only to identify and document those species most in need of conservation attention if global extinction rates are to be reduced, but also to provide a global index of the state of degeneration of biodiversity. The Red List is web accessible, and contains over 18,000 species and subspecies, including all known birds and mammals. Rather depressingly, 10,000 of these are regarded as threatened.[35]

Some of those threatened species have served as very effective flagships of wider conservation efforts. The history of conservation in the second half of the 20th century abounds with examples of single-species projects. These held a particular attraction for conservation organizations hard-pressed to influence government, and lacking secure and substantial resources. Conservation organizations, like the wider environmental movement of which they were forerunners, therefore worked hard to influence public opinion. By launching appeals, making use of the print and increasingly the television media, they were able at a stroke to win citizens in the First World to their cause, build a constituency that might pressure their governments into action, and raise funds to take specific action. By clever selection of targets for action, this could itself become an object lesson in conservation's beliefs both about the urgency and moral rightness of their task. The most effective, and emotive, subjects for public conservation campaigns were individual species of animal.

The power of the species focus to capture and hold the attention of conservationists and their supporters is shown by the remarkable enthusiasm for bats shown by conservationists in the 1980s. IUCN formed a Chiroptera Specialist Group in 1975, with support from WWF and the Fauna and Flora Preservation Society (FFPS).[36] Although not perhaps immediately charismatic, bats offered the advantage of novelty to the FFPS, then a small organization with big ideas but little money, and a bat project was developed in 1982.[37] A Bat Conservation Officer was appointed in 1984, and FFPS led a campaign to make the United Kingdom legislation protecting all bat species effective (including the memorable bumper sticker 'bats need friends', also the title of a BBC documentary in 1987).[38] There was an upsurge of interest in bat conservation across the country, with the formation of numerous local bat groups: in 1985 the London Bat Survey (FFPS) was launched by Ken Livingstone (then Leader of the Greater London Council).

The high point for bats as conservation icons in the United Kingdom was 1986, declared 'National Bat Year', launched by FFPS with funding help from WWF, the Nature Conservancy Council, and the Vincent Wildlife Trust. A six-week exhibition at the British Museum of Natural History was attended by 30–40,000 people, and there were lectures in the Queen Elizabeth Hall, along with bat-themed films, poetry, graphic art and antiques. Hundreds of 'bat walks' were held all over the country as well as fundraising events such as dances and barbeques, and bat stalls at county shows; schoolchildren were encouraged to make bat boxes. FPS claimed that 'national bat year' received over 10,000 column inches of newsprint in its first six months and was publicized internationally on TV and radio in Europe, Australia and Canada. Arguably, National Bat Year was good for bats, although not so good as a fundraiser for the FFPS itself, for people installed bat boxes individually and supported local initiatives rather than contribute to the central FFPS fund for bat boxes and roost protection grilles.

Bat enthusiasts however proved persistent. Globally, the 100 species of bats face a diverse array of threats, ranging from habitat loss or modification, disturbance of roost sites, persecution, to excessive harvesting for food (bats are considered a delicacy, especially on Indian Ocean and some Pacific islands: between 1981 and 1989, 13,000 flying foxes were imported into Guam annually). The IUCN and the Species Survival Commission published Action Plans for megachiropteran bats (167 species) in 1992, and microchiropterans (834 species) in 2001: over 200 species were classified as threatened, with 29 critically endangered, particularly island endemics.[39] Bats have many enemies, but they also have friends. They are a testament to the power of species to motivate conservation action.

OPERATION SAVE THE SPECIES

Campaigns to 'save' particular species were an important feature of conservation action on the ground in many instances after the Second World War, and within the fairly specific goals of species-based conservation, a successful one. The language of these various campaigns was characteristically militaristic: these were 'operations', 'campaigns' or 'projects'. They had neat titles, and used the language of targets, goals and logistics. In part this reflected the public respect in the United States and Europe for the power of military planning (with its specific focus, realism, energy, commitment, resources and technology), as well as a sense of the redemptive possibility of beating swords into ploughshares.[40] In part it also reflected the military experience of some of those involved in conservation planning.

The classic example of conservation action being driven by a charismatic species is probably the WWF 'Project Tiger campaign', launched in 1972, aiming to raise US$1 million.[41] A census in 1970 showed that the population of tigers in India had fallen from an estimated 40,000 in 1930 to only 1800, in directly inverse proportion to the growth in rural population and habitat change. Within 18 months, £800,000 had been raised for tiger conservation worldwide. Project Tiger won support at the highest level in India, with a special task force appointed by Mrs Indira Gandhi. With scientific and technical support from IUCN and WWF, the Indian Government created 11 new reserves explicitly for tigers. Most of these were small (the largest 2840 square kilometres), and in total covered 16,000 square kilometres. Even so, 33 villages were moved, creating a store of social and political problems that reverberate to the present day. In biological terms, the programme was reported to be successful, with a rise from 268 tigers in nine reserves in 1872 to 749 in 11 reserves in 1980.[42] Project Tiger was described in 1973 as a 'multi-national co-operative project', with India, Nepal, Bhutan and Bangladesh creating reserves, and WWF national appeals in 18 countries raising money.[43] China joined the project in 1979, following a visit from Sir Peter Scott, chair of the World Wildlife Fund, the Survival Service Commission of IUCN and the FPS.

There have been many other such 'operation save the species' schemes. In 1972 the FPS backed 'Operation Blackbuck', an attempt to reintroduce blackbuck to India.[44] In the same year, the FPS sought funds from readers of *Oryx* for an IUCN campaign by Russel Mittermeier to save the lion marmoset by creating a 3000 hectare reserve and captive breeding programme. In many cases these campaigns were shared between organizations, often with WWF taking the lead. Thus in 1980, when the FPS and the People's Trust for Endangered Species launched an appeal for the scimitar-horned oryx in West Africa, an anonymous German donor gave US$0.45 million to the WWF for this purpose in Niger.[45] West Africa had been rather ignored by international organizations obsessed with the plains game of East Africa: many mammals in arid West Africa were endangered by lack of protection, lack of reserves, poor management, availability of improved firearms and motor vehicles, and the increased guarding of water holes for livestock by nomads.[46] Not all campaigns however were so exotic: 1985 saw 'Operation Tortoise' launched, with a smaller FPS spinoff campaign on the Mediterranean Tortoise, with car stickers funded by Citroen.

The 1960s were the heyday of costly and flamboyant capture-release programmes for individual species. The classic group subjected to the indignity of salvation in this way were rhinoceroses. The various species of rhinoceros held pride of place on the Survival Service's first list of endangered species in

1948, and were repeatedly in the news in subsequent decades. The Sumatran, Indian and Javan rhinoceros were a major focus of Lee Talbot's work in the 1950s. The status of Indian rhinoceros in India itself was relatively well known, with about 400 animals in a series of reserves at the end of the 1950s. A special mission to Nepal by E P Gee for the Survival Service Commission in 1959 showed declining numbers in shrinking habitat, but not the collapse that had been feared.[47]

By the end of the 1950s, it was the two African rhinoceros species that were of greatest concern internationally. Poaching of the white rhinoceros for its horn (important in eastern medicine and for dagger handles in the Persian Gulf) had brought it to the verge of extinction across much of its range. Even in game reserves and national parks the species was not secure, and conservationists began an unprecedented and intensely physical campaign to capture those that remained, and move them to new locations where they could be protected, and also to create captive populations.

In Uganda in the early 1960s, white rhinoceros numbers had declined catastrophically west of the Nile. The decision was therefore taken to capture and move them into the Murchison Falls National Park. At first animals were lassoed from moving vehicles, and three of the eight animals captured died. Later, tranquillizing drugs were developed, and rhinos were darted with a crossbow from helicopters and land rovers, the whole operation being filmed by Anglia Television for their *Survival* series of wildlife documentaries.[48] At the same time, a major programme began to capture white rhinos in the Umfolozi Game Reserve in Natal, South Africa.

When the Umfolozi reserve was declared in 1895, it was the last refuge of the white rhino, shot out elsewhere in southern Africa (in 1898 Frederick Selous suggested there might be only 20 left).[49] The 1893 game law had taken white rhinoceros off the list of protected 'royal game', and sport hunters led a newspaper campaign (aimed against the Zululand administration) for its preservation that became unified with the proposal for game reserves.[50]

The problem in Natal was in a sense the reverse of that in Uganda: the population of white rhinoceros was large and growing (437 were counted in an aerial survey in 1953, in a reserve of only 29,000 hectares). By the 1960s, the reserve was becoming increasingly isolated in settled and farmed land; until 1962 it was unfenced, and rhinos moved freely onto adjoining farmed land. That became increasingly unacceptable, and rhino numbers had to be reduced. As they were extinct elsewhere in Africa, and globally threatened, capture and release for restocking was an obvious strategy for the Natal Parks Board. As Ian Player, leader of the programme, put it in 1972, 'fortunately for the white rhino and mankind, scientific advance made the latter possible.[51]

The Natal Parks Board relocation programme drew on the expertise of A M Harthoorn in tranquilizing animals for capture in Uganda. Work began in 1960, with a gun delivering a dart that contained a diverse cocktail of drugs. The idea was to dart the animal and pursue it (on horseback) until it stopped, then manhandle it into a crate and onto a truck for transportation to holding pens. There was a considerable death toll until a suitable mixture and dosages were devised, and ways were found to minimize the perils of hostile traffic policemen, inclement weather, infected dart wounds and other injuries. Ian Player's account of the operation, *The White Rhino Saga*, tells it as a series of deeds of derring-do, with a fair role call of human and animal casualties. But the technology eventually worked, and by the end of March 1962 18 white rhino had been captured and shipped off to game reserves across Natal. Orders began to come in from further afield. Kruger National Park ordered 12, the Orange Free State four and Southern Rhodesia eight (in 1962 the FPS contributed to the cost of moving eight animals to Southern Rhodesia). Zoos all over the world (including Bronx, San Diego, Berlin, Milwaukee and Chester) were also cabling in orders, despite an asking price of 6000 rand per pair. By 1965, IUCN declared the white rhino 'saved'.[52]

But the value of the white rhino export was material as well as cultural: Ian Player notes that the experience shows that investment in conservation of a rare species can reap handsome dividends. By the end of 1970, a total of 400 white rhino had been captured and released into their former habitat, and 150 sold to zoos. There were still over 2000 at large in Umfolozi and Hluhluwe Reserves. In 1969, Ian Player travelled to Europe and North America on a sales campaign for the Natal Parks Board, offering groups of 20 rhinos at a time to safari parks and zoos such as London Zoo's Whipsnade, San Diego Zoo's San Pasqual Animal Park and Lion Country Safari of Los Angeles. Enquiries came in from Peking and Moscow, and the whole operation was geared up, with 58 white rhino exported in 1970 and 78 in 1971. Between 1970 and 1972, the trade was worth £250,000, and it won important benefits in international goodwill for Apartheid South Africa.

The techniques for rhino capture developed in Uganda and South Africa have been applied elsewhere. In 1970, for example, the Southern Rhodesian government began their 'Operation Rhino', to capture black rhinos at risk from poaching in the Zambezi Valley, and remove them to the newly-created GonareZou National Park in the southeast Lowveld. Unlike their relatively placid grazing cousins, black rhinos are aggressive and hard to capture, especially in the broken terrain they favour. Darting technology had improved by 1970, but the work remained hazardous for both man and beast. Forty-one animals were successfully translocated in 1970, and 38 in 1971.[53]

Rhinos were moved again in 1970, when survivors from the poaching of white rhinos in Garamba National Park in Congo by Sudanese rebels were taken to temporary safety in Murchison Falls National Park in Uganda, and in 1979, when poaching had begun to threaten extinction of black rhino in East Africa.[54] A new 'Operation Rhino' was launched in 1980, led by the WWF, who had raised US$1.3 million for this purpose within a year. The FPS and the People's Trust for Endangered Species were also involved, and a campaign for action was developed across eight countries, including the creation of anti-poaching units and guard posts, investigation units modelled on criminal investigation departments, and international intelligence services, as well as programmes of public education and research. The FPS initially gave £20,000 with a further £20,000 promised for the future, urging its members to support the campaign.[55]

Population translocation as a conservation strategy continues to develop in its complexity. In the 1990s, the George Adamson Wildlife Preservation Trust and Tony Fitzjohn/George Adamson African Wildlife Preservation Trust funded importation of black rhinoceros from South Africa into a secure 7000 hectare sanctuary within the Mkomazi Game Reserve in Tanzania.[56] Four animals were moved to Mkomazi in November 1997 from the Addo Elephant National Park. They are actually originally East African animals *Diceros bicornis michaeli*. Their translocation will allow Addo to re-stock with the southern African subspecies, purchased from game ranches in Namibia. Such introductions are not, however, without controversy. In the Mkomazi case, the rhino sanctuary was placed in a protected area whose strict 'wilderness' management is strongly opposed by local people (see Chapter 5). The eviction of pastoralists from the Mkomazi Game Reserve by the Tanzanian government in 1988 has been the subject of a protracted legal battle, which reached the Tanzanian High Court in 1999.[57] What might seem at one level an inspired strategy for rhinoceros conservation can also be viewed as a very different (and quite unacceptable) story of imperialistic conservation. The costs of this kind of 'fortress' conservation area also daunting: the expenses of fencing the sanctuary capture, veterinary fees, transport and security all added up to nearly US$90,000 per animal in the first year.

Nonetheless, rhinoceros translocation is in many ways a conservation success story. There are now more than 8440 southern white rhinos in 247 wild populations, with an additional 704 animals in captive breeding institutions worldwide. Numbers are increasing in protected areas, and the white rhino is now classified as 'Lower Risk – Conservation Dependent' by the IUCN African Rhino Specialist Group.[58] White rhinos are the jewel in the crown of many large private wildlife ranches, and group wildlife 'conservancies' in southern Africa. These businesses, providing both wildlife viewing holidays and hunting safaris, proved commercially very successful in South Africa, Namibia and Zimbabwe in the 1990s, and have been able to pay for sufficient security staff to deter poaching, which has drastically reduced populations elsewhere.

The northern white rhino subspecies however remains classified as 'Critically Endangered'. In 1960, there were an estimated 2250 animals in the wild; today there is only one wild population of only 25 animals. Furthermore, there are only nine ageing and non-breeding animals in captivity, in two zoos.[59] The black rhino is doing a little better, although numbers have fallen drastically since the 1960s, when there were over 100,000 black rhino in the wild. In the 1970s, it was estimated that global consumption of rhino horn was about 7.75 tonnes, representing 2580 animals.[60] In 1997 there were estimated to be only 2600 animals left in the wild and 235 in captivity. Furthermore, of the four black rhino subspecies, the western black rhino was reduced to about 10 animals scattered across northern Cameroon. The south-central subspecies is the most numerous, with a stable estimated population of 1360. Despite all the costly efforts to capture and protect black rhino, the species was classified as Critically Endangered in the 1996 Red List of Threatened Animals.

THE WILD CAPTIVE

There is, of course, an irony in the whole idea of capturing wild species in order to save them. As has been described in previous chapters, the very 'wildness' of nature has been an important element in conservation concern throughout its history. That wildness has for many been epitomized by large mammals roaming abroad. Once captive and enclosed, or pacified to be treated by veterinarians, that wildness is somewhat compromised. The distinction between nature reserve and farm, between cage and national park, is, in a sense, eroded. Indeed, that erosion has been quite deliberate, the artifice of the naturalized zoo enclosure creating an illusion of naturalness for the visitor, while the scientific knowledge and skill of the zoo keeper established a healthy and calm environment for wild animals that would allow them to behave in a ways they had evolved to do, and to breed.[61]

The capture of white rhinos in Umfolozi and Uganda, as of black rhinos in southern Rhodesia, was initially for translocation to other game reserves. The captivity of these animals was partial and temporary. Only latterly did the Natal Parks Board extend their sales to zoos, and create a captive 'virtual herd', distributed across the world. In other instances, the last representatives of wild species were captured explicitly for such destinations, hauled aboard a zoological Noah's ark as the founders of a captive breeding programme.

Reputable zoos were in the forefront of attempts to promote conservation throughout the 20th century. The New York Zoological Society's Bronx Zoo, opened in 1899, was created in the ancient woodland of south Bronx Park, a place in which wild animals could be kept in conditions 'most closely approximating those with which nature usually surrounds them'. The zoo was imagined as a place that would cultivate in New Yorkers the knowledge and love of nature.[62] In 1946, the SPFE asserted grandly that 'zoos should be regarded as places of instruction through which the peoples of the world may be led to take an interest in wild life, leading up to the determination to preserve it in all its pristine beauty and grandeur in its natural environment for the benefit of present and future generations of men'.[63] Many leading conservationists found their platform in zoological associations. In the 1920s and 1930s such people included William Hornaday and William Beebee at the New York Zoological Society, Chalmers-Mitchell or Julian Huxley at the Zoological Society of London. Sir Peter Chalmers-Mitchell, Director of the London Zoo for 32 years, believed that 'properly-directed' zoos could play a valuable part in national education, especially where animals could be shown in 'comparative freedom'. His work at Whipsnade Park was a direct outworking of this view, and was of a piece with his involvement with the Conference that resulted in the Africa Convention of 1933, and the attempt to extend this to southeast Asia and Australasia through a further conference in 1939.[64] Chalmers-Mitchell saw a common ground between zoos and reserves, envisaging 'protected stations' established in reserves where visitors could be transported by silent elevated electric railways from viewpoint to viewpoint, and a continuity between city zoos and country parks (of which Whipsnade was perhaps the model).[65]

In the 1950s and 1960s, Bernhard Grzimek was Director of the Frankfurt Zoological Gardens, but also a leading advocate of *in-situ* conservation in national parks. Notably in this case he was a passionate polemicist for the integrity of the Serengeti-Mara ecosystem in the Serengeti National Park (see Chapter 5).[66] For such people, concern for conservation in game parks and reserves was linked to their interest in zoological collections. They saw national parks, rural wildlife collections and urban zoos as part of a continuum of opportunities for people to see and become interested in the fate of wildlife. From 1948, the President of the New York Zoological Society was Fairfield Osborn, son of the founder and a leading advocate of environmentalism well before it became a mass movement in the 1960s. The Bronx Zoo's naturalistic 'African Plains' exhibit (opened in 1941) both set new standards for the exhibition of animals to the public, and demonstrated the link that could be made between conservation *ex situ* (in zoos) and *in situ* (on the ground). In 1963, the New York Zoological Society established an 'Exhibition and Graphic Arts Department' to develop the verisimilitude of the zoo's human-made nature, its exhibits have included the World of Darkness (1960s), World of Birds and Wild Asia in the 1970s, Jungle World (1980s) and Congo Gorilla Forest (1990s).[67]

Rather like the game-hunting conservationists of the first half of the century, zoo-loving conservationists therefore faced important decisions. They had to differentiate between the specialized and extremely careful animal collecting that might serve the conservation objectives of proper zoos, and the reprehensible behaviour of cowboys seeking only their own profit from an unreasonable trade. Keith Caldwell noted in 1927 that the willingness of animal collectors to buy young animals for zoos could lead to excessive shooting of adults.[68] Furthermore, for the first decades of the century, zoos were as much a drain on wild animals as museums. Zoological Gardens could not be done away with, if only because they were so valuable for education, but at that time 'very few specimens of wild animals can be established in Zoological gardens to the extent of rendering importation from wild stock unnecessary'.[69] Indeed, and ironically, this need for animals was itself an argument for conservation on the ground: 'one contemplates with alarm the time when the splendid animals of Africa will have so far been wiped out that it will be impossible to replenish our stocks in the various Zoological Gardens'.[70] However, that trade could not be in improper hands: in 1928, the Secretary of State for the Colonies accepted the SPFE's suggestion that the Director of the British Museum of Natural History should be asked to advise the governors of colonies on the standing of those applying to collect animals, and the scientific merits of their applications.[71]

In the second half of the 20th century, zoos across the world were energetic in self-regulation and improvement. Thus in the United Kingdom, the Zoo Federation of Great Britain and Ireland was established in 1966, and acted as a club supportive of well-run conservation-minded zoos, and hostile to menageries. Eventually, in 1981, the Zoos Licensing Act was passed, giving local authorities the power to regulate, inspect (and if necessary close) zoos. Speaking for conservationists who saw zoos as both historically part of the problem as well as potentially part of the solution to conservation, the Fauna and Flora Preservation Society believed that this was not stringent enough, although they hoped that pressure would build up for stronger measures.[72]

The common ground between zoos and field conservation was the idea of captive breeding of endangered species for re-introduction to the wild. This idea was well established. The director of the Bronx Zoo, William T Hornaday, acquired bison for the Bronx Zoo in October 1899, the year the zoo opened. In 1905, the New York Zoological Society sponsored the founding of the American Bison Society, which pushed for national protection for the bison (then reduced to about 1000 animals in the wild) and its habitat. In 1907, 15 bison bred at the Bronx Zoo were released in the Wichita Mountain Preserve in Oklahoma, with further releases in other refuges in Montana, South Dakota and Nebraska.[73]

By the 1960s, the idea of captive breeding in zoos was familiar, at least in theory. It was generally accepted by conservationists, but only if the purpose was re-introduction into the wild.[74] Zoos might be a means to further conservation, but such '*ex-situ*' strategies were not to be confused with the real thing. In 1946 the SPFE noted 'it is no part of the policy of the Fauna Society to preserve wild life as a reservoir from which to draw animals for exhibition in zoos... It is Nature we seek to protect, not museums of live, still less of dead animals'.[75]

A symposium on 'zoos and conservation' in London in June 1964 addressed the role of zoos in conservation explicitly. The Director of Basel Zoo noted that advances in nutrition, hygiene and veterinary science (particularly tranquillizers) meant that captive animals could be bred successfully, and the Director of the New York Zoo pointed out that some captive-bred introductions into the wild had been successful.[76] On the other hand, the Chief Game Warden of Kenya, Ian Grimwood, pointed out that the death toll in animal capture could be huge, with many animals dying in transit.[77] The debate was continued at a major conference at San Diego Zoo in October 1966, attended by Lee Talbot, Ian Grimwood and many luminaries of international conservation. The keynote address was given by Peter Scott. He identified six ways in which zoos could contribute to conservation. The first five were: education, promotion of aesthetic appreciation of animals, the study of threatened species, the breeding of threatened species, and fundraising. The sixth was by 'maintaining an acute sense of their responsibility' by not exhibiting rare animals with little prospect of breeding.[78]

In 1969, the Survival Service Commission issued guidelines on animal capture programmes. Capture was acceptable when animals were in danger of extinction, in order to establish captive breeding populations in captivity or to transfer to safer areas. Captive breeding could be a step towards the maintenance of viable populations in the wild, if it strengthened the viability of existing populations, diversified the fauna in the interests of good management or conserved a population whose existing habitat was threatened. Captures for commercial reasons were only acceptable if they fulfilled these criteria.[79]

Zoos found captive breeding an increasingly important justification for their existence. There were many advocates of this strategy, most notably Gerald Durrell, whose dissatisfaction with the zoos to which his animal collecting expeditions dispatched specimens led him to establish his own, on the island of Jersey.[80] The FPS and Jersey Wildlife Preservation Trust held a conference on breeding endangered species in captivity at Jersey Zoo in 1972, with a follow-up in London in 1976, and in San Diego in 1979.[81] At that meeting, Gerald Durrell described the success of the Jersey Wildlife Preservation Trust in breeding endangered endemic species of the Indian Ocean islands, including the pink pigeon, Meller's duck and Rodrigues fruit bat, while in Mauritius there was further success to report with breeding the Mauritius kestrel.[82]

SAVING THE UNICORNS

The classic single-species captive breeding story of the 20th century is probably the Arabian oryx,[83] partly because of the high profile of *Operation Oryx*, the attempt led by the FPS in the 1960s to capture wild Arabian oryx to provide the nucleus of a captive herd. The Arabian oryx is one of four oryx species, and the only one to occur outside Africa.[84] It had long been high on international conservation's list of species of concern, and was a specific focus of Lee Talbot's attention in 1954. In common with other mammal species, it had been in decline for many decades, the combination of rifle and motor vehicle making it vulnerable to hunters. It shared this fate with other mammals, such as the Asiatic lion, which was extinct in Arabia by the middle of the 19th century and the Asiatic cheetah, the last wild Saudi Arabian animal being shot in the early 1950s.[85] Three separate populations of oryx were believed to exist in the 1950s within the Aden Protectorate, but the last individuals were reported (or reported killed) from two of these between 1947 and 1951.[86] By the 1960s, the oryx was believed to be close to extinction throughout its range, with at most 80–100 animals in the Wadi Shuwait and Mitan.

In 1960, Michael Crouch, a member of the FPS, was posted as Assistant Adviser, Northern Deserts, East Aden Protectorate (today part of the Yemen

Republic, then under British colonial rule). In 1961 he reported to the tireless Lieutenant Colonel Boyle of the FPS that a large motorized hunting party from Qatar had shot no less than 48 oryx in December 1960.[87] A second expedition, led by D W A Johnson, on leave from the Hadhrami Bedouin Legion, caught two oryx (by throwing a shark net over them from a Land-rover), although both of them (one a pregnant female) died within a few days. Boyle informed the press and the Foreign Office of the threat to the oryx, but no official action was taken. The idea of establishing a reserve in Arabia was floated, but the difficulties involved were found to be too great. Boyle then, through both the FPS and the IUCN Species Survival Commission, conceived the notion of supporting an expedition to capture some of the few surviving oryx to build a captive breeding population.[88] The hope was to eventually re-establish the oryx in some part of the original habitat.

A meeting in July 1961 estimated the cost of such an expedition at £6000. The FPS publicity officer John Hillaby persuaded the *Daily Mail* Newspaper group to put up the money in exchange for exclusive rights to the story, and help in kind was received from a number of sources, particularly the Royal Air Force (who flew people and equipment into the desert, and eventually flew the oryx out to Kenya), and the East African Wildlife Society (who lent their small spotting plane). Then *The Times* reported in January 1962 that a further hunting party had killed 16 more oryx, and a story was circulated that the animal was finally extinct. The *Daily Mail* withdrew the balance of the grant, but the FPS decided to meet the cost from its own resources, and in April 1962 the expedition set out into the desert from the port of Mukalla.[89]

The expedition's members were widely experienced, and if Anthony Shepherd's engaging, slightly *Boys' Own* style, account of their adventures is to be believed, they needed to be. They were led by Major Ian Grimwood. He had read biology at Imperial College London, before joining the Frontier Force regiment of the Indian Army in 1935. He had survived forced labour Japanese prison camps and ended up commanding the regiment before leaving to join the Rhodesian Game Department as a biologist, and moving in 1960 to be Chief Game Warden of Kenya. He was an extremely hardy man, bouncing round the desert on the expedition's catching truck with broken ribs. The expedition's other members were as colourful: the deputy leader, Michael Crouch, for example, unusually a graduate of Limuru Girls' School in Kenya, Oxford and Cambridge; Peter Whitehead, who left school in England at the age of 14 for Australia, became a contractor breaking horses, and came via the Australian Army Supply Corps and Royal Australian Air Force to the job of agricultural extension officer in Nigeria and game ranger in Northern Rhodesia, Tanganyika and Kenya. The expedition was chronicled by Captain G A Shepherd of the Armoured Car Squadron of the Federal Regular Army (formerly Aden Protectorate Levies).[90]

The expedition met its share of logistical problems. They had decided to catch the oryx by roping them from a moving truck. The team had experimented with this technique in the Northern Frontier District of Kenya with the larger beisa oryx (courtesy of the wild animal dealer John Seago). A vehicle was converted by Ker and Downey Safaris in Nairobi and shipped out to Aden. Eventually this, and its successor (botched together in the field) failed, as did ground and aeroplane radios and a radio-location beacon. Nonetheless, the expedition spent a month searching an area of about 6000 square miles of stone and sand desert, with transport and signals support from the Hadhrami Bedouin Legion under Lieutenant Colonel Quaid (Pat) Gray. Four oryx were eventually captured, three bulls and one cow. Most chases were short, if hairy. One was long, lasting almost 20 minutes and covering several miles. That animal, one of the bulls, died from exhaustion soon after capture. The risk of exhaustion was recognized, but Ian Grimwood commented 'under the peculiar circumstances … when the species appeared doomed and the individual appeared certain to fall victim to the raiders on their next visit, it seemed justifiable to continue'.[91]

The other three oryx prospered, and were eventually flown to Nairobi by the Royal Air Force, with the aim of moving them to the Veterinary Quarantine Station at Isiolo in the arid north. However, an outbreak of foot and mouth disease put paid to this, and they were forced to remain in the damp cold of Nairobi. Infra-red lamps were eventually obtained to keep them warm, but over the first weekend, volunteers had to hang electric ovens (supplied by the East African Power and Lighting Company) around the walls to heat their quarters. In July of 1962 they were eventually moved to Isiolo, while an FPS committee was formed to decide where their ultimate destination should be.

In 1963, the Shikar-Safari club provided funds to transport the three captured oryx to the Maytag Zoo in Phoenix, Arizona, to form the core of a captive breeding herd. Sheikh Jabir Abdullah of Kuwait then donated his one remaining captive female to the FPS, and the Zoological Society of London allowed one of their female oryx to join the breeding group at Phoenix Zoo. Late in 1963, King Saud of Saudi Arabia offered four more oryx to the Arizona herd. The four new animals (2 males and 2 females) were transported through a special charter of Pan American Airways in 1964, with the cost shared by the Shikar-Safari Club and the American National Appeal of the WWF.[92] Ironically, when picking up the animals in Saudi Arabia, Ian Grimwood discovered that there were no fewer than 13 oryx in excellent condition living at the new Riyadh Zoo. Two of the donated animals had been born in Riyadh.

By 1962 therefore, there were small herds of oryx in captivity, in Phoenix and in Riyadh. However, the oryx proved not only, in Ian Grimwood's words, 'extraordinarily easy to catch', but also extraordinarily docile. Captive life apparently suited them. By 1967 eight calves had been born to the Phoenix herd, and although the first seven were all males, the challenge of building up a viable captive herd had begun.[93]

This was fortunate, because hunting of the remaining wild oryx continued. In 1962 there were reports of a small herd of oryx still in the wild in a remote area of Oman, around the Wahiba Sands. Publicity led to further field surveys (especially associated with oil exploration), and by 1967 there were thought to be up to 200 animals in the wild in Muscat and Oman.[94] However, hunting persisted, and the last animals were reported killed or captured in October 1972. However, the 'World Herd', established at Phoenix, San Diego and other zoos, was growing fast. It was managed by five trustees, the Arizona Zoological Society, the FPS, the Shikar-Safari Club of California, WWF-US and the Zoological Society of London. Controversially, in 1965 the Los Angeles Zoo had obtained a pair of oryx from Riyadh, via a Dutch animal dealer and at a very high price. They had also bred, producing a string of females. Rapprochement was eventually negotiated in 1971 at the instance of Lord Willingdon, Chairman of the FPS, and a male and female were exchanged. By 1972, the world herd was 34 animals, and oryx began to be loaned out to other zoos, initially San Diego and then Brownsville. In 1979, the stud book listed 159 males and 163 females in captivity, with 48 calves born in the year. Animals were dispersed to East Berlin, Rotterdam, Hamburg and Zurich. There were also a number of herds within Arabia itself, in Qatar, Abu Dhabi and Dubai, with between 80 and 100 animals in all. The first calf was born in London Zoo in 1985, just two years before the 25th anniversary of *Operation Oryx*.[95]

Captive breeding of oryx, both within and outside the world herd, was so successful that it was agreed in the late 1970s that the ownership of the animals in the World Herd would be turned over to the zoos that held them, provided that they arrange for adequate exchange of stock for breeding purposes.[96] By 1992 there were 1600 captive Arabian oryx worldwide.[97] It is not, however, the success of the captive breeding that makes the oryx interesting – it is the sustained attempt to return animals to the wild. In a sense this should have been easier than it is for many species, for the main threat to the oryx was not loss of habitat or conflict with people over land use, but simply relentless and thoughtless hunting by a small elite. Apart from oil extraction, the desert was not being converted for other uses, so if the hunting threat could be dealt with, the oryx might be returned to its old haunts again with some success.

In Jordan, the Royal Society for the Conservation of Nature (formerly the Royal Jordanian Hunting Club) acquired a 22 square kilometre block of semi-desert land as the Shaumari Wildlife Reserve, 118 kilometres from Amman and close to the new Biological Station at Azraq. In 1974 they approached Phoenix Zoo about the introduction of oryx to the site. In 1975 the project began with funding from WWF.[98] In 1978 the trustees of the World Herd sent four animals to Jordan.[99] In the same year, Los Angeles Zoo sent four pairs of oryx to Israel to found a herd in the Hai Bar reserve. The Jordanian animals were bred in captivity at Shaumari, until in 1983, 31 oryx were released into the fenced reserve.

In 1977, the Director of WWF's Department of Conservation carried out a feasibility study for re-introduction to the wild for the Government of Oman. The proposed reintroduction area was the bleak stony plateau of the Jiddat al Harasis.[100] Holding pens were built, and in 1980 San Diego Zoo sent ten oryx to

Oman, followed by a further five the following year. The first calf was born in Oman in 1981. In January 1982, ten animals were released into the open desert. By 1984 this herd numbered 13, and was completely independent, although subject to intensive scientific enquiry and protection by a veritable army of 42 bedouin guards. In April 1984, a further ten animals were released at this site.[101] By 1995 there were 280 animals in the wild, including 22 surviving founders.[102]

The Jordan and Oman releases were followed by others, particularly in Saudi Arabia.[103] Since 1990, 38 oryx from zoo collections and 34 oryx bred at a special National Commission for Wildlife Conservation facility have been released in a 2200 square kilometre fenced area in western Saudi Arabia, and since 1995 a further 83 animals have been released into a vast 12,000 square kilometre reserve in the south at 'Uruq Bani Ma'arid. This contains a core of 2000 square kilometres where all human activity is banned, a 5000 square kilometre zone around it where livestock are permitted, and a 5000 square kilometre controlled hunting reserve around that. The goal of the National Commission for Wildlife Conservation is to re-establish free-ranging self-sustaining populations of oryx within a framework of protected areas across their former range.

However, the oryx saga is by no means over. Hunting remains a threat, ironically in part in the form of capture of specimens for private collections. At least 40 oryx were taken from the wild in Oman in 1996. Shooting and hunting from vehicles also increased, causing drastic population decline. By September 1998, the wild population of oryx in Oman had been reduced to 138 animals, of which only 28 were females. Animals were once again taken from the wild to form a new captive herd.[104]

RELEASING THE CAPTIVE

Captive breeding both works and doesn't work for conservation. It works, in the sense that if great care is taken, animals can be captured, brought into captivity and bred, and re-released into the wild. However, there are two major snags. First, it is prohibitively expensive, and therefore wholly dependent on public support, either through sponsorship, membership of zoo charities, or visitors to a zoo collection. It is impossible to think of breeding more than a few species, and captive breeding tends to have been done for high-profile species like the Arabian oryx or hyper-rare island fauna like the Mauritius kestrel.[105] The second snag is that captive breeding, *ex-situ* conservation, is only a contribution to conservation if populations can be re-established in the wild. Otherwise it is little more than a farming technique to artificially maintain a gene pool, a living version of cryogenic storage of genetic material. Indeed, botanists use the latter technique (rather than botanic gardens) much more readily, and with less embarrassment, than animal conservationists.

In 1974, Richard Fitter reviewed progress with the conservation of the list of 14 threatened mammals and 13 threatened birds drawn up at the Lake Success

Conference in 1949.[106] What had happened in the intervening 25 years? Of the 27 species or subspecies, two were no longer regarded as taxonomically distinct from their near relatives (the Addo Bush elephant and the Marianas mallard) and three were extinct (Caribbean monk seal, thylacine or Tasmanian tiger and North African hartebeest). Three were so near extinction that nothing could be done (Arabian ostrich, pink-headed duck and Eskimo curlew), and the status of two more was unknown (Cuban ivory-billed woodpecker and Marianas megapode). Of the 18 remaining species, five were formally protected, but without active management (Mediterranean monk seal, kagu, eastern ground parrot, western banded anteater and chinchilla). That left ten that conservationists had actually done something active about. Six had been the subject of successful conservation programmes (mountain zebra, Javan rhinoceros, European bison, nene goose, Laysan duck and whooping crane). Programmes for the other four had been less successful (Indian rhinoceros, Asiatic lion, Bermuda petrel (cahow) and California condor). Fitter's analysis suggested that the most successful strategy had been the establishment of protected areas, then law enforcement. Captive breeding had played a role in the conservation of seven species (chinchilla, Asiatic lion, Indian rhinoceros, European bison, ne-ne, Laysan duck and whooping crane), but only three of these species had been returned to the wild (chinchilla, European bison and ne-ne).

Interestingly, Fitter argued that the direct intervention of the Survival Service Commission had been important in the survival of only two species, the Javan rhinoceros and Asiatic lion. It was governments that had sought to save the rest. Governments were, of course, inevitably the leading actors in conservation during the 20th century, with the powers to legislate to protect species and to designate protected areas. However, species-based conservation, and especially captive breeding, had a particular appeal to governments. Whatever their general convictions about the desirability of conservation, the extirpation of species within national borders provides unequivocal evidence of failure, and a clear focus for action. Once that focus is agreed, government scientists and others can be targeted to deal with it. Furthermore, rare and near-extinct species provide a valuable ideological focus for popular support for conservation. Rare species that can be presented as having a distinctive national identity attract elite government and public support. It helps if they are distinctive, charismatic or engaging.

By the 1960s, captive breeding was an accepted useful weapon in national conservation agencies' armoury, although a costly one. The potential, and the problems, of this approach can be seen in the case of four classic case studies, the swift fox in Canada, the black-footed ferret, the California condor and the Antiguan racer.

Swift foxes were once widely distributed in the Canadian prairies. They declined as the Great Plains grasslands were ploughed up, and they suffered from campaigns of trapping, poisoning and shooting of 'vermin' that accompanied settlement and land 'improvement'. By 1978, they had disappeared from their Canadian range, and by 1995 they had disappeared from over 90 per cent of their historic range in the United States.[107] Captive breeding began in western Canada in 1972, using animals from the United States (Colorado, Wyoming and South Dakota). Between 1983 and 1997, 841 captive bred and 91 relocated swift foxes had been reintroduced. In south central Saskatchewan, 420 animals were released between 1990 and 1997. A wild population was established, and breeding successfully, but its sustainability is not proven. A survey in 1997 showed a wild population in the area of 87 animals.

Black-footed ferrets are predators of prairie dogs, needing about 50 hectares of prairie dog colony to raise a litter. However, during the 20th century, as ranchers across the North American prairies poisoned prairie dogs and destroyed their towns, the ferret declined to tiny numbers. A captive breeding programme was begun in the 1970s, but was unsuccessful. By 1979 the ferret was believed extinct in the wild, and in captivity. Fortuitously, a further wild colony was discovered in 1981, and in 1985 captive breeding began again. By 1991, ferrets were being released into the wild. Despite this relative success, the species remains highly vulnerable to disease (canine distemper and sylvatic plague), and the effects of the genetic bottleneck the surviving population has undergone.[108]

The other classic example of captive breeding and re-release into the wild in recent decades has been the California Condor Recovery Program.[109] Condor numbers declined in the 20th century due to loss of habitat and food, shooting, lead poisoning and poison baits used to kill predators. They were listed as an endangered species in 1967, under a law that pre-dated the 1973 Endangered Species Act. In 1982, the condor population fell to only 22 birds, and the US Fish and Wildlife Service started collecting chicks and eggs for a captive breeding programme. By late 1984, only 15 condors remained in the wild. Seven of these died in rapid succession, and (amidst considerable controversy, in the adopted state of John Muir, and spiritual home of the Sierra Club) the remaining birds were captured for the captive breeding program. By 1987 no Californian condor was flying free.

Fortunately, the condor was persuaded to breed in captivity, and the US Fish and Wildlife Service began releasing California condors back into the wild in 1992. By 2002, 218 condor chicks had been raised in captivity; 66 birds had been released, with 14 in field pens ready for release and a further 103 in captivity at the Los Angeles Zoo, San Diego Wild Animal Park and the Peregrine Fund's World Center for Birds of Prey in Boise, Idaho. The first wild-laid California condor egg for 18 years was hatched in April 2002, and there were further nests in California and in the Grand Canyon, Arizona.

On 1 May 2002, the last of the birds captured from the wild (romantically named AC9) was released after 15 years in captivity, into the Sespe Condor Sanctuary near Fillmore, California, together with three juvenile birds. One of these was from an egg laid in the wild in the Santa Barbara back country but raised by AC9 in Los Angeles Zoo. The Fish and Wildlife Service laid great store by family ties and mentoring: AC9's mate in the wild was released in April 2000 from the same release site.[110]

Perhaps the swift fox, black-footed ferret and California condor are obvious candidates for the demanding investment in species recovery programmes, but the same logic seems to work for less obviously charismatic species. One such is the Antiguan Racer Conservation Project, which seeks to conserve the harmless but critically endangered snake, the Antiguan racer.[111] Asian mongooses were introduced to Antigua (in the Lesser Antilles in the eastern Caribbean) in the late 19th century to control introduced black rats. Within 60 years, the Antiguan racer had vanished completely from Antigua and most of its offshore islands. It was reported extinct in 1963, one of many island endemics to fall victim to introduced predators. However, a small colony survived on the 10 hectare Great Bird Island, 2.5 kilometres offshore. In 1995 a survey at the behest of the Antiguan Forestry Unit (part of the Ministry of Agriculture, Forestry and Fisheries in the Government of Antigua and Barbuda) located about 50 racers, and the Antiguan Racer Conservation Project was set up to secure the species' survival. The project involves a mix of local and international, government and non-government organizations (the Antiguan Forestry Unit, Environmental Awareness Group, the Island Resources Foundation, Fauna and Flora International, Black Hills State University and the Durrell Wildlife Conservation Trust).

The project has a range of goals. Black rats were eradicated from Great Bird Island by the end of 1995, and then (with mongoose where they occurred) from nine other offshore islets. In 1996, five racers were captured for a breeding programme at Jersey Zoo, with hopes to reintroduce the snake on small rat-free islands. So far so ordinary. More interestingly, a major public awareness campaign was instituted, aimed at both Antiguans and tourists. In addition to visits to Great Bird Island and conventional wildlife talks, an intensive schools campaign has been organized. Children have been taught about the snake and its conservation, and shown a live specimen. Studies suggest that this has had a significant effect on attitudes and awareness.[112]

SPECIES *IN SITU*

Captive breeding is only one dimension of species-focused conservation. Species have also been highly effective in providing the focus for *in-situ* conservation, for example to gather and direct support for a national park. The classic charismatic species in terms of habitat conservation in the 20th was probably the mountain gorilla. The importance of mountain gorillas to conservation in the past century was outlined briefly in Chapter 1. At different periods they have epitomized the challenges facing conservation, and the strategies proposed for their conservation have tended to lead discussions about conservation more generally. In particular, mountain gorillas have been a test case for *in-situ* conservation. The threat posed by the collection of specimens for display outside Africa was clearly recognized by the 1920s. In 1924, C W

Hobley informed the Museums Association that 14 mountain gorillas had recently been shot for museums, and four caught alive to sell to zoos. He estimated that 50 had been killed since the end of the First World War, and that 'if strict preservation is not instituted they will soon disappear'. This was already by then a public issue – he noted that there had been recent debate in *The Times*.[113]

Once the Parc National Albert had been declared in the Belgian Congo in 1925, Belgian conservationists were indefatigable in urging similar protection for forest habitat in adjacent British territory, in southwest Uganda. Thus in 1929, Baron de Cartier de Marchienne again brought forward the question of declaring a portion of Uganda abutting the Belgian Congo a National Park for the protection of the gorilla. The SPFE Chairman stated that while the Executive Committee had discussed this, there was nothing yet to communicate to the society.[114] In 1931, Peter Chalmers-Mitchell repeated the call for a national park adjacent to the Parc National Albert in 1931 – indeed, not just a national park, but an international one.[115] However, while the Ugandan side of the Virunga volcanoes was made a game sanctuary and a forest reserve in the 1930s, no national park was created, despite the efforts of Major Hingston, Chalmers-Mitchell, and the Belgian government in the 1930s, and despite protection on the Rwandan slopes of the Virunga volcanoes.

International conservationists addressed themselves to the problem periodically, but poaching, forest loss and intensifying human use of forest environments grew in all three countries. Wild gorilla populations were falling. It was only in 1978 that the issue of gorilla conservation won sufficient public attention to stimulate decisive action. As narrated in Chapter 1, the critical event was the killing by poachers in December 1978 of a young male mountain gorilla that was part of Dian Fossey's habituated research group in the Parc National des Volcans in Rwanda. Digit, one of a group that Fossey had been studying since 1967, was something of a television star, having featured in a film by Anglia TV, playing with Fossey's pencil and notebook. His photograph had also been turned into a tourist poster with the slogan 'come and see me in Rwanda' by the government. When Brian Jackman wrote of his death in the *Sunday Times*, the severity of the problem of poaching received a burst of publicity. The bizarre nature of the trade in gorilla body parts, the patent barbarity of the amputation and economic absurdity that someone would kill for a trivial sum an animal capable of sustaining a long-term tourist market, made Digit's death an ideal subject for a public campaign. In a letter to the FPS, Dian Fossey wrote, that the loss of Digit from the Karisimbi population could be 'the beginning of the end' for the surviving mountain gorillas in Rwanda.

The FPS, with the People's Trust for Endangered Species (PTES) set up an appeal, publicized by the *Sunday Times*, and quickly raised £8000. Encouraged, FPS set up the Mountain Gorilla Project, and launched a larger appeal for £50,000 'to help save the mountain gorillas of Rwanda'. In August 1978 FPS, working closely with WWF, sent its Vice-President, Kai Curry-Lindahl, the gorilla biologist Sandy Harcourt and Brian Jackman to Rwanda to assess the situation on the ground.[116] On arrival, they discovered that two further members of the Karisimbi gorillas had been killed. The trade in gorilla hands and heads was recent, dating back only to 1976, but it was extremely destructive. Schaller had estimated a population of 400–500 gorillas in the Virungas in 1960: by 1973 Dian Fossey estimated 290, and with the upsurge in poaching the number was probably below 250.[117]

The mission to Rwanda identified a number of critical problems in the Virungas: the Parc National des Volcans cost twice as much to run as it received in revenue. Patrols (necessarily on foot) were ineffective, and the game guards ill-trained and un-motivated. Farmland abutted the park boundary, and 10,000 hectares had been excised by the government for pyrethrum, with further cuts planned for cattle grazing land. Tourist guides were poorly trained, and tourists behaved foolishly and badly, antagonizing and sometimes being attacked in return by irritated gorillas. The park needed new buildings (offices, accommodation for guards and tourists), entry gates and boundary notices and signs. Guards needed to be equipped and trained. More gorilla groups needed to be habituated, and tourism managed properly. Research was urgently needed to provide the basis for a proper management plan.

By 1979, the Mountain Gorilla Fund contained £24,000, raised by the FPS and PTES. In addition the WWF had raised £26,500, and the African Wildlife Leadership Foundation (AWLF) about £10,000. The different organizations collaborated, and divided the work in Rwanda, with FPS and PTES providing equipment and education materials (including a Renault van for films), WWF funding buildings and AWLF managing projects in the field and training rangers.[118] By the end of 1979 the appeal was nearing the £50,000 target, and the trade in gorilla heads as tourist trophies appeared to have been stopped.[119]

The Mountain Gorilla project had four dimensions. First, to train and equip a Park Guard Force; second, conservation education; third, tourism development and education; fourth, a building programme to construct offices and housing for the park guards.[120] Progress was made with all four, with audiences of up to 2000 for slide and film presentations in towns around the park, improved patrols and tourism development. Belgian aid had added to the funds available, as had the Lions Club and Round Table.[121] By 1983, the situation in Rwanda was largely stabilized, and tourism was increasing: in ten months of 1983, there had been over 3700 visitors to the Parc National des Virungas, including Princess Paola of Belgium.[122] In 1983, tourist income was £78,000, eleven times that at the start of the project, although the problem of poaching persisted.[123]

It was recognized by all parties in the Mountain Gorilla Conservation Project from the outset that the work in Rwanda needed to be extended to Congo and Uganda. The international boundary between Rwanda and Zaire passed close to Dian Fossey's research station. Rwandan guards could not go into the Parc des Virungas, Zaire to patrol or pursue poachers, but this part of the Parc des Virungas was so remote that it was barely patrolled from Zaire.[124] FPS proposed extending the work to include the adjoining Ugandan Mgahinga Gorilla Game Reserve.[125]

In 1984 the now-renamed Fauna and Flora Preservation Society (FFPS) hosted a meeting in London and refined the objectives of the Mountain Gorilla Project. Fundraising events were held in 14 towns around the United Kingdom, including a parachute jump, sponsored silences, quizzes and walks, jumble sales and village clean-ups. Paul Getty Jnr donated US$17,000 to the project. In the following year, Dian Fossey was murdered, and, as described in Chapter 1, the intensity of international concern about gorilla conservation grew further. Work began in Uganda in 1986, with the foundation of the Impenetrable Forest Conservation Project, modelled on the Rwandan Mountain Gorilla Project, and in Zaire in 1989 with funds from WWF and the Frankfurt Zoological Society.[126]

In 1989, the International Gorilla Conservation Programme was formed, a joint programme of the FFPS, African Wildlife Foundation (AWF) and WWF. This brought together the various projects into a single support system for government conservation agencies in the three countries. Remarkably, the programme has survived, overcoming the differences in language and the lack of communication and trust between neighbouring governments, and survived the fearsome and seemingly endless political turbulence of civil war and the genocide of 1994. Over the years, no less than 16 park rangers have lost their lives, and government salaries have been eroded by inflation and have often gone unpaid. Tourism has been a fickle engine of wealth generation. And yet the national parks are still patrolled, and despite periodic incidents of poaching, the gorillas are still there. It is a remarkable testament to the power of a single charismatic species to focus the energies and resources of conservationists, both in-country and internationally.

SPECIES AND IDENTITY

The conservation of particular species, sometimes called 'flagship species', can have importance for conservation strategies that goes beyond the immediate biodiversity preservation benefits.[127] Cynically, it is clear that action for particular species is a proven way to stimulate financial support for conservation activities from donors and the members of conservation organizations. More importantly, the plight of particular charismatic species can draw attention to more diffuse, generalized conservation issues. Threats to species such as primates (lemurs or orang-utans for example) have been extremely effective in raising public awareness of the problem of tropical forest loss, particularly in the industrialized countries. The humanitarian potential of appeals based on threats to species like primates strengthen their importance as emotive symbols of wider land cover change. Indeed, species are central to the humanitarian dimension of arguments for conservation. In 1962, when over 1 million lesser flamingos moved from Lake Natron in Kenya to Lake Magadi to breed, large numbers of chicks became crippled by the accumulation of soda around their legs. A campaign to raise money to 'Save the Flamingo' was launched. Was this, as one contemporary correspondent a waste of money, an unwarranted interference in natural processes and scientifically pointless? Possibly, but in reply Peter Scott noted how vital it was for conservation to respond when the ordinary citizen showed that they cared, pointing out that 'men cannot be expected to stand by and watch suffering if there is an obvious remedy'.[128]

Flagship species can also help legitimize conservation action, and provide the catalyst for local communities to recognize the significance of conservation action. Thus, on Pemba Island in Tanzania, the endemic flying fox (prominent, familiar and hunted for food) provided a focus for a conservation project supported by FFI that extended into the wider environment. Bats provided the entry point for work with hunters and schoolchildren, and effectively provided a 'brand' for the project, appearing on stickers, t-shirts and leaflets.[129] In the Golden Stream Corridor Preserve in southern Belize, purchased with money from FFI's Arcadia Fund in late 1998, the ceiba tree was identified as a species that had significance for Mayan people. The NGO running the reserve changed its name to the Ya'axche Conservation Trust, to reflect the tree's Mopan name.[130]

In many countries, conservation organizations are seeking to re-establish connections between society, culture and history. In the United Kingdom, for example, the organization Common Ground has developed the idea of local distinctiveness, promoting links between art and conservation, and drawing attention to the conservation and cultural significance of habitats such as orchards.[131] Species are critical to many such endeavours. In 2002 the NGO Plantlife asked the public to vote for a wild flower emblem for each county in the United Kingdom.[132] The largest vote nationally was for the bluebell, a spring flower that grows in dazzling carpets in ancient broadleaved woodlands. Plantlife's hope is that nationally, and in each locality, flowers will awaken and strengthen the concern of ordinary people for nature. Trees have also been widely used in this way.[133] The US National Arbor Day, for example, has been an important stimulus for habitat creation.[134] This dates back to 1872, when J Sterling Morton proposed a tree-planting holiday to be called 'Arbor Day' at a meeting of the Nebraska State Board of Agriculture. On 10 April 1874, the first Arbor Day, more than 1 million trees were planted in Nebraska. Arbor Day was officially proclaimed a public holiday in Nebraska in 1885. Other states passed legislation to observe Arbor Day in the 1870s, and the tradition began in schools nationwide in 1882.

As I was growing up in London, stories of captive breeding and species 'saved from the brink', seemed heartening evidence of what conservation and environmentalism might do.[135] They gave a young conservationist something to believe in. In retrospect, it is clear that I, and perhaps many like me, were over-credulous. These missions of rescue were glorious, but they were military

Chapter 7

The Demands of Development

All over the world today, vast numbers of fine and harmless wild creatures are losing their lives or their homes as a result of thoughtless and needless destruction. In the name of advancing civilization they are being shot or trapped out of existence on land taken to be exploited, or drowned by new dams, poisoned by toxic chemicals, killed by poachers for gain, or destroyed in the course of political upheaval (Morges Manifesto, 1961).[1]

SPACESHIP EARTH

A colleague has a remarkable poster on their office wall, an image of the world in deep blue, spattered with patches of creamy white. This is a composite satellite image of the Earth at night, showing the sources of human-made light. It is an amazing record of human activity, an illuminated advertising hoarding for technology and consumerism, flashing in the darkness of space.[2] The United States, Western Europe, India, China and the southwest Pacific Rim are lit up like a nightclub: here are streetlights, office buildings, factories, suburbs and supermarkets. Here too is the hot motor of the world economy, and behind the glow lie computers, telephones, banks and corporations, as well as the intricate capillary geography of consumption – cars, televisions, airports and Jacuzzis. Most of tropical Africa is dark, as is all but the edge of South America, the high latitudes and the oceans.

This image of the Earth's city lights was created by NASA with data from the Defense Meteorological Satellite Program, originally designed to pick up moonlight on clouds to help military aircraft navigate.[3] It is the fruit of a programme by researchers at NASA's Goddard Space Flight Center to map the extent and impacts of urbanization in the United States and globally.[4] In order to distinguish between cities and their surroundings, researchers had to manipulate the image to deal with the saturation of relatively bright city lights. In the US, satellite images were compared with 1990 US Census data to distinguish urban areas (1000 people or more per square mile), from peri-urban areas such as low-density suburbs, and non-urban areas.

Views of the Earth from space have often been used to drive environmental debates. Indeed, space exploration had a unique place in the development of environmental consciousness in the 20th century. In his book *Earth Rising*, David Oates describes the significance of the Apollo 8 photograph of the earth rising over the edge of the moon in December 1968.[5] This mission was a forerunner of the moon landings the following year, a figure-of-eight loop around the dark side of the moon. Oates considers the photograph one of the most significant things to arise from the Apollo extravaganza. For the first time, it was possible to see an actual image of the Earth as a body set in space. The mission commander, Frank Boorman, said 'When you are privileged to view the earth from afar, when you can hold out your thumb and cover it with your thumbnail, you realize that we are really, all of us around the world, crew members on the space station Earth'.[6]

The metaphor of space fitted the apocalyptic fears of the growing community by environmentalists in North America and Western Europe. In *The Limits of the Earth*, published in 1954, Fairfield Osborn wrote: 'man is becoming aware of the limits of his earth'.[7] The term 'spaceship Earth' was used by Kenneth Boulding in 1966 precisely to capture this sense of the finite nature of the Earth, and to express the need for common action for shared human welfare.[8] The image of the Earth as a blue sphere spinning in the cold darkness of space has become commonplace, usually now in the form of a synthesized false colour satellite image. However this image was once novel and even shocking, and became the icon of the environmentalism of the 1960s and 1970s. The cover of my edition of *Only One Earth*, the book written by Barbara Ward and René Dubos for the 1972 UN Conference on the Human Environment in Stockholm, shows a real-colour NASA image of the earth against black.[9] Max

Nicholson's book *The Environmental Revolution: a guide for the new masters of the world* (published in 1970) has an image of a vast freeway intersection imposed on a globe on its cover. In it, he uses the device of an imaginary aerial journey spiralling, like one of Apollo's orbiting astronauts, seven times around the globe to describe the ways humans use the Earth. He castigates the world leaders for their lack of geographical or ecological education, describing them as little better than absentee managers.[10]

Images of the Earth as a planetary body made the finite state of the biosphere self-evident. In the 1960s and 1970s, environmentalists rediscovered the ideas of Thomas Malthus, the 18th century cleric and author of *An Essay on the Principle of Population*.[11] The idea of limits to growth, and the wider neo-Malthusian concern about population growth, led to what one determined sceptic called the 'doomsday syndrome' in the 1970s.[12] In 1970 the world population was 3.5 billion, and 'Spaceship Earth' was said to be 'filled to capacity and beyond and is running out of food'.[13] There were precocious attempts to produce global computer models of the 'world system', notably Forrester's *World Dynamics*[14] and the work of the Massachusetts Institute of Technology for the 'Club of Rome', *The Limits to Growth*.[15] The idea that there was a limit to growth was fiercely opposed by mainstream political commentators and economists. To Wilfred Beckerman (1974) the Club of Rome report was 'guilty of various kinds of flagrant errors of fact, logic and scientific method'. The editor of *Nature* dismissed prophets of doom for lack of scientific evidence, saying 'the doomsday cause would be more telling if it were more securely grounded in facts'.[16] To the cornucopian Julian Simon, it was 'a fascinating example of how scientific work can be outrageously bad and yet be very influential'.[17]

HUMAN SPACE

From the perspective of the 21st century, with its 6 billion plus global population and spendthrift energy economy, it is easy to sneer at the naïve predictions of resource depletion and disaster of the environmentalists of the 1960s and 1970s. However, they were absolutely right about one thing; that the human demands on the biosphere are massive and have accelerated rapidly during the 20th century. In *Our Plundered Planet*, back in 1948, Fairfield Osborn commented: 'the tide of the earth's population is rising, the reservoir of the earth's living resources is falling'. He was quite right, although environmentalists would now point to the saturation of the Earth's capacity to absorb pollutants (such as atmospheric carbon dioxide, radionuclides or persistent organic carbons) rather than its ability to generate the feedstock for industry, as the key problem.[18]

Urbanization is a critical factor in the human impact on earth, through resource depletion, pollution (not least with carbon dioxide) and waste.[19] The majority of people on every continent live in urban areas, with Africa the last continent to make the transition. In the Third World, urban living is not accompanied by an escape from poverty: Third World cities hold increasing proportions of the growing absolute numbers of the world's poor. In the First World, however, urban and suburban sprawl bring with them massive rises in consumption and energy use. In the United States, the percentage of people living in urban areas has risen from 39 per cent to more than 73 per cent. Rural land has progressively been taken over for subdivisions, freeways, strip malls and parking lots.

It is a truism that by the end of the 20th century, humans dominated the Earth. No ecosystem on Earth was free from human influence. In 1994, Lee Hannah and others calculated that natural habitats had been displaced by human disturbance over nearly three-quarters of the habitable surface of the planet: although just over half the area was undisturbed, most of that was ice, rock or blowing sand.[20] Subsequent attempts to map the human 'footprint' on Earth, calculating a 'human influence index', suggest that human impact is greater, and rising. In total, 83 per cent of the land surface is affected in some way by human activity, and 98 per cent of the area where grain agriculture (wheat, rice and maize) is possible is directly influenced by humans.[21] If these scores are re-calculated for each of the world's major biomes, the resulting 'human footprint' map shows the relative scale and significance of human influence: the map shows what the satellite image shows, the amazing spread of human transformation of the biosphere.

The important issue, however, is not really the location of the most-transformed and least transformed area (no prizes for guessing where the eastern seaboard of the United States, or the depths of the Amazon or the Sahara, score), but the overall impact. In 1986, Peter Vitousek and others estimated that 40 per cent of potential terrestrial net primary production was used directly by human activities, co-opted or forgone as a result of those activities. Consumption is direct (for example crops, fish, wood), indirect (for example through livestock), and incidental (for example fire or human-induced soil erosion). They comment: 'an equivalent concentration of resources into one species and its satellites has probably not occurred since land plants first diversified'.[22]

By the end of the 20th century, it was simply the case that the structure and functioning of the Earth's ecosystems could not be understood without reference to human impacts. The Earth was a managed (or, as environmentalists would put it, a mis-managed) space: a backyard, a world made microcosm. Human impacts include the transformation of land cover, the alteration of the oceans (it is notable that 60 per cent of the world's people live within 100 kilometers of the sea), alteration of global biogeochemical cycles, and additions and losses of biota, regionally and globally. Critically, these changes do not simply accumulate as a series of individual impacts, but they interact. Peter Vitousek and others comment that 'the rates, scales, kinds and combinations of changes occurring now are fundamentally different from those at any other time in history; we are changing the earth more rapidly than we are understanding it'.[23]

Humans have now gone beyond the clearing of the forest and the draining of the fen, to start to fiddle with the engine of biodiversity change. Impacts on the extent of ecosystems have developed into impacts on ecosystem function, up to the global scale (for example in anthropogenic climate change). Human activities are even having measurable impacts on the process of evolution itself, accelerating evolutionary change in other species, especially in commercially important, pest and disease species.[24] Bacteria, retroviruses, fish (commercially caught and farm escapees), and species affected by exotic escapees, have all evolved as a direct result of human activity. The development of techniques of genetic engineering, particularly cross-taxa gene transfer, will increase both the scale and speed of such impacts.

The nature and scale of human impacts on the biosphere have extended beyond the wildest imaginations of early conservationists. They are unlikely to decline, and by any sane analysis need to be managed very carefully. Moreover, as the impacts expanded during the 20th century, they have ceased to be understood only as particular threats to particular places and species, but are seen to embrace the lives of conservationists themselves, and the economic systems within which they are embedded. The human footprint is vast, and the most destructive feet have proved to be those of the wealthy, greedy, First World consumer.[25] By the end of the 20th century, conservation could no longer be credible simply as a concern of gentlemen of private means, or of wildlife fanatics with secure incomes and First World consumerist lifestyles. Conservation had to address not just the fate of wildlife, but the fate of the Earth. It did so in the guise of environmentalism.

DEVELOPMENT, COLONIZATION AND CONSERVATION

Environmentalism is one of the big ideas of the 20th century. It is not as significant as the great political movements of communism or fascism, or the neoliberal notion of the unfettered market, nor does it bear comparison with the ideas of universal suffrage or feminism. But it is important, and wildlife conservation is a significant element within it, one flower on the sprawling bush of environmental concern. The unprecedented upsurge in environmentalism in the last three decades of the 20th century took as its starting point the scale and severity of the impacts of industrial technology on nature: pesticides, nuclear waste, oil, pollution, PCBs, acid rain. A whole litany of environmental ills were understood to be direct consequences of industrialization and human greed. The first 'post-scarcity' generation, the children of the post Second World War baby boomers, the generation of rock music, sexual liberation and flower-power was also the generation of environmental concern. And tangled with it, claiming its iconic place on the new public galleries of radicalism, T-shirts and environmental protest banners, was a new level of popular care about wildlife.

Worry about resource depletion, at the way human society and economy made unsustainable demands on nature, were not new in the 1960s. Where did they start? As discussed in Chapter 2, the destructive power of human activities was evident and widely remarked upon in North America and Europe by the second half of the 19th century. The most famous formulation of the problem was by the American lawyer, politician, diplomat and essayist, George Perkins Marsh.[26] Marsh had watched the lumber industry clear the primary forests of Vermont in his youth, and had observed the consequences for river erosion and fish populations. He saw the impacts of industrialization first hand, and when he later travelled in Turkey, Italy and France, he absorbed classical European thought about the destructive power of human action. His book *Man and Nature* (1894) was a rational environmentalist critique of human capacity to destroy nature through unwise use. Marsh observed: 'man has too long forgotten that the earth was given to him for usufruct alone, not for consumption'.[27] He admitted the possibility that human action could maintain and enhance environmental conditions, and might do much to restore the 'disturbed harmonies' of nature; however, his critique was trenchant: 'of all organic beings, man alone is to be regarded as essentially a destructive power';[28] humans were 'everywhere the disturbing agent'; having 'ruthlessly warred on all the tribes of animated nature whose spoil he could convert to his own uses'.[29]

Beyond industrial Europe and North America, the key issue at the start of the 20th century was colonization. As discussed in Chapter 2, where the settler farmed, nature – or at least the larger warm-blooded creatures that the early conservationists cared for – fled. This story was familiar to Theodore Roosevelt, reflecting on the decline of the freebooting American west in the 1890s. Along the Little Missouri, settlers, miners and branded cattle had replaced the buffalo (and the Indian), the west had been 'won' and settled, the continent laced together from sea to sea by railroads and commerce.[30] The pattern was familiar too in southern Africa. In both North America and South Africa, white settlement transformed landscapes and ecosystems. In comparing the environmental history of the two regions, William Beinart and Peter Coates describe how grazing (particularly sheep grazing) drove the 'mobile, expansive, plundering frontier' forwards.[31] Wool was South Africa's main export from 1840 to 1930, and by then by the land supported no less than 45 million nibbling Merino mouths. They left little room for wild life.

If the depletion of game was the driving issue for conservation in the second half of the 19th century, this was the big problem of the 20th. As economies prospered and 'developed', demands on nature grew. There seemed to be a zero-sum game, with humans progressively annexing land and ecosystem production to divert them for their benefit. Land was settled, demarcated, developed. Nature was converted, tamed, eradicated. The Earl of Onslow told the SPFE in 1928 'the whole world is becoming so speedily opened up to travelers, traders, tourists and settlers, and so much uncultivated land is coming under the plough that unless some more or less drastic measures are taken to preserve the distinct fauna it must obviously disappear entirely'.[32] What had taken place gradually in 18th and 19th century Australia, North America and South Africa was accelerated in places like East Africa, where white settlement at the start of the 20th century was extremely rapid.[33] In 1908, the editor of the Society's journal noted 'phenomenal extensions of white development', and the correspondingly urgent need for game protection.[34] As argued in Chapter 4, in such circumstances, it was vital for conservation to make an early claim for territory, to set up reserves before 'the whole country is settled up', as Edward Buxton put it in 1905.[35] Here, as more generally, colonial conservationists should learn from the United States, and the problem of extending Yellowstone National Park once white settlement has expanded in the low valleys to its East and South.[36]

The speed of settlement brought an urgent new dimension to conservationists' concern about the loss of wildlife. It was not simply the shooting of game that was the problem (the wrong animals by the wrong people in the wrong places), but the much larger issues of the ways economies, landscapes and ecosystems were transformed. The central problem was the possibility that conservation was fundamentally in conflict with development. The concept of 'development', in the sense of the betterment of human living conditions, particularly in what has come to be called the 'Third World', or the 'developing' or 'less developed world', had become to most people self-evident by the end of the 20th century.[37] In this sense, however, the phrase has a very specific and quite recent history. It dates from the 18th century with a meaning of unfolding and organic growth, and evolved through the 19th to reflect ideas of progress, indeed a quintessentially Western and linear idea of progress.[38] Central to the idea of the possibility (and the desirability) of progressive human improvement was the principle of the rational use of resources for human benefit. Ever since the enlightenment, Western thinkers have taken for granted that there is a clear distinction between 'human' and 'non-human', between nature and the cultural and social world that humans create and within which they live and reflect on their actions. It has been assumed that humans stood above the natural world, the capacity for human reason enabling humanity to escape from nature, and to re-order it to their best advantage.[39] The conservation movement, of course, was itself the product of this idea of human super-status, both in its sense of responsibility for nature, and its argument that nature needs to be handled right for best human advantage. Debates about how the great European empires should be run reflected very directly this profound belief in the possibility of re-structuring nature, and re-ordering it to serve human needs and desires.

Agriculture was the most favoured means of organizing the proper government of nature, whether in Tudor England, Irish or American plantations, or (by the mid-20th century) in the intricately jumbled fields of

African peasant farmers. The idea of agricultural improvement emerged in medieval England (as an argument for the enclosure of common land), and it came to underpin the economics of Empire in India, Australia and Africa. Agriculture could reclaim wastelands, and make barbarous peoples civilized.[40] In its 20th century guise this same impulse towards order and improvement was re-expressed as 'development', an all-conquering ideology of modernization and change.

WILDLIFE AND DEVELOPMENT

The idea of development in its 20th century form is commonly dated to the inaugural speech by US President Harry Truman in January 1949, in which he referred to the Southern hemisphere's 'underdeveloped areas'.[41] Arguably, the idea of 'underdevelopment', the idea that the world could and should attain the forms of economy and society of the West, also began with Truman's speech (although he was not the first to coin the word).[42] In practice, the meaning of development soon shrank to the promotion of economic growth, and the escape from measurable poverty by enlarging the economic cake. That is still its dominant meaning, although by the end of the 20th century, development theorists were losing faith with that vision. Wolfgang Sachs, for example, describes the project of development as 'a blunder of planetary proportions'. By the 1990s, the whole optimistic roadshow of development was obsolete, standing 'like a ruin in the intellectual landscape'.[43]

In 1903, Lord Cromer pointed out that colonially-imposed peace was problematic for the particular purpose of game preservation. In the Sudan, he held that warfare between 'barbaric' tribes had laid waste the country: '*Pax Britannica* can never do for African game in the future what the Zulu impis, the Masai Moran, the slave raiders, and the dervishes have done in the past'.[44] With misplaced romantic nostalgia, he pointed out that 'barbaric power', which 'makes solitude and calls it peace', was the best game preserver. While colonial legislation could protect game from the rifle, it was 'powerless to save it from giving way to civilization'.[45]

It was recognized as soon as conservation began to be established as a legitimate concern of colonial government, that it potentially clashed with forms of land use necessary for settlers to make a living, for development and for generating revenue for the government. Moreover, as game departments began to develop in size and the range of their activities, it became clear that conservation cost money. In colonial Africa, conservationists were rarely in doubt that if there was a straight choice between wildlife and the interests of development, wildlife would lose out. That was true whether 'development' was conceived of in terms of the rights and needs of settlers (which were rather forcefully expressed in newly-established colonies such as Kenya or Rhodesia), the interests of commercial undertakings endeavouring to develop the resources of the country (also well represented), or the interests of indigenous people (often rather archly referred to as 'the native question' and discussed later in this chapter). All these were interests of greater importance than game preservation, and an advocate of nature reserves in 1908 pointed out that to 'press game preservation to the detriment of any of these' would do 'an infinity of harm' and lose public opinion.[46]

From early in the 20th century, conservationists therefore learned to preface their remarks by avowing commitment to development, and arguing that conservation could be done without holding business interests back. In 1924 Keith Caldwell noted that the Kenyan Game Department sought to do its work 'in such a way that it does not in any way retard or interfere with the economic development of the country, or place any difficulties in the way of stock-breeding or crop-growing'.[47] The SPFE deputation to the Secretary of State for the Colonies in 1930 said they 'fully recognized that the development of civilization in East Africa should not be imperiled by an undue regard for the preservation of wild and destructive game' although they went on to urge that game should be preserved as far as possible anyway.[48] James Stevenson-Hamilton (doughty fighter for game reserves in the Transvaal) maintained that the argument that game reserves hindered development of a country did not bear investigation, for no government would want 'to crowd out white settlers in order to maintain a paradise for wild animals'.[49] As an editorial in the Society's Journal in 1948 argued 'we shall serve no useful purpose by unreasoning insistence on the sanctity of wild animal life. We have always recognized that real human interests must prevail when there is a conflict between the two'.[50]

There were, of course, positive arguments that could be marshalled in favour of conservation. These included imperial duty, and the value of wild species to science, but a case could also be made for the possibility of economic return: there was both 'a scientific and economic duty' to preserve the wild fauna'.[51] It was commonly argued that conservation also generated income, from license fees, the sale of ivory and other wildlife products, and more generally from the economic activity associated with hunting, and (from the 1930s) game viewing tourism. Conservationists repeatedly used this revenue to argue that conservation was not just a legitimate concern of government, but that it could contribute to development.

The British government's white paper on colonial development and welfare in 1941 opened the way for greatly increased expenditure on development.[52] This was both an opportunity and a threat to conservation, depending (as the SPFE's Journal pointed out) 'how the word "development" is to be interpreted'.[53] The SPFE was quick to argue that with 'scientific conservation', wildlife could provide a steady source of revenue from visitors (with gun or camera), and income from exports of ivory, horns or pelts. The new policy gave the Imperial Government the opportunity to support them 'to their lasting benefit as well as to the benefit of the whole world'.

Development remained, however, a threat to wildlife. By the 1940s, the language of ecology was starting to be used to express its impact. The Earl of Onslow noted that: 'great damage may be done on a more comprehensive scale through operations, undertaken to develop a region for occupation and exploitation by men, which gravely interfere with the natural ecology'.[54] Onslow had in mind particularly deforestation and soil erosion. The former was the old concern of the 18th and 19th centuries (see Chapter 2). The latter had become a big concern in colonial Africa as the implications of the American Dust Bowl were vigorously disseminated within the colonial service from the 1930s onwards.[55] Neo-Malthusian concerns about overgrazing and overcrowding came to drive colonial perceptions of African management of land, and to justify coercive and unpopular imposed soil conservation regimes.[56] Outside Africa, drought and soil erosion were more obviously the consequences of inappropriate agricultural technologies wielded by European settlers. In Australia, repeated droughts destroyed the hopes of farming settlers, and they in their turn drew down soil fertility and left land sterile behind them. Soil conservation authorities were established in New South Wales in 1938, and Victoria in 1940.[57] In Canada, attempts to boost smallholder settlement to grow wheat in the dry belt of southeast Alberta and southwest Saskatchewan proved disastrous.[58] The environmental impacts of development were increasingly clear.

GAME, DISEASE AND DEVELOPMENT

Game preservationists struggled through the early 20th century to safeguard the natural world, to keep it safe from harm at the hands of unprincipled game hunters, greedy settlers and local farmers, using two tools, game reserves and shooting regulations. In Africa, by and large, they had considerable success in preventing local people from hunting, certainly from hunting with guns and hunting in game reserves. They were less successful in reconciling the dilemma of the impact of colonial development on nature, for the very apparatus of the colonial state that they used to pursue their ends was also the chief mechanism for the destructive transformation of landscapes that they deplored. Conservationists, typified by the SPFE, were a pressure group within the elite of a colonizing power. They worked within its imperial mindset, and yet the fruits of imperial development were themselves profoundly destructive to their interests.

Nowhere is this dilemma more clearly demonstrated than in the long-running debate about the role of game animals in the transmission of sleeping sickness to people and their livestock. Sleeping sickness is caused by trypanosomes (protozoans) that infect humans and animals through the bites of blood-sucking flies of the genus *Glossina*, tsetse flies. Tsetse flies are like large horseflies, fast-moving but quick to settle. Trypanosomes spend part of their life-cycle in the gut of the fly, before entering a new host when it feeds. In the host's bloodstream, the trypanosomes are to an extent able to confuse the immune system by changing their antigenic coating, leading to successive peaks and troughs of infection.[59]

Sleeping sickness has been extensively studied by African historians – indeed, it is probably the subject that has most clearly led the realization that human and natural history cannot be separated.[60] The disease was the focus of a huge medical effort right across colonial Africa, and the measures taken to control it were draconian. Sleeping sickness was known for centuries as a killer of people, particularly in West Africa. In 1894, David Bruce established the sleeping sickness of cattle, called by the Zulu word *nagana*, was caused by a trypanosome. In 1912, the Luangwa Sleeping Sickness Commission in Northern Rhodesia showed that the tsetse fly *Glossina morsitans*, carrying trypanosomes, could feed off both wild animals and humans, and in 1913 research in Nyasaland and South Africa showed that the same parasite, *Trypanosoma rhodesiense*, caused *nagana* and human sleeping sickness.[61] Suddenly, game populations were a threat to development.

That threat was twofold. First, tsetse were a threat to human life, both that of settlers and that of Africans. Second, they were a threat to livestock, in particular because they stopped land being used for cattle. In Central and East Africa, attempts to control sleeping sickness primarily involved attempts to control the movements of Africans. In the Belgian Congo, a mission from the Liverpool School of Tropical Medicine arrived in 1903 to assess the extent of the epidemic, and recommended a policy of containment, the idea of a *cordon sanitaire* between the diseased and the healthy. In 1907, settlements were established to which infected people were forcibly consigned. They were soon seen as death camps, 'true asylums for the doomed'.[62] Similar methods were, however, used elsewhere. An epidemic of sleeping sickness broke out in Uganda in 1903, and from 1907, 24,000 people were forced to move to create concentrated settlements.[63]

Such strategies were disastrously misplaced, and based on a misunderstanding of the epidemiology of sleeping sickness. John Ford's monumental study in 1971 showed that researchers studying both tsetse and trypanosomes failed to see them in the context of the changing landscape ecology of the late 19th and early 20th centuries. The rapid political changes that took place in so many places in the second half of the 19th century, combined with the multiple disasters of its final decades (particularly the arrival of another cattle disease, rinderpest) had a massive impact on the ecology of the African savannas. They changed established patterns of field and bush, changed patterns of grazing and burning, and disrupted precolonial methods of environmental management. In areas such as northeast Tanzania, pre-colonial African societies had worked out how to live with vector and disease parasites. Some historians have suggested that the extent of agriculture led to its eradication from most areas in the 19th century, but it seems that control was achieved through occasional exposure of people and cattle that maintained resistance.[64]

Sleeping sickness expanded in the early 20th century in direct response to the political ecology of the late 19th. Rinderpest killed the vast majority of both wildlife and cattle hosts of *Glossina*, and tsetse initially declined. However, famine and disease drastically reduced human populations, pastures were lightly grazed, and cultivated land was abandoned. John Ford comments that when Rhodes' column arrived in Matabeleland in 1890, they took over a country emptied by famine and disease, and shortly afterwards rinderpest arrived to complete the devastation.[65] Bush developed in many areas, and tsetse expanded with it. As economic conditions recovered (and as Europeans tried to annex 'empty' land), they brought in, from tsetse-free regions, animals that were new to the area and had no disease resistance.[66] They suffered from a renewed outbreak of sleeping sickness. It was therefore depopulation that brought about the advance of 'fly belts', and the strategy of concentrating population led only to their expansion. Where (as in Northern Rhodesia) Africans were moved to reservations with landholdings too small for subsistence (to make way for white settlers, and to guarantee men's willingness to accept labour in the mines) this led to land exhaustion and soil erosion, while leaving them exposed to tsetse from surrounding, once-cultivated, bush.[67] Moreover, that bush was alive with crop-raiding animals that they were not allowed to hunt.

The realization that wild animals could host trypanosomes led almost immediately to calls to shoot game out. David Bruce was a leading advocate of slaughter, memorably arguing that 'it would be as reasonable to allow mad dogs to live and be protected by law in our English towns and villages'.[68] Game removal began in Rhodesia south of the Zambezi in 1901, when game laws were suspended in an area described by Buxton to the Colonial Secretary as 'twice as large as Wales'.[69] The programme was expanded between 1905 and 1908, and from 1910 to 1915.[70] Systematic game control measures (shooting and fencing) were to continue until the 1960s in Rhodesia, restricting tsetse to the low veld, particularly the Zambezi Valley, the land largely allocated for African reserves.[71]

Conservationists fought against game removal because of tsetse the length of the 20th century. They used a range of arguments. They challenged the link between tsetse and wildlife. They argued that there was no correlation between high wildlife densities and high fly densities. They argued that removing game would make very little difference: 'supposing, as has been suggested, certain reserves were to be thrown open, and the game exterminated within them is there any really sound reason for believing that the tsetse fly would thereby be eradicated?'.[72] Indeed, game removal might make the problem worse because it would force the tsetse to slake their hunger on people.[73]

The Society for the Preservation of the Wild Fauna of the Empire (SPWFE) lobbied tirelessly against the idea of game shooting in the name of sleeping sickness eradication. It was keen to show that it was not 'anti-science'. One of their members, E E Austen of the Natural History Museum, was a leading entomologist and (by happy chance) also a hunter. The SPWFE held to the widespread scientific view that there were varieties of parasites, not all of which caused sleeping sickness, that these were carried by only some species of tsetse, each of which had specific habitat requirements and appetites. They called for more and better scientific research, ensuring a delay in execution of control programmes. They argued that game removal was premature, and judgements of its necessity 'unscientific'.[74] In the early years they were hampered by the fact that Rhodesia, where game control policies were dominant, was run by the British South Africa Company, and even their privileged access to the Colonial Office was no guarantee of influence. Other lobby groups also opposed their views, particularly the central African missions.

By 1913, scientific research on sleeping sickness, and scientific debate, were in full swing. So too was the SPWFE's lobbying. In 1911, the Livingstonia Mission of Nyasaland sent a deputation to the Colonial Secretary in London to report a serious outbreak of sleeping sickness, and to blame regulations preventing natives from shooting game. In 1913, the Colonial Secretary established an Inter-Departmental Committee to consider the research, by Bruce's Commission among others, and the SPWFE decided to 'adopt an attitude of suspended judgement' until the report of the Sleeping Sickness Commission on the relation between tsetse flies and big game was published.[75] They could be sanguine about its conclusions, for they had won four places on the Committee, notably for Buxton and Austen, and established a subcommittee to prepare evidence.[76] The science of game removal was not clear, or at least, the Committee's majority report found it so. The committee proposed more research, an experiment of limited destruction of game to test the importance of game as a trypanosome reservoir.[77]

Meanwhile, game extermination continued, and not just in Rhodesia. In South Africa for example, the unattractiveness of land infested with tsetse had allowed game reserves to be set up at Umfolozi and Hluhluwe in Zululand, but pressure from settlers against their existence, and against the tsetse their wildlife were believed to harbour, was relentless.[78] In Natal, there was a huge game drive in 1920, when some 500 white people came from all over South Africa to shoot.[79] In 1925, the society lectured the Under Secretary of State for the Colonies, the Hon W G A Ormsby-Gore, about the inappropriateness of abolishing the Sabi Game Reserve to get rid of *nagana*. They suggested that hasty action to exterminate game was unnecessary and unwise, and proposed 'the fullest scientific investigation'.[80] Ormsby-Gore was not very helpful, suggesting that the society talk to the South African High Commissioner. An SPFE deputation did this less than three weeks later on 6 May 1925, giving a very forceful and powerful scientific argument into the tsetse fly question and the high commissioner agreed to take their case before the government.[81]

The arguments made about game and that 'pertinacious and greedy bloodsucker' the tsetse (of which they noted that there were 19 different species) were carefully presented within an overall commitment to development, and to science. Major Austen noted that they did not have 'the slightest wish to be unreasonable' – if 'the well-being of settlers in the districts concerned were incompatible with the continued existence of wild game, it was obvious that the game must go'. However, a 'stay of execution' was urged to allow for further research.[82] Chalmers-Mitchell argued that the pre-war Harcourt Committee (on which he had served) had failed to make the case for game destruction to eradicate the reservoir of sleeping sickness.[83] The experience of clearing game from the Transvaal was not necessarily relevant to Zululand. Perhaps, indeed, game-feeding tsetse were forced to attack humans and livestock by lack of wild food? Anyway, important hosts such as bush pig could not easily be eradicated, and game could help suppress tsetse by browsing undergrowth. Lastly, Sir Sidney Harmer offered a classic argument drawing on holist ecological ideas, observing that 'the balance of nature is a very delicate thing, and that if you interfere with it by taking away an important element you do not know what the result might be'.[84]

None of these arguments had much effect where game slaughter policies were well-established. In Southern Rhodesia, the programme was extensive by the 1930s and continued to the 1960s, with 750,000 head of game being killed and 26,000 square kilometres being cleared. It was also a major policy in South Africa from 1929 to 1946, in Botswana from 1937 to 1967, in Zambia from 1944 to 1974, in Tanzania from 1945 to 1951, in Mozambique from 1949 to 1958 and in Uganda from 1944 to 1970.[85] After the Second World War, SPFE members were told 'the fight against this revolting destruction in defence of which so-called expert opinion is invoked, will demand both skill and courage'.[86] Their case was still that 'strict scientific justification' was needed for any policy of destruction. But that destruction continued. Large areas of bush were cleared in Uganda Botswana and Tanzania.[87] In 1947 George Cansdale suggested (oddly perhaps in the light of subsequent experience) that the progress with game conservation in West Africa was the result not of legislation, but because the tsetse fly panic (and the ritual of killing game to eradicate it) had not taken hold as it had elsewhere.[88] Even here, though, bush-clearance was extensive, for example in countries such as Nigeria and Ghana.[89]

Nature's conservationist

For the first half of the 20th century, wildlife conservationists therefore fought settlers, development planners, disease researchers and governments in Africa to prevent wildlife slaughter in the name of animal health and livestock-based economic development. In the 1960s their goal was achieved. Game shooting was finally superseded as a strategy for sleeping sickness and *nagana* control. However, this was not the result of the urgings of generations of conservationists. The fact was that shooting was extremely costly, and inefficient. Many animals were killed, but important hosts could not be eradicated. In effect, tsetse departments had been operating rather inefficient game-cropping programmes. A wide range of species were killed in the name of disease control (including elephant, baboon and ostrich), yet by the late 1950s research had shown that just six species were the most critical hosts of the relevant trypanosomes (giraffe, buffalo, bushbuck, kudu, warthog, and bushpig). Bush clearance was no more efficient as a means of controlling the disease, requiring large volumes of hand labour or costly and hard-to-maintain machines: hard work was rapidly undone by natural savanna bush regeneration.

The most important reason for an end to wildlife shooting and bush clearance for tsetse control, however, was the availability of an alternative strategy using insecticides. Toxic chemicals had been used broadcast across the African landscape before the Second World War: in the 1930s, for example, arsenic dust was sprayed from aeroplanes to kill locusts.[90] At that time, experts suggested that impacts on wildlife would be minimal, and the conservationists of the SPFE made no protest, although it turned out (perhaps unsurprisingly) that the impacts were in fact considerable.[91] Organochlorine insecticides such as lindane (Gamma-BHC) and DDT became available during the Second World War, and were being used experimentally against tsetse in South Africa in 1948. Large scale control of tsetse with organochlorine pesticides began in the 1950s. BHC smoke and DDT dust, with another organochlorine dieldrin, became stock weapons in the hands of tsetse control departments. By the mid-1980s, some 300,000 square kilometres of Africa had been sprayed with these chemicals. Tsetse eradication was starting to be a possibility, and conservationists were looking beyond game shooting to worry about the implications of removing the restrictions it had placed on the development of land.[92]

Organochlorine pesticides got rid of tsetse, but there was a considerable environmental cost. In the 1960s, research in industrialized economies began to reveal the extent to which organochlorines were persistent in ecosystems, and bio-accumulated in the tissues of predators at the top of food chains. Mass kills of birds that had eaten treated seed in countries like the UK brought attention of the problem. The demonstration that high levels of pesticide in birds of prey caused breeding failures and the catastrophic decline of wild populations, then transformed public debate about the environmental impacts of technology.[93] Rachel Carson's *Silent Spring* caught the First World's environmentalist zeitgeist, but even in the Third World, where the health benefits of pesticide use against disease vectors were (and are) stronger, the wisdom of broadcasting organochlorine dust began to be questioned.[94] Although there were few scientists to observe them, impacts on fish and birds and non-target organisms were being observed by the 1960s.[95]

Organochlorine compounds were duly replaced with organophosphates, sprayed from the air. These were far more toxic (to humans as well as insects), although they did not bioaccumulate. By the 1980s, synthetic pyrethroids were being used, although ground-spraying with cheaper DDT remained important in broken country. Since then, tsetse control has become more subtle, with pesticide-impregnated traps laced with synthetic ox-odour.[96] At last, the eradication of tsetse has been made possible without recourse to game slaughter or bush destruction, and without massive collateral damage to non-target species.

Was this good news for wildlife? Conservationists did not think so. The truth was that the removal of tsetse by whatever means opened land up to intensive human use. Despite their protestations of support for development, conservationists opposed such land use change in Africa throughout the 20th century. By the 1980s, when tsetse eradication without a gross by-kill had finally become feasible, conservationists recognized its consequences.[97] Ultimately, they concluded, intensive agriculture and livestock management were the problem for wildlife. Tsetse removal without meticulous land use planning could lead to 'the degradation and virtual destruction of the habitat by over-grazing and impoverishment of the soil'.[98] Conservationists accepted the eradication of tsetse from heavily settled areas, and control of *nagana* in draught animals, but suggested that it might be better to intensify livestock productivity in tsetse-free areas than to allow tsetse control to permit the spread of livestock on to marginal land at the expense of wildlife.[99] In arid fly country, conservationists argued that cattle-keeping was an unsustainable land use. A far better idea was to crop the wild game, and for that you only needed to control human trypanosomiasis. Ormerod and Rickman called for the control of tsetse without eradication, precisely the policy that John Ford had argued that pre-colonial African societies had developed with some success.

In fact, of course, the 'tsetse fly menace' had some positive implications for the preservation of game, because it restricted agricultural settlement. At the start of the 20th century it held back land acquisition by white settlers. By the end, once rural African populations had recovered their numbers and started to boom, it was the pastoralist and smallholder that tsetse kept at bay. The spread of intensive agriculture was the most secure means of ridding the country of tsetse, as the Director of the Sleeping Sickness Bureau had noted in 1913.[100] It was also, of course, the most effective way to remove game from the landscape: development, in that guise, was incompatible with conservation. Areas with tsetse were (as indeed they remain) rich in wildlife. Frederick Selous argued in 1905 that the Zambezi Valley was a natural game reserve 'owing to its natural conditions' because it is tsetse fly country, and 'can never be settled upon'.[101] Similar notions persisted – after a survey by aeroplane Captain Pitman referred to the Lwangwa Valley (closed by sleeping sickness) as 'resembling a vast zoo' in a lecture to the Society in March 1933.[102]

Conservation concern about game control for tsetse through the 20th century was never simple, or entirely coherent. It certainly overlapped with other concerns about game shooting. Conservationists mistrusted those who would kill without regard to the sporting code, and feared that unscrupulous hunters were using game control as a cover for short-sighted profiteering, in the form of killing for meat and hides.[103] Conservationists had an equivocal, almost indulgent attitude to tsetse, which jarred with contemporary concerns about humanitarian needs and about the merits of landscape transformation and development. Game was accorded considerable moral status. In Buxton's words, it seemed 'rather a strong measure to condemn and sentence game generally' for carrying sleeping sickness.[104]

Conservationists believed from the start of the 20th century that there was a path between the destruction of game and legitimate development. By the end of the century, in the wake of the UN Conference on Human Development in Rio, belief in that path, christened 'sustainable development' was commonplace. That belief surfaced in the 1960s in the deliberations of a new generation of conservation organizations (described in Chapter 3). These not only operated at the international scale, but were themselves international organizations. They were concerned with conservation not, like the SPWFE, as 'the Imperial obligation of guarding from wanton destruction the marvellous varieties of life which are still to be found within the circumference of His Majesty's Dominions beyond the seas',[105] but as the concern of a global community of independent states.

SUSTAINABLE DEVELOPMENT

The UNSCCUR meeting at Lake Success in 1949, described in Chapter 3, was a critical landmark in the rise of broad international environmental concern.[106] It offered a view of conservation that concerned the long-term management of natural resources in a wider sense than simply wildlife. This reflected the US experience of conservation as 'wise use' of resources, part of public life since the progressive conservation movement associated with Gifford Pinchot at the turn of the century. Within IUCN, this change in focus was reflected in the change of title in 1956 to International Union for Conservation of Nature and Natural Resources (IUCN), in response to US pressure.[107] This change followed discussion of population and resource issues at the 1963 IUCN General Assembly in Nairobi. The view that 'nature', in the sense of fauna and flora, should be viewed as merely one element of the living resources of the planet had prevailed. It made it self-evident that social and economic considerations must become part of the question of conservation.[108]

This view had already been present at the parallel IUPN meeting at Lake Success in 1949, where one resolution charged IUPN with considering (with development agencies) surveys of the ecological impact of development projects. By the 1960s, there was increasing recognition within IUCN of the need to make conservation more relevant to the problems of poverty and the demand for development in emerging Third World countries.

A special conference on African conservation problems was convened at Bukavu in the Belgian Congo in 1953 at the invitation of the Belgian government. This, the Third International Conference for the Protection of the Fauna and Flora in Africa was a follow-up to the 1933 Conference (see Chapter

4), and was attended by delegations from all the African colonial powers (Belgium, Egypt, France, Italy, Portugal, Southern Rhodesia, the United Kingdom and the Union of South Africa), with observers from the United States, Denmark and Anglo-Egyptian Sudan. The United Kingdom delegation was headed by Captain Caldwell, and included representatives from nearly all the British colonial territories in Africa.[109] The conference discussed revision of the 1933 Convention to regulate the sale, purchase, barter or exchange of trophies or meat, and the enormous importance of propaganda, It reviewed the listing of species in the Annexes of the 1933 Convention, rather surprisingly moving the lowland gorilla from Annex A to B (to allow hunting or capture under licence) at the behest of the French delegation, because numbers were increasing in West Africa and causing damage. Most importantly the conference recognized that the protection of flora and fauna, and the national parks then being created across Africa, were not enough to achieve the conservation of nature. John McCormick argues that the Bukavu Conference introduced 'a tangential departure from previous thinking' by its broadening of conservation from simply the preservation of fauna and flora to the wider environment, and including the needs of people to exploit vegetation, soil, water and other resources.[110]

One product of the Bukavu Conference was a proposal for a new convention to address the whole natural environment and focus on the needs of Africans.[111] In 1968, 38 heads of state signed the African Convention on the Conservation of Nature and Natural Resources in Addis Ababa. The aim of this was to bring the 1933 Convention up to date, it was led by IUCN, UNESCO, FAO and the Organisation of African Unity. It adopted a broad environmental focus, arguing that soil and water as well as wildlife were all resources to be managed 'in accordance with scientific principles' and 'with due regard for the best interests of the people'.[112] The IUCN General Assembly in New Delhi in 1969 took a similar broad stand, defining conservation as 'the management ... of air, water, soil, minerals, and living species including man, so as to achieve the highest possible quality of life'.[113]

Late in 1968, the Conservation Foundation and Washington University of St Louis organized a conference on 'the ecological aspects of international development' held at Airlie House in Virginia, organized by the Conservation Foundation and Washington University of St Louis, late in 1968. Its proceedings were published as *The Careless Technology: ecology and international development*.[114] This catalogued the environmental problems caused by economic development.,

The IUCN General Assembly in New Delhi adopted a new mandate, defined as 'the perpetuation and enhancement of the living world – man's natural environment – and the natural resources on which all living things depend'.[115] In his history of IUCN, Martin Holdgate points out that in adopting the principle of sustainability two decades before Rio, in this way, IUCN was explicitly seeking to move with the tide of environmentalist concern in the developed world, while carrying the support of developing countries. This balancing act, or sometimes more a conjuring trick, has been repeated at international meetings and in agreements many times since, up to and including the World Summit on Sustainable Development at Johannesburg in 2002.[116]

A series of meetings followed between international conservation, environment and development organizations, including IUCN, the Conservation Foundation, UNDP, UNESCO and FAO. In 1970 there was a meeting at the FAO headquarters in Rome of interested parties, including now USAID and the Canadian aid agency CIDA, to consider further the ecological impacts of development. It was decided that IUCN and the Conservation Foundation should publish guidelines for development planners. Rather than address what we would now consider the sustainable development agenda head on (exploring, as originally intended, 'interrelationships between economic development, conservation and ecology'), this confined itself to outlining ecological concepts 'useful in the context of development activities', particularly in moist tropical forests and savannas, for example agriculture and river basin development. These appeared as the book *Ecological Principles for Economic Development*.[117]

THE IMPACTS OF DEVELOPMENT

Ecological Principles for Economic Development summed up conservation thinking on the need to apply concepts and insights from the science of ecology to development activities. If the 'lessons' of ecology were ignored, unexpected consequences could result from what were intended to be beneficial activities. The book presented ecology as a way of bringing science into decision-making, offering an inter-disciplinary understanding of the environment for the forester, agricultural specialist, range manager, development economist or engineer. In development planning, ecology could both improve success in meeting the goals of development, and anticipate the impact of that development on natural resources and the wider environment. If the adverse impacts of development and technology on local and global environments could be anticipated in the planning process and evaluated, decisions about developments could be made in full knowledge of possible consequences. A decision to develop despite environmental impacts might be justified by counterbalancing benefits, but 'it should never be taken blindly'. Ecology would help planners 'to make sure of success'.[118]

The 1960s and 1970s were a crucial period for conservation, because for the first time they began to ask systematic questions of the development process as a whole. They began to stop paying lip-service to the old argument that conservation could be achieved in the corners development left alone, in places more or less useless for other purposes. They began to look systematically at the extent of the human transformation of nature, and to come up with unsettling conclusions. Technology was becoming more powerful, and economic change was speeding up. Development planning was transforming landscapes, ecosystems (and societies) wholesale.

There are many possible examples of the growing awareness of conservationists to the environmental impacts of the development process, but I have chosen one here, the issue of oil pollution. This arose from that most basic demand of industrial and urban society, convenient sources of energy – for the power to keep the lights blazing out on Earth into the cold distance of space.

In the United Kingdom, the impacts of oil spills were well known quite early in the century. The tanker *Thomas W Lawson*, which sank in the Scilly Isles in 1907, caused widespread pollution, and in the 1920s, speakers in the House of Lords told of impacts of oil on wildlife, fisheries and holiday beaches.[119] In 1922 Parliament passed the Oil in Navigable Waters Act, establishing fines for allowing oil to spill within three miles of the coast. However, the problem of oil pollution was international, and could not be contained within one national jurisdiction. In 1926 the US Government held an international conference, and drafted a convention. In the event, Germany, Italy, and Japan refused to sign, and the initiative lapsed, although the RSPB continued to lobby hard within the United Kingdom. In 1933 the RSPB and the SPFE put a resolution to the Board of Trade on better measures to control disastrous effects on seabirds around United Kingdom, pointing out the need for international cooperation.[120] In 1934 the British government laid the matter before the League of Nations, which drew up another convention, unfortunately losing the initiative against the growing prospect of war.

The issue of oil pollution continued to hold an important place in the work of the SPFE following the war. As in the case of game shooting, it was the sense of the arbitrary wastefulness of the damage of pollution that distressed conservationists, combined with a humanitarian sensibility at the cruelty of the plight of oiled animals and birds. Only half the ships surveyed were fitted with separators to clean oil from bilge water, and more than half the tankers serving the United Kingdom were foreign registered: only international action was needed.[121] In the 1950s, the FPS contributed to an Oil Pollution Campaign.[122] The FPS Secretary Lieutenant Colonel Boyle was appointed to the British Coordinating Advisory Committee on Oil Pollution, founded in 1952. The Ministry of Transport established an official committee soon afterwards.[123] The UK government called a conference on the problem in 1954, and secured a convention establishing zones where tankers would be forbidden to discharge oil into the sea. It also made provision at main ports of facilities for the disposal of oily wastes. The main aim of the campaign, a total ban on the discharge of oil at sea, remained unfulfilled.[124] Furthermore, while from September 1956, British ships were banned from discharging oil, other major oil countries such as the United States, Panama and Liberia still needed to take action.

The Oil Pollution Campaign continued, with an informal conference in Copenhagen in 1959. In 1961, Poland signed the treaty, and the US Senate finally agreed to ratify it. In 1962, an inter-governmental conference on the Prevention of Pollution by Oil was held in London, extending the 1954 convention to cover smaller ships and naval vessels, and establish larger no-discharge sea zones.[125] These amendments were passed in the House of Commons in 1963, by which time 22 states had acceded to the convention. Four years later, in 1967, the *Torrey Canyon* grounded on the Seven Stones Reef between Land's End and the Scilly Isles leaking Kuwaiti oil the length of southwest England.[126] The FPS joined WWF, the RSPB and the RSPCA, to establish a Torrey Canyon Fund to rescue seabirds and promote research.[127]

As the 20th century wore to its close, arguments about oil pollution broadened into debates about the sustainability of an energy economy built on the exploitation of fossil fuels. The links between profligate demands for carbon-based fuels and climate change became a staple element of environmentalist arguments. Debates about nuclear power following the disasters of Windscale (Sellafield, 1957), Three Mile Island (1979) and Chernobyl (1986), and about the local environmental impacts of wind power, made the environmentalist position a complex one.[128] Moreover, the power of the motorized society proved monolithic, with consumers in both established and newly industralized economies highly resistant to a move away from the motor car. Meanwhile, although the dumping of oil as part of normal tanker operations declined among reputable operators, cowboys and accidents persisted.[129] As the wrecks of the *Exxon Valdez*, the *Braer*, the *Amoco Cadiz*, the *Sea Empress* and the *Prestige* in recent years show, the problem of oil pollution from tanker accidents remained ever-present, part of the running cost to the global environment of an unsustainable dependence on cheap oil.

DAMNED BY DEVELOPMENT

The demand for power impinged on conservationists in a second important way in the 1960s, as they responded to the impacts of dams on the environment. Not all dams were built for hydro-electric power development (irrigation, water supply and flood control were other important purposes), but it was the prospect of plentiful, renewable and in many ways clean power that particularly attracted dam builders.

Conservation protests began in the American West, where the US Army Corps of Engineers and the Interior Department's Bureau of Reclamation were prodigal builders of dams for public-subsidised irrigation.[130] In the 1950s, conservationists fought the construction of two dams on the Green River in the Dinosaur National Monument, just as John Muir and the Sierra Club had the damming of the Hetch Hetchy valley in the Yosemite National Park in the United States in 1913 (see Chapter 4). The Sierra Club ran raft trips in 1953, and

David Brower challenged the Bureau of Reclamation's calculations on evaporation losses before Congress. The Sierra Club ran a massive public campaign, with books, films and legal challenges. The dams within the Dinosoar National Monument were axed – although controversially the Sierra Club withdrew its opposition to the Glen Canyon Dam on the Colorado, eventually flooded below Lake Powell.[131] It is the Glen Canyon Dam that the heroes of Edward Abbey's Monkey Wrench Gang are obsessed with destroying.[132]

The defence of the Green River places organizations such as the Sierra Club within a long tradition of opposition to major engineering schemes such as dams, one that is still current, as the dispute over the dams on the Narmada River in India shows.[133] However, the mainstream engagement of wildlife conservationists with engineers was much less dismissive of development. It involved a strongly technocentrist attempt to identify how developers could adapt their practices and plans to take account of wildlife. Thus the 1956 IUCN General Assembly in Edinburgh focused on the impact of hydro-electric schemes, admiring the fish passes and landscaping of the dams being built by the North of Scotland Hydro-Electricity Board.[134] This led the President of the Society to suggest that destruction to nature could be avoided if there were 'better and fuller understanding between the engineers and competent biologists'.[135] This became the main line of IUCN's argument, their entry into what became the sustainable development debate.

However, conservationists in Africa and London were alarmed in 1957 at the proposal to build a major dam on the Zambezi at Kariba, between Northern and Southern Rhodesia, creating a lake of 2500 square miles. The project, like the others being built in Africa at the same period, was quite carefully planned. Bulldozers cleared trees with anchor chains through the bush to remove savanna trees, and there was a major programme to stock the reservoir with fish in anticipation of a commercial fishery.[136] A large number of Tonga people lived in the valley, and there were plans to resettle them, at considerable cost and in accordance with the severe standards of the time, and as it turned out, not without coercion and violence.[137]

Yet conservationists were concerned not with these broader social impacts, but with the fact that there had been little attention to the game of the Zambezi Valley. The dam was closed in December 1958, and as the President of the Game Preservation and Hunting Association of Northern Rhodesia reported in 1959, wild animals marooned on the fast-disappearing islands began to starve and drown. The Southern Rhodesian government set up a team of game rangers to rescue them, increasing their expenditure when the Opposition asked questions in the Southern Rhodesian Parliament. However, little was done in the north, and public opinion among settlers was awakened to the plight of the animals.[138] The Game Preservation and Hunting Association asked the FPS for help, and they held a press conference in London in March 1959, resulting in a leader in the *Field* about 'the scandal at Kariba Dam'. The plight of the animals was featured widely in newspapers, and the FPS launched an appeal for

UK£10,000 for 'Operation Noah', to operate rescue teams to save animals marooned by the rising waters. Rescue work began in Northern Rhodesia in April 1960, with the FPS/Game Preservation and Hunting Association team supporting a government team. The project purchased a 45-foot metal boat, named the Erica after a donor, 'the first since the ark to be built especially for animal rescue work'.[139] Between 1959 and the end of 1960, Operation Noah had raised £13,868, most of which was sent to Africa with the exception of a few hundred pounds for administration costs.

Operation Noah was important for the FPS, because it provided a clear role in an uncertain post-war and pre-independence Africa. It was also important in the way that it symbolized the impacts of development to the environment. The project did not present these impacts dispassionately, in terms, for example, of the 'costs' of development, but in a way that emphasized the suffering of particular animals and the cruelty of the actions that caused that suffering. This linkage between animal welfare and conservation was made even more clearly in clones of the Operation Noah initiative, notably perhaps the work of the International Society for the Protection of Animals in rescuing animals from the lake behind the Akfokaba Dam, constructed in 1964 on the Pernambuco River in Surinam (former Dutch Guiana) to produce hydro-electric power to smelt aluminium. In their account of the rescue, Operation Gwamba, John Walsh and Robert Gannon emphasized the suffering of rainforest animals, rather than, for example, the balance of environmental costs and economic benefits, or the biodiversity impacts of the loss of 600–900 square miles of rainforest.

Many large dams were built in the emerging Third World in the 1960s, and conservationists were greatly exercised at their impacts. Over the last quarter of the 20th century, they openly campaigned against some of them, such as the Silent Valley in India, and the Gordon-below-Franklin Dam in Tasmania.[140] By the 1970s, engineers were starting to acknowledge the significant environmental effects of their beloved projects. The Man and Biosphere Programme designated Project 10 on the effects of major engineering works. In 1977 the UN Water Conference received a report on *Large Dams and the Environment: Recommendations for Development Planning*; in 1972, the International Commission on Large Dams appointed a committee on dams and the environment, and in 1981 published the nicely spun volume *Dam Projects and Environmental Success*.[141] Such initiatives reflected more general moves from the late 1960s to develop Environmental Impact Assessment techniques (EIA), for example under the US National Environmental Policy Act (NEPA) of 1969.[142]

The main opposition to dam construction came from human rights and not conservation organizations. Very substantial numbers of people have been moved to make way for reservoirs throughout the developing world. The controversial Three Gorges development on the Yangtze will displace 1.3 million people, and the Sardar Sarovar Dam and Narmada Sagar Dam on the Narmada River in India almost half a million. The human cost of dam construction can be devastating, and extremely controversial.[143] Protests against dam projects grew through the 1980s and 1990s, with particular pressure on the World Bank to cease funding. The Bank and IUCN were involved in setting up the World Commission on Dams, which worked between 1998 and 2000 to identify strategies for river basin development that combined maximum human benefit with minimum social and environmental cost: the classic sustainable development balancing act.[144]

RECONCILING CONSERVATION AND DEVELOPMENT

By the 1990s piecemeal opposition to destructive development by conservationists had been subsumed beneath the over-arching concept of 'sustainable development'. Following the Rio conferences in 1992, this was universally accepted as a way of framing debate about the impacts of development on nature. The term is not, however, as simple as it seems. It has always been a highly political concept. This is one reason for the frustration felt by conservation biologists like John Terborgh, who describes it as the mantra of the conservation movement, attractive like apple pie precisely because most people are unable to enunciate a technically precise definition.[145] He is quite right about its vagueness, but misses its importance. Michael Jacobs points out that sustainable development and sustainability were not originally intended as 'economic' terms. He says 'they were, and remain, essentially political objectives, more like 'social justice' and 'democracy' than 'economic growth'. And as such their purpose, or 'use' is mainly to express key ideas about how society – including the economy – should be governed'.[146]

The evolution of the ideas of sustainability and sustainable development is worthy of a history in itself.[147] They were central to the success of the Stockholm Conference on the Human Environment in 1972, in building bridges between industrialized countries responding to environmentalist fears about industrial pollution, and developing countries whose chief concern was poverty, and the *lack* of industry. The memorable phrase 'the pollution of poverty' was coined at this time to emphasize that industrial development brought benefits as well as problems. The idea of sustainable development was offered as an escape from the idea that development gains inevitably brought environmental costs. It was a statement of faith, not a road map.

Conservation and development was the theme of the 1972 IUCN General Assembly at Banff, Canada, and in 1975 IUCN joined UNEP, UNESCO, and FAO in an 'Ecosystem Conservation Group' to develop a strategy for nature conservation. In 1977 UNEP commissioned IUCN to draft a document to provide a global strategy for conservation. Preliminary drafts were discussed at the IUCN General Assembly in Ashkhabad (USSR) in 1978. At that stage the strategy was effectively still a textbook of wildlife conservation, concentrating on the conservation of species and protected areas. Between then and 1980, when the World Conservation Strategy was published by IUCN, UNEP and the World Wildlife Fund,[148] the focus broadened substantially to include questions of population, resources and development.

The World Conservation Strategy (WCS) argued explicitly that development could be 'a major means of achieving conservation, rather than an obstruction to it'. It tried to show the relevance of conservation to development, and to offer both 'an intellectual framework and practical guidance'.[149] The WCS identified three objectives for conservation: first, the maintenance of 'essential ecological processes and life-support systems' (food production, health, and other aspects of human survival and sustainable development) and the ecosystems on which they depended; second, the preservation of genetic diversity, both in domestic and wild species; third the sustainable utilization of species and ecosystems, particularly fisheries, wild species which are cropped, forests and timber resources and grazing land.

Mainstream ideas of sustainable development were further developed through the report of the World Commission on Environment and Development *Our Common Future* and the follow-up to the WCS, *Caring for the Earth*, before its appearance in *Agenda 21* at the Rio Conference in 1992.[150] *Agenda 21* became a vast and sprawling compendium of developmental and environmental ideas, running to more than 600 pages, although it was conceived by the Conference Chairman Maurice Strong as a relatively simple document setting out a strategy to make the planet sustainable by the start of the 21st Century.[151] The whole of the second section of *Agenda 21* (14 of the 40 chapters) concerns the 'Conservation and Management of Resources for Development'. These are long chapters, comprising almost half the total page-length, addressing everything from deforestation and desertification through toxic waste and the atmosphere to the conservation of biological diversity.

The main focus of wildlife conservationists at the Rio Conference was the Convention on Biological Diversity. In a sense this was unfinished business arising from the World Conservation Strategy in 1980. Its roots went back long before preparations for the Rio Conference began – indeed, in a sense its roots go back to the 1933 Conference and the 1900 Convention for the Preservation of Animals, Birds and Fish in Africa (Chapter 4). IUCN drew up a draft Convention in the mid-1980s, with WWF, UNEP, the World Resources Institute and the World Bank. The idea of a global conservation convention had been suggested in Bali in 1982, at the Second World Congress on National Parks (organized by IUCN's Commission on National Parks and Protected Areas). Between 1988 and 1992 there was intensive debate about the need for international agreement on effective measures to preserve global biodiversity, and specifically on the need for a convention among IUCN, UNEP, FAO, UNESCO, WWF, World Resources Institute, and the World Bank). The *Global Biodiversity Strategy*, published in 1992, made the case for international agreement.[152]

Negotiations over a Convention were initiated by UNEP in 1990, and at first the evolving draft reflected conservationist concerns about biodiversity loss. However, at the second Preparatory Committee meeting in Geneva, the 'G77' countries (the group of 128 less-developed and less-industrialized countries set up as a counter lobby to the developed 'G7' countries) demanded the inclusion of the issues of bioprospecting and the exploitation of genetic resources through biotechnology. This was a novel (and controversial) broadening of the conservation agenda, although in principle it extended earlier ideas about the sustainable use of species and ecosystems for human benefit. By 1992 rapid development in genetics had opened up vast new areas of potential exploitation at the molecular level, including the creation of novel organisms (which might perhaps be patented by the corporations that created them) and products such as drugs or cosmetics derived from wild species. This technology had the potential to generate vast wealth, however biotechnological capacity was almost uniquely held by industrialized countries (because of the high costs of research laboratories, research infrastructure and training), and moreover by private corporations within those countries and not by governments. Third World countries feared 'biopiracy', stripping of their genetic resources by bioprospectors, and loss of access to economic benefits derived by First World corporations.[153] On the other hand, First World countries (particularly the United States, which dominated in this area of science) feared restriction of economic opportunity if trade in biotechnology were restricted by a benefit-sharing agreement. The Convention was drafted to reflect the balance of these opposite fears, containing, among other things, provision for sharing benefits from the commercial exploitation of genetic resources.

The Convention on Biological Diversity was agreed and signed by 156 countries at the Rio Conference. The United States refused to sign at that time, although it did so subsequently (although it had still not ratified by 2003). The Convention is a slightly awkward marriage between conventional conservation concerns and novel issues of biotechnology, held together by the fragile term 'biodiversity'. The Convention seeks to conserve biological diversity, promote the sustainable use of species and ecosystems, and the equitable sharing of the economic benefits of genetic resources. Signatory nations committed themselves to the development of strategies for conserving biological diversity, and for making its use sustainable. The convention notes that biodiversity conservation can be achieved *in situ* (that is through conventional methods such as the designation of systems of protected areas, see Chapters 4 and 5) or *ex situ* (for example through captive breeding, see Chapter 6), although the Convention also requires cross-cutting measures (for example relating to forestry or fishing). All these elements of the Convention are qualified by a get-out clause (all is to be done 'as far as possible and appropriate'). This programme is a logical development of the traditional conservationist concern for sustainable ecosystems use, and draws directly on the thinking in the *World Conservation Strategy* and *Caring for the Earth*.

The Convention on Biological Diversity came into force on 29 December 1993, and by 1997 it had been ratified by 162 countries. This rapid progress reflected the level of concern about biodiversity loss, but more particularly the explosion of commercial interest in biotechnology in the 1990s, and the potential commercial value of genetic material in both its raw (wild) state, and as patentable 'improved' forms. Debate over the issues embraced by the Convention has continued to be fierce, addressing among other things how the Convention on Biological Diversity should be integrated with other biodiversity conventions (notably the Convention on Trade in Endangered Species, CITES, see Chapter 8), and on relations with the World Trade Organisation, and its agreement on Trade Related Intellectual Property Rights.[154] The 6th meeting of the Conference of the Parties in April 2002 adopted a strategic plan which commits Parties to achieve, by 2010, a significant reduction in the current rate of biodiversity loss at the global, regional and national level.

Following Rio, the United Nations Commission on Sustainable Development (CSD) was created as a commission of the UN Economic and Social Council (ECOSOC) to monitor and report on implementation of the Earth Summit agreements at the local, national, regional and international levels.[155] Progress was reviewed at a special session of the UN General Assembly in June 1997 (the so-called *Earth Summit + 5*) and more completely in the autumn of 2002 at the World Summit on Sustainable Development in Johannesburg. There were four Preparatory Committee meetings, the last of which, at Ministerial level, was held in Bali, Indonesia.

Meanwhile, sustainability had been selected as one of the eight Millennium Development Goals agreed at the United Nations Millennium Summit in September 2000.[156] These are intended to be yardsticks for measuring improvements in people's lives, and are associated with 18 targets and 48 indicators. Goal 7, to 'ensure environmental sustainability' involves three targets: first, the integration of the principles of sustainable development into country policies and programmes and reverse the loss of environmental resources; second, the halving of the proportion of people without sustainable access to safe drinking water by 2015; third, the achievement of a significant improvement in the lives of at least 100 million slum dwellers by 2020.[157] There are seven indicators relevant to these goals. Some have an obvious and direct development focus (for example the proportion of people with sustained access to an improved water source). Two have some relevance to biodiversity, the proportion of land area covered by forest (although the kind of forest is not specified) and the area of land protected to maintain biodiversity.

Over 22,000 people attended the Johannesburg Summit, including 100 heads of State and government. The meeting confirmed government endorsement of the Rio agreements, and issued the Johannesburg Plan of Implementation.[158] Signatories committed themselves to achieving poverty-related targets and goals, including those contained in *Agenda 21*, the relevant outcomes of other United Nations conferences and the United Nations Millennium Declaration. The Plan addressed poverty eradication, changing unsustainable patterns of consumption and production, protecting and managing the natural resource base of economic and social development, the issue of sustainable development in a globalizing world, and the links between health and sustainable development. It also addressed sustainable development of small island developing states, Africa and other regions, and the institutional framework required to achieve sustainable development.

The shift in debates about development and environment has been a fundamental (and rather astonishing) feature of the last decades of the 20th century. The rhetoric of sustainability is now ubiquitous, with all its rampant vigour and its infuriating vagueness. Conservatives and radicals both march beneath its banner, some preaching a mild green reform of profitable global business, others calling for a fundamental restructuring of social and economic systems, and a profound re-assessment of the relations between humans and biosphere.[159] For conservationists, there are whole new institutional ecosystems to explore, hunting the captains of industry in their boardrooms and coming back with funds for cherished projects or strategies to enhance corporate environmental performance. These are deep bureaucratic jungles, where the latter-day successors of Buxton and Hornaday struggle to turn their profound feelings about the need to conserve nature into coherent plans of action that governmental and intergovernmental organizations will sign up to, such as the need to integrate the UN's Millennium Development Goals and the Convention of Biological Diversity's '2010 Global Biodiversity Challenge'.[160]

By the end of the 1990s, wildlife conservation had become an inextricable part of debates about development. The question of the extinction of species was rightly seen to be part and parcel of wider questions about the sustainability of the biosphere in the face of human demands upon it. The state of Spaceship Earth and the fate of its burgeoning crew were seen to be different parts of the same question.

All well and good, but the most interesting issue in the whole rambling sustainability debate for conservation continues to be whether people can actually use species and ecosystems sustainably. This was the issue that led IUCN into debates about development, and it continues to be a vexed one within conservation. Put simply, can species be harvested sustainably, and can those harvests be made the foundation for the improvement in the human condition? That is the subject of the next chapter.

Chapter 8

Trading Nature

Trade is the arch-exterminator of animal life (R W G Hingston, 1931).[1]

The quickest and most certain way of wiping animals off the face of the earth was to commercialise their trophies (Keith Caldwell, 1927).[2]

A ZOO IN THEIR LUGGAGE

Probably few customs officers have much knowledge of wild plants and animals. Perhaps some are amateur ornithologists, or avid watchers of wildlife documentaries, but most of them, as most other people, only know the species they meet day by day. Even those tend to be divorced from their raw form, clad in fur, feathers or leaves. Pity then the unhappy lot of the customs officer at Stansted Airport opening a suitcase to find 90 Ibiza wall lizards stuffed inside, or a colleague peering into a dodgy-looking crate to find illegally imported butterflies.[3] What are they? Are they illegal? What is to be done with them? What of the suitcase at Heathrow, seeping blood from the meat inside? Is this beef or bushmeat? Duiker or mandrill? From an endangered species or not?

Conservationists passed much of the 20th century with a presumption that trade in endangered species was a spectacularly poor idea and needed tight control. That they did so reflects the eventual success of a set of arguments that began in the very earliest years of the century. The current regime to control wildlife trade is built upon the Convention on Trade in Endangered Species (CITES), signed in 1973.[4] The arguments for (and against) such legislation were protracted, and still resonate. The implications of the eventual success of its promoters are now in their turn highly controversial.[5]

CITES works by establishing international agreement on the control of the import and export of wild species listed in three Appendices. Species in Appendix I are believed to be on the brink of extinction, and may not be traded commercially. Appendix II includes species that might come to be in danger of extinction if trade is not prevented (and 'look-alikes', that is species that closely resemble Appendix I species), while Appendix III lists species subject to regulation by one country, and which it requests other parties to the Convention to also regulate.[6] It is a fine idea. Conservationists have believed for years that a great many species are being pushed rapidly towards extinction because people want to buy them, or bits of them. Pets, furs, medicines, specialized foods, rare woods, jewellery, knick-knacks – market demand exerts a huge pressure on rare species, one that tends to increase as they become rarer. If all those species in danger of extinction were listed clearly, then it should be possible to stop illegal trade. CITES does that, reducing one threat to wildlife, and one that through the 20th century conservationists saw as pretty important.

In practice, things have proved a great deal more complicated. There is a wonderful document (running to 119 pages) that lists all the species regulated by CITES.[7] Some things are simple – gorillas and chimps are in Appendix I, as are dugongs and rhinoceros. No problem there. No problem either with the black swan or the lammergeier (Appendix II). But there are four and a half pages of parrots, and almost three pages of crocodiles, plus 12 pages of plants. This is a taxonomist's Aladdin's cave, but it must be a customs officer's idea of hell.

Whatever the specific arguments about CITES (discussed further later in this chapter), it represents the implementation of a particular approach to the conservation of rare species, one that places great emphasis on the destructiveness of hunting and trade. This view is long-established. To conservationists, as Sir Clement Hill commented in 1909, it seemed self-evident that 'very great slaughter goes on when questions of trade are connected with the destruction of animals'.[8]

The historical pedigree of this view is clear. Stalwart of the Society for the Preservation of the Wild Fauna of the Empire (SPWFE), Sir Henry Seton-Karr, saw in western America a powerful parable of the damage that uncontrolled commercial hunting could cause. He had known the west from the days when 'big game of all kinds were plentiful, when no measures for their protection were even thought of, and when everyone killed according to his own sweet will'.[9] Since then, antelope, deer, and wapiti had been exterminated or driven away from many areas. Protective legislation came too late for the buffalo. Indians (when they obtained cheap rifles) and white settlers had a role in its demise, but the chief culprit was the professional white hide hunter. The people needed to make a living, but to Seton-Karr it was 'permissible to wonder at the shortsightedness of the State authorities and of the United States Government, who permitted the slaughter to go so far. The moral for us of the Empire is plain'.[10]

In the British Empire in the early 20th century, commercial hunting (whether African or European), was repeatedly condemned by conservationists as a threat to wildlife even greater than the greedy sportsman, the settler or the hungry native. In the Sudan, Lord Cromer stated that the principal threat to game came from 'organized hunting parties, well armed with rifles', coming over from the Abyssinian frontier 'slaughter[ing] game indiscriminately' in search of hides. He doubted if the illicit destruction of game in the Sudan could entirely be stopped, as long as the natives possessed firearms, and he noted that it would be 'difficult if not impossible to disarm them'.[11]

Trade in tropical Africa continued to provide a powerful incentive for such hunting. In Kenya, strategic roads into the North Frontier District allowed easy access for lorries by the 1920s, and it was easy to smuggle ivory into Italian Somaliland.[12] White hunters developed many ruses to allow them to shoot elephant without breaking the letter of the law. In Uganda in the 1920s, known *shamba*-raiding elephants were kept alive to provide a permanent excuse for shooting other elephants for their ivory, and elephant were also herded onto farms to provide an excuse for killing them.[13] However, for many conservationists by the 1920s the real problem was the 'native hunter', when stimulated by the profit motive – and in Kenya, the Somali and other traders who used local hunters and illegally exported rhino horn and ivory, or as Keith Caldwell put it, 'our ivory'.[14] Caldwell believed that the door to commercial hunting should be 'banged, bolted and barred'.[15] Within one territory, that might be done by regulation, as it was, for example, in 1930 in Tanganyika, where the sale of game meat without a licence costing 40 shillings per annum was banned, a move that the SPFE believed 'should do much to check the traffic in game meat illegally obtained'.[16] Between territories, or on the wider international stage, it was much harder to regulate trade.

Conservation was dominated for the first three decades of the 20th century by men who had hunted, and many features of the dominant gentlemanly sporting code were important influences on conservation thinking. They reserved particular hostility for the commercial hunting of game, what Captain Keith Caldwell termed in 1926 'the profit killers'.[17] However, there was more to the hostility of conservationists to wildlife exploitation than simply the spectre of over-hunting. It was hunting carried out without the social constraints of sportsmanship that woke real fear of destruction. This was a feeling shared not only by the *Boys' Own Paper* and *Scouting for Boys* style of imperial British sporting conservationists, but also by their patrician equivalents in the United States. Both denigrated hunting for profit and for subsistence, while they glorified hunting for sport.[18] They were, of course, members of the same spiritual and economic community.

The conservationists' sense of sporting values waxed particularly strong in the case of European commercial hunters. Inexplicably in the eyes of sporting conservationists, such people did not hunt for trophies, nor for meat to feed their farm hands or to protect their crops, but for profit. They exploited easy loopholes in Game Ordinances designed to allow farmers to protect their fields, and the development of local markets for horns, ivory and hides made export regulations ineffective. Commercial hunters did not run the personal risks that excused the true sportsman's killing, and they killed without concern for the exhaustion of the stock. They were seen to lack an acceptable moral compass, shooting indiscriminately, and they left wounded animals to die ('the profit killer cared nothing for the fact that many limped away with broken legs and other wounds').[19] The 'profit killer' could not be a gentleman. In his 1909 'sportsman's platform', William Hornaday wrote simply 'a game-butcher or a market hunter is an undesirable citizen, and should be treated as such'.[20] His focus was North America, and he also argued that there was no excuse for the sale of meat as food, nor (in contrast to the more patrician style of hunting on landed estates in the United Kingdom), for 'the maintenance of hired labourers on wild game'. For conservationists, particularly sports hunting gentlemen, trade in wildlife was both wholly unacceptable and inevitably destructive. It had to be stopped if conservation was to progress.

THE PROBLEM OF IVORY

One product was the centre of debate about wildlife harvesting and trade throughout the 20th century, and that is ivory. From its foundation, the SPWFE was concerned about the export and sale of horns and skins in Africa, but their chief concern was always the hunting of elephants and the trade in ivory. In particular, they worried that young and female elephants were being killed, something that was both unsporting and damaging to the capacity of elephant populations to sustain themselves. Thus in 1907, the Society wrote to the Colonial Office about the killing of inappropriate elephants in the Gambia, saying 'to preserve the African elephant from extinction in the near future it is highly necessary that cow elephants and young bulls should be protected'.[21]

To the SPWFE, the obvious solution to such hunting was to constrain the ivory trade, establishing a minimum weight for the sale of tusks, and stopping the trade in undersized ivory. If cow and immature elephants had to be killed to protect crops, so be it, but there should be no additional inducement from profit on the sale of small ivory.[22] In 1908, they proposed that no ivory under 25 pounds per tusk should be traded from any British port in Africa.[23] In reply, the Colonial Secretary pointed out that such a law would not be of much use without an international agreement, otherwise people would just smuggle the ivory across borders to territories that allowed lower minimums. Furthermore, such standardization would be difficult, even within the British possessions. While there might be a need for elephant protection in British East Africa (that is Kenya), in Uganda there was a problem keeping troublesome elephant numbers down and protecting crops.[24]

The argument about small ivory was sustained, however, and an international scheme for the protection of elephant and rhinoceros was proposed at a conference held in London just before the outbreak of the First World War. This decided that the export of tusks of less than 10 kilos (approximately 22 pounds) in weight would be prohibited, while at the same time settlers and natives might be protected against the ravages of elephants by the respective powers.

The war put paid to ratification of this protocol, as to so much else. But by the 1920s the trade in ivory and rhinoceros horn was buoyant, and not confined to Africa. In Lower Burma rhinoceroses were being 'rapidly exterminated', their horns in demand for their medical properties, 'largely due to the existence of Chinese superstitions'.[25] A letter was drafted to urge the India Office to enforce game laws properly.[26] In Africa, the Belgians were urged to prohibit the sale of rhino horn in the Belgian Congo to protect the white rhinoceros.[27] Meanwhile, the major channel for the export of illegal ivory from East Africa in the 1920s was via Italian Somaliland through the British possession of Aden, where, as long ago as 1909, the Society had urged the Colonial Secretary to stop the sale of horns and skins.[28] His successor reported that he found it strange that travellers to India, stopping at a port in Asia, should wish to buy horns and skins of African mammals, but it was so. In 1923 the Society heard that customs officers in Kenya had stopped inspecting baggage for trophies, and even when (following representations from the Society) searches were reinstated, duty was not charged, contravening the London pact of 1909 to levy a duty on all ivory and trophies at port of export.[29]

In response to these pressures, the Foreign and Colonial Offices began to take steps to establish the International Convention on the Sale of Ivory agreed before the First World War. They started first to try to reconcile the various British Imperial Authorities in Africa: the Union Government of South Africa did not wish to be included, claiming that elephants were adequately protected already.[30] British colonial governments were no longer as responsive as they had been to the siren call of conservation, and progress was slow. In 1922, the Society persuaded General Smuts (Governor-General of South Africa) to support its efforts to persuade the Foreign Office to call a conference on the international trade in ivory.[31] In 1924 they agreed to consider an Ivory Conference once the form of government to be established in Rhodesia was settled.[32] By 1928, the United Kingdom, France and Belgium had expressed themselves willing to cooperate on an agreement on the export of ivory, and the Colonial Office was in touch with Portugal and Italy.[33]

This was all too slow, and too parochial, confined within the comfortable bounds of European colonial legislators. If the global ivory trade was to be tackled, a wider platform was needed, such as the League of Nations, or an independent international organization.[34] This would take conservation out of the hands of individual national actors, even those with as long a reach as the British Colonial Office. Agreement on wildlife trade required truly international action. There was precedent for this, and for international action to regulate unbridled commercial harvesting, in a very different environment, the sea.

OUTCONSUMING NATURE

In 1883, the British biologist T H Huxley, President of the Royal Society, blithely argued that sea fisheries, for example for cod, herring, mackerel and pilchard, were effectively inexhaustible, and any attempt to regulate them was therefore pointless.[35] In the face of the rapacious demands of the 20th century, most notably perhaps in the catastrophic decline of the Newfoundland cod, this seems a farcically optimistic view.[36] The cod of the Newfoundland Grand Banks is now effectively extinct as a commercial fish, to the utter destruction of the economy of the Canadian fishing communities. The damage was done quite simply by over-fishing.

The northern cod is found in the waters of southern Labrador and eastern Newfoundland (the Grand Banks), mostly now within the 200 mile Canadian fisheries limit, where the cold Labrador current (from the Arctic) mixes with the warm Gulf Stream.[37] The fishery is centuries old, with European boats, from the Basque country in particular, crossing the Atlantic to prepare salt cod for the European market. It was a tough life. Until recent decades, most fishing was small-scale, and took place close to the coast in summer as fish moved inshore to feed, using traps, gill-nets and hook and line. Cod spawn in the winter and spring months when fog, storms and ice effectively prevented fishing. Technologies were too crude to threaten the fish population. There were no rules to regulate catches beyond those imposed by the weather and the sea, and competition for the best on-shore drying locations.

Cod populations undergo natural cycles of abundance. The traditional catch during the 20th century averaged 200,000 tonnes, but was highly variable (between 150,000 and 300,000 tonnes). Then, in the 1960s, foreign trawlers were introduced that were equipped for winter conditions. These were highly efficient catchers of fish, and their catches were still unregulated. The cod fishery was effectively an open-access regime, and there were no limits on the size of the harvest. Moreover, the trawls of the new boats scoured the spawning banks during the breeding season, catching the breeding stock and damaging the sea floor. Initially, catches grew, to a peak in 1968 at 783,000 tonnes. Then they started to fall, to 287,000 tonnes in 1975 and then catastrophically to 31,000 tonnes in 1982. Too late, in 1977, the Canadian Government declared a 200 mile exclusion zone, but unwisely it did not seek to close down the offshore industrial fishery. Instead it set out to 'Canadianize' it, making large investments in vessels (100 foot stern trawlers) and in fish processing. The catch effort rose, but the catch fell as the population crashed. In 1992, the fishery in the Canadian zone was finally closed, but even then heavy fishing continued outside it (mostly by EC vessels, especially from Spain and Portugal). From 1982 to 1991 catches regularly exceeded quotas: there were no effective controls on what was hauled from the sea.

The story is a depressing one if you want to believe in the capacity of fisheries science to model harvests. Models were poor, stocks and mortality were systematically underestimated, and stochastic variations in cod numbers were not taken into account. Cod was treated as a unit stock, whereas it in fact consisted of different populations. The problem of recruitment over-fishing (catching of spawning populations) was not recognized. But the story is depressing too if you want to believe in the possibility of effective regulation or self-regulation of ocean fishing, or even if you believe in limits to the crass stupidity of humankind. Depressing, but not unusual.

Leaving the spurious wisdom of hindsight aside, Huxley had already been proved quite wrong by 1863, if he had but known it. The industrial revolution in Europe stimulated demand and provided the technology to meet it, driving fishing in the North Sea further and further away from port. The purse seine net, invented in the 1850s, was effective and widely used by the 1870s. The reduction of flatfish stocks off the United Kingdom was clear by the 1880s, and a Parliamentary Select Committee was appointed in 1893 to recommend measures for the preservation and improvement of sea fish stocks. The steam trawler transformed the industry, and catch per unit effort in the English North Sea trawl fishery declined by 50 per cent in the decade 1888–1898. In North America, the fishery for pelagic menhaden and mackerel off the east coast, and later for halibut off the west, also led to stock depletion. Fish catchers built bigger boats and sailed further afield, seeking new grounds and improving their gear to maintain catch rates. They left exhausted stocks behind them.

The conservation of fish stock required two things. The first was a scientific understanding of population dynamics. This was developed in the late 19th century, with the first mathematical analyses of stocks, recruitment and exploitation. The second requirement was international cooperation, because most marine fisheries are international, and the fish populations unbounded. International concern for fisheries surfaced at the same time as concern for wildlife, at the turn of the 19th and 20th centuries. In June 1899, the Swedish Government called an International Conference for the Exploration of the Sea. This recommended rational exploitation of fish stocks, firmly based on science, and subject to international agreement. An

International Council for the Exploration of the Sea was established in 1902 in Copenhagen under German chairmanship, with committees on overfishing, migration, and Baltic fish.[38] In the north-east Pacific, an International Fisheries Commission was established in 1923 and an International Pacific Salmon Commission in 1937. In 1946, an Overfishing Convention was established in London, proposing minimal landing sizes for demersal fish and minimal mesh sizes for trawls. The International Fisheries Commissions were established for the northwest and northeast Atlantic in 1949 and 1953.[39] None of this made a great deal of difference: depletion through overfishing, by-catches, pollution and other examples of poor management of the open access free-for-all in the oceans have left scant promise of sustained harvests from the oceans.[40]

It was not only fish that were being flagrantly over-harvested for commercial purposes. The first international convention to control marine harvesting was the North Pacific Fur Seal Convention in 1911, between Russia, Japan, the United States and the United Kingdom (representing Canada). Fur sealing had begun in the sub-Antarctic in the late 18th century. Ships raided breeding rookeries on sub-Antarctic islands, killing hundreds of thousands of animals (Weddell, for example reported 350,000 animals killed by 91 British and American ships between 1819 and 1820). By the 1830s, the fur seal population had effectively been exhausted, and sealers began to seek elephant seals for oil instead. Meanwhile, the Russian hunt for northern fur seal in the north Pacific began soon after the discovery of the Pribilov islands in 1786, with the first regulations coming in 1872, five years after the United States purchased Alaska. Pelagic sealing began in the 1860s, and the stock declined until the convention stabilized offtake and stock until the middle of the 20th century.

Unlike fish, the fate of land-breeding sea mammals and birds was something that awakened the interest of wildlife conservationists. International agreement had been reached for the preservation of the northern fur seal, but the exploitation of elephant seals and king penguins in the sub-Antarctic seemed to conservationists to offer a serious threat of extinction.[41] Moreover, this was a problem within the purview of the British Empire, and it attracted the attention of the SPWFE. In 1913 they reported that whales and albatrosses, seals and penguins were being 'ruthlessly and quickly destroyed' in the South Shetland and South Orkney Islands and South Georgia (all under the Falkland Islands Government), without regulations in force 'to check their destruction', or officials at depots to check the numbers killed. The society decided to draft a memo for the Colonial Office and write a letter to *The Times* to draw publicity.[42] Between the First and Second World Wars, sea lions, seals and elephant seals continued to be killed commercially in the Antarctic by annual expeditions from Cape Town.[43] There were also lurid reports in the English papers that the Canadian government was shooting sea lions (believed to be serious predators of salmon) off British Columbia by machine gun fire.[44] Oregon and Washington States of the United States had offered bounties on these species for years. Hunting of harp seals off

Newfoundland, and grey seals off Cornwall also exercised the SPFE's hyperactive imperial sensibilities.[45]

By the 1920s, there were also concerns about the size of the harvests for the trade in furs – indeed the father of animal population ecology, Charles Elton, worked as a consultant for the Hudson's Bay Company trying to explain cycles in populations of arctic fur-bearing animals.[46] The Earl of Onslow, on becoming President of the SPFE, noted that the recent 'great slaughter' of fur-bearing animals might threaten the trade itself.[47] The Society discussed measures for the protection of the sea otter with the Foreign Office and the Hudson's Bay Company in 1928,[48] and formed a sub-committee to confer with representatives of a fur trade beginning to get nervous as to how much longer the supply would hold out.[49]

WITHOUT BORDERS

Much of the energy expended on conservation in the first half of the 20th century was essentially local in its focus. This is particularly true of the British Empire, where concern was focused on the hunting of particular species and particular reserves, actions being coordinated through the Colonial Office in London, where the arguments could be stimulated and steered by the SPWFE. Conservation problems perforce took a common form in different places, as did recommended legislative responses. However, conservation was mostly seen as something that could be undertaken through local action. From the first, however, there were problems that could not be solved locally, and demanded international coordination and action. As the century wore on, most areas of conservation became internationalized, but the initial stimulus for coordination and collaboration came from the concern about international trade in wildlife products that arose from the commercial harvesting of wild species.

This surfaced in many different guises. One was a concern about the importation of feathers for the millinery trade. In the United States, George Bird Grinnell, editor of *Forest and Stream*, founded the Audubon Society in 1886 to speak against the slaughter of birds for meat, eggs and feathers. He was overwhelmed by the response, recruiting 38,000 members before closing the infant society in 1888. However, a group of concerned women formed the Massachusetts Audubon Society in 1896, and similar societies started to spring up in states across the United States, forming an alliance in 1901.[50] In the United Kingdom, women founded the Plumage League in 1885 and the Society for the Protection of Birds in Manchester in 1889. Like the 'fur, fin and feather' afternoons held by ladies in Croydon, these were at first women's groups agitating within polite society about the use of feathers in ladies hats. This was a very significant trade. John Sheail reports that nearly 7000 birds of paradise, 0.4 million West Indian and Brazilian birds and 0.36 million East Indian birds were imported in the first quarter of 1884.[51] In 1909, hunting of birds for feathers in places like Jamaica and Panama was on the SPWFE's agenda for the Colonial Office alongside more muscular concerns such as game conservation.[52] The Society for the Protection of Birds set out to recruit members as converts to their cause, and by 1898 had 20,000 members and 150 branches, including one in India, which in 1902 obtained a government ban on skin and feather exports. In 1899, officers of the British army were ordered to stop wearing egret feathers, and in 1904 the society was granted a royal charter, becoming the Royal Society for the Protection of Birds (RSPB). In 1911 the society employed sandwich men on the streets of London and ran a poster campaign against the use of bird plumes in hats. In the United States, the Audubon Society also prospered and grew, establishing a Junior Audubon Club programme in 1910.

The SPWFE shared some of the RSPB's goals, and was strongly in favour of prohibiting the importation of birds in danger of extinction.[53] The society gave 'hearty support' to the principles of the British Importation of Plumage (Prohibition) Bill at a meeting in 1914, although it did not pass. The RSPB persisted, and the Act was finally passed in 1921, banning the importation of all feathers except those of ostrich and eider duck. Pressure continued, and in time this domestic legislation enabled acts elsewhere (for example in Australia) to bite by closing the UK market.[54] There were similar developments in the United States. New York State made the sale of the plumage of all birds native in the state illegal in 1918, and in 1916 an Anglo-American Convention for the Protection of Migratory Birds was agreed. In 1918 the US Federal Migratory Bird Treaty Act became law. The US Tariff Act prohibited importation of wild birds' plumage for commercial uses, the US Feather Millinery Chamber of Commerce 'very patriotically living up to both the letter and the spirit of the law'.[55]

THE DEVIL AND THE DEEP BLUE SEA

Marine mammals were also beyond easy protection under legislation passed in any one country, and their conservation was also necessarily conceived in the context of international collaboration. Despite its predominant interest in savanna game, the SPFE was also concerned about sea mammals and particularly whales in the open ocean. By the 1920s, it reported that these had 'come upon very evil days'. There was no convenient governmental authority, British or otherwise, to whom they could appeal to improve the situation. Moreover, in the open-access regime towards the high seas, how could any government in justice restrain its own nationals while foreign competitors retained a free hand? What was needed was universal agreement. Without it, 'doubtless only when the last whale has disappeared will tardy legislation at length emerge'.[56]

Whaling was long-established by the 20th century, both in the form of local subsistence production and larger-scale commercial industry. In Europe, for example, there was an important Basque whale fishery from the 12th century until the early 17th (based in towns such as Biarritz, San Jean de Luz, San Sebastian, all more familiar in the 20th century as tourist resorts). By the 17th century, right whales were rare in the Bay of Biscay, and hunters were reaching as far afield as Iceland, Newfoundland and Labrador.[57] In the 16th century a Dutch and English whale fishery was active in Spitsbergen, with the industry moving to the Davis Strait, East Greenland, Iceland and Jan Mayen in the 17th and 18th centuries. From the 17th century American whaling began, based in New England, especially Massachusetts: Nantucket, Long Island, Cape Cod. European and American whaling turned to the enormously valuable sperm whales of the Southern Ocean in the 18th century and the Pacific in the 18th and 19th.

Prior to 1873, whales were killed perilously from open boats sent out from a parent sailing ship, but in that year the explosive harpoon was invented, and with the steam catching vessel this allowed a new and aggressive expansion into the Southern Ocean, first of land-based and then open ocean or pelagic whaling, with factory ships processing whale carcasses at sea, mainly for their oil and meat. Steam ships were fast enough to catch fin whales such as the blue whale, and their awkward carcasses could be kept afloat for industrial processing with compressed air. By 1906 there were 14 whaling leases in South Georgia, South Orkney, South Shetland and the Falklands, and catches rose, to 23,000 animals in 1924–5 and 43,000 in 1930.

Whaling stopped in the First World War, but, ominously, stocks did not recover. In 1926, the International Council for the Exploration of the Sea established a Whaling Committee, although whale hunting continued unabated. In 1931, for example, 30,000 blue whales were taken worldwide.

In 1937, an International Whaling Conference was called, attended by South Africa, Argentina, Australia, Germany, Irish Free State, New Zealand, Norway, the United Kingdom and the United States. As a result, an International Whaling Convention was signed, establishing a sanctuary in the Antarctic Ocean, closing most of the Arctic to pelagic whaling and protecting Antarctic humpback whales for a year. After the Second World War (during which whale meat was sold widely in both the United States and the United Kingdom), the whaling nations met again in London in 1945, and then in December 1946 in Washington. At that meeting an International Convention for the Regulation of Whaling was signed, establishing the International Whaling Commission (IWC) 'to provide for the proper conservation of whale stocks and thus make possible the orderly development of the whaling industry'.[58]

The IWC has enjoyed a chequered and politically charged history, handling issues of scientific ignorance and uncertainty, and increasingly complex issues of ethics.[59] Membership of the IWC is open to any country in the world that formally adheres to the 1946 Convention. Its task is to review and revise measures for the conduct of whaling throughout the world, including issues of limits on the numbers and size of whales which may be killed, the open and closed seasons and areas for whaling, the designation of whale sanctuaries and the protection of certain species.

Although the IWC had, by the closing decades of the 20th century, evolved into an arena for debate about whether whaling was acceptable at all, it acted initially as a management agency for whales as a fishable stock. Hunting continued apace for several decades after the Second World War. Indeed, conservationists bemoaned the fact that Italy, Japan, Argentina and the Netherlands were building new whaling ships in 1951, and that catches of the blue whale in particular were increasing.[60] There is great uncertainty about the accuracy of catch data from some whaling nations, but probably the peak year for whaling was 1961–2, when over 66,000 whales were killed. The Australian humpback whale fishery collapsed in 1962–3. The blue whale was protected by the IWC in 1965, although in fact the USSR continued to hunt it. By that time, whalers had begun perforce to turn to smaller and less cost-effective species – the industrial capture of sei whales began in 1958, of Bryde's whale in the Pacific and minke whale in 1971.

However, an increasing number of countries decided to abandon whaling, the stocks being so depleted that government subsidy was uneconomic, and public opinion growing increasingly unhappy with the morality of the whole business. The United Kingdom, the Netherlands and New Zealand stopped whaling in 1963–1964, Norway stopped pelagic whaling in 1969 (although it continued coastal whaling), while in the 1970s, Canada, the United States, South Africa and Australia all stopped commercial whaling.[61] In most industrialized countries the shift in public opinion against whaling at this period was decisive. The 1970s saw the issue of whaling taken up by the environmental movement in industrial countries. Greenpeace began its high-profile anti-whaling campaign in 1975, pitting inflatable boats and drivers against harpoon ships, graphically claiming the role of nature-loving David to bloodthirsty industry's Goliath. In July 1979, radical environmentalists from the organization *Sea Shepherd* rammed the pirate whale ship Sierra in Portugal, one among several examples of 'ecotage'.[62]

The 1972 Stockholm Conference on the Human Environment called for a ten-year moratorium on whaling, and nine conservation bodies, including the Fauna Preservation Society (FPS), appealed for its implementation.[63] The FPS demanded more scientific research, especially that research should not be confined to dead whales and the work and itineraries of whaling ships.[64] In London, the British comedian Spike Milligan took a petition calling for the end of commercial whaling signed by 27 leading industrialists, trade unionists and financiers to the Japanese embassy in 1974.

In 1975, the IWC established a new management policy, intended to bring all stocks to the levels providing the greatest long-term harvests, by setting catch limits for individual stocks below their calculated sustainable yields. However, scientists could not deliver, for too little was known about stock sizes (and catches). Anyway, debates about quotas were as much political as scientific.[65] In

1980, Richard Fitter castigated the IWC for having 'stage-managed the commercial extinction of the blue whale, the humpback whale, the sei whale and all but the North Atlantic stocks of the fin whale'.[66] In 1981 the IWC set a quota of zero for sperm whales in the Southern Ocean and North Atlantic, and agreed to ban the cold grenade harpoon.[67] In 1982 this was extended to all commercial species.

The IWC itself describes the decision to stop commercial whaling completely from 1985–1986 rather nicely as a 'pause' or 'a moratorium', although most outside observers from non-whaling countries have remembered it as an end to whaling for all time. A Revised Management Procedure was accepted and endorsed in 1994, although not implemented. In the 1990s, a deadlock developed between countries (Norway, Iceland and Japan) that wished to return to whaling when stocks allowed (believing that this could be done now), and those (for example the United Kingdom, France and Australia) who believed that the humanitarian case against whaling wholly outweighed any economic or cultural case for the killing. In 1992 Iceland withdrew from the IWC and Norway re-commenced a commercial minke whale hunt. In 2001 Norwegian whalers hunted 549 minke whales (from two stocks) in five different areas, from the North Sea up to Spitzbergen and Jan Mayen. Japan also pursued an extensive scientific whaling programme whose purpose is described by opponents as commercial.[68] This is a long-established practice: in 1977 Japan awarded itself a quota of 240 Bryde's whales for 'scientific research' coincidentally replacing reductions made in their quota of 94 sei and 132 fin whales by the IWC.[69]

In the middle of the fierce debates about the science, and the moral acceptability of whaling, lie the ongoing practices of aboriginal whale hunting, just as cruel as the commercial hunt, although of tiny ecological significance. Aboriginal subsistence whaling is permitted in Greenland (fin and minke whales), the Russian Federation (grey whales), St Vincent and The Grenadines (humpback whales), the United States (Alaska, bowhead and occasionally grey whales). As Richard Fitter noted bitterly after the 1980 IWC meeting, the United States 'bulldozed through' a quota of 65 bowhead whales struck or 45 landed of the endangered bowhead whale, 'because Eskimos have votes and whales do not'.[70]

Whaling is a classic conservation issue. It brings into conflict the utilitarian approach to conservation (that it is acceptable to harvest whales so long as the stock endures), and the moral and aesthetic dimension (that whaling is cruel and unacceptable whatever the circumstances). It highlights the importance, and the limitations, of science and scientists as arbiters of what is sustainable and also (more obviously) of what is acceptable. It awakens fierce debate about the rights of indigenous people, and particular traditional communities (Norwegian or Japanese whalers or whale meat consumers for example), to treat wild animals as they have done in the past, regardless of changing mores elsewhere. It provides a perfect ground on which to debate whether the managed exploitation of species does or does not provide an effective basis for their preservation, and whether the short-term self-interest of a few can ever effectively be regulated, by themselves or their governments.

One thing is clear, that the conservation of the great whales, like other species of the open ocean, is not readily achieved through conventional protected area strategies, although over the years there have been various attempts to establish sanctuaries where whaling is forbidden. In 1938, an Antarctic Sanctuary was established south of 40°S between longitudes 70°W and 160°W, but in 1955 the IWC opened this area, initially for three years, to reduce the pressure of catches on the rest of the Antarctic whaling grounds. In 1979 an Indian Ocean Sanctuary was established for 10 years, extending south to 55°S latitude. It has since been extended twice. In 1994, the IWC adopted a Southern Ocean Sanctuary for 10 years. In 2001 the island of Nieu in the Cook Islands and French Polynesia announced sanctuaries in their territorial waters.

THE FUR FLIES

In the global commons of the open oceans, it was obvious from early in the 20th century that conservation of economically harvestable animals required international action. In the face of the logic of diverse industrial enterprises exploiting an open access resource, the promise of self-regulation proved illusory. From the 1970s, as whale stocks moved from decline to crash, much of the work of international regulation turned to banning exploitation. Here was the story of ivory re-told, with a population of animals scattered in an ocean of unknown territory beyond the bounds of feasible policing. With no question of self-control by hunters, and scant prospect of effective external regulation, conservationists' response was to push the IWC to suppress harvest and trade.

In the second half of the 20th century, conservationists lacked the easy access to the levers of power in the British Colonial Office previously enjoyed by the SPWFE. Britain was impoverished, and rapidly discharging itself of the duties and perquisites of empire. The new international conservation regime (described in Chapter 3), dominated by the United States, was influential in a number of ways, but it was subservient to the new trans-national institutions of the World Bank and the United Nations. As a result, neither conservation organizations based in Europe nor those in North America had privileged access to either their own governments (obsessed with their home economies and the complex strategic power games of decolonization and the Cold War), or the legion of new independent governments that thronged the United Nations. Conservationists were predominantly Northern, white and wealthy, and they comprised a growing global movement, but they lacked direct power and influence. The resurgence of the post-war world economy, however, was giving real energy to the consumer forces that had driven the wildlife products trade. It is perhaps not surprising therefore that debate about a conservation response to this trade took a very similar course to that on whaling. Two trends in particular engaged conservationists, the trade in live animals, for zoos and other purposes, and the trade in fur (and to a lesser extent feathers, for in the 1950s the plumage trade began to take off again).

By the 1940s, the live animal trade had taken over from the museum trade as a *bête noir* of conservationists (see Chapter 6). The problem was threefold, and related both to ethical and practical concerns. First, animal collectors and their local agents often had to kill adult animals to obtain the young specimens desired by zoos – in the case of primates in particular, the adult death toll in the attempt to obtain infants was (as it remains) significant. This struck conservationists as wasteful, but also as cruel (creating orphans from happy family groups). Second, many animals died in transit, at all stages of their journey, again both wasteful and cruel. Third, animal collectors created a demand for species that led to speculative hunting activities by local agents. To conservationists, this awakened their long-established fear of 'natives' with guns, rapacious, cruel and unthinking agents of the unscrupulous dealer.

Of course, zoos and their directors were, by the 1960s, leading advocates of conservation, both *in situ* (in protected areas) and *ex situ*. Captive breeding was a critical element in conservation strategies for the most endangered species (see Chapter 6).[71] However, a properly-managed zoological collection, that could both inform the public and breed rare species, was one thing; the collection of specimens from the wild, particularly by less reputable zoos without strong scientific programmes, was another. The old-fashioned wildlife menagerie as a money-making spectacle was not at all to be encouraged. Furthermore there were issues of both cruelty and waste to confront in the collection of specimens.

In 1949, for example, Colonel Richard Meinertzhagen drew attention to the poor conditions in which animals were kept in Kenya before shipping, put on show in small cages 'within reach of the public, who were able to prod them with sticks etc'. He argued that dealers should be licensed. In its customary style, the SPFE agreed to write to the Kenyan Game Department.[72] In the 1950s, the FPS began to focus attention on the regulations for live animal imports at the United Kingdom end of the supply chain in response to a request by the Wild Life Protection Society of South Africa to halt the importation of tortoises. In 1954, IUPN requested their help with controlling illegal traffic from a different direction, in orang-utans through Singapore. Although orang-utans could not be brought into Singapore without a permit, there was no ban against exporting them again. The FPS secured an assurance from the government that permission to re-export would only be given if there was evidence of permission to export from their country of origin. As a result, the price of orang-utans in Singapore dropped. However, this was one species, and one port – moreover, one at the time still under the quirky bureaucratic hegemony of the British Empire.

Barton Worthington raised the threat of trade to species more generally at the IUCN Board meeting in 1961, urging legal controls.[73] At the Arusha Conference in September of that year, many African delegates argued that the scale of illegal trade was undermining their efforts to control poaching. The capture and export of ten mountain gorillas from Kivu in November of 1961 added to the pressure for action.[74] In 1963, in the light of its own involvement in *Operation Oryx* (Chapter 6) the FPS agreed to discourage the capture of any endangered species if it would add to the risk of extinction, except in the extreme case that capture was essential to its continued survival.[75] The FPS continued to lobby the Commonwealth Office through the 1960s, and with the Zoological Society of London it supported a Private Members Bill in Parliament to restrict the import of rare animals in accordance with the export laws of the country of origin. In 1964 the Prime Minister of Singapore greatly tightened controls on smuggling, and in 1967 the Governor of Hong Kong made it an offence to possess, buy or sell orang-utans without a permit, closing a further loophole for the Borneo trade; Indonesian police ordered all captive animals to be seized.[76]

Meanwhile, at the IUCN General Assembly in Nairobi in 1963, there had been discussion of a number of wildlife trade issues, including the poaching of leopards, trade in turtles for soup, and more generally the importation of rare species. The FPS presented their work on the draft Parliamentary Bill, and in 1963 they started two new campaigns. The first was against the use of spotted cat skins in the fashion business, with the aim of ending the illicit trade in leopard and cheetah skins and the poaching that drove it. The second was against turtle soup.[77] The fur trade campaign followed a resolution by IUCN in 1963 that the trade should be halted. The Society wrote to leading fashion writers, and members of the Incorporated Society of London Fashion Designers, to ask them to help discourage the spotted cat fur trade. A leopard skin coat took from five to seven skins; some 50,000 being sent annually from East Africa alone, of which only 500 were killed legally.[78] The fashion fur industry was also strong in the United States, the successful attempt of furriers to make furs 'fun', in contrast to the 'square' mink coast of the older generation.[79] In 1965 *Oryx* cited an example of the style of the new fashion-conscious fur-lovers: 'a member of the FPS, visiting Nairobi, taxed an American lady about her leopard skin coat, pointing out what was happening to leopards in the wild. The answer was: yes, she supposed that leopards would be extinct shortly; that was why she was buying two coats *now*'.[80]

In July 1964 the UK Animals (Restriction of Import) Act, originally proposed by Lieutenant Colonel C L Boyle, was finally passed, making it illegal to import a wide range of animals without a licence awarded by the Board of Trade. The Act established a committee to advise the Board of Trade under Lord Cranbrook (appointed in 1965 to the FPS council), with Boyle and Richard Fitter as members. This was a major step forward, but it was not an international agreement. That had to wait another decade, and the trading in furs of endangered species continued.

In 1970 IUCN and the International Fur Trading Federation agreed on a voluntary ban on the use of skins of tiger, clouded and snow leopards, giant and La Plata otters, and a three year ban on leopard and cheetah skins.[81] In the same year, the British Board of Trade banned imports of vicuna skins and hair. The new pattern of international conservation lobbying is neatly demonstrated here – Felipé Benavides from Peru (made an FPS Vice-President in 1971) had lobbied the Society, and FPS council member Sir Berkeley Gage, ex-ambassador to Peru, had in turn lobbied the British government. Benavides lamented the trade in chinchilla fur, caiman and otter skins and the unequal exchange that meant a jaguar skin was exchanged for a couple of machetes, leaving the most impoverished citizens of the Third World (the Fourth World, as it has often been dubbed) no better off for the destruction of their wildlife. 'Are we', he asked rhetorically, 'to allow the vicuna, one of the most beautiful animals in the world, to suffer the same fate as the chinchilla?' He called for a strict ban on trade in vicuna wool and pelts.[82]

The question of live wildlife imports into the United Kingdom meanwhile remained an unresolved issue. In 1973 the FPS council decided to support a policy by WWF and IUCN on the catching and keeping of wild animals as pets. This would limit the trade to species that were sufficiently numerous in the wild state to withstand collection, those that had been shown through experience or controlled tests to be suitable as pets and represented no known danger to human or animal health or the environment if they escaped.[83] In 1973 Lieutenant Colonel C L Boyle suggested it was time to really push the British government.[84]

The Stockholm Conference in 1972 saw international agreement to move on a series of international treaties for conservation, as well as calling for an end to whaling. The Ramsar convention on wetlands had been adopted the year before at a meeting on the Caspian Sea in Iran, and now gained enough signatories to come into force.[85] The World Heritage Convention (an odd amalgam of UNESCO's concern with cultural heritage and IUCN's with natural heritage) was agreed in 1972.[86] A proposal to conserve certain islands for science, originally proposed by Max Nicholson at the Pacific Science Congress in 1966, was not eventually successful. The final convention to be proposed at Stockholm concerned international trade in endangered species. IUCN had recommended such a treaty in 1963, at the General Assembly in Nairobi, and a draft convention was in fact drawn up in 1964. This was widely circulated, but the US Department of the Interior found it 'very European', and sent an expert from the Audubon Society to Kenya to produce a new version with UNEP. It was that version that was adopted at an inter-governmental conference in Washington DC in February 1973 as the Convention on Trade in Endangered Species (CITES).[87]

CITES was hailed as a great achievement for the wildlife lobby. In the long run it seemed to promise an end to the scandals of the fur, pet and leather trades, however, in the short term it threatened to increase the peril for endangered wildlife, at least until sufficient countries had ratified it.[88] It was signed by 21 states, and came into force in July 1975. The United Kingdom ratified in 1976, and incorporated the provisions into law by the Endangered Species (Import and Export) Act 1977, although its requirements had been followed for several years by then.[89] Four FPS council members sat on the UK advisory board.[90] British ratification also brought in the Dependent Territories, those 'fragments of paradise' that were the tiny residuum of Empire, although they included important wildlife trade entrepôts such as Hong Kong.[91]

What CITES did was to establish controls on the import, export and re-export of species listed in three appendices, as described at the beginning of this chapter.[92] However, there was no organization to monitor trade, since the US-based Animal Trade Information Service (established in 1972) had become defunct. The Survival Service Commission therefore established a group of volunteer experts to gather and analyse wildlife trade data, TRAFFIC (Trade Records Analysis of Flora and Fauna in Commerce). However, this group was relatively inactive until John Burton, by then Secretary of the FPS, was appointed to chair it at the IUCN General Assembly in Zaire in 1975. He set about raising funds, and recruiting its first staff. For some months, indeed, the FPS provided space in its offices at London Zoo until TRAFFIC could establish itself independently in London. Initially, TRAFFIC's funding came from the FPS, with the RSPB, RSPCA and National Audubon Society.[93] Under John Burton's leadership, TRAFFIC grew in size and capacity, establishing a US office in 1979, and handling enquiries from governments and NGOs around the world. Its work has continued to expand. By the end of the century, TRAFFIC had grown into a network of 17 offices on five continents, and has played a major role in persuading governments all over the world to increase species protection and strengthen wildlife trade controls. CITES had also grown, with 160 Parties, and 500 animal and 25,000 plant species listed on its appendices.[94]

On the face of it, this is a great success, since, as the CITES Secretariat boasts, no listed species has gone extinct due to trade since the Convention was created. However, the whole idea of listing endangered species turned out to be a lot more complicated than had at first been anticipated. When CITES was signed in 1973, 1100 species were listed in the appendices, more or less following the species listed in the *Red Data Books*.[95] Through the 1970s, it became clear that much more definite rules were needed as to which appendix species should be listed in. Criteria for listing were agreed in 1976, but even so the lists soon got out of hand. What had been imagined as a relatively limited list of endangered species grew to nightmare proportions as governments sent in huge lists. Exporting countries (most of which were poor, and had limited capacity to train customs officers) could not cope, requiring developed nations to restrict trade. Few government administrators had realized that more than a handful of species would be involved – indeed, it must be admitted, few of the conservationists who had promoted the Convention had anticipated the problems that would follow their success.[96]

That success was anyway, arguably, rather illusory. A review at the end of the 1990s concluded that listing on Appendix I had been effective for African elephants (at least in West and East Africa, where populations were low and poaching rife), but not for rhinoceros, tigers and bears, each of which has remained subject to illegal exploitation for Asian medicine.[97] Those who had pushed for CITES had in mind the threat to species of particular trades – especially that in cat skins, ivory and rhinoceros horn. They felt sure that making such trade illegal would make it easier to stop. In some instances, it did, but in many more (ivory and rhino horn being the classic examples), it simply pushed the trade underground, where it was more or less impossible to stop. Illegal trade had in fact always been the problem, and it remained so. Many countries have weak, poorly-equipped and even corrupt regulatory regimes, and in large and small consignments, over untended borders or under the eyes of ignorant or bribed officials, through the work of numerous small traders or the intimates of Presidents, illegal trade flourished.

Nonetheless, through the 1980s and 1990s, conservationists came to see the listing of a species on CITES Appendix I as a success in itself. CITES Conferences became important to Northern conservation organizations in the way they presented their fight against extinction to their own members. They were opportunities to show that species were being 'saved', and the beauty of it was that it required relatively limited investment. In presenting their work in this way, conservation organizations made full use of the long-established synergies between concerns about extinction and about animal welfare. Concern about cat fur coats after the Second World War followed the tradition of opposition to the bird plumage trade before the First, and indeed Victorian protests about issues such as the shooting of nesting seabirds (Chapter 3). The issue of cruelty was central to debates about proper and improper hunting, and the distinction between legitimate hunters and illegitimate 'poachers' (Chapters 2 and 5). Animal rights became more prominent as a public issue in the 1980s, and conservationists were caught up in the value change.

As the animal rights movement deepened and broadened in the 1970s and 1980s, it expanded well beyond the emotional and moral range familiar to conservationists. Conservation organizations urging the need to place rare species on Appendix I of CITES made full use of the sensitivity among their members to humanitarian questions of the cruelty of hunting. It was not just that animals were being killed that were rare, and that they were being killed for the base purpose of trade, but that their very killing was cruel.

The best example of this is the African elephant, placed on Appendix I of CITES in 1989, as a result of campaigns by First World conservation and animal welfare organizations. The African Wildlife Foundation declared 1988 the year of the elephant, running a powerful television campaign in the United States about ivory poaching, to try to stop people buying and wearing ivory jewellery. This caught the attention of US animal rights organizations such as 'Friends of Animals', who urged their members to write to WWF-USA to make them campaign for an ivory trade ban. This led to some interesting politics between WWF International and their UK and US organizations with powerful contributions to the controversy from organizations such as the Environmental Investigation Agency (EIA), and subsequently Greenpeace and the International Fund For Animal Welfare (IFAW).[98] The acceptability of elephant hunting became increasingly important in debates about the listing of species under CITES into the 1990s, notably in the campaigning of the US Humane Society against the CITES down-listing of African elephants in southern African range states before and after the CITES meeting in Harare in 1997.[99]

Leaving aside the issue of ethics, CITES was of limited value as a means to achieve preservation. CITES listing of itself, of course, did nothing to actually affect the causes of extinction on the ground. Listed species were not 'saved' at all: CITES was not a measure to stop extinction, simply to allow international collaboration to regulate trade. For most species, it was habitat loss, pollution or even local consumption that comprised the main threat of extinction. It took conservationists some time to take this in.[100]

USE IT OR LOSE IT

It became clear during the 1980s that CITES not only affected illegal trade, but also made it extremely difficult to undertake legitimate trade, even where a species was abundant. Some species are rare in one place, but common elsewhere. Indeed, some species seemed dangerously over-abundant to the people who encountered them as part of their daily life. Thus in the 1980s, African states found themselves unable to trade in the skins of crocodiles legally hunted from locally abundant populations because the Nile crocodile was a listed species under CITES. This was particularly unfortunate since crocodiles were a significant hazard to human life, and, to local people, hunting them and selling the skins seemed a thoroughly sensible thing to do. This issue surfaced at the Conference of the Parties in Botswana in 1983, but it and cases like it remained a source of much debate and resentment.[101]

The enthusiasm of conservationists for seeing CITES listing as a measure of success in conservation was in some sense a parallel with the conventional approaches to protected areas described in Chapter 4. Neither the creation of a national park on paper nor the decision to make trade in certain species illegal were in themselves enough to ensure the conservation of anything. Moreover, the trade-control approach became increasingly unhelpful as conservation thinking began to embrace ideas of sustainable development in the 1970s (as discussed in Chapter 7). As we have seen, the idea of the sustainable utilization of animal and plant populations underpinned thinking about sustainable development.[102] In the 1980s, in contrast to the mainstream tradition of opposition to hunting and trade in wild species, some conservationists began to reflect upon the benefits of the extraction and consumption of species as itself a route to successful conservation.

It began to be argued that, while unregulated (or illegal) trade was directly responsible for pushing some species towards extinction, trade itself was not necessarily bad for conservation. Indeed, the reverse could be the case – trading in species, or their products, even in rare species, could be a vital source of revenue either for conservation or for other purposes. One early example of this success was the trade in rhinoceros from South Africa. The way in which the Natal Parks Board pioneered the translocation and sale of white rhinos has been described in Chapter 6. In 1986 they began to auction white rhinos to private landowners, to provide the basis for trophy hunting and wildlife viewing tourism on game ranches. In 1990 they began to do the same with black rhinos. A significant proportion of live animals of both species are now in private hands.[103]

Another conservation success story arising from wildlife trade were crocodiles. In the early 1970s there were over 2 million skins traded from wild populations of the 23 species of crocodilians worldwide, mostly from the South American caiman, *Caiman crocodilus*. Most populations were suppressed, some near extinction. However, in the late 1970s, crocodile 'ranching' projects began in many countries, with animals reared in captivity from eggs taken from the wild at levels of harvest that were low enough not to affect recruitment into wild populations. Through the 1980s, legally harvested skins began to suppress the illegal trade. By the end of the 1990s, 30 countries traded wild harvested, ranched or farmed crocodile skins of 12 crocodile species. The illegal trade has more or less disappeared.[104]

The debate about the place of extractive use of wildlife and its trade as a positive force for conservation is, at the start of the 21st century, a very vigorous one. It is also highly complex, since it overlaps with the debate about protected areas (whether they should be strict reserves or allow community-based natural resource management, see Chapter 5) and issues of sustainable development and poverty alleviation (Chapter 7). These questions have become central elements in debates about the future of conservation. They are the subject of the next chapter. The contemporary debate is taking place in the context of substantial changes in the nature of conservation organizations themselves, and the adoption of business models of organization and activity.

Chapter 9

Conservation's Plan

There is no substitute for enforcement. Without it we are lost (John Terborgh).[1]

CONSERVATION'S CORPORATE PLAN

A great strength of the conservation movement in the 20th century was its capacity for self-criticism, to pick over the past, and derive lessons from it. There has been enormous interest in self-improvement in both conservation science and practice. What kind of science do conservation planners need at different stages in the crisis of extinction?[2] What should conservation goals be and how should progress in reaching them be measured? How can resources be targeted better? How can planning procedures be improved? How should conservationists understand their own processes of thought and planning, becoming adept as individuals and institutions at adaptive management? Quite simply, how can conservationists learn to do conservation better?[3]

An increasingly important model for this regime of self-improvement has been the world of corporate business. Conservation NGOs have been remarkably successful in building relations with corporate donors. Some have had striking success in unlocking the corporate dollar, notably Conservation International (CI), set up in 1987. CI grew very fast (their revenue was $83m in 1999, a figure they maintained through 2002). Many of the world's leading American-based corporations joined CI as 'Conservation Partners', providing funds for its work. These include financial houses such as the Bank of America and J P Morgan Chase and Company, tropical agri-food businesses and food retailers such as the McDonalds Corporation, Chiquita Brands International, Starbucks Coffee Company and the Green Mountain Coffee Roasters, and entertainment businesses such as the Busch Entertainment Corporation, Home Box Office, Sony Pictures Entertainment and the Walt Disney Company Foundation. They also include industrial heavyweights of the old and new economies – the ExxonMobil Foundation and the Ford Motor Company, the United Airlines Foundation and the Intel Corporation.[4]

Not all engagements between conservation organizations and the corporate world have taken this line. Fauna & Flora International, for example, presents a different view of corporate partnerships. Through their Global Business Partnership, FFI seeks to build relationships with selected major companies whose activities have a major impact on biodiversity, for example in the resource extraction sector (eg BP or Rio Tinto), or organizations (eg British American Tobacco). FFI is also working with companies such as Vodafone and Hewlett Packard to develop ways to apply novel technologies to conservation problems.[5] Corporate relations are therefore stretched well beyond the conventional arena of corporate sponsorship to address the issue of the integration of biodiversity into corporate planning at all levels.

Whatever form the engagement with corporations takes, one effect has been that conservationists have begun to learn to think like business people. Corporate sponsors demand that conservationists present their ideas in comprehensive and target-orientated terms. Arguments about imperial responsibility, which the Society for the Preservation of the Wild Fauna of the Empire could blithely trot out to the Colonial Office, have scant purchase in the boardrooms of international companies. Conservationists have to make a convincing case that money given to them will deliver outcomes that can be specified, within predictable time-frames. Annual Reports are expensively presented, with a punchy corporate style.[6] Conservationists have become convinced that the strategic business approach works for them, as a means of enabling them to deliver results.

Furthermore, in the last two decades, conservation science has developed to such an extent that it is starting to be possible to predict outcomes from interventions in ecology, biology or land use. The insights of island biogeography and genetics of small populations have transformed thinking about nature reserve design since the 1970s.[7] Systematic conservation planning of protected area systems is now well-established in conservation biology, for example in approaches (often now using GIS) such as 'gap analysis', or the use of indicator groups to reduce demands for biodiversity data.[8] Advocates, such as Bob Pressey of the New South Wales Parks Service in Australia, argue that conservation needs to be planned in a structured framework that takes account not only of science but also of economic, land use planning and political factors. What is needed is a logical process of linked action, compiling data on biodiversity, identifying regional conservation goals, reviewing existing conservation areas, selecting additional areas, taking action to protect areas and maintaining their value by management.[9] Pressey comments 'today's conservation planners must adopt a new way of doing business if they are to maximize the biodiversity that survives through the next century and beyond'.[10]

Globally, this trend towards systematic conservation planning has stimulated a number of attempts to identify priority areas for conservation. The strategic and business-like approach to saving biological diversity is to focus on the best areas, and concentrate resources on them. The most famous such initiative is probably Conservation International's 'biodiversity hotspots'. In 1998, the Chairman of the Intel Corporation, Gordon E Moore, and his wife Betty gave CI the first of a series of gifts that will amount to £26m over 10 years. They founded the Center for Applied Biodiversity Science (CABS), to collect, order and disseminate science-based information to support its conservation goals.[11] One of CABS's first initiatives, on which CI has based all its other work, was the attempt to map 'biodiversity hotspots'.[12] This concept, and term, was coined by Norman Myers in 1988, in the context of tropical forests.[13] The CI team identified 25 areas globally, covering 2.1 million square kilometres, that contained 44 per cent of plant species (133,149 to be precise), and 35 per cent of vertebrate species (9645). Just under 40 per cent of these areas was already in protected areas.

The CI hotspots made quite a splash. They included all the usual suspects – the Cape Floristic Province and the Succulent Karoo, Madagascar, the Philippines, Mesoamerica, and the Caucasus. Furthermore, despite CI's hopes of setting the industry standard, they are in fact only one among a series of similar experiments. For example, BirdLife International had already developed a programme to identify 'Important Bird Areas', where limited range and endemic birds were concentrated.[14] In 1998, WWF had published their 'Global 200', an analysis of the most valuable examples within each major habitat type.[15]

Within the last few years, most of the major conservation organizations have adopted similar strategic approaches, or at least have packaged their work in similar strategic language. In 1998, the African Wildlife Foundation repackaged its work as its 'African Heartland Program', identifying 'large landscapes of exceptional natural value'.[16] By 1999, they had identified four 'Heartlands' (Kilimanjaro, Maasai Steppe, Samburu and Virunga); in 2000 it added a fifth, the 'Zambezi

Heartland', embracing parts of Zimbabwe, Zambia and Mozambique, and a year later a sixth, the 'Four Corners Heartland', between Botswana, Namibia, Zambia and Zimbabwe. A linked public advertising campaign began, rewarded by a £5m grant from the government of the Netherlands in 2002. In the same vein, The Nature Conservancy explains its reserve acquisition strategy in terms of a 'portfolio', and their aim is to protect a complete portfolio of reserves (described as 'functional conservation areas') in each 'ecoregion' of the world.[17] The corporate language here is both typical and deliberate: their 'Campaign for Conservation' aims to raise $1.25 billion to save 200 of the world's 'Last Great Places'.[18] Interestingly, FFI have refused to engage in centrally-planned scientifically-driven priority-setting exercises, instead developing a strategy that involves working with partners across the world to develop programmes that meet locally-defined goals as well as meeting broad global criteria.[19]

Of course, there are significant drawbacks to the corporate approach to conservation. It has led to duplication of effort, and even competition between rival corporate 'big ideas'. Rather like the battle between rival video cassette formats, there are considerable implications for corporation and consumer in the adoption of an industry standard. When the CI 'hotspots' were published, scientific critics were quick to point to the limitations of the work (for example problems of the scale of analysis and the lack of focus on ecological processes in favour of species), and possible improvements. They also urged collaboration. Only a structured debate between conservation organizations to identify common goals could make conservation effort cost effective.[20] But the pressures of corporate structure do not make this easy. The demands of corporate distinctiveness lead to a diversity of goals and make a common approach to global conservation problematic. The institutional landscape of conservation is hard to map, yet as Kent Redford and colleagues observe, 'we will lose the race to conserve nature unless we can develop systematic collaboration among conservation groups'.[21]

The problem is not simply one of competition between conservation's corporate giants, but, as discussed at the end of Chapter 3, of their relations with smaller partner organizations. First World conservation NGOs need partners on the ground in order to deliver their objectives, and very often they wish those partners to have local 'grassroots'. On the other hand Third World NGOs depend on larger and richer foreign partners for the resources to survive and do their work.

Third World environmental organizations typically lack funds, both core funds to run themselves, and operating funds to undertake any practical conservation programme. There are rarely sources of funds available within Third World countries that they can draw on, as First World NGOs do. Furthermore, they mostly lack the resources and the expertise to apply successfully for funds available internationally, for example from First World government aid programmes, or international organizations like the Global Environmental Facility (GEF). To these relatively small and impoverished potential 'partners', international conservation organizations offer an astonishing cornucopia of resources.

Although themselves cash-strapped, the modest resources of the large First World conservation NGOs represent considerable riches in a Third World context. Local salaries are low, and services tend to be available cheaply. First World NGOs provide capital and recurrent funding for projects and can exert considerable influence on their direction. Third World NGOs are often narrowly focused on single issues: international NGOs bring sophisticated and cleverly packaged ideas and values, clear goals and strategic plans as well as the all-important financial resources.

The effect of this uneven relationships is that local organizations learn to accommodate themselves to the aims of international organizations. In effect, even local policies become market driven.[22] There has been growing criticism of the power of the larger environmental NGOs to mingle with and potentially influence the corporations and First World governments, for example at the Rio Conference in 1992.[23] Only the largest NGOs had the financial reserves to attend the various Preparatory Commissions for the Rio Conference, and the experience and the expertise in the US-style lobbying process to voice their concerns effectively. Perforce, they spoke for the hordes of lesser organizations (there were 4200 accredited lobbyists), who were at best left to network and debate at the Global Forum and 'Earth Parliament', physically and psychologically distant from the main conference. Only the largest and most corporate organized NGOs (almost all of whom were North American) have much influence internationally. The so-called 'big ten' are the Sierra Club, National Audubon Society, National Parks and Conservation Association, Izaak Walton League, Wilderness Society, National Wildlife Federation, Defenders of Wildlife, Environmental Defence Fund, Friends of the Earth, the Natural Resources Defence Council, IUCN, WWF and the World Resources Institute.

BACK TO BARRIERS

One fruit of the new corporate thinking within conservation by the end of the 20th century was a re-assessment of both the community conservation debate (Chapter 5) and the idea of sustainable use (Chapter 8). A lively debate has developed between those who believed that conservation around and away from protected areas should be delivered through the community-based paradigm, and those who felt this was a mistake. Books such as John Oates' *Myth and Reality in the Rainforest*, on forest protected areas in West Africa, and John Terborgh's *Requiem for Nature*, drawing on his extensive experience in the rainforests of South America, carried conviction for many conservationists. Both were published in 1999. These were people who had devoted their lives to field research, and spoke with the passion of convinced conservationists and the impartial authority of their scientific credentials.

John Terborgh's conclusion after 'a lifetime of roaming the tropics in search of unspoiled nature' was that on the ground he found only 'inadequate parks, unstable societies and faltering institutions'. Many parks were not up the task assigned to them, and yet that task was vital, for strict protection of parks was the only viable strategy. Parks were 'the last bastions of nature'.[24] John Oates argued that the theory that wildlife could best be conserved though promoting human economic development was a myth, and seriously flawed.[25] He rightly noted that it made those who promoted it feel good, for it offered the best of both worlds, with both wildlife and people benefiting together. However, disastrously in his view, it led to a low priority for basic protection. Excessive emphasis on development can lead to a de-emphasis of conservation goals to the extent that they are no longer seriously addressed, as in the case of the Okumu Forest Reserve in south-west Nigeria.[26] While at a rhetorical level it might therefore be desirable to argue that conservation and development can go hand in hand through a joint programme, he argued that development expenditure for conservation purposes may not give results that are effective in conservation terms.

Advocates of a return to strictly protected parks with hard barriers argue that conservation organizations need to rethink the 'conservation with development' approach. They also needed to return to the principles on which conservation organizations were founded, preserving nature for its intrinsic value and the aesthetic pleasures it brings people. Some are fierce in their calls for a strong regime of policing. John Terborgh bluntly argues that 'parks cannot be maintained without order and discipline'.[27] This is not a discipline that can be generated from inside a local community – Terborgh is not a believer in woolly liberal ideas about people suddenly choosing to love nature, nor in the practical feasibility of creating institutions (such as markets) that will bring about conservation-orientated behaviour. Discipline needs to be imposed from above: 'active protection of parks requires a top-down approach because enforcement is invariably in the hands of police and other armed forces that respond only to orders from their commanders'.[28] He actually suggests an international conservation police force to enforce protection of areas of international importance.

The 'back to barriers' movement draws on one observation that is certainly true. Parks as a whole have not been successful in ending the loss of biodiversity, particularly of attractive larger mammal species. John Oates catalogues the clearance of forest and the extinction of large mammals, particularly primates, in West Africa. John Terborgh laments the slow degradation of Manu National Park in Peru: 'Having lost the luster that made it one of the world's premier rainforest parks, and swelling with an ever larger and more assertive indigenous population, the Manu will imperceptibly pass from being a national park to being a reserve for its indigenous inhabitants'.[29] One reason for the failure of protected areas to achieve their goals has been that planners have often not taken the true costs of conservation fully into account. In particular, despite the growth of ideas about 'community conservation' and 'parks for people' (Chapter 5), there has been too little recognition of who paid the costs of conservation.

The debate about protected areas therefore opens up the whole question of the relationship between conservation, sustainability, economy and poverty.

THE COSTS AND BENEFITS OF CONSERVATION

Viewed in economic terms, protected areas create both benefits and costs.[30] The methods used by environmental economists to estimate the value of species and ecosystems are still somewhat experimental, and the data used for calculations are often poor. However, there is no doubt that wildlife can generate significant economic benefits, in various ways. There are direct consumptive uses of wildlife (for example through hunting animals for meat, or cutting vegetation for timber, fuelwood or medicines). Most national parks forbid such direct use of wild species, although in a number of countries (Uganda for example), there are experimental programmes of direct use of high-value low-volume products such as medicines. Economic benefits can also come from direct use of wildlife obtained without physical consumption, for example through tourist enterprises based on wildlife viewing. In economic terms, however many people view a lion or a rainforest bird, it is (in theory) still there to be viewed again by someone else later. Economists also identify indirect use values (environmental services such as water yield from afforested catchments, or pollution control through wetlands), and existence values (the values people attach to the cultural or aesthetic attributes of species, ecosystems or natural landscapes).

In countries with a significant tourist industry, the importance of wildlife as an attraction can be very great. The classic African big game viewing 'safari' is extremely important in countries such as Tanzania, Kenya, Botswana, Namibia and South Africa. In Kenya, for example non-consumptive use benefits from wildlife (that is wildlife tourism) were estimated to be US$27 million in 1989, and the return of wildlife to the Kenyan economy 27 per cent.[31] The importance of such revenues has been recognized since at least the 1920s. The Secretary of the SPFE noted in 1928 that over half the 350,000 visitors to Canadian National Parks every year came from abroad, and estimated that they probably brought in over £1 million to the economy, of which £36,000 was direct revenue to the Canadian Parks Service. To the swelling civic pride at the national parks was added a growing national appreciation of national parks as essentially commercial assets.[32] As discussed in Chapter 4, the potential for a wildlife and landscape-based tourist industry was a central argument for the establishment of national parks internationally.

Wildlife tourism, particularly so-called 'ecotourism' (that is tourism that is designed to have negligible minimal negative environmental and social impacts) became extremely fashionable in the 1980s and 1990s.[33] In part, this was a clever piece of niche-marketing by the vast global tourist industry, recognizing the market for high-value holiday products for thoughtful and caring (and prosperous) first world travellers. Arguably it was also a reflection of the destructiveness of conventional mass tourism. From the 1960s, and the advent of cheap air fares, tourist resorts enjoyed a short boom and bust cycle where development destroyed the very values tourists came to see as relentlessly as any other industry. Sustainable tourism might have been presented as a contribution to the sustainability of environments and societies in remote areas of the world, but it was as much about trying to establish a means for the tourist industry to sustain itself.

Ecotourism is widely seen as a saviour of wildlife conservation, capable of generating a flow of revenue to pay the costs of conservation and to meet the needs of local communities. It allows conservationists to promote revenue-generation and community-oriented strategies, while maintaining traditional protectionist goals. In remote areas with charismatic species (such as the island of Komodo in the Laccadive Islands of Indonesia) small-scale high-value environmentally-sensitive tourism seems an obvious way to blend development and conservation goals together, giving local people a reason to love and not fear their vast goat-eating neighbourhood dragons.[34] On the other hand, accounts of the potential of tourism are often based on relatively informal assessments of local success, often over short timeframes. Reviews of the successes of wildlife tourism operations have often been carried out by the very people who have run the project, who do not necessarily bring the most hard-headed and critical eye to the case.

Appraisals by economists of the economics of community benefits and costs from wildlife, suggest more caution about assumptions that wildlife tourism will always bring substantial benefits.[35] In many rainforests, for example, wildlife viewing has limited potential to generate significant revenues. Forest environments, dark, wet and itchy, are only attractive to a few hardy types, and wildlife is hard to see. In central African forests, for example, the income from wildlife viewing is small, and while safari hunting (essentially an extreme form of adventure tourism) has a greater potential, even this can only manage to offset some of the costs of protected areas.[36] Many areas with urgent conservation problems in fact have very limited tourist potential: in West and Central Africa, for example, tourist infrastructure is poor, tourism is limited, and political instability is a significant problem. Even in well-known national parks, such as Royal Chitwan National Park in Nepal, tourism may not offer a long-term solution to the costs of conservation.[37]

There are two further problems with arguments for protected areas based on the magnitude of a potential tourist industry, or for that matter any other economic activity based on wildlife. The first is that the economic benefits of wildlife-based tourism are rarely equitably shared. They tend to be cornered by the businesses that run tourist operations, such as national or international hotel or tour operators, and the importers and traders in elite products for tourists. Indeed, the establishment of infrastructure to make a tourist economy possible (endless clean water, power, roads and airports) all demand investment by the state that potentially takes money away from other priorities (for example primary education, mass population water supply or primary health care). Certainly it is quite rare for the bulk of the benefits of tourism in a protected area to be shared with local people.

This is not because people have not tried to make this happen, for there are numerous examples of revenue-sharing projects to give local people a stake in wildlife tourism around protected areas. One of the best known is in Uganda, around the patches of forest preserved for the mountain gorilla (discussed in Chapter 1). Between 50 and 400 visitors a month reach Mgahinga, which is in a remote corner of Uganda. The vast majority of these (95 per cent) are foreign nationals, who pay handsomely for the right to see gorillas. In 1996, 1100 tourists generated US$140,000 in revenue at Mgahinga. Twelve per cent of that revenue was in theory set aside for revenue sharing (8 per cent to local community projects, 2 per cent to local District Administrations, and 2 per cent for a national pool), although in fact less than US$5000 was in fact spent on the construction of classrooms for primary schools. These schools were regarded as extremely important by local people. In practice the revenue sharing system at Mgahinga is very far from perfect, but there is no doubt that such wildlife resources can yield significant sums, and that with the right institutions in place these could be effectively shared with local people.[38]

However, the economic benefit of protected areas are in many cases outweighed by the costs. The early colonial conservationists of the SPWFE recognized very well that wildlife tends to generate low economic returns compared to alternative land uses. This is still true, and is a major cause of economic pressure on protected areas. In southwest Kenya, for example, the Maasai Mara National Reserve (1368 square kilometres) is surrounded by extensive Maasai group ranches (4566 square kilometres), held privately either by individual families or groups of families.[39] The group ranches are part of the larger ecosystem, and are vital seasonal grazing for migratory wildebeest in the dry season. The reserve itself generates US$20 million per year, the group ranches $US10 million. However, on some of these ranches, agriculture (mechanized wheat cultivation, and barley for the brewing trade) and livestock would be highly profitable. The current revenue on the group ranches as a whole is US$16 million, compared to US$118 million if the land were developed. In simple terms, conservation here makes no business sense. The incentives to convert land to intensive ranching are actually much greater than these overall figures suggest, for landowners control income from livestock, whereas they receive only fees from the companies running tourist facilities and services such as lodges, tours and safaris. In 1989, landowners received less than 2 per cent of the tourist revenues generated on their land. Agricultural profits, too, are enjoyed by commercial agribusiness concerns who lease land, although they pay about 5 per cent of their revenue to landowners. Across the group ranches as a whole, the profits enjoyed by landowners would be 15 times higher if appropriate land was converted either to arable and livestock. There is a huge economic incentive to change land use on these group ranches – or, to put it another way, group ranch owners pay a considerable opportunity cost for keeping the land in conservation management.

Not only are the opportunity costs of protected areas high, but they are extremely costly to establish, police and maintain.[40] Globally, US$3.2 billion is spent on protected areas, a mean of US$893 per square kilometre. However, much of this is spent in rich industrialized countries.[41] It is not entirely surprising to find that Canada spends US$1100 and the United States over US$2500 per square kilometre, almost a billion dollars in total between them. For comparison, Tanzania spends US$182 per square kilometre, Kenya US$94 and Ethiopia US$5 per square kilometre; in countries like Angola or Laos, expenditure is far less than the average (less than US$1 per square kilometre). Few countries can match the expenditures deemed necessary to maintain parks in rich countries such as the United States. Even with foreign aid, most poor countries do not spend anything like enough per hectare of protected area to ensure that biodiversity conservation is effective. So in poor countries with large protected areas designated, the burden of state expenditure is high, but still much less than is needed. For example, the total of government and donor investment in Central Africa meets only 30 per cent of the recurrent costs of the protected area network.[42]

In many countries conservation therefore represents a net cost to the national economy in terms of revenue forgone, and the direct costs of protected area management. The potential economic return on the 60,600 square kilometres of protected areas in Kenya is US$203 million, some 2.8 per cent of gross domestic product. This opportunity cost of conservation is far greater than the US$42 million returns from wildlife and forestry within the protected areas.[43] Under these circumstances, conservation has costs that need to be paid, either by the state (which may have more urgent welfare priorities), local people (who may be very poor and unable and unwilling to pay), or by conservationists either nationally or internationally (for example the members of developed country conservation organizations). Without demonstrable economic benefits from wildlife at national level, governments economists may well see conservation as a luxury they cannot afford.

Local communities pay the opportunity costs of conservation on land that they cannot use, or turn to higher value uses, as well as paying considerable costs as neighbours to parks (see Chapter 5). There is growing acceptance of the principle that these opportunity costs should be paid by those national and global interests who most passionately wish that biodiversity is preserved.[44] The gap between the sums available and the active and passive costs of conservation can be vast. A series of innovative ideas are being developed to increase funds, including the idea of environmental trust funds, tightly organized markets for environment-friendly products (for example product certification), and new ways to generate donations, for example using methods to link donors and recipients directly. Some economists argue that direct payments for habitat management would be cost-effective, essentially a global version of the conservation contracts with farmers common in the European Community such as set-aside.[45] Certainly, unless the full costs of conservation are paid, conservation efforts are likely to be ineffective. Logically, local people will oppose conservation, the financial incentives for illegal use will drive degradation of the wildlife resource, and governments will give preference to other forms of land use (for example mining or agriculture). Poorly-protected 'paper parks' will be just empty bureaucratic irrelevancies.

One thing was clear from research by the mid-1990s, that community-based conservation was much easier to achieve in theory than in practice.[46] Projects such as integrated conservation and development projects (ICDPs), which seek to achieve both development and conservation goals, are often disappointing.[47] They may not be cost effective ways to tackle indicators of poverty, and if they do not tackle poverty effectively, they may well fail to break existing economic and cultural logics driving illegal and unsustainable harvests. They are unlikely therefore to achieve species or ecosystem conservation goals. The positive impacts of ICDPs on local economies are typically transient and dependent on the supply of foreign aid flows.

None of these failings is unique to community conservation projects, although conservation organizations were slow to learn from the experience of development planners with community-level schemes. Community-based projects are inherently highly complex, require high levels of skill from project staff, substantial funds and a realistic (that is long-term) timescale. Participatory planning often generates high local expectations. Success is vulnerable to local perceptions of the project, and hence to any public failure in particular components.[48] They demand careful evaluation of the costs and benefits of project components at the level of the individual household, long-term commitments to funding and strong local participatory linkages.[49] They are usually not cheap to implement, in terms of cost per participant or per unit area, or in terms of specific conservation outputs. They tend to have high administrative costs as they demand significant numbers of high quality staff with locally-specific knowledge, and can be frustratingly slow to bear fruit. Project designers can be compromised by pressure from donors for results and at the planning stage set objectives for 3 or 5 year projects that they know will take 10 or 20 years to achieve.

Effective community-based conservation work also requires a change in the organizational culture of conservation agencies (so that they genuinely see local residents as partners not subjects) and in the social institutions of rural residents (to respond to wardens and rangers as partners and not as corrupt policemen). Neither of these changes is necessarily easily achieved, especially in a short-term project. Participatory planning may trigger debates about resource or land rights, or the awakening of political consciousness. These may be valuable things in themselves, but they tend to alter or slow down the carefully-planned pattern of project development. One of the appeals of the community-based approach to conservationists was as a way of placating local opinion, but in some circumstances it may inflame it as participants argue with the conservation agency (or with each other) about their rights, needs and aspirations.

The large (and growing) literature on community conservation, is still dominated by more or less optimistic descriptions of local level 'success', often early in a project's life, written by people involved in project development and perhaps without sufficient critical distance to provide a complete review. A few case studies have been repeated and disseminated internationally to great effect. This phenomenon, which is also common to rural development, leads to what Robert Chambers calls 'project bias', whereby successive evaluations of a region or programme look repeatedly at the same projects, and one anothers' reports, without properly questioning the nature of change on the ground. This leads to the narrowing of possible lessons that policy-makers and researchers can learn, and constrains the creativity and innovation needed in the ways protected areas are imagined and organized.[50]

THE WILDLIFE RESOURCE

The other side of the debate about the right way to link conservation to the needs of the poor, and particularly about how to manage parks, concerns the idea discussed in Chapter 8 of treating conservation in terms of the management of wildlife as a resource (Chapter 8). It has been pointed out at several points in this book that wildlife conservation draws on two distinct traditions. The utilitarian approach to nature suggests that other species are there to be used for human benefit, and that conservation involves the choice of the best way to maintain the flows of those benefits over time. The other romantic, aesthetic, preservationist tradition holds that (for a variety of reasons), other species are there to be looked after, not used. (There are also those, of course, who argue that the two are not really different, since any human choice reflects preferences, and even preserving wildlife 'for its own sake' in fact reflects human values and interests). Conservationists have argued about these things throughout the length of the 20th century.

At the start of the 21st century, there is a vigorous debate between those who would see conservation retrench in fiercely-defended protected areas, and those who argue that conservation should be built around the idea of 'sustainable use'. This phrase, like so much else in contemporary conservation, is rather fraught. It includes three separate ideas: the fact that wildlife use is an imperative or choice of people (particularly the poor) in the pursuit of their livelihoods; the issue of how populations and ecosystems are to be used and managed to achieve biological sustainability, and the possibility that use can provide incentives to conserve biodiversity.

The phrase 'sustainable use' derives from the work of the IUCN Sustainable Use Specialist Group.[51] As discussed in Chapter 7, the concept of sustainable use was first articulated in the World Conservation Strategy. IUCN's General

Assembly in Perth in 1990 adopted the idea of 'conservation of wildlife through wise use as a renewable natural resource', and called upon the Director General and the Chair of the Species Survival Commission (SSC) to prepare guidelines for sustainable use.[52] The follow-up to the World Conservation Strategy, *Caring for the Earth*, published in 1992 defined sustainable use as 'use of an organism, ecosystem or other renewable resource at a rate within its capacity for renewal'. In 1994, the SSC's Specialist Group on Sustainable Use of Wild Species prepared *Guidelines for the Ecological Sustainability of Non-consumptive and Consumptive Uses of Wild Species* for the 1994 General Assembly in Buenos Aires, Argentina.

These guidelines were rejected, and the IUCN Director General and SSC Chair appointed a Task Force to advise them on how to proceed. It was concluded that IUCN's goals in relation to sustainable use were to distinguish uses that are ecologically and socially beneficial from uses that are ecologically and socially harmful, and to assist IUCN's members and others to support and augment conditions that contribute to uses that optimize benefits to both ecosystems and people. A Sustainable Use Advisory Group was therefore appointed, and in 1995 it launched the IUCN Sustainable Use Initiative, implemented through Regional Sustainable Use Specialist Groups. A Pan-African Symposium on the sustainable use of natural resources was held in Harare in June 1996: 14 regional groups were established by the end of that year.

At the 2nd World Conservation Congress in Amman, Jordan, in 2000, a policy statement on the sustainable use of wild living resources was adopted by IUCN members (with the US government abstaining).[53] This recognized that, if sustainable, the use of wild living resources was an important conservation tool because the social and economic benefits derived from such use provide incentives for people to conserve them; that when using wild living resources, people should seek to minimize losses of biological diversity; that enhancing the sustainability of uses of wild living resources involves an ongoing process of improved management of those resources and that such management should be adaptive, incorporating monitoring and the ability to modify management to take account of risk and uncertainty. IUCN committed itself to ensuring any uses of wild living resources were equitable and ecologically sustainable. By 2003, the IUCN Sustainable Use Specialist Group comprised 17 decentralized networks of regional sustainable use groups, functioning under the auspices of IUCN's Species Survival Commission, working from FFI. Each group decides its own membership, chooses its own leaders, sets its own priorities and plans its own activities, within an overall global framework.

Many conservationists believe that it is unrealistic to imagine that human use of living resources will ever be sustainable, or at least they point out that past experience offers little prospect that it can be achieved.[54] Arguably, the neat phrase 'use it or lose it' presents a false dichotomy: wild species that are used are too often thereby lost.[55] This line of thinking suggests that it is only the preservationist road and not the utilitarian road that offers any chance for conservation in the 21st century: in as much as conservation has embraced the idea of sustainable use (especially community-based natural resource management) it needs a U-turn, back to parks, for nature's 'last stand'.[56]

The argument of enthusiasts for sustainable use is based on the argument that it is self-evident that people will continue to use wild living resources and, moreover that inevitably these will be over-exploited so that living resource stocks are depleted. In the face of such pressure, conservationists could continue to throw resources into the hopeless task of stopping people from using the wildlife they want or need. Alternatively, conservationists could try to figure out how to work with the economic, social and cultural pressures that drive human consumption, seeking to work with people to find sustainable ways to derive benefits from species and ecosystems.[57]

Arguably, conservation is better done (that is more cost effectively and equitably done) by carrots than sticks; better driven by incentives that reward sustainable management rather than by attempts to stamp out uses of nature that are vital to people's survival. On this interpretation, the challenge for conservation in the 21st century is to place sustainable use and incentive-driven conservation at the core of conservation activity.

By the end of the 1990s, there was one issue that brought debates about sustainable use into focus, and that was 'bushmeat' hunting in tropical forests. Bushmeat is an umbrella term for all wild-caught mammal meat, and it can range from cane rats to gorillas. The subject is extremely complex. There are obvious ethical issues associated (particularly in the minds of adequately-nourished Westerners) with both killing and eating apes, for example as explored by the Great Ape Project.[58] There are also health issues, since the inter-species transmission of viruses such as Ebola is a major problem for people (and indeed apes). There are issues of poverty and malnutrition (for much bushmeat is consumed by people for whom there is no immediate alternative protein source). There are issues of political representation, since the majority of those campaigning on bushmeat are white Americans and Europeans, and bushmeat consumers are mostly not. And there are, of course, issues of biodiversity and extinction, particularly in the case of great apes, for as favoured species become rarer, they acquire a rather bizarre rarity value. Demand, particularly among prosperous urban consumers, rises.

There is little question that if trends continue as at present, the bushmeat trade will lead to the extinction of large mammals across almost all tracts of tropical forest not tightly protected. Indeed, the so-called 'half-empty forest' is a reality in many countries in West Africa, and the problem is spreading very rapidly.[59] Under conditions of growing hunting pressure, biologists predict the collapse of hunted species populations: the classic boom–bust cycle of the Northern cod or the blue whale.[60]

The critical question in the case of bushmeat, however, is not whether the trade is on balance a good or bad thing, but what is to be done about it. Should it be banned, with an attempt being made to create new protected areas, and to defend those that exist more vigorously? Or is that a waste of effort – should the trade instead be made legal and controlled through regulation? If so, who should regulate it: governments, whose preservationist laws are so widely flouted? The traders who buy and sell? The middlemen who take the profit? The consumers, who would presumably like their desire for tasty, apparently healthy non-farmed protein to be satisfied in perpetuity? The conservation organizations – who can judge the true conservation priority? The communities who actually capture the animals and use them to build a scanty livelihood?[61] These are important questions, but they are not easy ones to answer.[62]

WILDLIFE AS A CROP

The debate about what economists call 'consumptive use' (because once used the resource is not there for the next consumer) and biologists prefer to call extractive use (because once used the animal or plant is no longer present in the ecosystem) is lively, but it is by no means new.[63] It was axiomatic to the first 20th century conservationists that a properly managed wildlife resource could yield a steady flow of income or other benefits such as meat.

Their model for this was, of course the private estate. The Earl of Onslow noted at a meeting of the SPFE in 1928 the 'general policy' that game on private land should be recognized as the property of the landowner. This was the world he knew, of pheasants, grouse and deer, of society house parties and well-managed rural estates.[64] Onslow, as we have seen, saw national parks as analogous to shooting estates (Chapter 4). He noted in 1928 that the allocation of game on private land to the landowners in South Africa was highly beneficial, for 'it gives the people a value and interest in the game on their land, and where the landowner has an interest in the game on his land he takes great care to preserve it'.[65]

European colonists far afield in Empire showed a persistent enthusiasm for the domestication of wild species, a *quid pro quo* perhaps for their sometimes disastrous interest for the acclimatization of species from home. P L Sclater proposed domestication as a bold scheme to further the preservation of elephant, rhinoceros, giraffe, eland and zebra. The eland simply provided 'succulent and delicious' meat, and had been bred in England, having been imported by the 13th Earl of Derby in 1842, with herds at Knowsley, Hawkstone and Woburn.[66] Sclater proposed bringing in a Keddah from India complete with 'officers, trained elephants and men' to capture and train elephants on the forested slopes of Mount Kenya. Less exotically, perhaps, Sir Charles Eliot noted experiments to domesticate zebras near Naivasha in Kenya in 1903, although he thought them too weak in the withers for rough work.[67] The Belgians made quite a success of the domestication of the African elephant at Garamba in the Belgian Congo.[68]

Such experiments did not endure, but there were many attempts to realize an economic return from wild game cropped for meat, and to ranch wild mammals. The attraction to conservationists of using wild animals rather than cattle for meat was the apparent incompatibility of cattle ranching and game, particularly because of tsetse (Chapter 7). They argued that wild animals would be more disease-resistant, and would also be better adapted to natural vegetation and conditions: game-raising would remove the need for clearance of pastures or costly water points and dipping, while at the same time maintaining populations of game. Conservation would be the basis of the economy, not its enemy. While to those planning dryland development in Africa, improved livestock industry was the solution, to conservationists, cattle were the problem, and unimproved local livestock were the least defensible representatives of the problem. African cattle were thin and carried little meat: Michael Crawford observed in 1972 that the fact that 'these little cattle were surrounded by fat wild animals many times their size did not penetrate the minds of our traditionalist administrators'.[69]

In fact, of course, African savanna cattle-keepers did not breed or manage their herds for meat, but for milk and blood, and as a walking bank account. Indigenous cattle breeds, too, have subsequently proved to be remarkably hardy, and to have been bred to cope well with poor quality forage, distant watering points and intermittent drought. To conservationists throughout the 20th century, however, it seemed self-evident that wild game was a far superior way of converting savanna vegetation into meat than any kind of domestic animal. Animals like eland offered substantial dressed carcass weights, and lean meat; moreover wild game meat was tasty – wart hog, for example, tasted of pork when warm and turkey when cold.[70]

A correspondent to the *Veterinary Record* in the 1950s reported that the Uganda Game Department produced just under 4000 tons of meat from game-shooting per year worth over £400,000 in 1956, and representing 13 per cent of the annual production of slaughtered meat in the country. The key to this bounty, and to significant future increases, was the buffalo, at half a ton on the hoof. There was therefore a need for studies of comparative weight gain of buffalo and cattle, because only then would the benefits of cattle herding become clear. A systematic programme of selective cropping of buffalo could be made to yield large quantities of meat without depleting their numbers: and (the sting in the tail) the indiscriminate slaughter of buffalo in the name of tsetse eradication to allow inefficient cattle ranching was improvident.[71]

In the 1960s, the idea of formally developing the use of wild animals as a source of meat in Africa was important to conservationists. There was never any doubt about the importance of bushmeat, even where it was illegal. G G Watterson, FAO's first Regional Forestry Officer for Africa, toured seven countries in West Africa and nine in East Africa as Stage I of the IUCN African Special Project in 1960 and 1961. He reported that 80 per cent of meat eaten in Ashanti (Ghana) came from wild animals, that the bushmeat trade (and export trade) in Dahomey was flourishing, while alternative sources of meat were scarce. In Ghana, Watterson proposed research on the relative productivity of wild game and domestic livestock under various conditions, on measures to create a feeling of 'right of use' among Africans so that they would see game as something to be harvested rationally, and on methods of game-meat processing and marketing.[72]

In Tanzania, however, illegal meat hunting was a large, highly organized and profitable business. Here Watterson did not argue that the trade needed to be controlled immediately, but he proposed that it be *converted*, with the establishment of 'schemes which are rational, sustained yield projects, benefiting local populations'. At a conference on land management problems in areas containing game, Watterson heard Chief Fundikira, Minister of Lands, Surveys and Water, argue that wildlife should be seen as one of Tanganyika's important natural resources, that 'must be worked, as an asset, for all it is worth'.[73]

By the 1960s, research of the kind that Watterson envisaged was already underway at the Fulbright Large Animal Research Unit in Southern Rhodesia. There were also significant wildlife cropping programmes within Africa. In Kenya, large-scale wildlife hunting for meat for labourers and prisoners of war had been undertaken during the Second World War for the War Supplies Board.[74] In 1958, Ian Parker, then Game Warden in Kalifi, proposed the Waliangulu Scheme, to allow traditional elephant hunters to harvest elephant.[75] With favourable mention at the IUCN Assembly at Athens, and funds from the Nuffield Foundation, the Galana Game Management Scheme began in 1960, under the Game Department. By then it had become tightly structured like a development project, and former elephant poachers were actually employed to crop elephants in the area, adjacent to Tsavo National Park.[76] Far fewer than the quota of 200 elephants a year were killed, and eventually the scheme was taken over by a private corporation as Galana Game and Ranching Ltd, in the late 1960s.

This was not an isolated development: in Uganda, culling of hippopotamus at Queen Elizabeth National Park began in 1959, because hippopotamus numbers were thought to be causing soil erosion: shooting was done by the warden, and local contractors bought the carcasses (for up to £10.00) and sold the meat (up to 2000 pounds in a large animal) locally.[77] The problem here was that the conservationists' need to reduce hippopotamus numbers was not matched by the limited local market for highly perishable meat. The survey and cropping of hippopotamus at Queen Elizabeth National Park was taken over by the Nuffield Unit of Tropical Animal Ecology, with extensive work on population ecology by R M Laws, although overall wildlife research in East Africa was not well tied to management.[78]

The British Nature Conservancy had responsibility for advising the British government on conservation in colonial territories (Chapter 4). When, to this end, Barton Worthington toured East and Central Africa in 1960, he drew attention to current ideas about the possibility of harvesting wild animals in game cropping schemes, as part of a more dynamic approach to conservation.[79] In his report, he emphasized that wildlife should be regarded and managed as a resource, through 'wise use'. He urged the importance of game cropping and controlled hunting as a source of meat, livelihood and therefore development, pointing out how former destructive and uncontrolled hunting, for example of red lechwe in the Kafue Flats, could be sustained if re-started under controlled conditions.[80]

Such programmes were subsequently developed in Africa, particularly in Zambia, after independence. Controlled hunting by local people (particularly of hippopotamus) was an element of the Lwangwa Integrated Resource Development Project (LIRDP), begun in 1987. Revenue from safari hunting in the Lupande Game Reserve was used for development projects in the local area, as well as to finance the cost of locally recruited game guards in the South Lwangwa National Park.[81] This experience led to the establishment of the ADMADE (Administrative Management Design) programme across ten other game management areas in Zambia in 1987. Revenue from safari and other hunting fees were used to meet the costs of wildlife management (40 per cent to the game management area,15 per cent to the National Parks and 10 per cent to the Zambian Tourist Bureau), and to generate revenue for local community projects (35 per cent). The consumptive-use and benefit-sharing approach of ADMADE has been seen as a valuable model for conservation elsewhere.[82] However, it is interesting that neither the LIRDP nor ADMADE have reduced illegal hunting by local people. Community benefits generated by ADMADE fail to compensate for the economic, social and political returns from hunting: hunting tactics have changed, but people still flout the law to hunt.[83]

The idea of 'community-based natural resource management' became important in the 1990s, part of the wider 'community-based conservation' approach (Chapter 5).[84] The idea that the best way to stop people from hunting illegally is to allow them to hunt legally, is not a new one, and it has obvious intuitive attractions. The approach has been widely used, although with very different degrees of community involvement. For example in Game Reserves around Serengeti National Park in Tanzania, a cropping operation was begun in 1993 in 14 villages, with game scouts and a project officer from the Serengeti Regional Conservation Project shooting wildebeest, zebra and topi from vehicles to provide meat for local villages. This is a highly centralized top-down operation, with little input by members of local communities. It is perhaps not surprising that it is not very successful. It is expensive to run, and makes only a minor contribution to the economy of project villages. While subsidised, cropped meat is still to expensive for poorer households, illegal hunting continues to be extremely attractive, and economically important.[85]

COMMUNITY-BASED SAFARI HUNTING

Whatever the economic benefits of meat from wild herbivores, the other revenue stream from wild animals has always been from game shooting. As we have seen, from early in the 20th century, conservationists argued that the revenue from game licences should be used for conservation – Theodore

Hubback pointed out that licence fees in the Federated Malay States was $20,000 per annum, and expenditure on the game warden's staff only $5000 (the Game Wardens themselves were honorary). He wrote in 1924 that 'there is no reason why the game should not be considered a source of revenue; one should not expect to protect game for nothing.[86] An investment in game preservation would pay dividends. Keith Caldwell argued that 'for an investment of £4000 a year you get £13,000, of which £9000 is profit', but you had to preserve the game to keep that income. He observed that once you 'let the game go, you will find that it is difficult to get it back again. You cannot rear it like pheasants in England'.[87]

C W Hobley reviewed the case in 1937. Between 1926 and 1935, £665,000 had been collected in revenue by the game departments of Kenya, Uganda and Tanganyika Territory, generating a net surplus of £373,000.[88] This income could, he argued, be maintained as long as a crop of ivory was available, and hunting remained a popular sport. Unfortunately, the same logic would not work everywhere: in territories such as Malaya, game was sparse and sportsmen scarce, while in India income was scattered.

Safari hunting can still raise surprising sums of money. Hobley was more right than perhaps he knew, when he wrote in 1928 'I can visualize the time when the grant of a permit to shoot a specimen of one or more species will be considered a great privilege and worth paying for'.[89] Today, a hunt of several weeks, culminating in the killing of an elephant cost in the order of US$29,000 in Zimbabwe in the 1990s, and up to US$40,000 in Cameroon. In South Africa (where the hunt would probably take place on a game ranch) it would cost only US$14,000.[90] In a world where many countries cannot meet the costs of their protected area network and wildlife and regulations, safari hunting can offer an interesting way of meeting the costs of conservation.

Of course, for this to work, a country has to have the large charismatic beasts that visiting wealthy hunters will want to kill – in Africa, this means effectively the 'big five': lion, leopard, buffalo, rhinoceros and (above all) elephant. So safari hunting will not work everywhere, but in countries (of which Africa in particular has many) where tourist facilities are minimal, where the risks of travel would put off all but the most hardy of adventure tourists, and where large animals abound, safari hunting is an attractive option.

The Earl of Onslow would probably have been pleased to note the rise of private game ranches in southern Africa, and the growth of 'Conservancies' (large tracts of jointly managed private game ranches), especially in Zimbabwe and Namibia. By the mid-1980s, there were between 7000 and 10,000 game farms in South Africa, holding significant numbers of wild animals, including a number of rare species such as rhinoceros, gemsbok and sable antelope.[91] In 1975, the Rhodesian Parks and Wildlife Act allowed private landowners (almost all at that time former European settlers) to own the wildlife on their land for the first time.[92] Prior to that, all game had been the property of the state (a legacy of its definition in colonial legislation as 'royal game'). Game ranchers or farmers can make money from their animals through cropping and sale of meat, safari hunting by paying clients, live animal sales to other farms, and game viewing. With clever management of land, clients and time, they can do all these things in the same area. Under management as game ranches, poor and arid low veld land in Zimbabwe became profitable, and the hated cattle gave way to burgeoning populations of game animals, safer behind high fences and with salaried guards than they would have been in a cash-strapped national park.

In the 1980s, independent Zimbabwe took a further step, and set up institutions that made it possible for smallholders on so-called 'communal' land (former African Reserves) to profit from the safari hunting industry like their much richer neighbours. Under the Communal Areas Management Programme for Indigenous Resources in Zimbabwe, known by its acronym CAMPFIRE, District Councils were allowed to apply for 'appropriate authority' over wildlife.[93] This allowed communities to set up CAMPFIRE Committees, apply to the Department of National Parks and Wildlife for a hunting quota, and auction the right to hunt to a safari company. This has been widely celebrated by conservationists internationally as a 'win–win—win' solution – a strategy that uses wildlife to tackle poverty, creates wealth from the poor quality land to which the majority of rural Zimbabweans were moved during the colonial period, and keeps buoyant wildlife populations outside as well as inside national parks.

However it is clear that CAMPFIRE is only a success in some places. In a sense, CAMPFIRE is not a community programme at all.[94] Harvest quotas are not set by the community, but by the Department of National Parks and Wildlife (although there are interesting experiments with community quota-setting).[95] More seriously, authority (and hence revenues) are devolved only to District level, not to communities themselves.[96] In a study of 46 wards, 53 per cent of CAMPFIRE revenue reached the wards, 22 per cent went to wildlife management, 13 per cent to the district council.[97] Local communities may well have different ideas about how revenues should be spent from those of the district council. District headquarters can be far away and difficult to get to, and there can be well-founded fears of lack of transparency and corruption. In practice, CAMPFIRE has often become yet another avenue for political patronage and graft.

James Murombedzi concludes that CAMPFIRE has only been successful in small, discrete, and relatively homogenous communities with access to extensive wilderness.[98] Here the potential for wildlife harvests to contribute to household incomes is greatest because there are people and lots of wildlife. Harvest levels even for long-lived species such as elephant can be both biologically sustainable and yield significant income. However, such situations are rare. Ivan Bond found that CAMPFIRE revenue comprised more than three-quarters of total revenue in only four wards out of 46 studied. In most wards, wildlife incomes are only supplementary, and the main beneficiary of the arrangement is the safari industry not the local community. Wildlife costs (for example crop raiding) often exceed benefits. Where incomes from wildlife are small, households tend to be reluctant to favour wildlife management over other forms of land use. Whatever the attractions of wildlife revenue at district or community level, in an individual household the best way to accumulate wealth, or simply to survive, is still agriculture and livestock keeping. Moreover, many rural people fear wild beasts and reject the whole idea of allowing wild animals to roam near houses in the uncertain hope of some future CAMPFIRE payout. Where communities are divided, the prospects for equitable outcomes from wildlife use projects are less good.[99]

The lesson of CAMPFIRE is clearly not that community-based natural resource management on this model is the salvation of conservation. Rather, that a strategy of development based on consumptive use (of which safari hunting is the best-paying example) can work in the right conditions: where resource values are very high, where there is no competing higher value land use, where population density is low. Like other kinds of community projects, CAMPFIRE works where there is inspired leadership and high levels of trust within the community. In places with strong local indigenous institutions, communities can control the way the wildlife resource is used, and maintain wildlife revenues and (the conservationist as opposed to the development bottom line) wildlife populations.

PROFITING WITH NATURE

At the start of the 21st century, the debate between advocates of 'consumptive use' and those who propose a move 'back to parks' is very spirited, especially because it intersects with debate about the impacts of conservation on unwilling rural people, and on issues of human rights. For a parks advocate such as John Terborg, the whole idea of sustainable use is profoundly dangerous. He argues that economic pressures will always push towards more intensive management and shorter rotation cycles. In his terms, it allows no 'line in the sand', no point at which loss of biodiversity simply has to stop. He believes that 'sustainable use' will do nothing to diminish the biodiversity crisis, that 'starting down the slippery road to sustainable use is stepping back from that crucial line in the sand that defines one's beliefs and principles'.[100] To Terborgh, this is a 'gray zone'. Conservation decisions should be driven by science, not politics, economics or society.

This is a despairing and distopian vision. The proposals he makes for 'internationally financed elite forces within countries, counterparts to the rangers who protect national parks in the United States and are legally authorized to carry arms and make arrests' essentially conjure up an ecofascist regime to protect nature.[101] It is also a vision that fails to take into account the fact that the forces driving global ecosystem change *are* precisely the politics, economics or society that he wishes had no influence on conservation decisions. In a world driven by the demands of the world economy, it is in 99 per cent of cases the economic values of biological diversity that will determine its future.[102] Juggernauts do not respect lines in the sand. Moral arguments, however genuine or passionate, tend to be swept away in their path. And there can be no doubt that the world economy is an all-consuming juggernaut of a scale and power unprecedented in evolutionary time (Chapter 7). Alongside its achievements (for example science and technology, human rights) and the savagery of war, genocide and totalitarianism, the 20th century brought in unprecedented resource depletion and biological impoverishment. As Edward Wilson comments, 'we and the rest of life cannot afford another hundred years like that'.[103]

However, the potential of a conservation strategy that puts economic demand in the service of conservation is considerable, and advocates of incentive-based conservation have much to point towards in support of their case.[104] Trade in wild animals and plants and their parts and derivatives is vast – worth US$160 billion. The regulation of trade, and non-regulatory initiatives such as eco-labelling and building awareness of 'commodity chains' between remote producers and consumers are important elements with conservation toolkits.[105] Some of these initiatives, such as the Forest Stewardship Council, founded in 1993, have real potential to restructure the face of international trade in ways that make sustainability more than an idealistic pipe-dream.[106]

It is not impossible to create opportunities for impoverished rural communities to replace an illegal trade in wild species with a legal one – and, in the process, to open the door to sustainability. One example of this is the idea of establishing indigenous propagation in Turkey to replace wild bulbs with cultivated specimens. In the mid-1980s, research by the Fauna and Flora Preservation Society, the World Conservation Monitoring Centre and TRAFFIC identified the trade in wild bulbs from Turkey as a serious conservation problem. *Sternbergia* and *Galanthus* species were added to Appendix II of CITES alongside *Cyclamen*.

In the classic pattern of the wild products marketing chain, bulbs were collected by villagers in the Taurus Mountains, who received a tiny proportion of their eventual value on the international market. The wild origins of these bulbs was not made clear when they were retailed. Meetings with members of the Dutch bulb trade led to agreements on the need for truthful labelling (so that wild bulbs are labelled as coming from a wild source) and improved monitoring of the trade. One result was the *Good Bulb Guide*,[107] and improved regulation of the wild bulb trade in Turkey and Georgia. Another was the Indigenous Plant Propagation Project, initiated by FFI in Turkey, in 1992, in collaboration with Dogal Hayati Koruma Dernegi (DHKD). The project was designed to develop a method of propagating bulbs in three villages, and thereby create a sustainable source of income and employment.[108]

Another innovative example of trade-based conservation work is FFI's SoundWood conservation programme, which seeks to safeguard the future of trees necessary to make musical instruments. Mahoganies, rosewoods, ebonies and other woods have been exploited to the point of commercial extinction. Other species are becoming increasingly scarce, including the African blackwood or *mpingo*, used for clarinets and oboes, and the endangered *pau brasil*, from which violin bows are made. SoundWood promotes sustainable management of timber resources in partnership with local communities and works with musicians and manufacturers to encourage the use of wood from independently certified well-managed sources (rather than, for example, attempts to ban trade, or substitute all natural with synthetic materials).[109]

The start of the 21st century has seen numerous attempts to harness the power of the market, particularly the international market, to conservation: to reverse the gearing of the engine of destruction that dominated the 20th century. There are also many examples of such attempts by outside organizations to reach into poor rural communities and seek to make trade sustainable, rather than banning it. These initiatives inevitably blur the boundaries between 'conservation' and 'development'. One example of such hybrid initiatives is the work of is PhytoTrade Africa, a non-profit trade association that promotes sustainable production and fair trade of natural products in southern Africa. It works with African rural producers and their organizations to refine and market wild natural products such as drinks, cosmetic oils, health care products, herbal teas, jams, nutritional supplements and medicinal products.[110] Like 'shade-grown coffee', dolphin-friendly tuna, the SoundWood guitar or the FSC-certified garden furniture, these show the scope of the new market-orientated approach to conservation.

These are new waters for conservationists to wade in, with new perils of illegality and over-harvesting, of deceit and mis-labelling, of labyrinthine commodity chains and ill-informed consumers. However, they show how far conservationists have moved. Now, seemingly, people are not the enemy of conservation, but its friend; and markets are not the source of nature's destruction, but its salvation. The truth is less simple: conservation debates have started to grow up. Conservationists have begun to accept the political nature of conservation's critique of development, and of its claims on human communities; to count the cost of conservation and think out ways to pay it; to begin to consider anew what conservation means. The century ahead holds familiar challenges, but also new and exciting opportunities. Some of these are outlined in the final chapter.

Chapter 10

Society with Nature

Like the great libraries of the world, which strive to preserve history's written traditions, we struggle against huge forces of destruction and forgetting (Jonathan Swift).[1]

To conserve biological diversity is an investment in immortality (Edward O Wilson).[2]

NATURE'S DEGRADATION

This book has told the story of conservation in the last hundred years. Like any story about the past, it also inevitably reflects ideas about the present, and the future. The achievements of the conservation movement in the last century have been legion: a global network of non-governmental and governmental organizations committed to the benign management of nature; a worldwide system of protected areas; a battery of national and international legislation to protect species, from CITES to the Convention on Biological Diversity; an integrated body of scientific research directly relevant to ecosystem management; a coherent set of ideologies about the conservation of nature that have achieved global recognition, and a high degree of acquiescence from citizens, governments and business interests.

What would the pioneers of conservation think of this litany of hard-won achievements? How would Edward North Buxton, hunter of chamois and defender of Epping Forest, founder of the Society for the Preservation of the Wild Fauna of the Empire, skilled denizen of the corridors of power in Whitehall regard the explosion of the conservation movement? How about his successors, the Earl of Onslow, who brought the society into the bright lights of London society, or Sir Peter Chalmers-Mitchell, from his fastness in the Zoological Society of London? What would William Hornaday of the New York Zoological Society, or James Stevenson-Hamilton, whose indefatigable energy brought the Kruger National Park into being, have thought of the worldwide spread of national parks and protected areas? Above all, what would they, or later comers such as Julian Huxley, Hal Coolidge, Victor Van Straelen, Frank Fraser Darling, Raymond Dasmann or Peter Scott think of the achievements of the conservation movement in the 20th century?

I suspect they would regard what has been done as remarkable, and mostly admirable. However, their congratulations would inevitably be heavily muted, tempered by admonishment, possibly tinged with exasperation. How could the problems of extinction be known for a hundred years, and yet remain unsolved? How could conservationists build so powerfully, talk and write so much, and yet change so little? How could their successors, forewarned and forearmed, have let the world get into such a state? The sober fact is that after ten decades of effort, a whole century of achievement, the threats to nature are not reduced, but redoubled. Some of the perils that the pioneers of formal conservation feared at the start of the century have passed away, or at least lie in abeyance, but each has been replaced by a legion of others, more fell than before.

The central irony of the 20th century for conservationists is that the remarkable growth in size and influence of their movement has been accompanied by accelerating destruction of nature. Indeed, strangely, it is that destruction that has fuelled the growth of conservation. The movement to protect has always lagged behind and drawn power from the changes wrought by development, just as it was made possible by the freedom from want that development brought. The processes of human transformation of nature have not slowed. As Edward Wilson comments, it is clear at the start of the 21st century that the juggernaut of technology-based capitalism will not be stopped.[3] The power of consumption, driven by consumer demand in industrialized economies and subsistence needs in the world's poorest countries has flensed the biologically diverse world, laying bare the very bones of ecological resilience.

Our technologies have allowed us to transform land use, streamline food webs, and re-direct and privatize flows of benefits from nature. They have given us unprecedented powers to pollute and degrade, and for those of us in formal employment in industrialized economies, to escape the consequences of our actions for our own generation, and perhaps the generation of our privileged children. Aeroplanes plough the stratosphere, carrying the wealthy between comfortable house, global office and holiday paradise, bringing commodities the length of the earth, through complex and untraceable chains of exchange. Goods and products are created and marketed with dizzying speed, detached from the toiling hands that made them and the ecosystems that supplied their raw material and absorbed the waste products of production. The global communications revolution allows far-flung circuits of production and consumption to be controlled, and disseminates the fashions and advertising that feed capitalism's endless search for profit.[4]

Humans have proved much cleverer inventors and much more systematic rationalizers of society and nature than many would have expected a hundred years ago. We have literally become the planet's ecosystem engineers, although, in too many ways, incompetent ones.[5] Humans are clever, but also, it turns out, shortsighted and arrogant. Moreover, those with their hands on the levers too rarely look up, either to see how their different decisions interact, or to see whether the world outside the control room is actually changing as they would wish. At the end of the 20th century, humans manage the world like the Pentagon warriors viewing the Iraqi battlefield through the video-cameras of pilotless robot drones. We don't get out much to smell the air, and when we do, we smell the US East Coast, not the war zone. Things don't look too bad if you stand back far enough.

On the ground, however, as conservationists know only too well, the natural world is a mess. Rates of ecosystem change and rates of fossil energy use are high, and not slowing. The implications of anthropogenic climate change for biodiversity are profound, with the prospect of the world's species being reduced to a weedy fast-dispersing subset of the recent whole.[6] Even leaving aside the well-known problems of habitat destruction and pollution, the interactions of humans and other species hold novel threats to both, as the recent outbreaks of Ebola haemorrhagic fever in the forests of Central Africa, demonstrate. Neither people nor wild gorillas and chimpanzees can survive this killer, which they have the misfortune to share.[7]

Rates of extinction due to all causes are high, between 100 and 1000 times background levels. Despite the importance of the issue, the data are not available to predict future extinction rates for sure, but the prognosis is poor.[8] The modern world system has imposed standardization and uniformity on both living diversity and society in the past two centuries. Technology, quantification, bureaucratic control, the mastery of nature and the expansion of capitalism have gone hand in hand.[9] It is not just species that are at risk in our fast-moving globalized technosphere, for languages (and by analogy human cultural diversity) are under even greater threat of extinction; interestingly, the areas of fastest loss, and greatest diversity, tend to overlap.[10] Ecological and cultural uniformity seem to be the cost of feeding the global machine.

It seems clear that global development has come at a terrible cost. Yet this is not even a good Faustian bargain, for the 'magic' of development has not worked for the vast majority of the world's citizens. There have never been more people living in absolute poverty; and the United Nations Development Programme *Human Development Report* charts the failure of the stuttering engine of the global economy to extend its reach to the global poor.[11] Life expectancy at birth in 2001 was 77 years in OECD countries, but only 64 years in sub-Saharan Africa, 44 in Tanzania and 39 in Malawi; Gross Domestic Product per capita was over US$23,000 in OECD countries, $1800 in Sub-Saharan Africa, and only $520 in Tanzania.

The problems facing conservation at the start of the 21st century are only too familiar. Mostly they are the same problems recognized and faced by conservationists a century ago. What is more worrying is that the same is true of conservation's solutions. These too are well-tried and familiar. Protected areas, controls on hunting, regulations about trade, the attempt to educate all and sundry about the importance of other species, are the stock-in-trade of conservation. None of them is a bad idea. All of them are evolving, becoming more sophisticated, adapting to changing circumstances. However, none of them promises any kind of scale shift in the endless chess game of extinction.

In its efforts to combat the impacts of human development on nature, conservation began at the end of the 20th century to take on the same corporate methods that had become standard in business and modern government, pursuing efficiency and cost effectiveness, harnessing science and technology to achieve defined goals (Chapter 9). This is not surprising – David Orr points out that it is logical that the drive for standardization and uniformity might someday impose a grid-like pattern on the ecology of our minds 'until we are permitted to have no thoughts without right angles'.[12] But conservation needs to think in curves, and it is not clear how well corporate conservation is adapted to do this. The way forward may be through both a combination of a more systematic reorganization of individual businesses (through better and more sophisticated goal definition and more effective targeting of resources), or through new institutions of cooperation. Certainly, effective collaboration between conservation's corporate giants requires rather more than the exchange of letters that would once have sufficed to link William Hornaday to Peter Chalmers-Mitchell, although now, as then, the circle of key players is remarkably small, and dominated by the trans-Atlantic axis.

NATURE'S RENEWAL

There is no shortage of agendas for action for conservation in the second Millennium. Edward Wilson, for example, calls for the salvage of the world's biodiversity hotspots, the maintenance of the world's remaining frontier forests intact, an end to all old-growth logging, a concentration on lakes and river ecosystems and on marine hotspots. He calls for a complete mapping of the world's living diversity, an investigation of ways to make conservation profitable, particularly for those who live near reserves but also as a contribution to the world economy, a focus on ecological restoration, on wild animal and plant collections. He proposes the promotion of population planning, helping humanity achieve 'a smaller biomass, a lighter footstep'.[13] This is a sound and challenging agenda. Some of its ideas are already part of forward-looking conservation initiatives around the world, and others are being actively discussed. But is it enough?

The 20th century saw conservation's creation, but nature's decline. The refinement and extension of existing conservation strategies, however energetically pursued, may halt that decline, but it will do so only in a few favoured places. Globally, the natural capital of the biosphere will continue to be drawn down through consumption and pollution. Successful pursuit of conventional conservation goals will mean at best the preservation of scattered tufts of diversity in a world of uniformity. If the conservation planners get their algorithms right, and the various hotspots and key wilderness areas are identified and protected, we could keep a lot of species that way. But most of us, wherever we live, will know them only at second hand, through electronic transmission on film or web cam, through the ideas and words of commentators. Even if the diverse jewels of the earth are 'saved', we will still face a gloomy trudge through the new century accompanied by the steady leaching of natural diversity on every hand. This conserved world will not be one of self-generating living diversity. It will not be a world which retains the capacity for evolution that created the species and ecosystems we knew and started to describe and explain in the 20th century. That conserved world will not hold the natural vibrancy that once allowed humans to reach their technological and spiritual zenith.

Standard recipes for conservation are increasingly calling on the ethics of triage. On the battlefield, it is necessary to focus scant medical resources on those wounded who will survive, for if spread equally none will be saved. Thus conservationists tell each other that they face hard choices, that they must dismiss lost causes: West Africa, for example, can be regarded as 'a conservation disaster', where the conservation dollars invested have negligible benefits, and would be better spent elsewhere.[14] Edward Wilson notes the importance of the same absolute determination and focus. Standard thinking about the environment since the 1980s might suggest that the job of governments is to take no action that knowingly endangers biodiversity. For Wilson, that is not enough. He suggests that the commitment must be much deeper 'to let no species knowingly die, to take all reasonable action to protect every species and race in perpetuity'.[15]

Yet nature's renewal needs something different from existing models of sustainability; something more than triage, more than sharper visions of business-as-usual, more than better fundraising, better education, better reserve selection, better targeting of resources. David Orr recently argued that something like spiritual renewal was needed if humankind is to make a transition to sustainability.[16] Conservation needs new thinking about what nature is.

This is not as radical as it sounds, nor as vague. The seeds of new thinking set themselves decades ago, indeed they have been actively propagating throughout the 20th century, although conservationists have mostly been oblivious to them. Let me suggest some of the new thinking we need to do, in terms of new ways of imagining nature, a renewed engagement with its restoration, and a new sense of ourselves as co-dwellers with other species in the biosphere.

NATURE'S IMAGE

The first step is in many ways the hardest, at least for many conservationists trained as biologists, and it is to accept that what we understand by nature is socially constructed. This has become a commonplace thought in the social sciences and humanities, but it is one that shocks and alarms many natural scientists, for it cuts deep into the ideas about truth, evidence and proof that they accept as essential foundations for scientific understanding. Take away the belief that science tells the truth, and they fear that demons of unreason will be let loose. In conservation, scientists fear that all their hard-won arguments about extinction and biodiversity, ecological change and sustainable harvest will be swept away. Once admit that nature is socially constructed, and they fear that Pandora's Box will be opened, nothing can ever be the same.

Michael Soulé wrote in 1995 that there were two assaults on nature, the first was overt and physical (as described in this book). The second was covert, ideological and social. He was concerned that the 'wave of relativistic anthropocentrism' sweeping the humanities and social sciences would influence the way policymakers and technocrats would manage biodiversity and 'the remaining fragments of wilderness'.[17] Soulé's co-editor, Gary Lease took a more favourable view of these developments, quite rightly describing the engagement between the humanities and social sciences on the one hand and the natural sciences on the other over the question of nature 'tense but unavoidable.[18] Interestingly, the essays in their volume by Donald Worster, Gary Nabhan and Stephen Kellert among others that explore postmodern thinking about nature do not suggest that all moral argument about the worth of nature is extinguished,[19] or that 'informed, compassionate decisions about the future of wild nature' become less possible.[20] They do suggest a need to broaden the frame of reference for conservation decisions, and they show that glib formulaic decisions about what nature is like, and what it ought to be like, quite unacceptable.

It is possible to base arguments for conservation on grounds other than capitalist or scientific rationality.[21] The fact that conservation in the 20th century was largely an elite discourse, between those holding different ideas about the right balance between nature and development in a colonial world, and between world leaders at international meetings, does not mean that such people should have a monopoly on arguments about nature. The fact that conservation arguments have predominantly been expressed in the abstract logics of science and economics does not mean that these are the only ways in which conservation claims can be understood. When people feel passion for nature, the arguments that carry conviction, and also the possibility of broad democratic support, are those that make sense to ordinary people. Conservation urgently needs to make sense to ordinary people.

Conservationists therefore need to take a deep breath, and admit that nature is a social construction. By that I mean that the way we understand nature depends on who we are, on what we know, on the people we meet with. Our science, just as our childhood, our fiction, our newspapers, leads us to certain understandings of the way nature is, and ought to be. This does not make all ideas about nature of equal worth. The existence of centaurs in the forbidden forest at Hogwarts is no more reliable a guide to ecology than the idea that there are trolls under the bridge, although both are likely to affect the way susceptible children approach a walk in the country at night.[22] Scientists, like grown-ups, know better. But both can be wrong. Nature is full of surprises, some of them interesting in a scientific sort of way, some of them thoroughly alarming.

Ecologists know this, of course, and have coined the concept of resilience to refer to the way ecosystems react to surprises and shocks.[23] The normal language to speak of such responses is to say that ecosystems 'recover' from such surprises to continue to function and provide ecological services. This suggests that perturbations are a temporary loss of equilibrium. Another view is that ecosystems are nothing like so commonly stuck in equilibrium as ecologists like to assume. Arguably, shocks and surprises are an integral part of the way many ecosystems work, with extreme events pushing ecosystem states from one temporary equilibrial point to another. The point about these changes in ideas about ecosystem dynamics is that natural science tells us almost everything we know in a formal sense about the way ecosystems work. But what it tells us keeps changing. Science at any moment never tells us everything – it never tells us the whole truth.

Natural science must be seen as just one among several ways of understanding nature. The views of scientists about conservation matter, but not uniquely so. There is a need to broaden the community of those whose views about nature are taken seriously. Conservation thinking needs to open up to new ideas, from new partners. This is the one big lesson that needs to be drawn from the long-running debate about 'community' and 'participation' in conservation (Chapters 5 and 9). Conservationists need to recognize that concepts like 'biodiversity' shut out other ideas about nature just as effectively as rooms full of Western-salaried conservation scientists mapping hotspots shut out other people.

Jane Guyer and Paul Richards point out that while conservationists fully recognize that different people understand nature in different ways, they cannot cope with that knowledge. They do not have the mental categories to understand and cope with the variety of ways in which people engage with the non-human world. People are treated as uniform, 'phenomenally lumped together', like light across the spectrum: we know the colours are there, but we can't see them, at least not until we take steps to see differently.[24] Conservationists know that different people's ideas about nature matter, but they want to be able to treat this diversity efficiently. They therefore, at best, tend to put human ideas about and relations with nature in a box marked 'indigenous knowledge', and try to draw some standard conclusions about how they should respond to this singularized position. Ironically, in doing so, conservationists miss seeing the diversity of human engagement with natural diversity.

I suggest that conservationists need to re-think their dependence on standard Western assumptions about the 'divide' between people and non-human nature. They need a more pluralist understanding of different understandings, meanings and values of biodiversity.[25] There is already widespread acceptance that indigenous or traditional knowledge is highly relevant to ecosystem conservation.[26] Compared to modern science, such knowledge may be holistic and adaptive, gathered over many generations by observers whose lives depended on its use. Like modern science, such knowledge accumulates incrementally, and is passed on to future generations, mostly in this instance orally and through shared practice (like the practical skills of laboratory working that are needed in addition to the formal abstracted 'methods' of scientific papers). It is awkward for modern conservation planners that local knowledge is mostly inside people's heads, not in books, but the solution is to work with people, not try to write it all down and take it away.[27] It is a folksy observation, but a true one, that once you get talking to people, you learn a lot of things. Sometimes you learn that the question you were asking is the wrong one. Sometimes you learn that the categories you have used to frame the question are wrong as well.

Conservation needs to be based on a fusion of local and external, traditional and scientific knowledge, and that knowledge should be used within decision-making processes that include the widest possible range of stakeholders. To achieve that, conservation thinking and action needs to be flexible and adaptable, to accommodate both complex ecological systems and diverse stakeholder interests.[28]

It is only too easy for conservationists, like scientists working as biodiversity prospectors for commercial companies, to exploit indigenous or traditional knowledge about nature. The search for equity and fairness in biodiversity prospecting was an important element in debate about the Convention on Biological Diversity, and is now an important issue for conservationists, worked through for example in the People and Plants Initiative.[29] However, there is more to such engagements between scientists and others than the issue of commercial rights and benefits. The act of attempting to interpret local knowledge about nature into 'peasant scientific knowledge', and translating it into modern scientific categories and recording systems is not only potentially unfair, but it implies that all such local knowledge is *only* scientific in a Western sense. This is like the idea that the existence of indigenous reserves or 'sacred groves' automatically means that people are really conservationists in the sense used in this book, and will therefore automatically sign up to externally-defined biodiversity conservation goals; such groves may contain many species, but they cannot simply be treated by outsiders as local biodiversity hotspots and added to a tally of 'protected areas'.[30]

Even a passing engagement with the work of anthropologists reveals that people outside the Western tradition often understand nature in quite different ways from all Western patterns of thought and understanding. For many societies, nature is not simply something understood as a set of objects to be classified, through some kind of 'peasant taxonomy'. People's concrete knowledge of the world they live in, their ideas about nature, cannot be tied in any simple way to Western categories of 'human' and 'nature', of 'facts' and 'myths'. Shamanistic belief systems, for example, cut right across such reductionist frames of reference. If nature is not 'out there', separate from us, how can it be made the subject of abstract debate about management or conservation? Woe betide the conservationist who arrives in a community expecting to find their own mental categories replicated. They might as well expect to find a troll under the bridge.[31]

NATURE'S NEIGHBOURS

Nature's renewal demands that conservationists break through the limitations of existing strategies. Not only do conservationists need to learn to look differently at nature, therefore, but also to think differently about people. Specifically, they need to foster new relationships between people and nature. The challenge is not to preserve (or even restore) 'the wild', but peoples' *relationships* with the wild.

Throughout the 20th century, conservationists saw nature as something beleaguered, and needing protection. They had little doubt that nature occurred in a given state and within fixed bounds, and that human action was changing the first and eroding the second. The whole ethos of game and nature reserves and national parks (Chapters 4 and 5) left no doubt that their prime concern was to conserve nature in the special places where it still thrived. Even today, conservationists often believe that the preservation of all components of biodiversity can only be achieved in areas largely free of human alteration, and they focus their efforts on lands with minimal human presence.[32] But such areas are few, and the prodigious effort devoted to the conservation of distant lands and species detaches conservation from the world's urban majority, and imposes it on often unwilling rural people. Nature cannot be preserved only in parks, however well-located.[33]

Living nature's only limit is the earth itself. Inside the biosphere, nature is continuously in flux, changing at multiple scales in response to internal and external forces. No protected area system can capture and contain that diversity. Conservation therefore cannot be restricted to the protection of diverse places or rare species alone. As discussed in Chapter 5, this has become an accepted element in thinking about protected areas, with increasing interest in landscape-scale conservation initiatives, 'conservation beyond parks'.[34] Quite apart from the various ecological arguments for landscape scale conservation, the critical reason why what British policy-makers call 'the wider countryside', outside designated reserves and conservation areas, is important is simply that most people live there. Without conservation action where they live, they are destined forever to live in landscapes stripped of their natural diversity. Why does this matter? Because without contact with nature, people's capacity to understand and engage with it withers.

This has been argued many times by conservationists, but it bears repeating. Edward Wilson notes that although the destruction of living diversity is anathema to conservationists, most people regard it as perfectly acceptable.[35] This is as likely to be true of the New York taxi driver, the Texan golfing executive, the malnourished Mumbai rubbish picker or the Brazilian rainforest smallholder settler. Some are rich, others poor, but it is likely that none would feel directly engaged with or responsibility for other species, beyond the few for which they have immediate need. Why do they not feel more broadly and deeply about the fate of nature? Because they do not know it. Edward Wilson argues that the better an ecosystem is known, the less likely it will be destroyed.[36] In her book exploring why people love nature, Kay Milton points out that knowledge is not emotionally neutral. She argues that we perceive meanings in our environment as we engage with it, indeed it is these meanings that enable it to become known. Those meanings give things value, and from value follow emotion and feelings, which in turn motivate action.[37] In a world where British schoolchildren are better at recognizing imaginary Pokémon characters than wildlife, the implications for their willingness to engage with and champion nature are grim.[38]

The future of conservation will turn on the extent to which a strong individual connection to nature and natural processes is maintained for the world's people in the 21st century. Robert Pyle suggests that such a sense withered in the 20th century. Moreover, even the enthusiasm for the environment demonstrated by the growth of the Western environmental movement (Chapter 3) masks a profound change in the nature of the contact between people and nature. In the industrialized world, engagements with nature are superficial, epitomized by nature recreation, and 'shallow contact leads to shallow conservation'.[39] Those who know less, recognize less, care less and therefore act less, a cycle of loss and disconnection from nature that Pyle calls 'the extinction of experience'.[40] When that happens, 'hope, spirit and existence all suffer'.

On the other hand, Edward Wilson observes that wilderness 'settles peace on the soul because it needs no help; it is beyond human contrivance'.[41] This is an illusion, of course. The very idea of wilderness reflects the scale of the human appropriation (both physically and conceptually) of nature (Chapter 5). Wilson's view of the importance of the idea of wilderness is as a metaphor, speaking of unlimited opportunity in nature. Such nature is not only found in remote areas, and conservationists must not confine their concern for nature to areas that they feel comfortable defining as 'wilderness'. As Robert Pyle argues, reconnection with nature cannot be achieved by any strategy that is solely confined to special nature in special places. The solution for conservation cannot be some idealistic 'return to Eden', whatever the theoretical merits of conservation efforts in the biodiverse shards of habitat remaining on the Earth. Much of the opportunity facing conservationists lies not in remote regions of the world, but much closer to home.

Once conservationists start to devise strategies for conservation where people actually live, they have to face the fact that 'nature' is usually profoundly influenced by human action. Where land is converted to agriculture, or a mix of agriculture and other uses, charismatic larger species such as primates and large carnivores and herbivores tend to have disappeared. However, other adaptable and fast-reproducing mammals usually persist, as do many birds, plants, insects and a whole taxonomic miscellany of lesser organisms, above, on and below the earth.[42] The fact that wildlife habitats in northwest Europe were not (in North American terms) very 'wild' never bothered conservationists in the United Kingdom much, because many millennia of agriculture had created diverse and sometimes stunningly attractive wildlife habitats. Indeed, much of the effort of the conservation scientists from the 1950s onwards was spent working out how to protect such anthropogenic habitats, and replicate such benign systems of land management once the economy had made the activities that created them uneconomic.[43]

Elsewhere, of course, human action has left severely degraded landscapes of low diversity. Here habitat restoration, or what Robert Pyle rather nicely refers to as 'resurrection ecology', the bringing back of extinct habitats, has a real potential.[44] Throughout the 20th century, conservationists used the argument that nature was pristine, and foully threatened by human action. In the 21st century, the usefulness of this myth will decline. It is already a constraint on conservation vision. Where humans have been destructive, they must be creative to restore the diversity of nature. The enhancement of the living diversity of unreserved lands is a vital challenge.[45] Edward Wilson urges us to go beyond beyond 'mere salvage' to begin the restoration of natural environment, to 'enlarge wild populations and stanch (*sic*) the haemorrhaging of biological wealth'. There can be, he argues, 'no purpose more inspiriting than to begin the age of restoration, reweaving the wondrous diversity of life that still surrounds us'.[46]

If conservation is to take seriously diverse ideas about what nature is, it is local people who should be the originators of restoration projects, the arbiters of what nature, their nature, should be like. Nature does not just come in fixed formats. As John Rodwell comments, 'biodiversity is not the recipe found in a book, it is the many dishes that can be made from it; not the musical score but the multifarious performances'.[47] The engagement between people and nature can be genuinely creative, proof that it is the process that matters most, not just the pattern that conservationists have so long concentrated upon.

Conservation internationally needs to recognize that people care about the nature around them. The British organization Common Ground has long argued that the distinctiveness of local environments matters.[48] Sue Clifford points out that everyday places are as vulnerable as the rare. It is when people lose identification with place that ownership changes hands and a spiral of decline begins. Unless a place has meaning for people, it is unlikely to be well cared for. This is becoming a recognized element of conservation in busy industrialized countries like the United Kingdom, but is has profound implications internationally. Whatever efforts are made to enforce the defence of protected areas, or to create genuinely participatory community conservation, they will come to naught unless place and the nature in it have meaning for people.

John Cameron believes that it might be possible to engender love of place as a means of achieving conservation objectives. Arguably, experiencing a deeper relationship with one place can open someone up to a deeper affiliation with all places.[49] Landscapes, and the stories embedded within them, provide an opportunity for conservation in the 21st century to build a new constituency in the public mind.[50] As Sue Clifford points out, community involvement presupposes the existence of a community: conservationists must re-imagine their thinking and practice to find and support communities that value their local place and local nature.[51]

Enthusiasm for biodiversity hotspots and protected areas should not therefore blind us to the conservation importance of more mundane landscapes. Even farmed land in the Third World matters in terms of its living diversity. Since the Sahel drought of 1974, it has been known that trees and shrubs in the Sahel are important for migratory warblers such as the whitethroat. The management of fields and pastures, and of woody vegetation within the landscape, are highly significant to the Palaearctic-African migration system.[52] The ways people micro-manage areas such as African farmlands therefore has a global conservation importance, not for hugely rare species, but for the survival of the wider local living connections that comprise the biosphere.

Such intensively-managed land is both a challenge and an opportunity in the search for a strong popular foundation for conservation in the developing world. Conservation in Europe and North America is empowered by a broad social movement. In the South it is powered by international (largely European and American) ideas promoted by tiny national minorities in turn driven by international conservation NGOs and aid donors. The costs of conservation are so great that beyond such 'hotspots' as foreign subsidy pays for, the only landscapes and species that are conserved in poor countries will be what ordinary people in those countries themselves think is important, and are willing (and able) to pay for. People in some countries may come to want the national parks that international conservation has persuaded their governments to set aside, and their economies may develop to such an extent that they can be paid for. But how will ordinary people in those countries build the close engagements with nature that might lead them to care enough for wildlife to make this happen? A concern for nature comes first from wildlife close to home, not from remote biodiverse hotspots. The conservation and enhancement of the biodiversity of ordinary landscapes in the developing world is a vitally important challenge for conservation in the 21st century.

SOCIETY WITH NATURE

'Nature' is an emergent property of sets of ecosystems evolving in real space and time, never constant, never quite the same. So, too, conservation is the product of human societies, something that emerges from the happenstantial accumulation of billions of human engagements with other species every day.

Conservation is the term we use to describe the choices we make about the terms of engagement between people and other species. There can be no one conservation strategy. There is no single set of priorities or decisions that will guarantee perfection. Conservation is not like that. Indeed, nature is not like that. There will always be disputes, confusions, mistakes. There will always be diversity in the things humans want to see in nature, and in the space nature makes for humans to exercise those choices.

The key point about all this is that the biosphere is not an endlessly elastic envelope. It is not even particularly vast, comprising only one part in ten billion of the earth's mass, a thin layer of soil, water and air just a kilometre thick stretched over a half billion square kilometres of the earth's surface.[53] The resilience of the ecosystems that make up that layer must be the ultimate concern of humans, whether on ethical or simply self-interested grounds. It is the diversity of life that, somehow, creates that resilience.[54]

In 1976, Raymond Dasmann, a pioneer and leader in conservation through the second half of the 20th century, spoke to a technical meeting at the IUCN General Assembly in Kinshasa, Zaire. He set out the distinction between what he called 'ecosystem people' and 'biosphere people'. Ecosystem people are those who depend on the resources and ecosystems where they live. Biosphere people on the other hand, draw on resources from across the planet, and bring great amounts of energy and materials to bear on any one point. The result is all too often degradation, even devastation. Dasmann pointed out that all those tied into the global network of technological society are biosphere people. They are people 'who preach conservation, but often do not practice it'. Is there, he asked, 'any point in preaching conservation if you live in a style that wastes energy and materials and places excessive demands upon the world's living resources?' His challenge to the conservation movement is still valid almost three decades later.[55]

We need to place at the centre of conservation's concern the relationship that humans (every human, not just those appointed or self-appointed as nature's guardians) have with other species. It is vital to reconnect people and nature, although as Robert Pyle points out, ultimately this is a nonsense phrase, 'for people and nature are not different things, and cannot be taken apart. The problem is, we haven't yet figured that out'.[56] Conservationists have consistently failed to see the linkages between specific conservation problems and the broader drivers of global economic life. They have only slowly come to understand that their problem cannot be tackled piecemeal.

The central question for conservationists in the 20th century was how to stop extinction. They stood against the tide of destruction that was driven by the greatest achievements of humankind, as the processes of development steamrollered the terrestrial globe (and we even stuck exploratory hands out towards other planets). The big question for conservation in the 21st century must be broader. Not just how to stop the loss of species, but how to prevent our dazzling technical capacity, and our seemingly endless desire to consume nature's diversity, from fatally undermining the resilience of the biosphere.

Notes

PRELIMS

1 Edward O Wilson (1992) *The Diversity of Life*, Penguin, Harmondsworth.
2 For a discussion of this point, see Kay Milton (2002) *Loving Nature: towards an ecology of emotion*, Routledge, London, and for an example see William M Adams (2003) *Future Nature: a vision for conservation*, revised edition, Earthscan, London.
3 This point has been well made by Robert M Pyle (2003) 'Nature matrix: reconnecting people and nature', *Oryx* 37: 206–214.

CHAPTER 1 THE CHALLENGE OF NATURE

1 Not quite unnoticed: see www.fauna-flora.org/press_pub/press_news_mountain_gorilla_frame.htm.
2 This event is described by George Schaller (1963) *The Mountain Gorilla: ecology and behavior*, University of Chicago Press. Von Beringe's account of the expedition was published in *Deutsches Kolonialblatt* in 1903. The mountain gorilla was described by Matschie in 1903.
3 Jared Diamond (1991) *Rise and Fall of the Third Chimpanzee*, Radius, London.
4 Lynn Merrill (1989) *The Romance of Natural History*, Oxford University Press, Oxford, p117.
5 Mary L Jobe Akeley (1929) 'Summary of talk given for Society for the Preservation of the Fauna of the Empire by Mary L Jobe Akeley, 10 December 1928', *Journal SPFE* (1929): 15–23.
6 Akeley (1929) p16.
7 Donna Haraway (1995) 'Universal donors in a vampire culture: it's all in the family: biological kinship categories in the twentieth century United States', in W Cronon (ed) *Uncommon Ground: toward reinventing nature*, W W Norton, New York, pp321–366. The gorilla diorama is described more fully in Donna Haraway (1989) *Primate Visions: gender, race and nature in the world of modern science*, Routledge, New York.
8 George Schaller (1963) *The Mountain Gorilla: ecology and behavior*, University of Chicago Press.
9 See Kay Anderson (1995) 'Culture and nature at the Adelaide Zoo: at the frontiers of "human" geography', *Transactions of the Institute of British Geographers* NS 20: 275–294. Adelaide Zoo's website is www.adelaide-zoo.com.au/AdelaideZoo/default.htm. It was founded in 1886, and is run by the Royal Zoological Society of South Australia, originally formed in 1878 as the Acclimatization Society of South Australia.

10   See Anderson, (1995, p290). The Adelaide Zoo has a range of primates: golden-lion, black-lion and cotton-top tamarins, spider and squirrel monkeys, mandrills and baboons, dusky langurs, lion-tailed macaques, siamang, chimpanzees, orang-utans, and ring-tailed lemurs (www.adelaide-zoo.com.au/AdelaideZoo/The+Animals/default.htm).

11   www.biodiv.org/convention/articles.asp, 30 January 2003.

12   E N Buxton (1902) *Two African Trips: with notes and suggestions on big game preservation*, E Standford, London.

13   www.iucn.org/themes/wcpa/wpc2003/staging/about.html, 30 January 2003.

14   Dian Fossey (1983) *Gorillas in the Mist*, Hodder & Stoughton, London. The Dian Fossey Gorilla Fund International website is: www.gorillafund.org/000_core_frmset.html. You can adopt a gorilla from one of the Karisoke Research Center's groups for US$50.

15   The IGCP was a successor the the Mountain Gorilla Fund (set up in 1977) and the Mountain Gorilla Project (1978). The World Wildlife Fund subsequently became the Worldwide Fund for Nature (www.panda.org), now WWF: The Global Environment Network. African Wildlife Foundation: www.awf.org/. Fauna & Flora International: www.fauna-flora.org/.

16   His widow certainly saw it this way; Mary L Jobe Akeley (1929) 'Summary of talk given for Society for the Preservation of the Fauna of the Empire by Mary L Jobe Akeley, 10 December 1928, *Journal SPFE* 9, 15–23 (p15).

17   Richard S R Fitter and Peter Scott (1978) *The Penitent Butchers: the Fauna Preservation Society 1903–1978*, Collins, London.

18   Akeley (1929) 'Summary of talk given for Society for the Preservation of the Fauna of the Empire by Mary L Jobe Akeley, 10 December 1928', p16.

19   Akeley (1929, p15).

20   Akeley (1929, p17).

21   Akeley (1929, p17) (capitals in the original).

22   *Oryx* (1964) 'Victor van Straelen: an international conservationist', *Oryx* 7: 212.

23   Akeley (1929) 'Summary of talk given for Society for the Preservation of the Fauna of the Empire by Mary L Jobe Akeley, 10 December 1928', p21.

24   K Curry-Lindahl, (1964) 'The Congo National Parks since independence', *Oryx* 7: 233–239.

25   Baron Cartier de Marchienne's Address to the Meeting on 10 December 1928, *Journal SPFE* (1929): 21–23 (pp22, 23).

26   T M Butynski and J Kalina, (1993) 'Three new mountain parks for Uganda', *Oryx* 27: 214–224.

27   A McNeilage (1996) 'Ecotourism and mountain gorillas in the Virunga Volcanoes', in V J Taylor and N Dunstone (eds) *The Exploitation of Mammal Populations*, Chapman and Hall, London, pp334–344. Wildlife viewing tourism is discussed further in Chapter 9.

28   Gorillas are coprophagic, which doesn't help. See T M Butynski and J Kalina, (1998) 'Gorilla tourism: a critical look', in E J Milner-Gulland and R Mace (eds) *Conservation of Biological Resources*, Blackwell, Oxford, pp294–313; M H Woodford, T M Butynski and W B Karesh (2002) 'Habituating the great apes: the disease risks', *Oryx* 36: 15–160.

29 500 people visited Bwindi in 1998. Eight foreign tourists and a Ugandan guard were killed in March 1999. The park re-opened to tourists a month later, its security increased by 1000 soldiers; John Odyek (1999) *New Vision* 20 April, p29.

30 Butynski and Kalina (1993) 'Three new mountain parks for Uganda': 214–224.

31 E J Gubelman, et al (eds) *Bwindi Impenetrable National Park Management Plan 1995–1999*, Uganda National Parks, Kampala.

32 The Game (Preservation and Control) Act 1964.

33 This use by local people was explicit in the 1967 working plan for the forest reserve. There were 80 bamboo licences, each to cut 900 bamboo stems. By 1991 it was estimated that 34,000 bamboo stems were being cut annually.

34 The same is true for the Parc National Albert, whose population was cleared in the name of sleeping sickness eradication in 1933, see James Fairhead and Melissa Leach (2000) 'The Nature Lords', *Times Literary Supplement* 5 May 2000: 3–4.

35 W M Adams and M Infield (2001) 'Park outreach and gorilla conservation, Mgahinga Gorilla National Park, Uganda', in D Hulme and M Murphree (eds) *African Wildlife and Livelihoods: the promise and performance of community conservation*, James Currey, Oxford, pp131–147.

36 Community conservation is discussed in Chapter 5; see W M Adams and D Hulme (2001) 'Conservation and communities: changing narratives, policies and practices in African conservation', in D Hulme and M Murphree (eds) *African Wildlife and Livelihoods: the promise and performance of community conservation*, James Currey, London, pp9–23.

37 See Adams and Infield (2001) 'Park outreach and gorilla conservation', pp131–47, and K Archabald and L Naughton-Treves (2001) 'Tourism revenue-sharing around national parks in Western Uganda: early efforts to identify and reward local communities', *Environmental Conservation* 28: 135–149. Wildlife tourism at Mgahinga is discussed in more detail in Chapter 9.

38 A B Cunningham (1996) *People, Park and Plant Use: recommendations for multiple-use zones and development alternatives around Bwindi Impenetrable National Park, Uganda*, People and Plants Working Paper 4, UNESCO, Paris.

39 Fikret Berkes (1999) *Sacred Ecology: traditional ecological knowledge and resource management*, Taylor and Francis, London. See also, for example, A Posey Darrell (ed) *Cultural and Spiritual Values of Biodiversity*, UNEP, Nairobi.

40 The Society's journal was published as the *Journal of the Society for the Preservation of the Wild Fauna of the Empire* until 1913, then, in a new series, as *Journal of the Society for the Preservation of the Fauna of the Empire* (61 volumes, 1921–1950). In footnotes, these titles have been shortened to *Journal SPWFE* and *Journal SPFE* respectively.

41 I have provided extensive footnotes, for what Dick Chorley would have called 'the alert student' to pursue.

42 Wilson (2002) *The Future of Life*, Little Brown, London, p39.

43 Wilson (1992) *The Diversity of Life*, Penguin, Harmondsworth, p326.

CHAPTER 2 GOOD HUNTING

1   H Seton-Karr (1908) 'The preservation of big game', *Journal SPWFE*, 4: 26–28 (p26).

2   Jonathan Kingdon (1997) *The Kingdon Guide to African Mammals*, Academic Press, London. The South African Museum in Cape Town is leading an attempt to selectively breed plains zebras to create animals that resemble the quagga in appearance (and possibly genetically). See: www.museums.org.za/ sam/quagga/quagga.htm

3   www.museums.org.za/sam/quagga/tring.htm. See Miriam Rothschild (1983) *Dear Lord Rothschild: birds, butterflies and history*, London, Hutchinson.

4   The last record of capture was 1662. The dodo made poor eating, and its demise was probably due to introduced pigs, although cats, dogs, horses, goats, mongoose and crab-eating macaques cannot have helped, see Anton Gill and Alex West (2001) *Extinct*, Channel 4 Books, London; Graeme Caughley and Anne Gunn (1996) *Conservation Biology in Theory and Practice*, Blackwell Oxford.

5   Gill and West (2001). On the dodo, see www.internationaldove society.com/Misc%20Species/Dodo.htm. On the solitaire, see: www.internationaldovesociety.com/Misc%20Species/Reunion%20Solitaire.htm. On Steller's sea cow see: animaldiversity.ummz.umich.edu/accounts/ hydrodamalis/h._gigas$narrative.html. On the great auk, see: www.birds ofna.org/excerpts/auk.html. On the passenger pigeon, see Clive Ponting (1992) *A Green History of the World*, Penguin Books, Harmondsworth, and the Passenger Pigeon Society, www.passengerpigeon.org.

6   S H Whitbread (1907) 'The Year', *Journal SPWFE* 3: 10–13 (p12).

7   This period is well described by John MacKenzie (1988) *The Empire of Nature: hunting, conservation and British imperialism*, Manchester University Press, Manchester.

8   MacKenzie (1988, p92).

9   W Beinart and P Coates (1995) *Environment and History: the taming of nature in the USA and South Africa*, Routledge, London.

10   John MacKenzie describes the social cachet of hunting in Victorian society, and the importance of hunting trophies.

11   W C Harris, Sir (1839) *The Wild Sports of Southern Africa: being the narrative of an expedition from the Cape of Good Hope, through the territories of the Chief Moselekatse, to the Tropic of Capricorn*, J Murray, London; R G G Cumming, (1850) *Five Years of a Hunter's Life in the Far Interior of South Africa: with notices of the native tribes, and anecdotes of the chase of the lion, elephant, hippopotamus, giraffe, rhinoceros, &c.*, J Murray, London.

12   W C Baldwin (1863) *African Hunting, from Natal to the Zambesi: including Lake Ngami, the Kalahari Desert, &c. from 1852 to 1860*, R Bentley, London.

13   MacKenzie (1988) *The Empire of Nature*; A M Whitehouse and G I H Kerley (2002) 'Retrospective assessment of long-term conservation mangement of elephants in Addo Elephant National Park, South Africa', *Oryx* 36: 243–248.

14   H A Bryden (1893) *Gun and Camera in Southern Africa*, London.

15   Kingdon (1997) *The Kingdon Guide to African Mammals*. The Cape mountain zebra is *Equus zebra*.

16   John M MacKenzie (1997) 'Empire and the ecological apocalypse: the historiography of the imperial environment', in T Griffiths and L Robin (eds) *Ecology and Empire: environmental history of settler societies*, Keele University Press, Keele, pp215–228.

17   The ecological impact of empire is well argued by A W Crosby (1986) *Ecological Imperialism: the ecological expansion of Europe 1600–1900*, Cambridge University Press, Cambridge. The clearance of forests in the USA is analysed in detail by Michael Williams (1989) *Americans and their Forests: a historical geography*, Cambridge University Press, Cambridge.

18   T R Dunlap (1997) 'Ecology and environmentalism in the Anglo settler colonies', in Griffiths and Robin (eds) *Ecology and Empire*, pp76–86. See also Tim Flannery (1994) *The Future Eaters: an ecological history of the Australasian lands and people*, Reed Books Australia, Sydney (New Holland Edition, Sydney, 1997), and W Beinart, and P Coates, (1995) *Environment and History*.

19   See especially the work of Richard Grove, for example R H Grove (1992) 'Origins of western environmentalism', *Scientific American*, 267: 42–47; R H Grove, (1995) *Green Imperialism: colonial expansion, tropical island Edens and the origins of environmentalism, 1600–1800*, Cambridge University Press, Cambridge; R H Grove (1997) 'Conserving Eden: the (European) East India Companies and their environmental policies on St Helena, Mauritius and in Western India, 1660–1854', in R H Grove *Ecology, Climate and Empire; colonialism and global environmental history 1400–1940*, White Horse Press, Knapwell, pp37–85; R H Grove (1998) 'The East India Company, the Raj and the El Niño: the critical role played by colonial scientists in establishing the mechanisms of global climate teleconnections 1770–1930', in R H Grove, V Damodaran and S Sangwan (eds) *Nature and the Orient: the environmental history of South and Southeast Asia*, Oxford University Press, Delhi, pp301–323.

20   Gregory R Barton (2002) *Empire Forestry and the Origins of Environmentalism*, Cambridge University Press, Cambridge, p29. See also R Rajan (1998) 'Imperial environmentalism or environmental imperialism? European forestry, colonial foresters and the agendas of forest management in British India 1800–1900, in Grove, Damodaran and Sangwan (1998) (eds) *Nature and the Orient*, pp324–371.

21   Barton (2002). The title of this chapter is of course taken from Kipling's story in *The Jungle Book* 'Kaa's Hunting'.

22   R H Grove (1987) 'Early themes in African conservation: the Cape in the Nineteenth Century', in D M Anderson and R H Grove (eds) *Conservation in Africa: people, policies and practice*, Cambridge University Press, Cambridge, pp21–40.

23   MacKenzie (1988) *The Empire of Nature*.

24   R Nash, (1973) *Wilderness and the American Mind*, Yale University Press, New Haven, CT.

25   Richard S R Fitter and Peter Scott (1978) *The Penitent Butchers: the Fauna Preservation Society 1903–1978*, Collins, London.

26   R Boardman (1981) *International Organisations and the Conservation of Nature*, Indiana University Press, Bloomington, Indiana, p28.

27   John MacKenzie reports that the number of pianos being built in the USA rose from 20,000 per year in 1850 to 370,00 in 1910.

28   MacKenzie (1988) *The Empire of Nature*.

29   R Pankhurst and D H Johnson (1988) 'The great drought and famine of 1888–92 in Northeast Africa', in D Johnson and D Anderson, (eds) *The Ecology of Survival*, Lester Crook, London, pp47–70; R T Waller (1988) Emutai: crisis and response in Maasailand 1883–1902', in Johnson and Anderson *The Ecology of Survival*, pp72–112.

30   A R E Sinclair, and M Norton-Griffiths, (1979) (eds) *Serengeti: Dynamics of an Ecosystem*, University of Chicago Press, Chicago.

31   MacKenzie (1998) *The Empire of Nature*, p134.

32   *Saturday Review* 24 November 1906 'The dying fauna of an empire', reprinted in *Journal SPWFE* 3: 75–77

33   E N Buxton, (1902) *Two African Trips: with notes and suggestions on big game preservation*, London, E Stanford, p11. The text of the Convention is in *Journal SPWFE* 1903.

34   MacKenzie (1988) *The Empire of Nature*, p208.

35   Graeme Caughley and Anne Gunn (1996) *Conservation Biology in Theory and Practice*, Blackwell, Oxford.

36   Popular environmentalist angst about extinction has been enhanced by ideas of North American Pleistocene 'overkill', which researchers now widely reject, see Donald Grayson and David J Meltzer (2003) 'A requiem for North American overkill', *Journal of Archaeological Science* 30: 1–9.

37   Gill and West (2001). On the thylacine's web presence, see for example www.naturalworlds.org/thylacine/. On attempts to clone the thylacine see for example www.irysec.vic.edu.au/sci/goneill/thylacine.htm.

38   The evolution of that symbol of conservation is shown at www.wwf.org.uk/core/about/whoweare.asp.

39   Gerald Durrell (1960) *A Zoo in my Luggage*, Rupert Hart-Davis, London, p10.

40   E O Wilson and F M Peter et al (1988) *Biodiversity*, National Academy Press, Washington.

41   Wilson and Peter (1988, pvi).

42   Edward O Wilson (1992) *The Diversity of Life*, Harvard University Press, Cambridge, MA.

43   www.biodiv.org/convention/articles.asp

44   Myers, N (1988) 'Tropical forests and their species: going, going …?' in Wilson and Peter, *Biodiversity*, pp28–35.

45   Wilson (1992) *The Diversity of Life*, p327; Richard Leakey and Richard Lewin (1995) *The Sixth Extinction*, Doubleday, New York.

46   Secretariat of the Convention on Biological Diversity (2001) *Global Biodiversity Outlook*, Secretariat of the Convention on Biological Diversity, Montreal.

47   Fraser D M Smith, Robert M May, Robin Pellew, Timothy H Johnson, Kerry S Walter (1993) 'Estimating extinction rates', *Nature* 364 (5 August): 494–496.

48   Extinct, extinct in the wild, critically endangered, endangered, vulnerable, lower risk, data deficient and not evaluated.

49   Stuart L Pimm, Gareth Russell, John L Gittleman and Thomas M Brooks (1995) 'The future of biodiversity', *Science* 269 (21 July): 347–350.

50 For those with a literal mind, Bjorn Lomborg's (2001) *The Sceptical Environmentalist*, Cambridge University Press, Cambridge, is a mine of fascinating details.

51 Wilson (1992) *The Diversity of Life*, p327.

52 Wilson (1992, p327).

53 *Journal SPFE* (1924).

54 E N Buxton (1898) *Short Stalks: comprising trips in Somaliland, Siani, the eastern desert of Egypt, and Crete, the Carpathian Mountains, and Daghestan*, [Second series] E Stanford, London; E N Buxton (1902) *Two African Trips*.

55 Buxton (1902, p115).

56 Buxton (1902, p117).

57 John Sheail (1976) *Nature in Trust: the history of nature conservation in Britain*, Blackie, Glasgow.

58 For the origins of conservation in the UK, see David E Allen (1976) *The Naturalist in Britain*, Penguin, Harmondsworth, and John Sheail (1976).

59 W Addison (1991) *Epping Forest: Figures in a landscape*, Robert Hale, London.

60 See E N Buxton, (1923) *Epping Forest*, E Stanford, London. On his deathbed, Buxton purchased Hatfield Forest in Essex for the National Trust, 'The Late Mr E N Buxton', *Journal SPFE*, 4: 23–24 (1924).

61 *Journal SPWFE* (1905), 2.

62 H Seton-Karr (1908) 'The Preservation of Big Game', *Journal SPWFE*, 4: 26–28 (p26)

63 Buxton (1902) *Two African Trips*.

64 Buxton (1902, p127).

65 Buxton (1902, p128).

66 For details see MacKenzie (1988) *The Empire of Nature*, p223.

67 Whitbread (1907) 'The Year', p10.

68 Whitbread (1907, p10).

69 See Mark Toogood (2003) 'Decolonizing Highland Conservation', in William Adams and Martin Mulligan (eds) *Decolonizing Nature: strategies for conservation in a post-colonial era*, Earthscan, London, pp152–171.

70 For Quatermain see H Rider Haggard (1886) *King Solomon's Mines*, London; for Peter Piennar see John Buchan (1919) *Mr. Standfast*, Oxford University Press, Oxford.

71 MacKenzie (1988) *The Empire of Nature*, p134.

72 M S S Pandian (1998) 'Hunting and colonialism in the nineteenth-century Nilgiri Hills of South India, in R H Grove, V Damodaran and S Sangwan (eds) *Nature and the Orient: the environmental history of South and Southeast Asia*, Oxford University Press, Delhi, pp273–297.

73 Pandian (1998).

74 In 1890 the US Census Bureau announced that there was no longer a contiguous frontier line in the west. In 1893, Frederick Jackson Turner articulated the idea that the frontier was fundamental to the development of the USA, at the Columbian Exposition in Chicago, marking the 400th anniversary of the voyage of Columbus, see Frederick Jackson Turner (1920) *The Frontier in American History*, Henry Holt, New York (and Dover Publications, London, 1996).

75   Karl Jacoby (2001) *Crimes Against Nature: squatters, poachers, thieves and the hidden history of American conservation*, University of California Press, Berkeley, p58.

76   H Paul Jeffers (2003) *Roosevelt the Explorer: Teddy Roosevelt's amazing adventures as a naturalist, conservationist, and explorer*, Taylor Trade Publishing, Lanham NewYork.

77   Quoted in Paul Jeffers (2003, p46).

78   See Jeffers (2003); the Boone and Crockett Club's lobbying eventually led to passage of the Park Protection Act of 1894.

79   Donald Goddard (1995) 'A great campaign of conservation' in Donald Goddard (ed) *Saving Wildlife: a century of conservation*, Harry N Abrams with the Wildlife Conservation Society, New York, pp42–46.

80   William T Hornaday (1887) 'The passing of the buffalo' from *The Cosmopolitan*, October 1887 in Goddard (ed) (1995) *Saving Wildlife*, pp47–50.

81   Paul Jeffers (2003) *Roosevelt the Explorer*, p70.

82   William T Hornaday (1921) 'Post-war game conditions in America', *Journal SPFE* 1 1: 53–8 (pp56, 54).

83   Hornaday (1921, pp54, 57).

84   Buxton (1902) *Two African Trips*, p115.

85   SPWFE (1907) 'The Dying Fauna of an Empire', *Journal SPWFE*, 3: 75–77, p76; *Saturday Review* 24 Nov 1906.

86   This phrase was taken as the title of the history of the Fauna Preservation Society written in 1978 by Richard Fitter and Peter Scott, *Penitent Butchers: 75 years of wildlife conservation*, Collins, London.

87   H Seton-Karr (1908) 'The preservation of big game', *Journal SPWFE*, 4: 26–28 (pp26, 26–27).

88   Buxton (1902) *Two African Trips*, p121. Gamekeepers hang the carcasses of vermin on a gibbet.

89   Buxton (1902, pp115, 116).

90   Major Stevenson-Hamilton (1907) 'Opposition to game reserves', *Journal SPWFE* (1907): 53–9 (p54).

91   Minutes of proceedings at a deputation from the SPWFE to the Right Hon Alfred Lyttelton (His Majesty's Secretary for the Colonies), 2 February 1905, *Journal SPWFE* (1905) (2): 9–18 (p12).

92   Lord Hindlip (1905) 'Preservation of the fauna of British East Africa from the point of view of a settler', *Journal SPWFE*, 2: 51–57 (p51).

93   'Preservation of Game', Extract from Lord Cromer's Report for Egypt and the Sudan for the year 1902, Item 11, *Journal SPWFE* 3: 61–67 (p65).

94   Stevenson-Hamilton (1907) 'Opposition to game reserves', (p53).

95   Lord Hindlip (1905) 'Preservation of the fauna of British East Africa from the point of view of a settler', *Journal SPWFE*, 2: 51–57 (pp51, 52).

96   Lord Hindlip (1905, p52).

97   Lord Hindlip (1905). Grogan is famous for driving from the Cape to Cairo. Among other things, Lord Delamere shot lions with live donkeys as bait, and established the Masara pack of foxhounds in Kenya, see C McKenzie (2000) 'The British Big-Game Hunting Tradition: Masculinity and fraternalism with particular reference to "the Shikar Club"'. *The Sports Historian*, 20(1): 70–96.

98   Seton-Karr (1908) 'The preservation of big game', p27.

99   'The Year', *Journal SPWFE* (1905): pp 5–8 (p8).

100 Extract from Sir Charles Eliot's reports on the British East Africa Protectorate for the years 1902 and 1903, *Journal SPWFE* (1903) 1(7): 49–54 (p50).

101 The Editor (1909) 'Introduction', *Journal SPWFE* (1909).

102 Sir J Hayes Sadler to Earl of Crewe 3 October 1908, *Journal SPWFE* 4: 37–48 (p37).

103 'Export of Game Hides – Crops destroyed by game', Colonists' Association (*East African Standard* 14 August 1909) *Journal SPWFE* 5: p28–29. The motion was seconded by Mr Tarlton, who had guided President Roosevelt on his safari.

104 Extract from letter 28 August 1909, *Journal SPWFE* 5: 29.

105 Lord Hindlip (1905) *Journal SPWFE* 2: 51–57 (p52).

106 Stevenson-Hamilton (1907) 'Opposition to game reserves', p54.

107 C W Hobley (1924) 'The protection of wild life', Paper to the Museums Association 14 July 1924, *Journal SPFE* 4: 26–34 (p29).

108 Lord Hindlip (1905, p52).

109 'Extract from a letter from a correspondent in East Africa', *Journal SPWFE* (1903) 1: Item 4, pp39–40 (p39).

110 Lord Hindlip (1905).

111 Whitbread (1907) 'The Year', p11.

112 Hayes Sadler (1908, p41).

113 Minutes of proceedings at a deputation from the SPFE received by the Right Hon the Earl of Crewe K G (Principal Secretary of State for the Colonies), 26 February 1909 *Journal SPWFE* 1909 (4): 11–27 (p19).

114 Buxton (1902) *Two African Trips*, p117.

115 E N Buxton, (1908) Minutes of a meeting of the Society for the Preservation of the Wild Fauna of the Empire held in the House of Commons on 21 July 1908. Unpublished.

116 McKenzie (2000). Shikar-Safari Club International was founded in 1952. The Club membership is limited to 200 (see www.conservationforum.org/nwcp/partners/.) A book of hunting reminiscences was published in a limited edition in 2002 (Phillips, (2002) *A Hunting Heritage: fifty years of Shikar-Safari Club*, Safari Press, Ohio. I have not seen this book.

117 W T Hornaday's Letter and Fifteen Cardinal Principles, *SPWFE Journal* 5: 56–8, (p57).

118 Minutes of meeting SPFE 17 February 1928, *Journal SPWFE* 7: 20–27.

119 General Meeting SPFE London Zoo, 15 October 1928, *Journal SPFE* 9: 5–12 (p12).

120 Meeting SPFE 27 January 1936, *Journal SPFE* 28: 7–8. The proposal was bounced to the Executive Committee on 25 May, which recommended a more measured approach.

121 C W Hobley (1938) The conservation of wild life: retrospect and prospect, Part II', *SPFE Journal* 33: 39–49, (p47).

122 Hobley (1938, p43).

123 Jeffers (2003) *Roosevelt the Explorer*, see Samuel P Hays (1959) *Conservation and the Gospel of Efficiency: the progressive conservation movement 1890–1920*, Harvard University Press, Cambridge, MA.

124   Whitbread (1907) 'The Year', p11.

125   Buxton (1902) *Two African Trips*, pp117, 116.

126   SPWFE (1907) Minutes of proceedings at a deputation of the SPWFE to the Right Hon the Earl of Elgin, His Majesty's Secretary of State for the Colonies. *Journal SPWFE*, III: 20–32.

127   'The Year', *Journal SPWFE* (1905) 2: 5–8 (p7).

128   Minutes of proceedings at a deputation from the SPWFE to the Right Hon Alfred Lyttelton (His Majesty's Secretary for the Colonies), February 2 1905, *Journal SPWFE* (2): 9–18 (p10).

129   Rhys Williams to the Secretary of State for the Colonies, 9 June 1906, *Journal SPWFE*, 14–19 (p15).

130   Minutes of proceedings, *Journal SPWFE* 2: 9–18 (p13).

131   Minutes of proceedings, *Journal SPWFE* 2: 9–18 (p14).

132   Minutes of proceedings at a deputation from the Society for the Preservation of the Fauna of the Empire received by the Right Hon the Earl of Crewe KG (Principal Secretary of State for the Colonies), 26 February 1909, *Journal SPWFE* 4: 11–27 (p14).

133   Seton-Karr (1908) 'The preservation of big game'.

134   *Saturday Review* November 24 1906, reprinted as 'The Dying Fauna of an Empire', *Journal SPWFE* (1907) 3: 75–77.

135   SPWFE (1908) 'Editorial note', *Journal SPWFE* 4: 9–10 (p9).

136   John Henry Patterson (1907) *The Man-eaters of Tsavo and other East African Adventures*, Macmillan, London. The incident was the subject of a film starring Val Kilmer called *The Ghost and the Darkness* (1996). J H Patterson's later adventures are widely held to be the inspiration for Ernest Hemingway's story of adultery and murder on a Kenyan safari in *The Short Happy Life of Francis Macomber* (1936).

137   See Jeffers (2003) *Roosevelt the Explorer*, p191.

138   Compiled as *African Game Trails* in 1910.

139   They shot 512 head of big game, MacKenzie (1988) *The Empire of Nature*, p162.

140   This section draws extensively on Kenneth M Cameron (1990) *Into Africa: the story of the East African Safari*, Constable, London.

141   Cameron (1990) John MacKenzie has a fine photo of the Duke and Duchess of York with a shot black rhinoceros, *The Empire of Nature* (1988) p295.

142   General Meeting SPFE London Zoo, 4 November 1929, *Journal SPFE* (1930) 10: 5–10.

143   General Meeting SPFE London Zoo, 15 April 1929, *Journal SPFE* (1929) 9: 23–29 (p27).

144   General Meeting SPFE London Zoo, 3 March 1930, *Journal SPFE* (1930) 10: 5–11 (p9).

145   Deputation to the Secretary of State for the Colonies 5 March 1930, *Journal SPFE* (1930) 11: 11–16 (p12).

146   General Meeting SPFE London Zoo, 10 December 1928, *Journal SPFE* (1929) 9: 12–14.

147   Onslow to AGM SPFE 7 March 1932, *Journal SPFE* 16: 5–12.

148   General Meeting SPFE London Zoo, 3 March 1930, *Journal SPFE* (1930) 10: 5–11 (p8).

149 Markham, B (1942) *West With the Night*, republished Penguin Books, Hemel Hempstead, 1988.

150 'The King and Queen in East Africa', *Journal SPFE* 31 (1937): 7–10.

151 Both stories were first published in 1936, and collected in 1938 in *The Fifth Column* and *The First Forty-Nine Stories*. 'The Snows of Kilimanjaro' was made into a film in 1952 starring Gregory Peck and Ava Gardner.

152 'The Year', *Journal SPWFE* 2: pp5–8 (p8). See K G Schilling (1922) *Mit Blitzlight und Büsche im Zauber des Elelescho*, Voigtlander, Leipsig.

153 See for example S Metcalfe (1994) 'The Zimbabwe Communal Areas Management Programme for Indigenous Resources (CAMPFIRE)', in D Western, R M White and S C Strum (eds) *Natural Connections: perspectives in community-based conservation*, Island Press, Washington, pp161–192; David Hulme and Marshall Murphree (eds) (2001) *African Wildlife and Livelihoods: the promise and performance of community conservation*, James Currey, Oxford.

CHAPTER 3 THE GLOBAL CONSERVATION REGIME

1 Barbara Ward and René Dubos (1972) *Only One Earth: the care and maintenance of a small planet*, Penguin Books, Harmondsworth.

2 Secretariat of the Convention on Biological Diversity (2001) *Global Biodiversity Outlook*, Convention on Biological Diversity, Montreal.

3 www.biodiv.org/events/biodiv-day.asp. The USA did not sign the Convention.

4 C W Hobley (1924) 'The protection of wild life', paper to the Museums Association 14 July 1924, *Journal SPFE* 4: 26–34 (p26).

5 General Meeting SPFE London Zoo, 15 October 1928, *Journal SPFE* (1929): 5–12 (p6).

6 Objects of the Society, *Journal SPFE* 16 (1932), frontispiece.

7 The Convention on International Trade in Endangered Species of Wild Fauna and Flora, see www.CITES.org.

8 In Australia, the Field Naturalists Club of Victoria was established in 1880, the Gould League of Bird Lovers (in Victoria) and the Wildlife Preservation Society (in Sydney) in 1909; see Martin Mulligan (2001) 'Re-enchanting conservation work: reflections of the Australian experience', *Environmental Values* 10: 19–33.

9 Martin Holdgate (1999) *The Green Web: a union for world conservation*, Earthscan, London.

10 Holdgate (1999). See www.birdlife.net.

11 The best account of the development of the international conservation movement is by Martin Holdgate (1999); but see also John McCormick (1992) *The Global Environmental Movement: reclaiming Paradise*, Belhaven, London (first published 1989, Indiana University Press, Bloomington, Indiana).

12 The Society sent delegates, and a letter recording their adherence to the principles of the Conference (SPFE Meeting 10 April 1923). Their experiences reported Minutes of Meeting SPFE December 3 1925, *Journal SPFE* (1926).

13 The development of international conservation in Holland is described by Paul Jepson and Robert J Whittaker (2002) 'Histories of protected areas:

internationalisation of conservationist values and their adoption in the Netherlands Indies (Indonesia)', *Environment and History* 8: 129–172.

14   Holdgate (1999) *The Green Web*.

15   W M Adams, (1996) *Future Nature: a vision for conservation*, Earthscan, London.

16   This paragraph draws extensively on Holdgate (1999) but see also R Boardman, (1981) *International Organisations and the Conservation of Nature*, Indiana University Press, Bloomington, IN.

17   Aldo Leopold (1933) *Game Management*, Scribners, New York; Aldo Leopold (1949) *Sand County Almanac: and sketches here and there*, Oxford University Press, Oxford, Aldo Leopold died in 1948.

18   Although a proposal was made by Miss C Buxton to shorten the Society's name in 1928 it was rejected by the Executive Committee who felt that its aims could not be expressed in a shorter form, General Meeting SPFE London Zoo, 10 December 1928, *Journal SPFE* 9: 12–14.

19   Meeting 26 March 1920, *Journal SPFE* 1: 19.

20   Lord Grey of Fallodon had turned down the position for lack of time, *Journal SPFE* 7: 11. Lord Grey had been Foreign Secretary from 1905 to 1916.

21   General Meeting SPFE London Zoo, 15 April 1929, *Journal SPFE* 9: 23–29.

22   For example Report of Executive Committee to General Meeting 17 February 1928, *Journal SPFE* 8: 28–29.

23   See for example; Meeting 17 February 1928, *Journal SPFE* (1928) 8: 28.

24   General Meeting SPFE London Zoo, 15 October 1928, *Journal SPFE* 9: 5–12.

25   General Meeting April 27 1928, *Journal SPFE* (1928) 8: 32–33.

26   General Meeting SPFE London Zoo, 3 March 1930, *Journal SPFE* 11: 5–11, (p6).

27   General Meeting SPFE London Zoo, 15 April 1929, *Journal SPFE* (1929) 9: 23–29 (p26).

28   See Gregory Barton (2002) *Empire Forestry and the Origins of Environmentalism*, Cambridge University Press, Cambridge.

29   General Meeting SPFE London Zoo, 15 April 1929, *Journal SPFE* 9: 23–29 (p25).

30   Roderick P Neumann (1996) 'Dukes, Earls and ersatz Edens: aristocratic nature preservationists in colonial Africa', *Environment and Planning D: Society and Space* 14: 79–98.

31   See John MacKenzie (1988) *The Empire of Nature: hunting, conservation and British imperialism*, Manchester University Press, and David K Prendergast and William M Adams (2003) 'Colonial Wildlife Conservation and the Origins of the Society for the Preservation of the Wild Fauna of the Empire (1903–1914)', *Oryx* 37(2): 251–260.

32   Deputation to the Secretary of State for the Colonies 5 March 1930, *Journal SPFE* 11: 11–16 (p15).

33   Editorial, *Journal SPFE* 11: 16–18 (p17).

34   CRS Pitman (1933) report of address to SPFE 13 March 1933, *Journal SPFE* 19: 8–10

35   AGM SPFE 13 March 1933, *Journal SPFE* 19: 7–13.

36   Holdgate (1999) *The Green Web*.

37   Holdgate (1999) *The Green Web*.

38   C L Boyle (1959) 'The Survival Service Commission', *Oryx* 5: 30–35. The New York Zoological Society changed its name to the Wildlife Conservation Society in 1994.

39   John McCormick (1992) *The Global Environmental Movement: reclaiming paradise*, Belhaven, London.

40   On Huxley see J L Huxley (1977) *Memories II*, Harper and Row, New York; on UK conservation see John Sheail (1984) 'Nature reserves, national parks and post-war reconstruction in Britain', *Environmental Conservation* 11: 29–34.

41   Julian L Huxley (1930) *African View*, Chatto and Windus, London, E Barton Worthington (1983) *The Ecological Century: a personal appraisal*, Cambridge University Press, Cambridge.

42   McCormick (1992) *The Global Environmental Movement*.

43   Society for the Preservation of the Fauna of the Empire (1948) 'International Union for the Protection of Nature', *SPFE Journal* 58: 12–17.

44   Holdgate (1999) *The Green Web*.

45   McCormick (1992) *The Global Environmental Movement*.

46   Holdgate (1999) *The Green Web*.

47   Max Nicholson is a central figures in the development of conservation in the UK, founding the British Trust for Ornithology, was a leading figure in post-war planning in the UK and a member of the Wildlife Conservation Special Committee for England and Wales (the 'Huxley Committee') that recommended establishment of the Nature Conservancy in 1947 (Cmd 7122), and was the Nature Conservancy's second Director General (J Sheail (1976) *Nature in Trust: the history of nature conservation in Great Britain*, Blackie, Glasgow). Among other achievements he also led British involvement in the establishment of the International Union for the Protection of Nature, and was central to the success of the International Biological Programme (E Barton Worthington (1983) *The Ecological Century*).

48   Holdgate (1999) *The Green Web*.

49   SPFE (1950) 'Conservation and Lake Success', *Journal SPFE* 61: 31–33.

50   Editorial, *Journal SPFE* 58: 4–10 and article *Journal SPFE* (1948) 58: 12–17. The committee drafting the IUPN constitution was chaired by an SPFE Council member, Dr Herbert Smith.

51   In the March issue of the magazine of the American Museum of Natural History.

52   *Journal SPFE* 59: 5–7 (p5).

53   SPFE (1950) 'Conservation at Lake Success', *Journal SPFE* 61: 31–33 (p32).

54   General Meeting 21 November 1946, *Journal SPFE* 55: 43–44.

55   General Meeting on 5 June 1950. The Privy Purse indicated that the king agreed to continue as Patron of the Society under its new name in 1951.

56   Appendix 'Rules of the Fauna Preservation Society', *Oryx* 1(4): i–iv (1951).

57   Annual Report for the year ending 32 December 1953, *Oryx* 2 (4): 261–263. The proceeds from a collection at the door were £23 18s 2d, divided equally).

58   See William M Adams and Martin Mulligan (2003) *Decolonizing Nature: strategies for conservation in a post-colonial era*, Earthscan, London.

59   www.eawildlife.org

60   Donald Goddard (1995) 'Field science comes of age' in Donald Goddard (ed) *Saving Wildlife: a century of conservation*, Harry N. Abrams with the Wildlife Conservation Society, New York pp42–46.

61   *Oryx* 6: 260

62   See www.awf.org.

63   See for example A R E Sinclair, and M Norton-Griffiths, (eds) (1979) *Serengeti: dynamics of an ecosystem,* University of Chicago Press, Chicago.

64   Holdgate (1999) *The Green Web.*

65   The debate about Serengeti is described more fully in Chapter 4. The establishment of the park is described by Roderick Neumann (1998) *Imposing Wilderness: struggles over livelihood and nature preservation in Africa*, University of California Press, Berkeley.

66   McCormick (1992) *The Global Environmental Movement.*

67   Quoted in Holdgate (1999) *The Green Web,* p72.

68   Deputy Director of the UK Nature Conservancy, and with extensive experience of limnological research in East Africa.

69   *Oryx*, 6 (3): p143.

70   In 1960 G G Watterson visited Ghana, Ivory Coast, Dahomey, Togo, former French Cameroun, Central African Republic and Nigeria. In 1961 he visited Sudan, Kenya, Tanganyika, Uganda, Northern and Southern Rhodesia, Ethiopia and Somalia (The International Union for the Conservation of Nature and Natural Resources African Special Project, Stage 1, 1961, *Oryx* 6 (3): 143–170.

71   Worthington (1983) *The Ecological Century*, p154.

72   John Hillaby (1962) 'African Special Project, Stage Two – the Arusha conference', *Oryx* 6: 211–214 (p213).

73   Hillaby (1962, p213).

74   Hillaby (1962, p212).

75   Hillaby (1962, p213).

76   Richard S Fitter and Peter Scott (1974) *The Penitent Butchers*, Collins, London.

77   McCormick (1992) *The Global Environmental Movement.*

78   WWF became the Worldwide Fund for Nature in 1986. The United States and Canada retained the old name. For WWF see www.wwf.org.

79   *Daily Mirror*, 9 October 1961; Holdgate (1999) *The Green Web*, p84.

80   Holdgate (1999, p82).

81   Holdgate (1999, p83).

82   See A N James, K J Gaston and A Balmford (1999) 'Balancing the Earth's accounts', *Nature* 4012: 323–324.

83   Holdgate (1999) *The Green Web*, p70; Van Straelen died soon after the launch, to be succeeded by Jean Dorst. The government of Ecuador declared its first national park in the Galápagos Islands (see www.galapagospark.org).

84   Grant of US$131, in 1962 E P Gee recorded 870 animals; by 1975, numbers had dropped to 400; a wild ass sanctuary was established, and by the mid-1980s, the population had risen to an impressive total of well over 2000 (www.panda.org).

85   Roderick P Neumann (1998) *Imposing Wilderness: struggles over livelihood and nature preservation in Africa*, University of Calidfornia Press, Berkeley and wwf.panda.org.

86   1001 individual donors each contributed US$10,000 for this project.

87   In 1973 Indira Gandhi set up a task force to implement a six-year conservation plan for tigers, and the government established nine tiger reserves (later adding six more). Nepal created 3, Bangladesh 1; see www.panda.org. Project Tiger is discussed further in Chapter 6.

88   This led to representative areas of tropical moist forest in Central and West Africa, Southeast Asia, and Latin America being managed as national parks or reserves. By 2003, the WWF Forest Programme supported 350 projects all over the world (www.panda.org).

89   Leading to the establishment of marine sanctuaries for marine mammals, and the protection of marine turtle nesting sites (www.panda.org).

90   Which raised over US$1 million to combat rhino poaching.

91   Examples of debt-for-nature swaps include Zambia, Madagascar, Ecuador and the Philippines.

92   The Conservation Stamp Collection, launched in 1983 in collaboration with Groth AG, has helped over 200 countries select threatened species to feature on official postage stamps. The programme has raised over US$13 million (www.panda.org).

93   See history on www.panda.org.

94   While conservationists in conference might ask 'has the panda had its day?' (Abigail Entwistle and Nigel Dunstone (eds) (2000) *Priorities for the Conservation of Mammalian Diversity: Has the Panda had its Day?*, Cambridge University Press, Cambridge), it has survived as conservation's chief icon. However, the panda has had several public-relations makeovers, becoming increasingly less the helpless cute focus of last-ditch rescue and more the tough doughty survivor of corporate sustainability, see www.panda.org/about_wwf/who_we_are/history/40th_anniversary.cfm.

95   Friends of the Earth UK was set up by Graham Searle in 1970, Greenpeace in the UK in 1977 (Meredith Veldman (1994) *Fantasy, the Bomb and the Greening of Britain: romantic protest 1945–80*, Cambridge University Press, Cambridge). The RSPB and the Naturalists' Trusts were not holistic environmental organizations in the 1960s.

96   By that time, FPS had members in over 87 countries.

97   Sir Peter Scott retired as Chairman of FFPS at the end of 1980, and was made a Vice President. Lord Craigton succeeded him as chairman. Scott died in 1989.

98   Lord Greenwood to FPS AGM 1973, *Oryx* 12: 165–166):

99   Holdgate (1999) *The Green Web*.

100   Holdgate (1999).

101   'News and Views' *Oryx* (1980) 15(3).

102   Hobley (1924) *Journal SPFE* 4 (pp28, 32); C W Hobley (1938) 'The conservation of wild life: retrospect and prospect, Part II', *Journal SPFE* 33: 39–49 (p4).

103   See, for example, Fairfield Osborn (1948) *Our Plundered Planet*, Faber and Faber, London; John Terborgh (1999) *Requiem for Nature*, Island Press; Edward Wilson (2002) *The Future of Life*, Little, Brown, London.

104   Sir Peter Chalmers-Mitchell (1931) 'Zoos and National Parks: British Association meeting, London, 1931', *Journal SPFE* 15: 21–43.

105　Meetings SPFE 20 July 1923, 2 November 1923, 22 January 1924.

106　Armand Denis (1963) *On Safari: the story of my life*, Collins, London.

107　MacKenzie, C (2000) 'The British Big-Game Hunting Tradition: Masculinity and fraternalism with particular reference to "the Shikar Club"', *The Sports Historian*, 20 (1): 70–96.

108　Minutes of meeting SPFE December 3 1925, *Journal SPFE* (1926): p20.

109　Hobley (1924) SPFE Journal 4 (p32).

110　*Journal SPFE* 9: 5; General Meeting SPFE London Zoo, 4 November 1929, *Journal SPFE* 10: 5–10 (p6).

111　General Meeting SPFE London Zoo, 4 November 1929, *Journal SPFE* 10: 5–10 (p11).

112　Meeting of SPFE 21 November 1938, *Journal SPFE* 35: 14.

113　M A Wetherall to AGM SPFE 7 March 1932, *Journal SPFE* 16: 5–12.

114　Hobley (1938) 'The conservation of wild life', p4.

115　C W Hobley (1932) 'The need for censorship of "jungle" films: cinematic records that are marred by cruelty and bad taste', *The Field* 16 January 1932, reprinted in *Journal SPFE* 16: 42–5.

116　Hobley (1932, pp54–55).

117　Executive Committee 4 December 1933, *Journal SPFE* 21: 11–14.

118　Denis (1963) *On Safari*.

119　In gratitude, the FPS Council proposed electing him a Vice President.

120　The film was produced by James Hill. Joy Adamson's book was published in 1960, *Born free: a lioness of two worlds*, London. It included a foreword by Charles Pitman, of the Uganda Game Department. I am grateful to Liz Watson for suggesting the importance of this film.

121　Denis (1963) *On Safari* (p316).

122　David Attenborough (2002) *Life on Air: memoirs of a broadcaster*, BBC Books, London. The programmes also generated a series of best-selling books published by the Lutterworth Press, such as *Zoo Quest to Guiana* (1956), *Zoo Quest for a Dragon* (1957) and *Zoo Quest in Paraguay* (195).

123　The development of wildlife film on television is described in David Attenborough (2002) *Life on Air*.

124　Gail Davies (2000) 'Narrating the Natural History Unit: institutional orderings and spatial strategies', *Geoforum* 31: 539–551.

125　Subsequently Young Ornithologists Club and then Wildlife Explorers.

126　Sheail (1976) *Nature in Trust*.

127　There are now 48 Wildlife Trusts, including several in urban areas such as London. RSNC is now branded 'The Wildlife Trusts'.

128　David Evans (1992) *A History of Nature Conservation in Britain*, Routledge, London.

129　The growth of the Wildlife Trusts is discussed by Philip Lowe and Jane Goyder in *Environmental Groups in Politics*, Allen and Unwin, Hemel Hempstead, 1981.

130　RSPB Annual Reports.

131　*Independent* 7 October 2002, p6; for National Trust see www.nationaltrust.org.uk/main/nationaltrust/.

132　See Peter Rawcliffe (1994) *Swimming with the Tide: the changing nature of national environmental pressure groups in the UK 1984–1994,* Unpublished PhD Thesis,

University of East Anglia, and HMSO (1994) *Social Trends 24*, HMSO, London.

133 See Ramachandra Guha and Martinez-Alier (1997) *Varieties of Environmentalism: essays North and South*, Earthscan, London. The middle class is also important in the Indian environmental movement.

134 Ramachandra Guha (2000) *Environmentalism: a global history*, Oxford University Press, Delhi.

135 These and other cases are discussed in W M Adams (2001) *Green Development: environment and sustainability in the Third World*, Routledge, London. On the Narmada dams see www.narmada.org; on the Ogoni, see www.mosopcanada.org.index/html

136 Of course, even in countries where wildlife environmentalism is strongly supported, the political climate is extremely variable, and has been fiercely anti-environmentalist as in the United States under the Reagan and Bush administrations.

137 'Editorial', *Journal SPFE* (1945) 52: 9.

138 G P Chapman, K Kumar, C Fraser and I Gaber (1997) *Environmentalism and the Mass Media: the North–South Divide*, Routledge, London.

139 See www.birdlife.net

140 www.fauna-flora.org/around_the_world/asia/world_main_cebu_frame.htm. The best-known animal species are the Cebu black shama (*Copsychus cebuensis*), the Cebu flowerpecker (*Dicaeum quadricolor*), believed extinct until a sighting in the Tabunan forest in 1992, and the Cebu hanging parakeet (*Loriculus philippensis chrysonatus*), believed extinct until a flock of five birds was sighted in Tabunan in 1998. Tabunan forest holds the last known stand of the endemic Cebu cinnamon tree (*Cinnamonum cebuense*), described only 10 years ago and at least 200 threatened native plant species.

141 See www.fauna-flora.org/around_the_world/eurasia/world_main_kyrgyzstan_frame.htm.

142 www.conservation.org

143 P Chatterjee and M Finger (1994) *The Earth Brokers: power, politics and world development*, Routledge, London.

144 See James Fairhead and Melissa Leach (2000) 'The Nature Lords', *Time Literary Supplement*, (5 May 2000): 3–4.

CHAPTER 4 NATURE IN ITS PLACE

1 John Terborgh (1999) *Requiem for Nature*, Island Press, Washington DC.

2 Bernard and Michael Grzimek (1960) *Serengeti Shall Not Die*, Hamish Hamilton, London. On film, see the 1994 Imax/Omnimax film *Africa: the Serengeti*, directed by George Casey.

3 On research see A R E Sinclair and M Norton-Griffiths (eds) (1979) *Serengeti: Dynamics of an Ecosystem,* University of Chicago Press, Chicago. On film, see the 1994 Imax/Omnimax film *Africa: the Serengeti*, directed by George Casey.

4 The human rights issues associated with the creation of Serengeti National Park are reviewed by Roderick P Neumann (1995) 'Ways of seeing Africa: colonial recasting of African society and landscape in Serengeti National Park',

Ecumene 2: 149–169, and Roderick P Neumann (1998) *Imposing Wilderness: struggles over livelihood and nature preservation in Africa*, University of California Press, Berkeley. The general issue of evictions from national parks is discussed in Chapter 5.

5   'Editorial Notes', *Journal SPFE,* 56: 5.

6   The Secretary [C L Boyle] (1956) 'What of the Serengeti?', *Oryx* 3 (6): 303–318. The SPFE regarded this as a significant achievement, see Lord Greenwood, *Oryx* 12 (2): 165–166.

7   Pearsall had been a member of the British Nature Reserves Investigations Committee and the British Ecological Society's special committee on nature conservation in the 1940s, and was a member of the Nature Conservancy after the war. He was the first President of the Field Studies Council in 1943, J Sheail (1976) *Nature in Trust: the history of nature conservation in Great Britain*, Blackie, Glasgow. Pearsall's report was published in *Oryx* 4: 71–136.

8   The SPFE continued to protest, see 'The Serengeti', *Oryx* (1958) 4 (6): 351–352. The issue of land rights in the Ngorogoro Conservation Area remains current, the latest moves to ban cultivation and evict Maasai coming in 2001, see Kathy M Homewood and William A Rodgers (1991) *Maasailand Ecology: Pastoral Development and Wildlife Conservation in Ngorogoro, Tanzania*, Cambridge University Press, Cambridge; see also Anon (2002) 'Are there too manyu animals and people in Ngorogoro?', *Haramata* 43, March, 2003: 16–19.

9   E Ray Lankester (1914) 'Nature reserves', *Nature*, March 12: 33–35.

10   See John Sheail (1976) *Nature in Trust: the history of nature conservation in Great Britain*, Blackie, Edinburgh.

11   Lionel Rothschild eventually took a leading role in both the SPNR and the Society for the Preservation of the Fauna of the Empire; see Sheail (1976) *Nature in Trust* and Miriam Rothschild (1983) *Dear Lord Rothschild: birds, butterflies and history*, London, Hutchinson.

12   On the SPNR's surveys see Miriam Rothschild and Peter Marren (1997) *Rothschild's Reserves: time and fragile nature*, Harley Books, Colchester; on the nature reserve in the UK, see Sheail (1976) *Nature in Trust*.

13   Extract from Sir Charles Eliot's reports on the British East Africa Protectorate for the years 1902 and 1903, *Journal SPWFE* 1: 49–54.

14   P L Sclater (1905) 'On the best mode of preserving the existence of the larger mammals of Africa for future ages', *Journal SPWFE* 2: 46–50 (p49).

15   Major Stevenson-Hamilton (1907) 'Opposition to game reserves', *Journal SPWFE*: 53–59 (p53).

16   Lord Hindlip (1905) 'Preservation of the fauna of British East Africa from the point of view of a settler', *Journal SPWFE* 2: 51–57.

17   F Gillet (1908) 'Game reserves', *Journal SPWFE* 4: 42–45.

18   Sir J Hayes Sadler to Earl of Crewe 3 October 1908, *Journal SPWFE* 4: 37–48.

19   Minutes of proceedings at a deputation from the SPWFE received by the Right Hon the Earl of Crewe KG (Principal Secretary of State for the Colonies) at the Colonial Office, 26 February 1909, *Journal SPWFE*, 4: 11–27 (p14).

20   SPWFE Deputation to the Earl of Crewe 26 February 1909, *Journal SPWFE*, 5: 11–27. The SPWFE carried the argument: Lord Crewe (Colonial Secretary)

declared that no alterations to the reserves under his authority would be made
without agreement of either himself or his successors in the Colonial Office.

21 Gillet (1908) 'Game reserves', p42.

22 Minutes of proceedings at a deputation of the Society for the Preservation of
the Wild Fauna of the Empire to the Right Hon the Earl of Elgin, His
Majesty's Secretary of State for the Colonies, *Journal SPWFE* 3: 20–32 (p31).

23 On parrots, see SPWFE deputation to the Earl of Crewe, 26 February 1909,
Journal SPWFE (1909) (4): 11–27 (p126). The problem of tsetse fly and
livestock is discussed in Chapter 7.

24 H Seton-Karr (1908) 'The preservation of big game', *Journal SPWFE* 4: 26–28.

25 T H Henfrey (1928) 'Is game preservation compatible with the agricultural
development, with special reference to Tanganyika Territory', *Journal SPFE* 8:
117–119.

26 Extract from letter 28 August 1909, *Journal SPWFE* (1909): (p27).

27 Meeting 20 June 1924.

28 Minutes of proceedings at a deputation from the SPWFE to the Right Hon
Alfred Lyttelton (His Majesty's Secretary for the Colonies), 2 February 1905,
Journal SPWFE (1905) (2): 9–18 (p13).

29 C W Hobley (1938) 'The conservation of wild life: retrospect and prospect,
Part II', *Journal SPFE* 33: 39–49.

30 Gillet (1908) 'Game reserves', p43.

31 Major Stevenson-Hamilton (1907) 'Opposition to game reserves', *Journal
SPWFE* (1907): 53–99 (pp54, p59).

32 Stevenson-Hamilton (1907, p59).

33 Minutes of proceedings at a deputation from the Society for the Preservation
of the Fauna of the Empire to the Right Hon the Earl of Elgin (His Majesty's
Secretary for the Colonies), 15 June 1906, *Journal SPWFE* 3: 20–32 (p21).

34 'Editorial notes', *Oryx* 1 (6): 262–263

35 Extract from the report of Sir Alfred Sharpe, the Commissioner in British
Central Africa 1901–1902, and Major F B Prance for 1903, 'Game
preservation', *Journal SPWFE* 1: 58–60 (p59).

36 Hesketh Bell, Governor of Uganda, to Lord Elgin (Extract from Blue Book
No 44, *Journal SPWFE* 5: 30–31 (p30).

37 C R S Pitman (1933) Report of address to SPFE 13 March 1933, *Journal SPFE*
19: 8–10.

38 Extract from the report of Col Hayes Sadler for the Uganda Protectorate for
the years 1902 and 1908, 'Preservation of Game', *Journal SPWFE* 1: 55–57
(p55).

39 Extract from the report of Col Hayes Sadler (p55).

40 Extract from the report of Col Hayes Sadler (p55).

41 Luise White (1995) 'Tsetse visions: narratives of blood and bugs in colonial
Northern Rhodesia, 1931–9', *Journal of African History* 36: 219–245; Henrietta
Moore and Megan Vaughan (1994) *Cutting down Trees: gender, nutrition and
agricultural change in Zambia*, James Currey.

42 Henfrey (1928) 'Is game preservation compatible with the agricultural
development' *SPFE Journal* 8: 117–119.

43 Henfrey (1928).

44   Minutes of meeting SPFE 17 February 1928, *Journal SPWFE* 7: 20–27 (p26).

45   Hesketh Bell, Governor of Uganda, to Lord Elgin (Extract from Blue Book No 44, *Journal SPWFE* 5: 30–1 (p30).

46   Reported by E N Buxton (1913) 'Further Correspondence relating to the preservation of wild animals in Africa', presented to Parliament March 1913, *Journal SPWFE* 6: 72–75 (p74).

47   The British South Africa Company defended itself against the SPWFE's accusations of weakness in game laws in Rhodesia in 1905 precisely because the ban on firearms made slaughter by natives effectively impossible, 'Correspondence with British South Africa Company', *Journal SPWFE* (1905) 2: 68–69.

48   Henfrey (1928) 'Is game preservation compatible with the agricultural development', p118.

49   Minutes of Meeting of Executive Committee SPWFE 22 February 1921, *Journal SPFE* 1: 19–20.

50   Minutes of Meeting of Executive Committee SPWFE 22 February 1921, *Journal SPFE* 1: 19–20. The meeting of 22 June 1921 heard that the Lake Chad Reserve was definitely abolished, and another in exchange marked out in Bedde Emirate 150 Miles to the west.

51   Henfrey (1928) 'Is game preservation compatible with the agricultural development', p118.

52   See Hobley (1938) 'The conservation of wildlife', p44.

53   See for example Thomas J Bassett and Donald E Crummey (eds) (1983) *Land in African Agrarian Systems*, Wisconsin University Press, Madison, WI, particularly Thomas J Bassett 'The land question and agricultural transformation in sub-Saharan Africa' (pp3–34), and John W Bruce 'Do indigenous tenure systems constrain agricultural development?' (pp35–56).

54   Henfrey (1928) 'Is game preservation compatible with the agricultural development', p118.

55   Henfrey (1928, p118) (1906).

56   Minutes of proceedings at a deputation from the SPWFE to the Right Hon the Earl of Elgin, *Journal SPWFE* 3: 20–32.

57   Minutes of proceedings at a deputation from the SPWFE to the Right Hon the Earl of Elgin (1906, p24).

58   Peter Chalmers-Mitchell, Vice Chairman of SPFE to AGM 27 February 1931, *Journal SPFE* 13: 5–11 (p6).

59   H G Maurice 'Man-made Edens' *Journal SPFE* 34: 41–46 (p43).

60   General Meeting SPFE London Zoo, 3 March 1930, *Journal SPFE* (1930): 5–11 (p9).

61   'The Year', *Journal SPWFE* 2: 5–8 (p7).

62   Minutes of proceedings at a deputation from the SPWFE to the Right Hon Alfred Lyttelton (His Majesty's Secretary for the Colonies), February 2 1905, *Journal SPWFE* 2: 9–18. This was not in fact true – Yellowstone was poorly managed and lacked funds for decades. See Alfred Runte (1987) *National Parks: the American experience*, University of Nebraska Press, Lincoln.

63   Rhys Williams to the Secretary of State for the Colonies, 9 June 1906, *Journal SPWFE*: 3: 14–19 (p15).

64   William T Hornaday (1921) 'Post-war game conditions in America', *Journal SPFE* 1: 53–8 (p56).

65   Runte (1987) *National Parks*, pxix.

66   Cited in Runte (1987). Catlin's ideas that people had a place within the 'natural' landscape was something only taken up in national park thinking well into the 20th century.

67   Andrew C Isenberg (2000) *The Destruction of the Bison: an environmental history, 1750–1920*, Cambridge University Press, Cambridge.

68   Anne Whiston Spirn (1995) 'Constructing nature: the legacy of Frederick Law Olmstead', in William Cronon (ed) *Uncommon Ground: toward reinventing nature*, W W Norton, New York, pp91–113 (p95).

69   Runte (1987) *National Parks*, p44.

70   Runte (1987).

71   Richard Fitter and Peter Scott (1974) *The Penitent Butchers: 75 years of wildlife conservation*, Fauna Preservation Society, London; Martin Mulligan (2001) 'Re-enchanting conservatin work: reflections of the Australian experience', *Environmental Values* 10: 19–33.

72   Karl Jacoby (2001) *Crimes Against Nature: squatters, poachers, thieves and the hidden history of American conservation*, University of California Press, Berkeley.

73   The Forest Service and War Department did not hand over monuments under their jurisdiction until 1933 Runte (1987) *National Parks*, p103.

74   Jacoby (2001) *Crimes against Nature*, p87.

75   Alfred Runte (1990) *Yosemite: the embattled wilderness*, University of Nebraska Press, Lincoln.

76   See for example Jerome A Greene (1991) *Yellowstone Command: Colonel Nelson A. Miles and the Great Sioux War 1876–1877*, University of Nebraska Press, Lincoln.

77   Jacoby (2001) *Crimes against Nature*.

78   Jacoby (2001, footnote 60, p235). Smokey the Bear is a cartoon figure long used to warn the public about the dangers of fire, see www.smokeybear.com.

79   Runte (1990) *Yosemite*.

80   J G Nelson (1968) 'The National Parks movement in Canada', in J G Nelson and R G Scace (eds) *The Canadian National Parks: today and tomorrow*, National and Provincial Parks Association of Canada, Calgary, pp35–65 (p35).

81   Robert Craig Brown (1968) 'The doctrine of usefulness: natural resource and National Park Policy in Canada 1887–1914', in Nelson and Scace *The Canadian National Parks*, pp94–110.

82   J G Nelson (1968) 'Man and landscape change in Banff National Park: a national park problem in perspective', in Nelson and Scace *The Canadian National Parks*, pp111–150.

83   K McNamee, (1993) 'From wild places to endangered spaces: a history of Canada's national parks', in P Dearden and R Rollins (eds) *Parks and Protected Areas in Canada*, Oxford University Press, Oxford, pp17–41.

84   R W Sandford (1990) *The Canadian Alps: the history of mountaineering in Canada, Volume 1*, Altitude Publishing, Banff, Canada.

85   Runte (1987) *National Parks*.

86   Runte (1987).

87   'The Canadian National Parks: progress in 1926', *Journal SPFE* (1926): 53–5
88   On Indian Days, see Runte (1990) *Yosemite*.
89   On the Model T see www.wiley.com/legacy/products/subject/business/ forbes/ford.html. On the motor car more generally, see James J Flink (1988) *The Automobile Age*, MIT Press, Cambridge, MA.
90   On Olmstead, see Spirn (1995) 'Constructing nature', p91.
91   See for example Alexander Wilson (1992) *The Culture of Nature: North American landscape from Disney to the Exxon Valdez*, Blackwell, Oxford.
92   The Secretary [of the SPFE] (1953) 'An international conference on the protection of nature', *Oryx* 2: 150–154 (quotes pp150–151).
93   P E Davidson (1957) 'The impact of visitors on game in national parks', *Oryx* 4: 189–195 (p194).
94   Wilko Graf von Hardenberg (2003) 'Nature in fascist regime: concepts and policies', unpublished first year PhD report, Department of Geography, University of Cambridge.
95   C W Hobley (1924) 'The protection of wild life', paper to the Museums Association 14 July 1924, *Journal SPFE* 4: 26–34 (p33).
96   S H Prater (1933) 'The preservation of wild life in the Indian Empire', in *The Wild Animals of the Indian Empire, and the problem of their preservation*, reprinted from the *Journal of the Bombay Natural History Society* 36 (4): 1–11, (p5).
97   The story of the creation of the Kruger National Park is told by James Stevenson-Hamilton (1937) *South African Eden: from Sabi Game Reserve to Kruger National Park*, Cassell, London and Jane Carruthers (1995) *The Kruger National Park: a social and political history*, Natal University Press, Durban. The issue of tsetse and wildliffe is discussed in Chapter 7.
98   On Stevenson-Hamilton, see Jane Carruthers (2001) *Wildlife and Warfare: life of James Stevenson-Hamilton*, University of Natal Press, Durban; Stevenson-Hamilton died in 1957. See also his own book, (1952) *South African Eden, from Sabi Game Reserve to Kruger National Park*, Cassell, London.
99   Major Stevenson-Hamilton (1924) 'The Transvaal Game Reserve', *Journal SPFE* 4: 35–44 (p42).
100   See Jane Carruthers (1997) 'Nationhood and national parks: comparative examples from the post-imperial experience', in T Griffiths and L Robin (eds) *Ecology and Empire: environmental history of settler societies*, Keele University Press, Keele, pp125–138. For a full account see Jane Carruthers (1995) *The Kruger National Park*.
101   Comparisons between conservation in South Africa and the United States are made explicitly by William Beinart and Paul Coates (1995) *Environment and History: the taming of nature in the USA and South Africa*, Routledge, London. Kruger, and the private conservancies around it, are still major tourism destinations, see the Kruger National Park homepage www.ecoafrica.com/ krugerpark/index.html (especially perhaps its 'virtual safari').
102   Jane Carruthers (1995) *The Kruger National Park*.
103   J Stevenson-Hamilton (1939) 'Address at Rotary Club luncheon, Pretoria, 17th November, 1938', *Journal SPFE* 36: 18–25 (p20).
104   James Stevenson-Hamilton (1930) 'The management of a national park in Africa', *Journal SPFE* 10: 13–20.
105   Jane Carruthers (1995) *The Kruger National Park*, p79.

106 J Stevenson-Hamilton (1939) 'Address at Rotary Club luncheon', p20.
107 The problematic heritage of the clearances for conservation thinking is discussed by Mark Toogood (2003) 'Decolonizing Highland conservation', in William M Adams and Martin Mulligan (eds) *Decolonizing Nature: strategies for conservation in a post-colonial era*, Earthscan, London, pp152–171.
108 Charles Stewart (1909) *In the Evening*, Murray, London, quoted in Sheail (1976) *Nature in Trust*.
109 Harry Johnston (1909) 'Reserves for wild fauna at home and abroad', *Journal SPWFE* 5: 103–5. He also proposed national parks in the West Indies, particularly Jamaica.
110 General Meeting SPFE London Zoo, 15 October 1928, *Journal SPFE* (1929): 5–12 (p6).
111 Edward North Buxton was a keen mountaineer, and had a particular liking for hunting chamois: his obituary noted that 'in later life the attraction of a *mauvais pas* was increased for him by the chance of a chamois at the other end of it' (*Journal SPFE* (1924) 4: 23–4).
112 Earl of Onslow (1941) 'Science and the conservation of the wild life of the world', *Journal SPFE* 44: 8–14 (p13). National parks were 'inalienably dedicated to nature; strict nature reserves (a category developed by the French, particularly in Madagascar) were absolute sanctuaries not open to the public, while in game reserves wildlife could be shot under licence.
113 Hobley (1924) 'The protection of wildlife', p27.
114 General Meeting SPFE London Zoo, 15 October 1928, *Journal SPFE* 9: 5–12 (p7); General Meeting SPFE London Zoo, 4 November 1929, *Journal SPFE* 10: 5–10 (p6).
115 General Meeting SPFE London Zoo, 4 November 1929, (p7).
116 General Meeting SPFE London Zoo, 4 November 1929, (p8).
117 General Meeting SPFE London Zoo, 4 November 1929, (p6).
118 Quoted in Sheail (1976) *Nature in Trust*.
119 Sheail (1976).
120 Benny Rothman died in January 2002 (www.guardian.co.uk/Print/0,3858,4342755,00.html). The current Duke of Devonshire apologized for his grandfather's action in April 2002 (www.ramblers.org.uk/news/Kinder29Apr02.html). Kinder Scout is now within the Peak Distict National Park.
121 Although a true 'right to roam' on open land was only granted six decades later, in the Countryside and Rights of Way Act 2000, and even then was controversial (W M Adams *Future Nature: a vision for conservation*, Earthscan, London, revised edition 2003).
122 'Evidence on the preservation of fauna and flora submitted by the British Correlating Committee for the Protection of Nature', *Journal SPFE* (1931) 13: 49–55. On the work of the Committee, see Sheail (1976) *Nature in Trust*.
123 Executive Committee SPFE 7 June 1937, *Journal SPFE* 32: 11–12.
124 Martin Duncan (1937) 'The New Forest', *Journal SPFE* 32: 12–20.
125 Sheail (1976) *Nature in Trust*; John Sheail (1991) *Rural Conservation in inter-war Britain,* Clarendon Press, Oxford; John Sheail (1998) *Nature Conservation in Britain: the formative years*, The Stationery Office, London.

126 See David Evans (1992) *A History of Nature Conservation in Britain*, Routledge, London; D Poore and J Poore (1992) *Protected Landscapes in the UK*, Countryside Commission, Cheltenham (CCP 362).

127 The Broads is not strictly a National Park, but functions under the Broads Authority as if it were one.

128 See John Moir (1991) 'National Parks north of the border', *Planning Outlook* 34: 61–67; and Sir J Douglas Ramsey (1945) *National Parks: a Scottish Survey; a report by the Scottish National Parks Survey Committee*, HMSO, London. The website of the Loch Lomond and the Trossachs National Park is www.lochlomond-trossachs.org/.

129 J Sheail (1995) 'War and the development of nature conservation in Britain', *Journal of Environmental Management* 44: 267–283.

130 Geoffrey Dent (1941) 'Conservation of British fauna and flora: its place in post-war reconstruiction',' *Journal SPFE* 42: 29–32 (p30).

131 A G Tansley (1945) *Our Heritage of Wild Nature: a plea for organized nature conservation*, Cambridge University Press, Cambridge (p41). On Tansley's work with Freud, see Laura Cameron and John Forrester (1999) '"A nice type of the English scientist": Tansley and Freud', *History Workshop Journal* 48: 65–100.

132 Julian Huxley (1947) *Conservation of Nature in England and Wales*, Cmd 7122, HMSO, London, (para 192). The Chair of the committee was later taken over by A G Tansley.

133 John Sheail (1996) 'From aspiration to inspiration – the establishment of the first National Nature Reserves in Britain', *Landscape Research* 21: 37–54.

134 *Nature Conservancy Council 16th Annual Report, 1 April 1989–31 March 1990*, NCC, Peterborough.

135 See J Sheail (1993) The management of wildlife and amenity – a UK post-war perspective', *Contemporary Record* 7: 44–65.

136 Mark Toogood (2003) 'Decolonizing Highland conservation', in William M Adams and Martin Mulligan (eds) *Decolonizing Nature: strategies for conservation in a post-colonial era*, Earthsan, London, pp152–171.

137 Hobley (1938) 'The conservation of wildlife', p4.

138 Vice Chairman of SPFE to AGM 7 December 1931, *Journal SPFE* 15: 4–11.

139 'Report of deputation to the High Commissioner for S. Rhodesia, Sir Francis Newton', *Journal SPFE* 6: 22.

140 General Meeting SPFE London Zoo, 15 October 1928, *Journal SPFE* 9: 5–12 (p9). James Stevenson-Hamilton's views about national parks are set out in 'The management of a national park in Africa', *Journal SPFE* 10: 13–20.

141 Deputation to the Secretary of State for the Colonies 5 March 1930, *Journal SPFE* 10: 11–16 (p12).

142 Sir Peter Chalmers-Mitchell (1931) 'Zoos and National Parks: British Association meeting, London, 1931', *Journal SPFE* 15: 21–43.

143 Chalmers-Mitchell (1931).

144 R W G Hingston, (1930) 'The Oxford University expedition to British Guiana', *Geographical Journal* 76: 1–24.

145 R W G Hingston, (1931) 'Proposed British National Parks for Africa', *Geographical Journal* 77: 401–428.

146 Hingston (1931, p402).

147 Hingston (1931, p402).
148 Hingston (1931, p402).
149 Hingston (1931, p 406).
150 Hingston (1931, p 406).
151 Hingston (1931, p 407).
152 Hingston (1931, p.408).
153 Hingston (1931, p413).
154 See Vice Chairman of SPFE to SPFE 7 December 1931, *Journal SPFE* 15: 4–11, and AGM SPFE 7 March 1932, *Journal SPFE* 16: 5–12.
155 Meeting SPFE 6 June 1932, *Journal SPFE* 7–10. Lord Rothschild thought perhaps the resistance to a park for the Ugandan Mountain Gorillas would be eased when Lord Passfield ceased to be Colonial Secretary, but Chalmers-Mitchell said not: the opposition was deep within the Colonial Office, not just as the top.
156 Vice Chairman of SPFE to AGM 7 December 1931, *Journal SPFE* 15: 4–11.
157 The text of Ramsay MacDonald's letter, with the 1931 Conference resolutions, are printed in *Journal SPFE* (1931) 15: 43–52.
158 *First Report of the Preparatory Committee for the International Conference for the protection of the Fauna and Flora of Africa, 1933*, Economic Advisory Council, London (EAC [C] 75), 12 January 1933.
159 The Rt Hon the Earl of Onslow (1938) 'Preservation of African Fauna', *Journal of the Royal African Society* July 1938 (*Journal SPFE* (1938) 34: 24–30). I am grateful to Caroline Cowan for information on the 1933 Conference; see Caroline Cowan (2001) *Game Preservation or Nature Conservation? Colonial conservation policy in East Africa*, MPhil Thesis, University of Cambridge.
160 *First Report of the Preparatory Committee* 1933.
161 *Second Report of the Preparatory Committee for the International Conference for the protection of the Fauna and Flora of Africa, 1933*, Economic Advisory Council, London (EAC [C] 78, March 9, 1933.
162 Report of Preparatory Committee of 1933 Conference, para 9.
163 *Second Report of the Preparatory Committee* 1933.
164 The Final Act of the Conference is printed in *Journal SPFE* (1934) 21: 19–47.
165 On the Parks Bill see *Journal SPFE* 25: 55–61; On the Conference see 'All India Conference for the Preservation of Wild Life, Delhi 28–31 January 1935, *Journal SPFE* 25: 23–33; see also comment of the Belgian Ambassador Baron de Cartier de Marchienne at the SPFE AGM, 28 January 1935, *Journal SPFE* 25: 5–9.
166 Jim Corbett (1946) *Man-Eaters of Kumaon*, Oxford University Press, London; the United Provinces park was renamed the Corbett National Park in 1957 (John MacKenzie (1988) *The Empire of Nature: hunting, conservation and British imperialism*, Manchester University Press, Manchester).
167 Paul Jepson and Robert J Whittaker (2002) 'Histories of protected areas: internationalisaton of conservationist values in their adoption in the Netherlands Indies (Indonesia)', *Environmental History* 8: 129–172.
168 Executive Committee SPFE 27 January 1936, *Journal SPFE* 28: 8–13
169 Executive Committee SPFE 8 February 1937, *Journal SPFE* 31: 12–15; Executive Committee SPFE 27 July 1937, *Journal SPFE* 30: 8–11.

170 Onslow (1939) 'To the members of the Society', *Journal SPFE* 36: 5–8; Report of Executive Committee to AGM SPFE 19 February 1940, *Journal SPFE* 39: 49.

171 J G Nelson (1968) 'The National Parks movement in Canada', in Nelson and Scace *The Canadian National Parks*, pp35–65.

172 E O Shebbeare (1946) 'Malayan National Park', *Journal SPFE* 53: 41–45 (p43).

173 Nina Ryasentseva (1945) 'Nature Reservations in the USSR', *Journal SPFE* 52: 41–43.

174 M H Cowie (1949) 'National Parks and reserves in Kenya', *Journal SPFE* 69: 14–20.

175 Cowie (1949).

176 *Oryx* 2 (6): 342.

177 A lively eye-witness account of the origins of Ugandan national parks is given by Bruce Kinloch (1972) *The Shamba Raiders: memories of a Game Warden*, Collins, London.

178 Princess Elizabeth was, of course, on safari in Kenya, at Treetops Lodge in the Aberdares National Park, when the announcement of her accession was made.

179 Prater (1933) 'The preservation of wild life in the Indian Empire', *Journal of the Bombay Natural History Society* 36(4) (p2).

180 Extracts from the Report of the Second IUPN General Assembly, Brussels, October 1950, *Oryx* 1(3): 152–5 (p153). Paul Jepson and Robert J Whittaker (2002) 'Histories of protected areas: internationalisation of conservationist values and their adoption in the Netherlands Indies (Indonesia), *Environment and History* 8: 129–172.

181 See for example 'Warning words from the Belgian Congo', by an anonymous correspondent , in the *Journal SPFE* (1949) 60: 84–85.

182 J-P Harroy (1964) 'Victor Van Straelen: an international conservationist', *Oryx* 7 (5): 212.

183 See Harroy (1964) and Kai Curry-Lindahl (1964) 'The Congo National Parks since independence', *Oryx* 7: 233–239.

184 Grzimek and Grzimek (1960) *Serengeti Shall Not Die* (p176).

185 R M Bere (1957) 'The national park idea: how to interest the African public', *Oryx* 4: 21–27 (p22).

186 John A Pile (1962) 'Wild life conservation education in Southern Rhodesia', *Oryx* 6: 279–282.

187 Erica Critchley (1961) 'A camp for schoolchildren in the Kafue National Park, Northern Rhodesia', *Oryx* 6: 35–38.

188 G D Hayes (1967) 'How independence saved an African reserve', *Oryx* 9: 25–7.

189 See Clark C Gibson (1999) *Politicians and Poachers: the political economy of wildlife policy in Africa*, Cambridge University Press, Cambridge.

190 Sir Dawda Jawara, *Oryx* 14 (1): 9.

191 Minutes of proceedings at a deputation from the SPWFE to the Right Hon the Earl of Elgin (His Majesty's Secretary for the Colonies), 15 June 1906, *Journal SPWFE* 3: 20–32 (p24).

192 T Ranger (1999) *Voices from the Rocks: nature, culture and history in the Matopos Hills of Zimbabwe*, James Currey, Oxford.

193 Holdgate (1999) *The Green Web* (p69).

194 www.iucn.org/themes/wcpa

195 The United Nations List of National Parks; see Martin Holdgate (1999) *The Green Web*. See also www.wcmc.org.uk/protected_areas/data/cnppa.html

196 www.unep-wcmc.org/protected_areas/categories/

197 Jeremy Harrison, Kenton Miller and Jeffrey McNeely (1982) 'The World. Coverage of protected areas: development goals and environmental needs', *Ambio* 24–245.

198 'A park to save the Arabian Tahr', *Oryx* 12 (5) and 'Plan for reserves in Oman', *Oryx* 13 (3).

199 Robert Poirier and David Ostergren (2002) 'Evicting people from nature: indigenous land rights and national parks in Australia, Russia and the united States', *Natural Resources Journal* 42: 331–351.

200 For data on the global extent of protected areas, see the UNEP-WCMC Protected Areas Programme: www.wcmc.org.uk/protected_areas. The 2003 UN List is available at: www.iucn.org/themes/wcpa/wpc2003/pdfs/unlistpa2003.pdf.

Chapter 5 Poachers to Partners

1 J S Adams and T O McShane (1992) *The Myth of Wild Africa: conservation without illusion*, W W Norton and Co.

2 www.conservation.org. R A Mittermeir, C G Mittermeier, P R Gil, J Pilgrim, G Fonseca, T Brooks and W R Constant (2003) *Wilderness: Earth's last wild places*, University of Chicago Press, Chicago. See also Eric W Sanderson, Malanding Jaiteth, Marc A Levy, Kent H Redford, Antoinette V Wannebo and Gillian Woolmer (2002) 'The Human footprint and the last of the wild', *BioScience* 52: 891–904.

3 www.conservation.org

4 Mathis Wackernagel and William Rees (1996) *Our Ecological Footprint: reducing human impact on earth*, New Society Publishers, Gabriola Island, British Columbia. Such analyses are discussed in Chapter 7.

5 These meaning of wilderness are analysed by Simon Schama (1995) *Landscape and memory*, HarperCollins, London, and by William Cronon (1995) 'The trouble with wilderness, or, getting back to the wrong nature', in W Cronon (ed) *Uncommon Ground: toward reinventing nature*, W W Norton and Co, New York, pp69–90. The phrase 'fruited plain' is from Gordon G Whitney (1994) *From Coastal Wilderness to Fruited Plain: a history of environmental change in temperate North America from 1500 to the present*, Cambridge University Press, Cambridge.

6 W M Adams (2003) *Future Nature: a vision for conservation*, Earthscan, London.

7 See, for example, Michael Bunce (1994) *The Countryside Ideal: Anglo-American images of landscape*, Routledge, London.

8 Jonathan Bate (1991) *Romantic Ecology: Wordsworth and the environmental tradition*, Routledge, London.

9   On Tansley, ecology and conservation, see J Sheail (1976) *Nature in Trust: the history of nature conservation in Great Britain*, Blackie, Glasgow, and J Sheail (1987) *Seventy-five Years of Ecology: the British Ecological Society*, Blackwell Scientific, Oxford. On Tansley's vegetation work, see A G Tansley (1911) *Types of British Vegetation*, Cambridge University Press, Cambridge, and A G Tansley (1939) *The British Islands and their Vegetation*, Cambridge University Press, Cambridge.

10   On settlement and conservation, see T R Dunlap (1999) *Nature and the English Diaspora: environment and history in the United States, Canada, Australia and New Zealand*, Cambridge University Press, Cambridge, and T Griffiths and L Robin (1997) (eds) *Ecology and Empire: environmental history of settler societies*, Keele University Press. On indigenous people and conservation in Australia, see Marcia Langton (2003) 'The "wild", the market and the native: indigenous people face new forms of global colonization', in William M Adams and Martin Mulligan (eds) *Decolonizing Nature: strategies for conservation in a post-colonial era*, Earthscan, London, pp79–107.

11   See R Nash (1973) *Wilderness and the American mind*, Yale University Press, New Haven, CT.

12   On the history of the West see, for example, William Cronon's *Nature's Metropolis: Chicago and the Great West*, Norton, New York, on Pinchot and Muir, see Samuel P Hays (1959) *Conservation and the Gospel of Efficiency: the progressive conservation movement 1890–1920*, Harvard University Press, Cambridge, MA.

13   See, for example, Whitney (1994) *From Coastal Wilderness to Fruited Plain*.

14   T R Dunlap (1999) *Nature and the English Diaspora*.

15   S J Pyne (1997) 'Frontiers of fire', in Griffiths and Robin *Ecology and Empire*, pp19–34 (p33).

16   D M Anderson and D H Johnson (1988) 'Ecology and society in northeast African history', in D Johnson and D M Anderson (eds) *The Ecology of Survival: case studies from Northeast African history*, Lester Crook, pp1–26.

17   See, for example, R P Neumann (1998) *Imposing Wilderness: struggles over livelihood and nature preservation in Africa*, University of California Press, Berkeley.

18   Roderick P Neumann (1995) 'Ways of seeing Africa: colonial recasting of African society and landsacape in Serengeti National Park', *Ecumene* 2: 149–169, and (1998) *Imposing Wilderness*.

19   H G Maurice 'Man-made Edens' *Journal SPFE* 34: 41–46. On Kruger see James Stevenson-Hamilton (1937) *South African Eden: from Sabi Game Reserve to Kruger National Park*, Cassell, London and Major Stevenson-Hamilton (1924) 'The Transvaal Game Reserve', *Journal SPFE* 4: 35–44 (p42).

20   Mervyn Cowie (1955) 'Preserve or Destroy?', *Oryx* 3: 9–11 (pp9, 10).

21   Julian Huxley (1970) *Memories*, Allen and Unwin, London.

22   Ian Parker and Stan Bleazard (2001) *An Impossible Dream: some of Kenya's last colonial wardens recall the Game Department in the British Empire's closing years*, Librario, Kinloss.

23   A good long-timeframe perspective on human extinctions is provided by Edward O Wilson (1992) *The Diversity of Life*, Penguin, Harmondsworth. The persistence of large mammals in Africa into the 20th century is the reason for its central position in the history of global conservation concern. I am grateful to Dan Brockington for pointing me to Donald Grayson and David J Meltzer (2003) 'A requiem for North American overkill', *Journal of Archaeological Science*

30: 1–9, which shows that the old theory of 'Pleistocene overkill' by the first human settlers in North America is now abandoned by most scholars; the causes of these particular extinctions are clearly complex, as in Europe.

24 B McKibben (1990) *The End of Nature*, Penguin Books, Harmondsworth.

25 Cronon (1995) 'The trouble with wilderness', in W Cronon (ed) *Uncommon Ground*, W W Norton, New York (p69).

26 G W Burnett, and K wa Katg'ethe (1994) 'Wilderness and the Bantu mind', *Environmental Ethics* 16: 145–160.

27 Burnett and wa Katg'ethe (1994, p155).

28 See, for example, Elisabeth Croll and David Parkin (1992) 'Anthropology, the environment and development', in E Croll and D Parkin (eds) *Bush Base: Forest Farm; culture, environment and development*, Routledge, London, pp3–10, and Tim Ingold (2000) *The perception of the environment: essays on livelihood, dwelling and skill*, Routledge, London.

29 Edward O Wilson (2002) *The Future of Life*, Little Brown, London (p133).

30 James Stevenson-Hamilton (1946) 'A game warden reflects', *Journal SPFE* 54: 17–21 (p17).

31 Sir Peter Chalmers-Mitchell (1931) 'Zoos and National Parks: British Association meeting, London, 1931', *Journal SPFE* 15: 21–43.

32 See Susan L Flader (1974) *Thinking like a Mountain: Aldo Leopold and the evolution of an ecological attitude toward deer, wolves, and forests*, University of Missouri Press, Columbia, MS.

33 W M Adams (2003) *Future Nature: a vision for conservation* (revised edition), Earthscan, London.

34 E B Worthington (1961) *The Wild Resources of East and Central Africa*, HMSO, London, (Colonial No 352). Involvement of the Nature Conservancy in colonial conservation is discussed by Mark Toogood (2003) 'Decolonizing Highland conservation', in Adams and Mulligan *Decolonizing Nature*, pp152–171. The importance of managerialism and control in conservation is discussed by W M Adams (2003) 'When nature won't stand still: conservation, equilibrium and control', in Adams and Mulligan *Decolonizing Nature*, Earthscan, London (pp220–246).

35 E Walter Russell (1968) 'Management in National Parks – a policy for Tanzania', *Oryx* 9: 398–403 (p401).

36 The phrase is from Karl Jacoby (2002) *Crimes Against Nature: squatters, poachers, thieves, and the hidden history of American conservation*, California University Press, Berkeley, who describes the creation of poachers in the United States; examples from Africa are legion, but see, for example, Neumann (1998) *Imposing Wilderness*; for East Africa see, for example, 'Extract from a letter from a correspondent in East Africa, *Journal SPWFE* 1: 39–40.

37 R W G Hingston, (1931) 'Proposed British National Parks for Africa', *Geographical Journal* 77: 401–428 (p404).

38 Richard Jefferies (1978) *The Amateur Poacher*, Oxford University Press, Oxford (first published 1948; Jefferies died in 1897); John Buchan (1925) *John Macnab*, Hodder and Stoughton, London.

39 Hingston (1931) 'Proposed British National Parks for Africa', p404.

40 E N Buxton (1902) *Two African Trips: with notes and suggestions on big game preservation*, London, E Stanford (p139).

41　Minutes of proceedings at a deputation from the SPWFE to the Right Hon. Alfred Lyttelton (His Majesty's Secretary for the Colonies), 2 February 1905, *Journal SPWFE* 2: 9–18 (p12).

42　Henry Seton-Karr (1908) 'The Preservation of Big Game', *Journal SPWFE*, 4: 26–28 (p27).

43　Minutes of proceedings at a deputation from the SPWFE to the Right Hon Alfred Lyttelton (His Majesty's Secretary for the Colonies), 2 February 1905, *Journal SPWFE* 2: 9–18 (p17).

44　Sir Alfred Sharpe (1905) 'Slaughter by natives', *Journal SPWFE* 2: 18.

45　'Extract from a letter from a correspondent at Barberton in South Africa, *Journal SPWFE* (1903) 1 (Item 5): 40–41 (p41).

46　Mervyn Cowie (1955) 'Preserve or Destroy?', *Oryx* 3: 9–11 (p11).

47　Minutes of proceedings at a deputation from the SPWFE to the Right Hon the Earl of Elgin (His Majesty's Secretary for the Colonies), 15 June 1906, *Journal SPWFE* (1905) (3): 20–32 (p22).

48　W T Hornaday (24 March 1909, letter to Rhys Williams, *Journal SPWFE* 5 (1909): 56–58, (p57).

49　*Second Report of the Preparatory Committee for the International Conference for the Protection of the Fauna and Flora of Africa, 1933*, Economic Advisory Council, London (EAC [C] 78), March 9, 1933.

50　Earl of Onslow (1941) 'Science and the conservation of the wild life of the world', *Journal SPFE* 44: 8–14 (p11).

51　Deputation to the Secretary of State for the Colonies 5 March 1930, *Journal SPFE* 11: 11–16 (p13).

52　Vice Chairman of SPFE to AGM 27 February 1931, *Journal SPFE* 13: 5–11 (p6).

53　General Meeting SPFE London Zoo, 15 October 1928, *Journal SPFE* 1929: 5–12 (p9).

54　C W Hobley (1937) 'The conservation of wild life: retrospect and prospect, Part I', *Journal SPFE* 32: 38–44, (p39).

55　Examples of writers portraying the horrors and threat of poaching are numerous, see, for example, Bernhard and Michael Grzimek (1960) *Serengeti Shall Not Die*, Hamish Hamilton, London, and John Gordon Davis in his account of black rhino translocation in Rhodesia because of poaching pressure (*Operation Rhino*, Michael Joseph, London, 1972).

56　A fine example of the latter is Bruce Kinloch's (1972) *The Shamba Raiders: memories of a Game Warden*, Collins, London.

57　Dan Brockington (2002) *Fortress Conservation: the preservation of the Mkomazi Game Reserve, Tanzania*, James Currey, Oxford.

58　D Brockington and K Homewood (1996) 'Wildlife, pastoralists and science: debates concerning Mkomazi Game Reserve, Tanzania', in M Leach and R Mearns (eds) *The Lie of the Land: challenging received wisdom in African environmental change*, James Currey, Oxford, pp91–104 (p104).

59　Brockington (2002) *Fortress Conservation*.

60　On the Selous Game Reserve, see R P Neumann (1998) *Imposing Wildnerness* (Table 4, p147). On the Serengeti, see K M Homewood and W A Rodgers (1991) *Maasailand Ecology: pastoralist development and wildlife conservation in Ngorogoro, Tanzania*, Cambridge University Press, Cambridge. On involuntary resettlement from protected areas more generally see Marcus Colchester (2002) *Salvaging Nature: indigenous peoples, protected areas and biodiversity conservation*, World Rainforest Movement, Montevideo; Dawn Chatty and Marcus Colchester (2002) (eds) *Conservation and Mobile Indigenous Peoples: displacement, forced resettlement and sustainable development*, Berghahn Press, Oxford.

61   D Turton (1987) 'The Mursi and National Park development in the lower Omo Valley', in D M Anderson and R H Grove (eds) *Conservation in Africa: people, policies and practice*, Cambridge University Press, Cambridge, pp169–186.

62   Leslie Brown was a well-known Kenyan ornithologist (for example *The Mystery of the Flamingos*, East Africa Publishing House, Nairobi, 1959); Ian Grimwood was formerly Chief Game Warden of Kenya, and led the Fauna Preservation Society's *Operation Oryx* in 1962.

63   Turton (1987) 'The Mursi and National Park development', p179.

64   Turton (1987, p180).

65   Jane Carruthers (1995) *The Kruger National Park: a social and political history*, Natal University Press, Durban.

66   Hector Magome and James Murombedzi (2003) 'Sharing South African national parks: community land and conservation in a democratic South Africa', in Adams and Mulligan *Decolonizing Nature*, pp108–134.

67   See, for example, the impact of an aid-funded project to grow wheat in Tanzania, Charles Lane (1992) 'The Barabaig pastoralists of Tanzania: sustainable land use in jeopardy', in Dharam Ghai and Jessica M Vivian (eds) *Grassroots Environmental Action: people's participation in sustainable development*, Routledge, London, pp81–105.

68   On resettlement see Thayer Scudder (1991) 'A sociological framework for the analysis of new land settlements', in M Cernea (ed) *Putting People First: sociological variables in rural development*, Oxford University Press, Oxford, pp148–167; for one coercive example, the Kariba Dam on the Zambezi, see D Howarth (1961) *The Shadow of the Dam*, Collins, London.

69   See, for example, Robert Poirier and David Ostergren (2002) 'Evicting people from nature: indigenous land rights and national parks in Australia, Russia and the United States', *Natural Resources Journal* 42: 331–351.

70   Jacoby (2002) *Crimes Against Nature*, University of California Press, Berkeley (p191).

71   Kevin McNamee (1993) 'From wild places to endangered spaces: a history of Canadian National Parks', in Philip Dearden and Rick Rollins (eds) *Parks and Protected Areas in Canada: planning and management*, Oxford University Press, Toronto, pp17–44.

72   See Lucy Emerton (2001) 'The nature of benefits and the benefits of nature: why wildlife conservation has not economically benefited communities in Africa', in D Hulme and M Murphree (eds) *African Wildlife and Livelihoods: the promise and performance of community conservation*, James Currey, London, pp208–226.

73   See K Archabald and L Naughton-Treves (2001) 'Tourism revenue-sharing around national parks in Western Uganda: early efforts to identify and reward local communities', *Environmental Conservation* 28 (2), 135–149; W M Adams and M Infield (2003) 'Who is on the gorilla's payroll? Claims on tourist revenue from a Ugandan National Park', *World Development* 31 (1): 177–190.

74   Princess Margaret visited Mount Meru in 1958. Ngurdoto Crater National Park was strictly the first park declared after independence.
75   Neumann (1998) *Imposing Wilderness*, University of California Press, Berkeley.
76   See, for example, L Naughton-Treves (1997) 'Farming the forest edge: vulnerable places and people around Kibale National Park, Uganda', *The Geographical Review* 87: 27–46, or N U Sekhar (1998) 'Crop and livestock depredation caused by wild animals in protected areas: the case of Sariska Tiger Reserve, Rajasthan, India', *Environmental Conservation* 25: 160–171.
77   This social tension and distance is mutual: many 'community game guards' live isolated lives at the mercy of local communities whom they are supposed to police.
78   Neumann (1998) *Imposing Wilderness* (p272).
79   On the new thinking, see D Western, R M Wright and S C Strum (1994) *Natural Connections: perspectives on community-based conservation,* Island Press, Washington; and K B Ghimire and M P Pimbert (1996) (eds) *Social Change and Conservation*, Earthscan, London.
80   See W M Adams (2001) *Green Development: environment and sustainability in the Third World* (second edition), Routledge, London.
81   M Batisse (1982) 'The biosphere reserve: a tool for envirionmental conservation and management', *Environmental Conservation* 9: 101–111.
82   See for example J A McNeely and K R Miller (eds) (1984) *National Parks, Conservation and Development: the role of protected areas in sustaining society*, Smithsonian Institute Press, Washington DC, and Elizabeth Kemf (ed) (1993) *The Law of the Mother: protecting indigenous peoples in protected areas*, Sierra Club Books, San Francisco.
83   Adrian Phillips (2002) 'Turning ideas on their head: the new paradigm for protected areas', *George Wright Forum* 20(2): 8–32.
84   Sir Sridath Ramphal (1993) 'Para nosotros la patria es el planeta tierra', in J McNeely (ed) *Parks for Life: report of the IVth World Congress on National Parks and Protected Areas*, IUCN Gland, Switzerland, pp56–58 (p57).
85   See for example Langton (2003) 'The "wild", the market and native: indigenous people face new forms of global colonization', in W M Adams and M Mulligan (eds) *Decolonizing Nature: strategies for conservation in a post colonial era*, Earthscan, London, pp79–107.
86   Lawrence Berg, Terry Fenge and Philip Dearden (1993) 'The role of Aboriginal peoples in national park designation, planning and management in Canada', in Philip Dearden and Rick Rollins (eds) *Parks and Protected Areas in Canada: planning and management*, Oxford University Press, Toronto, pp225–255.
87   Berg, Fenge and Dearden (1993).
88   Poirier and Ostergren (2002) 'Evicting people from nature'.
89   Or at least only as a last resort and very carefully: World Bank (1984) *Tribal People and Economic Development: human ecologic considerations*, World Bank, Washington.
90   Javier Beltran (ed) (2000) *Indigenous and Traditional Peoples and Protected Areas: principles, guidelines and case studies*, IUCN, Gland, Switzerland.
91   Kevin McNamee (1993) 'From wild places to endangered spaces.
92   Barry J Heydenrych, Richard M Cowling and Amanda T Lombard (1999) 'Strategic conservation interventions in a region of high biodiversity and high

vulnerability: a case study from the Agulhas Plain at the southern tip of Africa', *Oryx* 33: 256–269.

93 www.fauna-flora.org/around_the_world/world_main_frame.htm.

94 Magome and Murombedzi (2003) 'Sharing South African national parks' in W M Adams and M Mulligan (eds) *Decolonizing Nature*, Earthscan, London.

95 A Agrawal and C Gibson (1999) 'Enchantment and disenchantment: the role of community in resource conservation', *World Development* 7: 629–649.

96 E F Schumacher (1973) *Small is Beautiful: economics as if people mattered*, Blond and Briggs, London (paperback edition published in 1974 by Abacus); for a more general discussion, see Adams (2001) *Green Development*.

97 R P Neumann (1997) 'Primitive ideas: protected area buffer zones and the politics of land in Africa', *Developmnent and Change* 28: 559–582.

98 William J Sutherland (2003) 'Parallel extinction risk and global distribution of languages and species', *Nature* 425 (15 May): 376–378.

99 E Roe (1991) 'Development narratives, or making the best of blueprint development', *World Development* 19: 287–300. The idea of environmental narratives is elaborated in M Leach and R Mearns (1996) *The Lie of the Land: challenging received wisdom on the African environment*, Heinemann/James Currey, London. A classic narrative is that surrounding desertification, inexorable breakdown in arid ecosystems is due to overgrazing, see Jeremy Swift (1996) 'Desertification narratives; winners and losers', in Leach and Mearns *The Lie of the Land*, pp73–90.

100 See A Hoben (1995) 'Paradigms and politics: the cultural construction of environmental policy in Ethiopia', *World Development* 23: 1007–1021.

101 D Western (1982) 'Amboseli National Park: enlisting landowners to conserve migratory wildlife', *Ambio* 11 (5): 302–308; W K Lindsay (1987) 'Integrating parks and pastoralists: some lessons from Amboseli', in D M Anderson and R H Grove (eds) *Conservation in Africa*, Cambrifhe University Press, Cambridge, pp149–167.

102 E Barrow, H Gichohi and M Infield (2001) 'The evolution of community conservation policy and practice in East Africa', in D Hulme and M Murphree (eds) *African Wildlife and Livelihoods: the promise and performance of community conservation*, James Currey, London, pp59–73.

103 See C S Barrett, and P Arcese (1995) 'Are integrated conservation-development projects (ICDPs) sustainable? On the conservation of large mammals in Sub-Saharan Africa', *World Development* 23 (7); 1073–1084; M Stocking and S Perkin (1992) 'Conservation-with-development: an application of the concept in the Usambara Mountains, Tanzania', *Transactions of the Institute of British Geographers N S* 17: 337–349; M Wells and K Brandon, (1992) *People and Parks: Linking Protected Areas with Local Communities*, World Bank, Washington DC.

104 See, for example, Lee Hannah (1992) *African People, African Parks*, Conservation International, Washington DC.

105 IUCN (1980) *World Conservation Strategy*, IUCN, Washington DC; United Nations (1992) *Agenda 21: the United Nations Plan of Action from Rio*, United Nations, New York.

106 E Barrow and M Murphree (2001) 'Community conservation: from concept to practice', in Hulme and Murphree *African Wildlife and Livelihoods*, pp24–37.

107 D Hulme and M Murphree (1999) 'Communities, wildlife and the "new conservation" in Africa', *Journal of International Development* 11 (2): 277–286.

108 For the prospects for grizzlies, see Bruce Mclellan and Vivian Banci (1999) 'Status and management of the brown bear in Canada', in Christopher Servheen, Stephen Herrero and Bernard Peyton (eds) *Bears: Status Survey and Action Plan*, IUCN/SSC Bear Specialist Group and IUCN/SSC Polar Bear Specialist Group, Gland, Switzerland, pp46–54.

109 David Western (1989) 'Conservation without parks: wildlife in the rural landscape', in David Western and Mary Pearl (eds) *Conservation for the Twenty-first Century*, Oxford University Press, New York, pp158–165.

110 L Hannah, G F Midgely, T Lovejoy, W J Bond, M Bush, J C Lovett, D Scott, and F I Woodward (2002) 'Conservation of biodiversity in a changing climate', *Conservation Biology* 16: 264–268.

111 Reed F Noss (1983) 'A regional landscape diversity approach to maintain diversity', *BioScience* 33: 700–706.

112 See Rosaleen Duffy (1997) 'The environmental challenge to the Nation-State: superparks and National Parks policy in Zimbabwe', *Journal of Southern African Studies* 23: 441–451; Magome and Murombedzi (2003) 'Sharing South African national parks'.

113 V S Rivera, P M Cordero, I A Cruz and M F Borrás (2002) 'The Mesoamerican Biological Corridor and Local Participation', *Parks* 12(2): 42–54. On the Golden Stream reserve see www.fauna-flora.org/around_the_world/world_main_frame.htm.

114 Achim Steiner (2003) 'Trouble in paradise', *New Scientist* 18 October (p21). For the recommendations and other outputs at the Fifth World Parks Congress in 2003, see www.iucn.org/themes/wcpa/wpc/2003/index.htm

115 See nature.org.

116 Neumann (1998) *Imposing Wilderness*.

117 www.acguanacaste.ac.cr/1997/principaling.html. See William Allen (2001) *Green Phoenix: restoring the tropical forests of Guanacaste, Costa Rica*, Oxford University Press, New York.

CHAPTER 6 TWO BY TWO

1 www.etni.org.il/music/animalsongs.htm

2 Haldane's most famous book was *The Causes of Evolution* (1937). He became disillusioned with Soviet Communism following the rise of Stalin, and rejected the anti-Mendelian genetics of Trofim Lysenko. He died in 1964 (www.wikipedia.org).

3 www.palaeos.com/Invertebrates/Arthropods/Insecta/Coleoptera.htm

4 www.mbayaq.org/efc/efc_fo/fo_ottr_brink.asp.

5 www.mbayaq.org/efc/efc_fo/ottr_brnk_recovery.asp.

6 J A Estes and J F Palmisano (1974) 'Sea otters: their role in structuring nearshore communities', *Science* 185: 1058–1060.

7 E J Milner-Gulland and Ruth Mace (1998) *Conservation of Biological Resources*, Blackwell, Oxford.

8   R Norman Owen-Smith (1988) *Megaherbivores: the influence of very large body size on ecology*, Cambridge University Press, Cambridge.

9   See www.bbc.co.uk/beasts.

10 Quoted in Milner-Gulland and Mace (1998) *Conservation of Biological Resources*.

11 See N Leader-Williams (2002) 'Animal conservation, carbon and sustainability', *Philosophical Transactions of the Royal Society of London A* 360: 1781–1806.

12 Renamed the Durrell Wildlife Conservation Trust in 1995, following Gerald Durrell's death, see www.durrellwildlife.org.

13 Interestingly, Philip Stott argues that the idea of 'rainforest' was itself quite deliberately created and fashioned by environmentalists to provide a stable basis for their ideological campaigns in the 1970s and 1980s; Philip Stott (1999) *Tropical Rainforest: a political ecology of hegemonic myth making*, Institute of Economic Affairs, London.

14 H Paul Jeffers (2003) *Roosevelt the Explorer: Teddy Roosevelt's amazing adventures as a naturalist, conservationist and explorer*, Taylor Trade Publishing, New York (p98).

15 Susan L Flader (1974) *Thinking Like a Mountain: Aldo Leopold and the evolution of an ecological attitude toward deer, wolves and forests*, University of Missouri Press, Columbia, Missouri.

16 'Preservation of Game', Extract from Lord Cromer's Report for Egypt and the Sudan for the year 1902, Item 11, *Journal SPWFE* (1903) 1: 61–67 (p66).

17 Extract from the report of Col Hayes Sadler for the Uganda Protectorate for the years 1902 and 1908, 'Preservation of Game', *Journal SPWFE* 1: 55–57 (p55).

18 Keith Caldwell (1924) 'Game preservation: its aims and objects', lecture to Kenya and Uganda Natural History Society 14 March 1924, *Journal SPFE* 4: 45–59 (p50).

19 Glover Allen (1942) *Extinct and Vanishing Mammals of the Western Hemisphere with the marine species of all the oceans*, American Committee for International Wild Life Protection, Washington, DC; Francis Harper (1945) *Extinct and Vanishing Mammals of the Old World*, American Committee for International Wild Life Protection, New York. A third volume by James C Greenway Jr *Extinct and Vanishing Birds of the World* was published in 1958, American Committee for International Wild Life Protection, New York.

20 SPFE (1948) 'International Union for the Protection of Nature', *Journal SPFE* 58: 12–17.

21 Article 1 of IUPN Statutes, see Holdgate (1999) *The Green Web: a union for world conservation*, Earthscan, London.

22 The source for much of this section is Holdgate (1999) *The Green Web*.

23 Harold Coolidge's work on expeditions to Africa and Asia in the 1920s had sealed his commitment to conservation; Holdgate (1999, p14).

24 R Boardman (1981) *International Organisations and the Conservation of Nature*, Indiana University Press, Bloomington, Indiana (p76).

25 The grant of US$700 came from Russell M Arundel, see Lee Merriam Talbot (1956) *A Look at Threatened Species: a report on some animals of the Middle East and southern Asia which are threatened with extermination*; the IUCN and Natural Resources Survival Service Field Mission of 1955 and subsequent inquiries, FPS for the IUCN and Natural Resources, London. (Reprinted *Oryx* 5(4))

26   Holdgate (1999) *The Green Web*, Earthscan, London.
27   Established at the Edinburgh General Assembly, with Lee Talbot and Jena-Jaques Petter as Assistant Secretaries.
28   Richard Fitter and Peter Scott (1974) *The Penitent Butchers: 75 years of wildlife conservation*, Fauna Preservation Society, London.They included mountain zebra, Javan rhinoceros, Indian rhinoceros, European bison, Gubal hartebeest, Indian lion, Mediterranean monk seal, Caribbean monk seal, Tasmanian tiger (thylacine), nene goose, Laysan duck, pink-headed duck, Eskimo curlew, Arabian ostrich, whooping crane, Bermuda petrel (cahow) and California condor. See also C L Boyle (1959) 'The Survival Service Commission', *Oryx* 5 (1): 30–35.
29   Minutes of Meeting SPFE December 3 1925, *Journal SPFE* 6: 17.
30   R S R Fitter (1963) 'The Survival Service Commission: September 1963 – January 1964', *Oryx* 7 (4): 157–159.
31   John Burton (2001) 'The Colonel's card files make Red List History', *World Conservation* (2001) (3): 4. Richard Fitter describes these as the brainchild of Peter Scott, see Fitter and Scott (1975) *Penitent Butchers*.
32   Fitter and Scott (1975).
33   This was originally at Kew Gardens, becoming the Conservation Monitoring Centre in 1981, with part moved to Cambridge.
34   www.redlist.org/info/introduction.html.
35   Anna Knee (2001) 'A tool for conservation action', *World Conservation* (2001) (3): 4. For the Red List see www.redlist.org.
36   Simon P Mickleburgh, Anthony M Hutson and Paul A Racey (2002) 'A review of the global conservation status of bats', *Oryx* 36 (1): 18–34.
37   *Oryx* had carried a number of articles on bats, notably by Bob Stebbings, Chair of the IUCN Chiroptera Specialist Group
38   Tony Huston (1989) 'The FFPS Bat Project' *Oryx* 23: 27–32.
39   Mickleburgh, Hutson and Racey (2002) 'A review of the global conservation status of bats', *Oryx* 36: 18–34.
40   The same phenomenon typified areas such as agricultural development in Africa in the 1940s, see W M Adams (1992) *Wasting the Rain: rivers, people and planning in Africa*, Minnesota University Press, Minneapolis.
41   *Oryx* 11 (6).
42   Guy Mountford (1983) 'Project Tiger: a review', *Oryx* 17: 32–33.
43   Guy Mountford (1973) 'Saving the tiger' *Oryx* 12: 109–110.
44   Anne Wright (1972) 'Operation Blackbuck' *Oryx* 11: 228–230.
45   In 1985 10 scimitar horned oryx were sent from Marwell and Edinburgh Zoos to a National Park in Tunisia. In December 1988 FFPS paid for a researcher from London Zoo to monitor the population.
46   John Newby (1980) 'Can Addax and Oryx be saved in the Sahel?' *Oryx* 15: 262–266.
47   C L Boyle (1959) 'Foreword', *Oryx* 5(2): 1.
48   G A W Guggisberg (1966) *S.O.S. Rhino*, Andre Deutsch, London.
49   Ian Player (1972) *The White Rhino Saga*, Collins, London.
50   Shirley J Brooks (2001) *A Critical Historical Geography of the Umfolozi and Hluhluwe Game Reserves, Zululand, 1887 to 1947*, Unpublished PhD thesis, Queen's University, Canada.

51 Player (1972) *The White Rhino Saga* (p16).

52 Player (1972).

53 John Gordon Davis (1972) *Operation Rhino*, Michael Joseph, London.

54 K Hillman and E Martin (1979) 'Will poaching exterminate Kenya's rhinos?', *Oryx* 15: 131–132.

55 See Notes and News (1980) 'Selling rhinos to extinction', *Oryx* 15: 322–3; Markus Borner 'Black rhino disaster in Tanzania', *Oryx* 16 (1): 59–66 and Notes and News (1981) 'SSC in New Delhi' *Oryx* 16: 14–15.

56 See Dan Brockington (2002) *Fortress Conservation: the preservation of the Mkomazi Game Reserve, Tanzania*, James Currey, Oxford.

57 The pastoralists lost: the High Court ruled that they were recent immigrants who did not have ancestral customary rights; see Brockington (2002) *Fortress Conservation*. The debate about Mkomazi grows in scale and passion: see Ian Parker (2002) 'Mkomazi – a cause célèbre?', *Swara*, 25 (3): 40–42.

58 www.rhinos-irf.org/technicalprograms/afrsg/.

59 www.rhinos-irf.org/technicalprograms/afrsg/.

60 Marcus Borner (1981) 'Black rhino disaster in Tanzania', *Oryx* 16 (1): 59–66.

61 This is discussed by, among others, Gregg Mitman (1996) 'When nature *is* the Zoo: vision and power in the art and science of natural history', *OSIRIS* 11: 117–143.

62 Donald Goddard (1995) 'A great campaign of conservation' in Donald Goddard (ed) *Saving Wildlife: a century of conservation*, Harry N Abrams with the Wildlife Conservation Society, New York, pp42–46 (p42).

63 Editorial Notes, *Journal SPFE* (1946) 54: 4–10, (p9).

64 Obituary Sir Peter Chalmers-Mitchell, *Journal SPFE* (1945) 52: 13–14.

65 P Chalmers-Mitchell (1929) *Centenary History of the Zoological Society of London*, Zoological Society of London, London.

66 Bernhard Grzimek (1956) *No Room for Wild Animals*, trans R H Stevens), Thames and Hudson, London; Bernhard Grzimek and Michael Grzimek (1960) *Serengeti Shall Not Die* (trans E L and D Rewald), Collins, London.

67 See wcs.org. The African Plains exhibit is analysed by Mitman (1996)'When nature *is* the Zoo', *OSIRIS* 11.

68 Captain K Caldwell (1927) 'The commercialization of game', text of lecture delivered in Nairobi August 1926, *Journal SPFE* 7: 83–90 (p97). He also felt that while it was acceptable for recognized zoos to have wild animals, the commercial interest in their collection was regrettable.

69 D Seth-Smith (1930) 'Zoological collections – the future outlook', *Journal SPFE* 10: 21–4 (p24).

70 Seth-Smith (1930).

71 Report of Executive Committee submitted to General Meeting, 17 February 1928, *Journal SPFE* 1928: 28–33.

72 *Oryx* 1981, 'Notes and news', *Oryx* 16 (2).

73 See wcs.org.

74 See Richard Fitter (1967) 'Conservation by captive breeding: a general survey', *Oryx* 9 (2): 87–96.

75 Editorial Notes, *Journal SPFE* (1946) 54: 4–10 (p9). This statement followed a letter from a Mr le Souef asking the Zoological Society of London to ask the British government to call a meeting to discuss international cooperation for

conservation, and outlining his plans for 'a series of large breeding establishments' for wildlife in Australia, Malaya, India, Nigeria, Uganda, Natal and British Guiana that could pay for themselves by selling surplus stock to zoos.

76   For a recent review of tranquilizers, see Steven A Osofsky and Karen J Hirsch (2000) 'Chemical restraint of endangered mammals for conservation purposes: a practical primer', *Oryx* 34 (1): 27–33.

77   'How can zoos help wildlife conservation?' *Oryx* (1964) 7: 215–217.

78   Peter Scott (1967) 'The role of zoos in wildlife conservation', *Oryx* 9: 82–86 (p86).

79   'Capture programmes for rare animals', *Oryx* (1969) 10: 175.

80   See Gerald Durrell (1964) *Menagerie Manor*, R Hart Davis, London; Douglas Botting (1999) *Gerald Durrell: the authorized biography*, HarperCollins, London.

81   Paul Leyhausen (1977) 'Breeding endangered species', *Oryx* 13: 427–428; R S R Fitter (1980) 'Breeding endangered species', *Oryx* 15: 230.

82   Fitter (1980).

83   The classic account of the reintroduction of the captive breeding and reintroduction of the Arabian oryx is by Mark Stanley-Price (1989) *Animal reintroductions: the Arabian oryx*, Cambridge University Press, Cambridge.

84   The Arabian oryx is *Oryx leucoryx*. The others are the gemsbok in South Africa, the scimitar-horned oryx of the Sahel and the Beisa oryx of the Horn of Africa and East Africa.

85   I A Nader (1989) 'Rare and endangered mammals of Saudi Arabia', in A H Abuzinada, P D Goriup and I A Nader (eds) *Wildlife Conservation and Development in Saudi Arabia, Riyadh*, NCWCD, Publication No.3, Riyadh, pp220–233.

86   Major Ian R Grimwood (1962) 'Operation Oryx', *Oryx* 6: 308–334.

87   To add insult to injury, they were hunting unsportingly from cars.

88   A narrative of the expedition is Anthony Shepherd's (1965) *Flight of the Unicorns*, Elek Books, London. He donated half the advance royalties of this book to the society.

89   By the end of 1962, donations of £3797 had been received, the balance of £853 being paid by the FPS General Reserve Fund.

90   Anthony Shepherd (1965) *Flight of the Unicorns*.

91   Grimwood (1962) 'Operation Oryx'.

92   Ian Grimwood (1964) 'Operation Oryx: the second stage', *Oryx* 7 (5): 223–225.

93   Ian Grimwood (1964) 'Operation Oryx: the three stages of captive breeding', *Oryx* 9 (2): 110–118.

94   Grimwood (1964) 'Operation Oryx: the three stages of captive breeding'.

95   Celebrated by a symposium at London Zoo

96   Richard Fitter (1980) 'Operation Oryx – End of Phase One' *Oryx* 15: 227–228.

97   Stéphanie Ostrowski, Eric Bedin, Daniel M Lenain and Abdulazis H Abuzinada (1998) 'Ten years of Arabian oryx conservation in Saudi Arabia – achievements and regional perspectives', *Oryx* 32 (3): 209–222.

98   John Clarke (1977) 'Reserve for the Arabian oryx', *Oryx* 14 (1): 31–35.

99   Richard Fitter (1982) 'Arabian oryx returns to the wild' *Oryx* 16 (5): 406–410.

100 H Jungius (1978) 'Plan to restore Arabian oryx in Oman', *Oryx* 14 (4): 329–336.

101 Richard Fitter (1984) 'Operation Oryx – the success continues', *Oryx* 18 (3): 136–137. The whole oryx reintroduction experience is reviewed by Mark Stanley-Price (1989) *Animal reintroductions: the Arabian oryx*, Cambridge University Press, Cambridge.

102 J A Spalton, M W Lawrence and S A Brend (1999) 'Arabian oryx reintroduction in Oman: successes and setbacks', *Oryx* 33: 168–175.

103 Ostrowski, Bedin, Lenain and Abuzinada (1998) 'Ten years of Arabian oryx conservation in Saudi Arabia', *Oryx* 32: 209–222.

104 Spalton, Lawrence and Brend (1999) 'Arabian oryx reintroduction in Oman'.

105 www.peregrinefund.org/conserv_maurkest.html.

106 Richard Fitter (1974) '25 years on: a look at endangered species', *Oryx* 12 (3): 341–346.

107 Clio Smeeton and Ken Weagle (2000) 'The reintroduction of the swift fox *Vulpes velox* to south central Saskatchewan, Canada', *Oryx* 34: 171–179.

108 Graeme Caughley and Anne Gunn (1996) *Conservation Biology in Theory and Practice*, Blackwell Science, Oxford.

109 See US Fish and Wildlife service website, news.fws.gov/NewsReleases/ R1/8DA3E747-C3F9-4AC4-8884C9410847B2B4.html (May 2003). The California Condor Recovery Program is a partnership between the US Fish & Wildlife Service, the Los Padres National Forest, California Department of Fish and Game, San Diego Wild Animal Park, Los Angeles Zoo, and the Peregrine Fund's World Center for Birds of Prey.

110 News.fws.gov/NewsReleases/R1/8DA3E747-C3F9-4AC4-8884C9410847 B2B4.html (May 2003).

111 Jenny C Daltry, Quentin Bloxam, Gillian Cooper, Mark L Day, John Hartley, McRonnie Henry, Kevel Lindsay and Brian E Smith (2001) 'Five years of conserving the 'world's rarest snake', the Antiguan racer *Alsophis antiguae*', *Oryx* 35 (2): 119–127. See also www.antinguanracer.org.

112 Daltry et al (2001).

113 C W Hobley (1924) 'The protection of wild life', Paper to the Museums Association 14 July 1924, *Journal SPFE* 4: 26–34 (pp33–34). He urged that not every museum should aim to possess specimens of rare species, and suggested that a limited number should be based where the benefit to science was greatest.

114 General Meeting SPFE London Zoo, 15 April 1929, *Journal SPFE* (1929): 23–29 (p28).

115 Vice Chairman of SPFE to AGM 7 December 1931, *Journal SPFE* 15: 4–11.

116 A H Harcourt and K Curry-Lindahl (1978) 'The FPS Mountain Gorilla Project – a report from Rwanda', *Oryx* 14 (4): 316–324.

117 Harcourt and Curry-Lindahl (1978).

118 A H Harcourt (1979) 'The Mountain Gorilla Project: a progress report', *Oryx* 15 (1): 10–11.

119 A H Harcourt (1979) 'The Mountain Gorilla Project: progress report 2', *Oryx* 15: 114–115.

120 A H Harcourt (1979) 'The Mountain Gorilla Project: progress report 3', *Oryx* 15: 324–325.

121   C Aveling and R Aveling (1981) 'Mountain Gorilla Project: Progress report 4', *Oryx* 16: 135–138.

122   Roger Wilson (1983) 'Mountain Gorilla Project: Progress report 5', *Oryx* 17: 52–53.

123   Roger Wilson (1983) 'Mountain Gorilla Project: Progress report 6', *Oryx* 18: 223–229.

124   'News and Views' *Oryx* (1978): 14 (p193).

125   Harcourt (1979) 'The Mountain Gorilla Project: progress report 2'.

126   Conrad, Veling Aveling and Rosalind Aveling (1989) 'Gorilla conservation in Zaire', *Oryx* 23: 64–70.

127   Nigel Leader-Williams and Holly T Dublin (2000) 'Charismatic megafauna as 'flagship species', in A Entwistle and N Dunstone (eds) *Priorities for the Conservation of Mammalian Diversity. Has the panda had its day?*, Cambridge University Press, Cambridge, pp53–81.

128   J M Pearson and P Scott (1965) '"Save the Flamingo": was it a good idea? Two views of a rescue operation', *Oryx* 8: 48–51 (p50).

129   Evan Bowen-Jones and Abigail Entwistle (2002) 'Identifying appropriate flagship species: the importance of culture and local contexts', *Oryx* 36 (2): 189–195.

130   Bowen-Jones and Entwistle (2002). On the reserve, see www.fauna-flora.org/around_the_world/world_main_frame.htm.

131   For Common Ground, see www.commonground.org.uk. The 'cultural turn' in British conservation is discussed in W M Adams (2003) *Future Nature: a vision for conservation*, Earthscan, London (revised edition).

132   www.plantlife.org.uk.

133   John Rosenow (12001) 'What role for national trees in promoting biodiversity conservation?' *Oryx* 35: 1–2.

134   See www.arborday.org.

135   One captive breeding icon of that era was Père David's deer, extinct in the wild in China since 1900, although famously preserved in captivity by the Duke of Bedford at Woburn Abbey in England. In 1998 deer were released experimentally into a reserve in Jiangsu Province, China. Maybe even that icon of captivity can be returned to the wild. Huijan Hu and Zhigang Jiang (2002) 'Trial release of Père David's deer *Elaphurus davidianus* in the Dafeng Reserve, China', *Oryx* 36: 196–199.

136   Julian Huxley (1963) address to IUCN 8th General Assembly in Nairobi, September 1963 *Oryx* 7: 154.

CHAPTER 7 THE DEMANDS OF DEVELOPMENT

1   Morges Manifesto, signed by Jean Baer, Charles Bernard, François Bourlière, Wolfgang Burhenne, Ed Graham, Kai Curry-Lindahl, Eurgen Gerstenmeier, Julian Huxley, Max Nicholson, Erico Nicola, Peter Scott and Barton Worthington in 1961, prior to the establishment of the World Wildlife Fund.

2   An image of this kind can be viewed on-line at NASA's Earth Observatory website see earthobservatory.nasa.gov/masthead.html. A version of a similar image can be downloaded from photojournal.jpl.nasa.gov/catalog/PIA02991.

3   The Operational Linescan System.

4   See John Weier (2000) 'Bright Lights Big City', earthobservatory.nasa.gov/ Study/Lights/, 19 October 2000.

5   David Oates (1992) *Earth Rising: ecological belief in an age of science*, Oregon State University Press, Corvalis, Oregon.

6   Quoted in David Oates (1992, p12).

7   F Osborn (1954) *The Limits of the Earth,* Faber and Faber, London, p11.

8   K E Boulding (1966) 'The economics of the coming spaceship earth', in *Environmental Quality in a Growing Economy*, reprinted in H E Daly (ed) (1973) *Towards a Steady-state Economy*, W H Freeman, New York, pp121–32.

9   B Ward and R Dubos (1972) *Only One Earth: the care and maintenance of a small planet*, André Deutsch, London.

10   E Max Nicholson (1970) *The Environmental Revolution: a guide for the new masters of the world*, Hodder and Stoughton, London, p83.

11   Thomas Malthus (1798) *An Essay on the Principle of Population, as it Affects the Future Improvement of Society with Remarks on the Speculations of Mr Godwin, M Condorcet, and Other Writers,* J Johnson, London.

12   J Maddox (1972) *The Doomsday Syndrome*, Macmillan, London; for classic neo-Malthusian work, see P R Ehrlich (1972) *The Population Bomb*, Ballantine, London.

13   Paul R Ehrlich and Anne H Ehrlich (1970) *Population, Resources and Environment: issues in human ecology*, W H Freeman, New York, p3.

14   J W Forrester (1971) *World Dynamics*, Wright-Allen Press, Cambridge, MA.

15   D Meadows, J Randers and W W Behrens (1972) *The Limits to Growth*, Universe Books, New York. The Club of Rome was backed by European multinational companies, see R Golub and J Townsend (1977) 'Malthus, multinationals and the Club of Rome', *Social Studies of Science* 7: 202–222.

16   J Maddox (1972) *The Doomsday Syndrome*.

17   W Beckerman (1974) *In Defence of Economic Growth*, Jonathan Cape, London, p242; J L Simon (1981) *The Ultimate Resource*, Princeton University Press, Princeton, NJ, p286.

18   See for example R J Goodland, H E Daly and S E Serafy (1993) 'The urgent need for rapid transition to global sustainability', *Environmental Conservation* 20: 297–309; A Jansson, M Hammer, C Folke and R Costanza (eds) (1994) *Investing in Natural Capital: the ecological economics approach to sustainability*, Island Press, Washington DC.

19   US Census Bureau, 1995: *Urban and Rural Population 1900–1990*, Suitland, MD.

20   L Hannah et al, (1994) 'A preliminary inventory of human disturbance of world ecosystems', *Ambio* 23: 246–250.

21   Eric W Sanderson, Malanding Jaiteth, Marc A Levy, Kent H Redford, Antoinette V Wannebo and Gillian Woolmer (2002) 'The Human footprint and the last of the wild', *BioScience* 52: 891–904.

22   Peter M Vitousek, Paul R Ehrlich, Anne H Ehrlich and Pamela A Matson (1986) 'Human appropriation of the products of photosynthesis', *BioScience* 36: 368–373 (p372).

23   Peter M Vitousek, Harold A Mooney, Jane Lubchenco, Jerry M Melillo (1997) 'Human domination of Earth's ecosystems', *Science* 277 (25 July): 494–499 (p498).

24   Stephen Palumbi (2001) 'Humans as the world's greatest evolutionary force', *Science* 293 (7 September): 1786–1790.

25   Mathis Wackernagel and William Rees (1996) *Our Ecological Footprint: reducing human impact on earth*, New Society Publishers, Gabriola Island, British Columbia.

26   G P Marsh (1864) *Man and Nature; or, physical geography as modified by human action*, Scribners, New York; Sampson Low, London (reprinted Harvard University Press, 1965).

27   Marsh (1864, p36).

28   Marsh (1864, p36).

29   Marsh (1864, pp36, 39).

30   H Paul Jeffers (2003) *Roosevelt the Explorer: Teddy Roosevelt's amazing adventures as a naturalist, conservationist, and explorer*, Taylor Trade Publishing, Lanham, New York.

31   William Beinart and Peter Coates (1995) *Environment and History: the taming of nature in the USA and South Africa*, Routledge, London, p56.

32   Minutes of General Meeting, 17 February 1928, *Journal SPFE* 1928: 20–27 (p21).

33   Lines, W (1991) *Taming the Great South Land: A History of the Conquest of Nature in Australia.* Allen and Unwin, Sydney; Gordon W Whitney (1994) *From Coastal Wilderness to Fruited Plain: a history of environmental change in temperate North America from 1500 to the present*, Cambridge University Press, Cambridge; Beinart and Coates (1995) *Environment and History.*

34   Editorial Note, *Journal SPWFE* (1908): 9–10 (p9).

35   Minutes of proceedings at a deputation from the SPWFE to the Right Hon Alfred Lyttelton (His Majesty's Secretary for the Colonies), 2 February 1905, *Journal SPWFE* (1905): 9–18 (p11).

36   'The Year', *Journal SWPFE* (1905): 5–8 (p7).

37   These terms are all potentially problematic, and to all intents and purposes interchangeable. To some people, the phrase 'Third World' is redundant given the collapse of the Iron Curtain (the communist 'Second World'). To others the concept of 'less developed' implies an inevitable linear path of change, the likelihood of continuous improvement, and that certain countries are lacking something that is by definition desirable.

38   Michael J Watts (1995) 'A new deal in emotions: theory, practice and the crisis of development', in Jonathan Crush (ed) *Power of Development*, Routledge, London, pp44–62; see also Michael P Cowen and Robert W Shenton (1996) *Doctrines of Development,* Routledge, London.

39   See Raymond Murphy (1994) *Rationality and Nature: a sociological enquiry into a changing relationship*, Westview Press, Boulder, CO.

40   R Drayton, (2000) *Nature's Government: science, imperial Britain and the 'improvement' of the World,* Yale University Press, New Haven.

41   Wolfgang Sachs (1992) *The Development Dictionary*, Zed Books, London, p2.

42   G Esteva, (1992) 'Development', in W Sachs (ed) *The Development Dictionary: a guide to knowledge as power*, Zed Books, London, pp6–25.

43   W Sachs (1992) 'Introduction', in W Sachs (ed) *The Development Dictionary: a guide to knowledge as power*, Zed Books, London, pp1–5 (p3, p1).

44 'Preservation of Game', Extract from Lord Cromer's Report for Egypt and the Sudan for the year 1903, Item 11, *Journal SPWFE* (1903) 1: pp 68–70 (p70).

45 'Preservation of Game', Extract from Lord Cromer's Report for Egypt, (p70).

46 F Gillet (1908) 'Game Reserves', *Journal SPWFE* 1908: 42–45 (p43).

47 Keith Caldwell (1924) 'Game preservation: its aims and objects', lecture to Kenya and Uganda Natural History Society 14 March 1924, *Journal SPFE* 4: 45–59 (p45).

48 Deputation to the Secretary of State for the Colonies 5 March 1930, *Journal SPFE* 11: 11–16 (p11).

49 James Stevenson-Hamilton (1907) 'Opposition to game reserves', *Journal SPWFE* 3: 53–59 (p55).

50 Editorial 'Hope deferred', *Journal SPFE* (1945) 52: 9.

51 Deputation to the High Commissioner for the Union of South Africa 6 May 1925, *Journal SPFE* 1925: 29–35 (p26).

52 Statement of Policy on Colonial Development and Welfare, Cd 6175, 1940.

53 Colonial Development and Welfare, *Journal SPFE* 39 (1940): 17–19, (p18).

54 Earl of Onslow (1941) 'Science and the conservation of the wild life of the world', *Journal SPFE* 44: 8–14.

55 See for example G V Jacks and R O Whyte (1938) *The Rape of the Earth: a world survey of soil erosion*, Faber and Faber, London; A Aubréville (1949) *Climats, Forêts et Désertification de l'Afrique Tropicale*, Société d'Edition Géographiques, Maritimes et Coloniales, Paris; J-P Harroy (1949) *Afrique: terre qui meurt: la dégradation des sols Africains sous l'influence de la colonisation*, Marcel Hayez, Brussels.

56 See for example D M Anderson, (1984) 'Depression, dust bowl, demography and drought: the colonial state and soil conservation in East Africa during the 1930s', *African Affairs* 83: 321–344, and W Beinart (1984) 'Soil erosion, conservation and ideas about development: a Southern African exploration 1900–1960', *Journal of Southern African Studies* 11: 52–84.

57 L Robin, (1997) 'Ecology: a science of empire?', in T Griffiths and L Robin (eds) *Ecology and Empire: environmental history of settler societies*, Keele University Press, Keele, pp63–75.

58 D C Jones (1987) *Empire of Dust: settling and abandoning the Prairie Dry Belt*, University of Alberta Press, Edmonton.

59 James Giblin (1990) 'Trypanosomiasis control in African history: an evaded issue?', *Journal of African History* 31: 59–80; the classic study of sleeping sickness is John Ford (1971) *The Role of Trypanosomiases in African Ecology: a study of the tsetse fly problem*, Clarendon Press, Oxford.

60 See Giblin (1990) 'Trypanosomiasis control in African history'.

61 Luise White (1995) 'Tsetse visions: narratives of blood and bugs in colonial Northern Rhodesia, 1931–9', *Journal of African History* 36: 219–245.

62 Martinez Lyons (1985) 'From "death camps" to *cordon sanitaire*: the development of sleeping sickness policy in the Uele District of the Belgian Congo, 1903–1914', *Journal of African History* 26: 69–91 (p81).

63 John MacKenzie (1988) *The Empire of Nature: hunting, conservation and British imperialism*, Manchester University Press; John Ford (1971) *The Role of Trypanosomiases in African Ecology: a study of the tsetse fly problem*, Clarendon Press, Oxford.

64 Giblin (1990) 'Trypanosomiasis control in African history'.

65   Ford (1971) *The Role of Trypanosomiases in African Ecology*, p338.

66   See Giblin (1990) 'Trypanosomiasis control in African history', and the fate of the cattle enterprise of the Spiritan Order in the Wami Valley, Uzigua, in the first decade of the century.

67   See Leroy Vail (1977) 'Ecology and history: the example of eastern Zambia', *Journal of African History* 3: 129–155, and White (1995) 'Tsetse visions', *Journal of African History* 36.

68   Quoted in Ford (1971) *The Role of Trypanosomiases in African Ecology* (p73).

69   SPWFE (1909) Minutes of proceedings at a deputation of the SPWFE received by the Right Hon the Earl of Crewe (Principal Secretary of State for the Colonies) at the Colonial Office. *Journal SPWFE* 5: 11–27.

70   MacKenzie (1988) *The Empire of Nature*, p237.

71   See Ford (1971) *The Role of Trypanosomiases in African Ecology* (p345, Map 20.2). Over half the extra land allotted to Africans under the Land Apportionment Act of 1930 was in the fly belt.

72   Major Stevenson-Hamilton (1907) 'Opposition to game reserves', *Journal SPWFE* 3: 53–59 (pp58–59).

73   See, for example, E N Buxton (1913) 'Further Correspondence relating to the preservation of wild animals in Africa', presented to Parliament, March 1913, *Journal SPWFE* 6: 72–5.

74   See for example E N Buxton in the Minutes of proceedings at a deputation of the SPWFE received by the Right Hon the Earl of Crewe (Principal Secretary of State for the Colonies) at the Colonial Office. *Journal SPWFE* 5: 11–27 (p12).

75   Editor (1913) 'Introduction', *Journal SPWFE* 6: A2.

76   SPWFE Meeting of 16 June 1913; the SPWFE's members of the Committee were Prof Mitchell, E E Austen, F C Selous, E N Buxton, and Rhys Williams; Manuscript, FFI Archives.

77   Society's meeting on 24 February 1914; Manuscript, FFI Archives.

78   See Shirley J Brooks (2001) *Changing Nature: a critical history of the Umfolozi and Hluhluwe game reserves, Zululand, 1887–1947*, PhD thesis, Kingston, Ontario.

79   Sabi (1922) 'Empire Fauna in 1922', *Journal SPFE* (1922) (2): 38–43; see also MacKenzie (1988) *The Empire of Nature*.

80   Deputation to the Secretary of State for the Colonies 21 April 1925, *Journal SPFE* 5: 25–28 (p27). The delegation also discussed other matters, including the administration of the Malay States Game Ordinance of 1925.

81   The SPWFE had dropped the word 'wild' from their title after the First World War. The Strategy was discussed at the SPFE meeting on 27 February 1925. The meeting with the Under Secretary of State for the Colonies, the Hon W G A Ormsby-Gore took place on 21 April 1925, *Journal SPFE* (1925): 25–28. The Deputation to the High Commissioner for the Union of South Africa took place on 6 May 1925, *Journal SPFE* 5: 29–35.

82   Deputation to the High Commissioner for the Union of South Africa 6 May 1925, *Journal SPFE* 5: 29–35 (p31).

83   Deputation to the High Commissioner for the Union of South Africa 6 May 1925, *Journal SPFE* 5: 29–35.

84   Deputation to the High Commissioner for the Union of South Africa 6 May 1925, *Journal SPFE* 5: 29–35 (p34).

85   P Matthiessen and B Douthwaite (1985) 'The impact of tsetse fly control on African Wildlife', *Oryx* 19: 202–209.

86   *Journal SPFE* Editorial: 1945: vol 52: p9.

87   P Matthiessen and B Douthwaite (1985) 'The impact of tsetse fly control on African Wildlife', *Oryx* 19: 202–209. Some 17,000 sq km was cleared in Uganda between 1947 and 1976.

88   For a contemporary and pessimistic view of conservation in West Africa, see John F Oates (1999) *Myth and Reality in the Rain Forest: how conservation strategies are failing in West Africa*, University of California Press, Berkeley.

89   Matthiessen and Douthwaite (1985). 'The impact of tsetse fly control on African Wildlife'. In Nigeria, 10,000 sq km of riverine forest was cleared 1912–1960.

90   Executive Committee SPFE 14 May 1934, *Journal SPFE* 23: 7–10.

91   Meeting SPFE 15 April 1935, *Journal SPFE* 26: 7–11. It was noted that Imperial Chemical Institute were seeking an alternative preparation.

92   *Oryx* (1957) 'Editorial Notes', *Oryx*, IV (1): 1–3.

93   See for example John Sheail's masterly account (1985) *Pesticides and Nature Conservation: the British experience 1950–1975*, Clarendon Press, Oxford.

94   Rachel Carson (1963) *Silent Spring*, Hamilton, London.

95   Matthiessen and Douthwaite (1985). 'The impact of tsetse fly control on African Wildlife'.

96   M Redfern (1986) 'Tsetse traps stop trypanosomiasis', *New Scientist* 27 February: 22.

97   For example W E Ormerod (1986) 'A critical study of the policy of tsetse eradication', *Land Use Policy* 3: 85–99.

98   W E Ormerod and L R Rickman (1988) 'Sleeping sickness control: how wildlife and man could benefit', *Oryx* 22: 36–40 (p36).

99   Matthiessen and Douthwaite (1985) 'The impact of tsetse fly control on African Wildlife', (p206).

100   In E N Buxton (1913) 'Further correspondence relating to the preservation of wild animals in Africa', presented to Parliament March 1913, *Journal SPWFE* 1913: 72–5 (p73).

101   Minutes of proceedings at a deputation from the SPWFE to the Right Hon Alfred Lyttelton (His Majesty's Secretary for the Colonies), 2 February 1905, *Journal SPWFE* (1905) (2): 9–18 (p16).

102   C R S Pitman (1933) Report of address to SPFE 13 March 1933, *Journal SPFE* 19: 8–10.

103   See E N Buxton and Lord Cranworth in the Minutes of proceedings at a deputation of the SPWFE received by the Right Hon the Earl of Crewe (Principal Secretary of State for the Colonies) at the Colonial Office, February 26 1909, *Journal SPWFE* 5: 11–27 (p13).

104   Minutes of proceedings at a deputation of the SPWFE received by the Right Hon the Earl of Crewe (Principal Secretary of State for the Colonies) at the Colonial Office, February 26 1909, *Journal SPWFE* 5: 11–27 (p12).

105   S H Whitbread (1907) 'The Year', *Journal SPWFE* 3, pp 10–13 (p.10).

106   John McCormick (1992) *The Global Environmental Movement: reclaiming Paradise*, Belhaven, London, (p37).

107   John McCormick (1992) *The Global Environmental Movement*, and Samuel P Hays (1959) *Conservation and the Gospel of Efficiency: the progressive conservation movement 1890–1920*, Harvard University Press, Cambridge..

108   Munro, D A (1978) 'The thirty years of IUCN's *Nature and Resources* 14(2): 14–18 (p14).

109   The UK delegation had met and discussed matters the preceding April at a conference in Tanganyika. Captain Keith Caldwell 'The Bukavu Conference', *Oryx* 2: 234–237.

110   John McCormick (1992) *The Global Environmental Movement*, p43.

111   Kai Curry-Lindajl (1969) 'The new African conservation convention', *Oryx* 10: 116–126.

112   McCormick (1992) *The Global Environmental Movement*, p46.

113   McCormick (1992, p46).

114   M T Farvar and J P Milton (eds) (1973) *The Careless Technology: ecology and international development*, Stacey, London.

115   M Holdgate (1999) *The Green Web: a union for world conservation*, Earthscan, London, p108.

116   On the evolution of sustainable development thinking, see below, and William M Adams (2001) *Green Development: environment and sustainability in the Third World*, Routledge, London; on the Johannesburg Summit see www.johannesburgsummit.org.

117   R F Dasmann, J P Milton and P H Freeman (1973) *Ecological Principles for Economic Development*, Wiley, Chichester.

118   Dasmann, Milton and Freeman (1973, pp21–22).

119   This section draws extensively on Sheail (1976) *Nature in Trust: the history of nature conservation in Britain*, Blackie, Edinburgh.

120   Executive Committee 4 December 1933, *Journal SPFE* 21: 11–14.

121   Lieut Col C L Boyle (1954) 'Sea Pollution: British call for action by all maritime countries', *Oryx* 2 (4): 212–215.

122   There was an appeal in *Oryx* for support for the Oil Pollution Campaign. Ten guineas were sent from FPS' own funds.

123   *Report of the Committee on the Prevention of Pollution of the Sea by Oil*, HMSO, London.

124   Boyle (1954) 'Sea Pollution'.

125   Oil Pollution Conference, *Oryx* 6 (5): 299 (1962).

126   See http://www.davidaxford.free-online.co.uk/torreycn.htm, 30 July 2001.

127   £54,000 was raised, including gifts from the New York Zoological Society (used on a survey of unpolluted marine life in Bantry Bay, Ireland).

128   On Windscale see Catherine Canfield (1989) *Multiple Exposures: chronicles of the radiation age*, Secker and Warburg, London. On Three Mile island see www.tmia.com. On Chernobyl, see www.chernobyl.com. For a sample of environmentalist positions on energy, see Friends of the Earth's website, www.foe.co.uk/campaigns/climate.

129   C L Boyle (1968) 'Oil pollution of the sea', *Oryx* (1969) 10 (1): 43–45.

130   Marc Reisner (1986) *Cadillac Desert: the American West and its disappearing waters*, Peregrine Books, New York.

131   Tom Turner (1991) *Sierra Club: 100 years of protecting nature*, Harry N Abrams with the Sierra Club, New York.

132   E Abbey (1975) *The Monkey Wrench Gang*, J B Lippincott, New York.

133   See, for example, P McCully (1996) *Silenced Rivers: the ecology and politics of large dams*, Zed Press, London, and www.narmada.org/.

134   A M V Boyle (1957) 'The International Union for the Conservation of Nature and Natural Resources Fifth General Assembly Excursions', *Oryx* 4 (1): 43–46. Surprisingly, Boyle suggested of Glen Lyon 'it is hard to think that the bare glen may not be improved by the small lochs which will result' (p44).

135   The Rt Hon Lord Hurcomb (1956) 'Hydro-electric works and nature', *Oryx* 3 (4): 188–191 (p189).

136   Tilapia, Melanopleura and Macrochir, at a rate of 10 tons per year. R A Critchley (1959) '"Operation Noah"', *Oryx* 5 (3): 100–107.

137   See D Howarth (1961) *The Shadow of the Dam*, Collins, London.

138   The Southern Rhodesian team consisted of six white game rangers, a vet and 48 African staff, with 4 boats (Critchley (1959) 'Operation Noah', *Oryx* 5: 100–107.

139   Critchley (1959, p102).

140   On the campaign against the loss of 530 hectares of species-rich rainforest in the Silent Valley Forest Reserve on the Nilgiri Plateau in India, see J S Singh, S P Singh, A K Saxena and Y S Rawat (1984) 'India's Silent Valley and its threatened rainforest ecosystems', *Environmental Conservation* 11: 223–33. In 1983, David Bellamy (council member and later Vice President of the FPS) was arrested protesting against the construction of the Gordon-below-Franklin Dam in Tasmania, which would flood one of the last three temperate rain forests on earth, and a World Heritage Site.

141   See P H Freeman (1977) *Large Dams and the Environment: recommendations for development planning*, Report for United Nations 1977 Water Conference, IIED, London; ICOLD (1981) *Dam Projects and Environmental Success*, International Commission on Large Dams, Paris.

142   R E Munn (ed) (1979) *Environmental Impact Assessment: principles and procedures*, SCOPE Report No 5, Wiley, Chichester; see J Barrow (1997) *Environmental and Social Impact Assessment: an introduction*, Arnold, London.

143   Patrick McCully (1996) *Silenced Rivers: the ecology and politics of large dams*, Zed Press, London; W M Adams (2001) *Green Development: environment and sustainability in the Third World*, Routledge, London.

144   World Commission on Dams (2000) *Dams and Development: a new framework for decision-making*, Earthscan, London.

145   John Terborgh (1999) *Requiem for Nature*, Island Press, Washington DC (p142).

146   M Jacobs (1995) 'Sustainable development, capital substitution and economic humility: a response to Beckerman', *Environmental Values* 4: 57–68 (p65).

147   Sources here and subsequently are primarily M Holdgate (1999) *The Green Web: a union for world conservation*, Earthscan, London; John McCormick (1992) *The Global Environmental Movement: reclaiming Paradise*, Belhaven, London; and William M Adams (2001) *Green Development: environment and sustainability in the Third World*, Routledge, London.

148   IUCN (1980) *The World Conservation Strategy*, International Union for Conservation of Nature and Natural Resources, United Nations Environment Programme, World Wildlife Fund, Geneva.

149   IUCN (1980, para i).

150 H Brundtland (1987) *Our Common Future*, Oxford University Press, Oxford, for the World Commission on Environment and Development); IUCN (1991) *Caring for the Earth: a Strategy for Sustainability*. International Union for the Conservation of Nature, Gland, Switzerland; N Robinson (ed) (1993) *Agenda 21: Earth's action plan*, Oceana Publications, New York (IUCN Environmental Policy and Law Paper No 27).

151 P Chatterjee, and M Finger (1994) *The Earth Brokers: power, politics and world development*, Routledge, London.

152 WRI, IUCN and UNEP (1992) *Global Biodiversity Strategy: guidelines for action to save, study and use Earth's biotic wealth sustainably and equitably*, World Resources Institute, Washington. On these developments, see Holdgate (1999).

153 V Shiva (1997) *Biopiracy: the plunder of nature and knowledge*, South End Press, Boston, MA.

154 See M Pimbert (1997) 'Issues emerging in implementing the Convention on Biological Diversity', *Journal of International Development*, 9: 415–425; S Bragdon (1996) 'The Convention on Biological Diversity', *Global Environmental Change* 6: 177–9. The Convention's website is www.biodiv.org.

155 www.un.org/esa/sustdev/csd/about_csd.htm.

156 www.developmentgoals.org/. The others goals are to eradicate extreme poverty and hunger, to achieve universal primary education, to promote gender equality and empower women, to reduce child mortality, improve maternal health, to combat HIV/AIDS, malaria, and other diseases, and to build a global partnership for development.

157 www.developmentgoals.org/Environment.htm.

158 www.johannesburgsummit.org/html/documents/summit_docs/2309_ planfinal.htm.

159 The radical and reformist strands within sustainable development are analysed by Adams (2001) *Green Development*.

160 See www.biodiv.org/meetings/gbc-2010/.

CHAPTER 8 TRADING NATURE

1   R W G Hingston (1930) 'The Oxford University expedition to British Guiana', *Geographical Journal* 76: 1–24 (p403).

2   Captain K Caldwell (1927) 'The commercialization of game', lecture delivered in Nairobi, August 1926, *Journal SPFE* 7: 83–90 (p86).

3   A real case from 1986: in the event Colchester Zoo looked after them and the FPS arranged that they be sent back to a wildlife sanctuary in Ibiza. In 1986 also, the FPS tipped off the Department of the Environment to stop the sale of illegally imported butterflies, some with the label 'protected fauna'. Arising from this, Sotheby's auction house considered a ban on all sales of natural history specimens.

4   See www.cites.org.

5   See Jon Hutton and Barnabas Dickson (eds) (2000) *Endangered Species, Threatened Convention: the past, present and future of CITES*, Earthscan, London; and Sara Oldfield (2003) *The Trade in Wildlife: regulation for conservation*, Earthscan, London.

6   R B Martin (2000) 'When CITES works and when it does not', in Hutton and Dickson (eds) *Endangered Species, Threatened Convention*, pp29–37.
7   World Conservation Monitoring Centre (1988) *Annotated CITES Appendices and Reservations*, WCMC, Cambridge.
8   Minutes of proceedings at a deputation from the SPWFE received by the Right Hon the Earl of Crewe KG (Principal Secretary of State for the Colonies), 26 February 1909, *Journal SPWFE* (1909) 4: 11–27 (p19).
9   H Seton-Karr (1908) 'The Preservation of Big Game', *Journal SPWFE* 4: 26–28 (p27).
10   Seton-Karr (1908, p27).
11   Seton-Karr (1908) Extract from Lord Cromer's Report for Egypt and the Sudan for the year 1902, Item 11, *Journal SPWFE* 1: 61–67 (p62 and 63).
12   Keith Caldwell (1924) 'Game preservation: its aims and objects', lecture to Kenya and Uganda Natural History Society 14 March 1924, *Journal SPFE* 4: 45–59 (p53).
13   Caldwell (1927) 'The commercialization of game', *SPFE Journal* 7. *Shamba* is Swahili for farm.
14   Caldwell (1924) 'Game preservation', *Journal SPFE* 4 (p51).
15   Caldwell (1924, p48).
16   Editorial, *Journal SPFE* 1930: 16–18 (p16).
17   Caldwell (1927) 'The commercialization of game', p83.
18   On American sporting versus subsistence and commercial hunting, see Karl Jacoby (2001) *Crimes Against Nature: squatters, poachers, thieves and the hidden history of American conservation*, University of California Press, Berkeley.
19   Caldwell (1927) 'The commercialization of game', p87.
20   W T Hornaday, 24 March 1909, letter to Rhys Williams, *Journal SPWFE* 5 (1909): 56–8 (p57).
21   Rhys Williams for the SPWFE to Colonial Office, 5 November 1907, *Journal SPWFE* 5: 49–50 (p49).
22   Rhys Williams for the SPWFE to Colonial Office, 5 November 1907, *Journal SPWFE* 5: 15 May 1908, *Journal SPWFE* 5: 52; see also Editorial Note, *Journal SPWFE* 4: 9–10 (p9).
23   Rhys Williams for the SPWFE to Colonial Office, 15 May 1908, *Journal SPWFE* 5: 52.
24   SPWFE (1909) 'Minutes of proceedings at a deputation of the SPWFE received by the Right Hon the Earl of Crewe (Principal Secretary of State for the Colonies) at the Colonial Office', *Journal SPWFE* 5: 11–27.
25   *Journal SPFE* New Series 1: 16.
26   The SPFE received a letter from the Revenue Secretary to the Government of Burma reporting that protection had been secured in 1922 at its meeting in October 1922.
27   Minutes of Meeting 20 July 1923, *Journal SPFE* 1924. It was resolved to write to the Musée du Congo.
28   Minutes of meeting 20 July 1923, *Journal SPFE* 1924. Minutes of proceedings at a deputation from the SPWFE received by the Right Hon the Earl of Crewe KG (Principal Secretary of State for the Colonies), 26 February 1909, *Journal SPWFE* 5: 11–27 (p14).
29   Meeting, 20 June 1924.

30   Editorial (1921) *Journal SPFE* 1: 15–17.

31   Letter requested October 1922 Meeting, reported received 10 April 1923.

32   Meeting, 22 January 1924.

33   General Meeting SPFE London Zoo, 10 December 1928, *Journal SPFE* 9: 12–14.

34   Minutes of meeting of SPFE, 24 March 1922. In 1927, Keith Caldwell called for a government monopoly on ivory, and an agreement under the league of nations to bring trade abuses to light, see Caldwell (1927) 'The commercialization of game', *Journal SPFE* 7.

35   Inaugural address to an international Fisheries Exhibition in London, reported in D H Cushing, (1988) *The Provident Sea*, Cambridge University Press, Cambridge.

36   The ancient rise and modern demise of the Newfoundland cod fishery is described by Mark Kurlansky (1999) *Cod: a biography of the fish that changed the world*, Vintage, London (originally published 1997).

37   This account is taken from A Finlayson and B J McCay (1998) 'Crossing the threshold of ecosystem resilience: the commercial extinction of northern cod', in F Berkes and C Folke (1998) (eds) *Linking Social and Ecological Systems: management practices and social mechanisms for building resilience*, Cambridge University Press, Cambridge, pp 311–337.

38   Cushing (1988) *The Provident Sea*.

39   Cushing (1988).

40   See, for example, Kai Curry-Lindahl (1982) 'A tale of mismanagement at sea', *Oryx* 16 (5): 415–420.

41   Minutes of proceedings at a deputation for the SPWFE received by the Right Hon the Earl of Crewe KG (Secretary of State for the Colonies) 26 February 1909, *Journal SPWFE* 5: 11–27 (p26).

42   Manuscript, FFI Archives.

43   Editorial, *Journal SPFE* 8: 30–37 (p35).

44   Editorial, *Journal SPFE* 8: 40–2; 2900 were killed in 1925, 1900 in 1926.

45   Meeting SPFE, 15 April 1935, *Journal SPFE* 26: 7–11.

46   C Elton (1927) *Animal Ecology*, Sidgwick and Jackson, London.

47   Minutes of meeting SPFE, 25 April 1927, *Journal SPFE* 7: 13–15.

48   Report of Executive Committee submitted to General Meeting, 17 February 1928, *Journal SPFE* 8: 20–23. The sea otter was protected by an order in Council under the Sea Fisheries Act, see Minutes of meeting SPFE, 17 February 1928, *Journal SPWFE* 1927: 20–27.

49   General Meeting SPFE London Zoo, 4 November 1929, *Journal SPFE* (1930): 5–10; see also Editorial, *Journal SPFE* 9: 30–37 (p35). The SPFE thought the salvation of fur-bearing species might come in the domestication of fur-bearing species and the fur-fabric industry.

50   www.audubon.org.

51   John Sheail (1976) *Nature in Trust: the history of nature conservation in Great Britain*, Blackie, Edinburgh.

52   Minutes of proceedings at a deputation from the SPWFE received by the Right Hon the Earl of Crewe KG (Principal Secretary of State for the Colonies), 26 February 1909, *Journal SPWFE* 5: 11–27 (p15).

53 Minutes of proceedings at a deputation from the SPWFE received by the Right Hon the Earl of Crewe KG (Principal Secretary of State for the Colonies), 26 February 1909, *Journal SPWFE* 5: 11–27 (p15).

54 Minutes of meeting SPFE, 17 February 1928, *Journal SPWFE* 1927: 20–27.

55 William T Hornaday (1921) 'Post-war game conditions in America', *Journal SPFE* (1921) 1: 53–8 (p55).

56 Editorial, *SPFE Journal* (1929): 30–37 (p35).

57 Randall Reeves (1982) 'What hope for the North Atlantic Right Whales?', *Oryx* 16 (3): 255–262.

58 See www.iwcoffice.org.

59 For example Sidney Holt (1983) 'Who really threatens whales and seals?', *Oryx* 17 (2): 68–77. See J Cherfas (1988) *The Hunting of the Whale: a tragedy that must end*, The Bodley Head; R F Nash (1989) *The Rights of Nature: a history of environmental ethics*, University of Wisconsin Press, Madison; P J Stoett (1997) *The International Politics of Whaling*, UBC Press.

60 Valerie Boyle (1951) 'The International Union for the Protection of Nature technical meeting, The Hague, 19th–22nd September, 1951', *Oryx* 1: 204–210.

61 The USSR did the same in 1987.

62 For the classic account of environmental sabotage see Edward Abbey (1975) *The Monkey Wrench Gang*, J B Lippincott, New York.

63 Richard Fitter (1973) 'Whaling – almost a victory', *Oryx* 12 (2): 186–187. The FPS contributed £200 towards the cost of the appeal for the implementation of the moratorium. Those who signed it included Peter Scott, Julian Huxley, and Frank Fraser Darling, the Duke of Edinburgh and Prince Bernhard of the Netherlands.

64 *Oryx* 12 (2): 187.

65 Richard Fitter reported in 1979 that the IWC adopted a nine-fold increase in whaling quotas against the advice of its scientific advisory committee as a result of Japanese claims (*Oryx* 14 (3)).

66 Richard Fitter (1980) 'Last profits in whales', *Oryx* 15 (5): 437–438.

67 Richard Fitter (1981) 'Whaling bans – another inch forward', *Oryx* 15: 1213–1214.

68 See Greenpeace, http://whales.greenpeace.org.

69 Richard Fitter (1974) Notes and Views, *Oryx*.

70 Richard Fitter (1980) 'Last profits in whales', p437.

71 Richard Fitter (1967) 'Conservation by captive breeding: a general survey', *Oryx* 9 (2): 87–96.

72 Minutes of general meeting SPFE, 14 July 1949, *Journal SPFE* 60: 39–40 (p49). Interestingly, Captain Caldwell argued that the treatment of animals after capture was not covered by a game licence, and that the alternative to sale to zoos was shooting.

73 Barton Worthington was an experienced tropical ecologist, with extensive experience in the East African Great Lakes. In the 1930s he had travelled the length of Africa with Lord Hailey, researching his *An African Survey* (1938, Oxford University Press), see E B Worthington (1983) *The Ecological Century: a personal appraisal*, Cambridge University Press, Cambridge.

74 Martin Holdgate (1999) *The Green Web: a union for world conservation*, Earthscan, London.

75   Annual Report of the Year ending 31 December 1963, *Oryx* 7 (4): 196–197.
76   *Oryx* (1967) 'Orang utans confiscated in Borneo', *Oryx* 9 (1): 18; Tom Harrison (1965) 'A future for Borneo's wildlife?', *Oryx* 8: 99–100.
77   Annual Report of the Year ending 31 December 1963, *Oryx* 7 (4): 196–197.
78   *Oryx* (1964) 'Fifty thousand leopards to make coats and handbags', *Oryx* 7 (4): 155–156.
79   *Oryx* (1967) 'Fun Furs', *Oryx* 9 (3): 189–192 (reprinted from the *New Yorker Magazine*).
80   *Oryx* 8 (1): 12.
81   Peter Scott and Richard Fitter acted as two of the negotiators for IUCN.
82   Felipé Benavides (1972) 'The persecuted majority', *Oryx* 11: (5).
83   *Oryx* (1973) 12 (2).
84   *Oryx* (1973) 12 (2).
85   The Ramsar Convention grew out of out of IUCN's Project Mar. This had a preliminary information collection stage, followed by a conference in the Camargue in 1962 (A. Daubercies (1963) 'Wetlands Conference in the Carmargue', *Oryx* 7 (1): 39–40). In 2003 there were 136 Contracting Parties to the Convention, with 1267 wetland sites, totaling 107.5 million hectares, designated for inclusion in the Ramsar List of Wetlands of International Importance, see www.ramsar.org.
86   See whc.unesco.org. The flooding of the Abu Simbel temples by the Aswan Dam in 1959 provided the stimulus for the convention.
87   Holdgate (1999) *The Green Web*.
88   *Oryx* (1973) 'Convention to control the rare animal trade', *Oryx* 12 (2): 188–194.
89   David Evans (1992) *A History of Nature Conservation in Britain*, Routledge, London.
90   These were Brambell, Corbett, Grandison and Fitter.
91   See Sarah Oldfield (1987) *Fragments of Paradise: A Guide for Conservation Action in the UK Dependent Territories*, British Association of Nature Conservationists and World Wildlife Fund, Oxford.
92   For details, see www.cites.org/eng/disc/how.shtml.
93   See the history of TRAFFIC at www.traffic.org. The first member of staff was Tim Inskipp. TRAFFIC's US office opened in 1979.
94   For the curious, and taxonomically gifted, these are listed on www.cites.org.
95   Chris Huxley (2000) 'CITES: the vision', in Jon Hutton and Barnabas Dickson (eds) *Endangered Species, Threatened Convention: the past, present and future of CITES, the Convention on International Trade in Endangered Species of Wild Fauna and Flora*, Earthscan, London, pp3–12.
96   'Notes and News', *Oryx* 14: 97–98.
97   Michael 't Sas-Rolfes (2000) 'Assessing CITES: four case studies', in Hutton and Dickson *Endangered Species, Threatened Convention*, pp69–87.
98   For Humane Society of the United States, see www.hsus.org; for Friends of Animals, see www.friendsofanimals.org; for IFAW see www.ifaw.org.
99   Rosaleen Duffy (2000) *Killing for Conservation: wildlife policy in Zimbabwe*, James Currey, Oxford.
100   See Chris Huxley (2000) 'CITES: the vision', in Hutton and Dickson *Endangered Species, Threatened Convention*, pp3–12; Morné A du Plessis (2000)

'CITES and the causes of extinction', in Hutton and Dickson *Endangered Species, Threatened Convention*, pp13–25.

101   The application of CITES in the case of the Nile crocodile is reviewed by Henriette Kievit (2000) 'Conservation of the Nile crocodile: has CITES helped or hindered?', in Hutton and Dickson *Endangered Species, Threatened Convention*, pp88–97.

102   The importance of ideas on sustainable utilization drawn from ecology for mainstream thinking about sustainable development is explored in W M Adams (2001) *Green Development: environment and sustainability in the Third World*, Routledge, London.

103   Michael 't Sas-Rolfes (2000) 'Assessing CITES', in Hutton and Dickson (eds) *Endangered Species, Threatened Convention*.

104   See Jon Hutton (2003) 'Crocodiles: legal trade snaps back', in Sara Oldfield (ed) *The Trade in Wildlife: regulation for conservation*, Earthscan, London, pp108–120.

CHAPTER 9 CONSERVATION'S PLAN

1   John Terborgh (1999) *Requiem for Nature*, Island Press, Washington DC, p170.

2   See for example Wayne L Linklater (2003) 'Science and management in a conservation crisis: a case study with Rhinoceros', *Conservation Biology* 17: 968–975. The model stages of crisis and response are population decline, crisis management, stabilization and recovery. Linklater argues that the distinction between pure and applied research is unhelpful.

3   For an example of such reflection, see Nick Salafsky, Richard Margoluis, Kent H Redford and John G Robinson (2002) 'Improving the practice of conservation: a conceptual framework and research agenda for conservation science', *Conservation Biology* 16: 1469–1479.

4   www.conservation.org

5   www.fauna-flora.org/our_partners/our_main_frame.htm.

6   See, for example, the Conservation International Annual Report, conservation.org/xp/CIWEB/about/annual_report.xml.

7   Reviewed by, for example, Graeme Caughley and Anne Gunn (1996) *Conservation Biology in Theory and Practice*, Blackwell Science, Oxford.

8   See M D Jennings (2000) 'Gap analysis: concepts, methods and recent results', *Landscape Ecology* 15: 5–20; Peter C Howard, Paolo Viskanic, Tim R B Davenport, Fred W Kigenyi, Michael Baltzer, Chris J Dickenson, Jeremiah S Lwanga, Roger Matthews and Andrew Balmford (1998) 'Complementarity and the use of indicator groups for reserve selection in Uganda', *Nature* 394: 472–475.

9   C R Margules and R L Pressey (2000) 'Systematic conservation planning', *Nature* 405: 243–253.

10   R L Pressey (1994) 'Ad Hoc reservations: forward or backward steps in developing representative reserve systems, *Conservation Biology* 8: 662–668 (p669).

11   www.biodiversityscience.org/xp/CABS/home. CABS also runs an open web-based 'Knowledge Management System' as a platform for users to search, organize, store and share conservation and scientific information and files

related to people (contacts, expertise directories), organizations, documents, datasets, projects, news and discussions – see cabs.kms.conservation.org// WOMBAT/application/home.cfm.

12   Norman Myers, Russell A Mittermeier, Christina G Mittermeier, Gustavo A B de Fonseca and Jennifer Kent (2000) 'Biodiversity hotspots for conservation priorities', *Nature* 403: 853–858.

13   Norman Myers (1988) 'Threatened biotas: "hotspots" in tropical forests', *Environmentalist* 8: 187–208.

14   For example Lincoln D C Fishpool and Michael I Evans (2001) *Important Bird Areas in Africa and Associated Islands: priority sites for conservation*, Pices Publications Newbury for BirdLife International.

15   David M Olson and Eric Dinerstein (1998) 'The Global 200: a representation approach to conserving the earth's most biologically valuable ecoregions', *Conservation Biology* 12: 502–515.

16   www.awf.org.

17   See nature.org.

18   Details of how to help on the TNC website, nature.org.

19   For details of FFI's thoughts on its methodology, see www.fauna-flora.org/about_us/about_main_frame.htm. The common characteristics of FFI projects are that they have global reach and scientific credibility, exhibit careful planning, long-term vision, pragmatism, quality assurance, and that there is effective local participation to ensure that conservation solutions are community driven.

20   G M Mace, A Balmford, L Boitani, G Cowlishaw, A P Dobson, D P Faith, K J Gaston, C J Humphries, R I Vane-Wright and P H Williams (2000) 'Its time to work together and stop duplicating conservation efforts', *Nature* 405: 393.

21   Kent H Redford, Peter Coppolillo, Eric W Sanderson, Gustavo A B de Fonseca, Eric Dinerstein, Craig Groves, Georgina Mace, Steward Maginnis, Russell A Mittermeier, Reed Noss, David Olson, John G Robinson, Amy Vedder and Michael Wright (2003) 'Mapping the conservation landscape', *Conservation Biology* 17: 116–131.

22   See, for example, Michael Edwards and David Hulme (eds) (1996) *Beyond the Magic Bullet: NGO performance and accountability in the post-Cold War world*, Kumarion Press, West Hartford, Connecticut.

23   P Chatterjee and M Finger (1994) *The Earth Brokers: power, politics and world development*, Routledge, London.

24   John Terborgh (1999) *Requiem for Nature* (pxi and title to Chapter 5).

25   J F Oates (1999) *Myth and Reality in the Rain Forest: how conservation strategies are failing in West Africa*, University of California Press, Berkeley.

26   J F Oates (1995) 'The dangers of conservation by rural development – a case study from the forests of Nigeria', *Oryx* 29: 115–122.

27   John Terborgh (1999) *Requiem for Nature* (p192).

28   John Terborgh (1999, p170).

29   John Terborgh (1999, p58). He believes the only solution is resettlement of indigenous communities within the park.

30   The costs and benefits of conservation are reviewed by Lucy Emerton (2001) 'The nature of benefits and the benefits of nature: why wildlife conservation has not economically benefited communities in Africa', in D Hulme and M

Murphree (eds) *African Wildlife and Livelihoods: the promise and performance of community conservation,* James Currey, London, pp208–226.

31   See Emerton (2001). Gross tourist revenues were US$419 million, half of which was estimated to be due to wildlife (US$210).

32   C W Hobley (1928) 'Game as a commercial asset', *Journal SPFE* 8: 94–97.

33   M Honey (1999) *Ecotourism and Sustainable Development: who owns paradise?* Island Press, Washington DC.

34   M J Walpole and H J Goodwin (2001) 'Local attitudes towards conservation and tourism around Komodo National Park, Indonesia', *Environmental Conservation* 28, 160–166; on ecotourism see Lisa M Campbell (2002) 'Conservation narratives and the "received wisdom" of ecotourism: case studies from Costa Rica', *International Journal of Sustainable Development* 5: 300–325.

35   Lucy Emerton (2001) 'The nature of benefits and the benefits of nature: why wildlife conservation has not economically benefited communities in Africa', in Hulme and Murphree *African Wildlife and Livelihoods*, pp208–226.

36   See the work by D S Wilkie and J F Carpenter (1999) 'Can nature tourism help finance protected areas in the Congo Basin'? *Oryx* 33 (4): 332–338, and 'The potential role of safari hunting as a potential source of revenue for protected areas in the Congo Basin?' *Oryx* 33 (4): 339–345.

37   On central Africa see D Brown (1998) 'Participatory biodiversity conservation: rethinking the strategy in the low tourist potential areas of tropical Africa', *ODI Natural Resource Perspectives* 33, August 1998, Overseas Development Institute, London; on Nepal see M P Bookbinder, E Dinerstein, A Rijal, H Canley and A Rajouria (1998) 'Ecotourism's support of biodiversity conservation', *Conservation Biology* 12: 1399–1404.

38   K Archabald and L Naughton-Treves (2001) 'Tourism revenue-sharing around national parks in Western Uganda: early efforts to identify and reward local communities', *Environmental Conservation* 28 (2): 135–149; T M Butynski and J Kalina (1998) 'Gorilla tourism: a critical look', in E J Milner-Gulland and R Mace (eds) *Conservation of Biological Resources*, Blackwell, Oxford, pp294–313; W M Adams and M Infield (2003) 'Who is on the gorilla's payroll? Claims on tourist revenue from a Ugandan National Park', *World Development* 31 (1): 177–190.

39   M Norton-Griffiths (1995) 'Economic incentives to develop the rangelands of the Serengeti: implications for wildlife conservation', in A R E Sinclair and P Arcese (eds) *Serengeti II: dynamics, management, and conservation of an ecosystem,* University of Chicago Press, Chicago, pp588–604.

40   A N James, K J Gaston and A Balmford (1999) 'Balancing the earth's accounts', *Nature* 401 (23 September), 323–324.

41   Alexander N James, Michael J B Green and James R Paine (1999) *A Global Review of Protected Area Budgets and Staff*, WCMC – World Conservation Press, Cambridge.

42   D S Wilkie and J F Carpenter (1999) 'Can nature tourism help finance protected areas in the Congo Basin?' *Oryx* 33 (4), 332–338.

43   M Norton-Griffiths and C Southey (1995) 'The opportunity costs of biodiversity conservation in Kenya', *Ecological Economics* 12, 125–139.

44   There is an excellent review of the position by Andrew Balmford and Tony Whitten (2003) 'Who should pay for tropical conservation, and how could the costs be met?', *Oryx* 37: 238–250.

45   Paul J Ferraro and R David Simpson (2000) 'The cost-effectiveness of conservation payments', *Resources for the Future Discussion Paper 00–31*.

46   Oates (1999) *Myth and Reality in the Rain Forest* (pxvi).

47   Discussions of this point include C B Barrett and P Arcese (1995) 'Are Integrated Conservation-Development Projects (ICDPs) Sustainable? On the conservation of large mammals in sub-Saharan Africa', *World Development* 23: 1073–1084; M Stocking and S Perkin (1992) 'Conservation-with-development: an application of the concept in the Usambara Mountains, Tanzania, *Transactions of the Institute of British Geographers N S* 17: 337–349; C Wainwright and W Wehrmeyer (1998) 'Success in integrating conservation and development? A Study from Zambia', *World Development* 26: 933–944.

48   M Stocking and S Perkin, (1992) 'Conservation-with-development'.

49   C C Gibson and S A Marks (1995) 'Transforming rural hunters into conservationists: an assessment of community-based wildlife management programs in Africa', *World Development* 23: 941–957.

50   Robert Chambers (1983) *Rural Development: putting the last first*, Longman, London.

51   See www.iucn.org/themes/ssc/susg.

52   www.iucn.org/themes/ssc/susg/timeline.html.

53   www.iucn.org/themes/ssc/susg/policystat.html.

54   See, for example, John G Robinson (2001) 'Using "sustainable use" approaches to conserve exploited populations', in J D Reynolds, G M Mace, K H Redford and J G Robinson (eds) *Conservation of Exploited Species*, Cambridge University Press, Cambridge, pp485–498.

55   C H Freese (1997) 'The "use it or lose it" debate', in C H Freese (ed) *Harvesting Wild Species: Implications for Biodiversity Conservation*, Johns Hopkins University Press, Baltimore and London, pp1–48.

56   On such arguments, see, for example, Randall Kramer, Carel van Schaik and Julie Johnson (1997) *Last Stand: protected areas and the defense of tropical biodiversity*, Oxford University Press, Oxford; Katrina Brandon, Kent Redford and Steven Sanderson (1998) *Parks in Peril: people, politics and protected areas*, Island Press, Washington DC; Terborgh (1999) *Requiem for Nature*.

57   See Jon M Hutton and Nigel Leader-Williams (2003) 'Sustainable use and incentive-driven conservation: realigning human and conservation interests', *Oryx* 37: 215–226.

58   See www.greatapeproject.org.

59   K H Redford and P Feinsinger (2001) 'The half empty forest: sustainable use and the ecology of interactions', in J D Reynolds, G M Mace, K H Redford and J G Robinson (eds) *Conservation of Exploited Species*, Cambridge University Press, Cambridge, pp370–399. On the failings of forest conservation in Africa, see Oates (1999) *Myth and Reality in the Rain Forest*.

60   Richard F W Barnes (2002) 'The bushmeat boom and bust in West and Central Africa', *Oryx* 36: 236–242.

61   See, for example, Evan Bowen-Jones (2003) 'Bushmeat: traditional regulation or adaptation to market forces', in Sara Oldfield (ed) *The Trade in Wildlife: Regulation for Conservation*, Earthscan, London, pp132–145.

62   On the growing debate, and the lack of simple answers, see for example the *Forum* papers in *Oryx* 36: 328–333, by Elizabeth Bennet et al, Stephen Ling

et al, Marcus Rowcliffe and John Robinson and Elizabeth Bennett. See also M Rao and P J K McGowan (2002) 'Wild meat use, food security, livelihoods and conservation', *Conservation Biology* 16: 580–583.

63   This distinction is drawn by Jon M Hutton and Nigel Leader-Williams (2003) 'Sustainable use and incentive-driven conservation: realigning human and conservation interests', *Oryx* 37: 215–226. They favour the phrase 'extractive use'.

64   Roderick P Neumann (1996) 'Dukes, Earls and ersatz Edens: aristocratic nature preservationists in colonial Africa', *Environment and Planning D: Society and Space* 14: 79–98.

65   Minutes of meeting SPFE 17 February 1928, *Journal SPWFE* 1927: 20–27, p26.

66   P L Sclater (1905) 'On the best mode of preserving the existence of the larger mammals of Africa for future ages', *Journal SPWFE* 1905: 46–50 (p49).

67   Extract from Sir Charles Eliot's reports on the British East Africa Protectorate for the years 1902 and 1903, *Journal SPWFE* (1903)1: 49–54. Interestingly, the eccentric Lord Rothschild trained zebras to pull a trap in rural Hertfordshire, see Miriam Rothschild (1983) *Dear Lord Rothschild: birds, butterflies and history*, Hutchinson, London.

68   See Jeremy Gavron (1993) *The Last Elephant: an African quest*, HarperCollins, London; Armand Denis (1963) *On Safari: the story of my life*, Collins, London.

69   Michael Crawford (1972) 'Conservation by utilisation', *Oryx* 11: 427–432, (p428).

70   Michael Crawford (1972, p428).

71   Letter from A M Harthoorn, Department of Veterinary Physiology, Makerere College Uganda to the *Veterinary Record* 27 October 1956 'comparison of food intake and growth-rate of the African buffalo (*Syncertus caffer*) with indigenous cattle: preliminary report', reprinted in *Oryx* (1959) 5: 18–19.

72   'The International Union for the Conservation of Nature and Natural Resources African Special Project, Stage I', *Oryx* 6: 143–170.

73   'The International Union for the Conservation of Nature and Natural Resources African Special Project, Stage I', *Oryx* 6: 143–170 (p159).

74   Peter Jenkins (2001) 'Wildlife use in World War II', in Ian Parker and Stan Bleazard (eds) *An Impossible Dream: some of Kenya's last colonial wardens recall the Game Department in the British Empire's closing years*, Librario, Milton Brodie, Kinloss, pp39–41.

75   Ian Parker (2001) 'The Galana Game Management Scheme', in Parker and Bleazard *An Impossible Dream*, pp165–174.

76   E B Worthington (1961) *The Wild Resources of East and Central Africa*, HMSO, London, Colonial Office No 352.

77   R M Bere 'The hippopotamus problem and experiment', *Oryx* 5 (3).

78   J Morton Boyd (1965) 'Research and Management in East African wildlife', *Nature* 208 (5013): 828–830.

79   E B Worthington (1960) 'Dynamic conservation in Africa', *Oryx* 6: 341–345.

80   Worthington (1961) *The Wild Resources of East and Central Africa*.

81   M Wells and K Brandon (1992) *People and Parks: linking protected area management with Local Communities*, World Bank, Washington.

82   Edward B Barbier (1992) 'Community-based development in Africa', in T M
      Swanson and E B Barbier (eds) *Economics for the Wilds: wildlife, wildlands, diversity
      and development*, Earthscan, London, pp103–135.

83   C C Gibson, and S A Marks (1995) 'Transforming rural hunters into
      conservationists: an assessment of community-based wildlife management
      programs in Africa', *World Development* 23: 941–957.

84   E Barrow and M Murphree (2001) 'Community conservation: from concept
      to practice', in Hulme and Murphree *African Wildlife and Livelihoods*, pp24–37.
      See D Western, R M Wright and S C Strum (1994) *Natural Connections:
      perspectives on community-based conservation,* Island Press, Washington; and K B
      Ghimire and M P Pimbert (1996) (eds) *Social Change and Conservation*,
      Earthscan, London.

85   Tomas Holmern, Elvin Røskaft, Job Mbaruka, Samson Y Makama and John
      Muya (2002) 'Uneconomical game cropping in a community-based conservation
      project outside the Serengeti National Park, Tanzania', *Oryx* 36: 364–372.

86   Letter from Theodore Hubback to Chairman of Fauna Society, 22 April 1924,
      on the preservation of the fauna of Malaya, *Journal SPFE* 4: 60–63.

87   Keith Caldwell (1924) 'Game preservation: its aims and objects', lecture to
      Kenya and Uganda Natural History Society, 14 March 1924, *Journal SPFE* 4:
      45–59 (p46).

88   C W Hobley (1938) 'The conservation of wild life: retrospect and prospect,
      Part II,' *Journal SPFE* 33: 39–49.

89   C W Hobley (1928) 'Game as a commercial asset', *Journal SPFE* 8: 94–97 (p97).

90   D S Wilkie and J F Carpenter (1999) 'The potential role of safari hunting as a
      potential source of revenue for protected areas in the Congo Basin?', *Oryx* 33:
      338–345.

91   Richard Luxmoore (1985) 'Game farming in South Africa as a force for
      conservation', *Oryx* 19: 225–231.

92   G Child (1995) Managing wildlife in Zimbabwe', *Oryx* 29: 171–177.

93   S Metcalfe (1994) 'The Zimbabwe Communal Areas Management Programme
      for Indigenous Resources (CAMPFIRE)', in D Western, R M White and S C
      Strum (eds) *Natural Connections: perspectives in community-based conservation*, Island
      Press, Washington, pp161–192.

94   M W Murphree (1994) 'The role of institutions in community-based
      conservation', in Western, White and Strum *Natural Connections*, pp403–427.

95   WWF (1997) *WWF Quota Setting Manual*, WWF Programme Office Zimbabwe,
      Zimbabwe Trust and Safari Club International, Harare.

96   J S Murombedzi (1999) 'Devolution and stewardship in Zimbabwe's
      CAMPFIRE Programme', *Journal of International Development* 11: 287–293.

97   I Bond (2001) 'CAMPFIRE and the incentives for institutional change', in
      Hulme and Murphree *African Wildlife and Livelihoods*, pp227–243. Data on 46
      wards 1989–1996; 10 per cent of money was unallocated, 2 per cent went to
      miscellaneous other uses.

98   Murombedzi (1999); J Murombedzi (2001) 'Why wildlife conservation has not
      economically benefited communities in Africa', in Hulme and Murphree
      African Wildlife and Livelihood, pp208–226.

99   James Murombedzi (2003) 'Devolving the expropriation of nature', in William
      M Adams and Martin Mulligan (eds) *Decolonizing Nature: strategies for conservation*

in a post-colonial era, Earthscan, London, pp135–151. On conflict see Sian Sullivan (2003) 'Protest, conflict and litigation: dissent or libel in resistance to a conservancy in North-West Namibia', in E Berglund and D M Anderson (eds) *Ethnographies of Conservation: environmentalism and the distribution of privelege*, Berghahn Press, Oxford.

100   Terborgh (1999) *Requiem for Nature*, p140.

101   Terborgh (1999, p199). The resonances between fascism and ecology and conservation are interesting – see David Pepper (1996) *Modern Environmentalism: an introduction*, Routledge, London.

102   This point is widely made by environmental and ecological economists. For a good exposition, see Edward B Barbier, Joanne C Burgess and Carl Folke (1994) *Paradise Lost? The ecological economics of biodiversity*, Earthscan, London.

103   Edward O Wilson (2002) *The Future of Life*, Little Brown, London, p29.

104   See Jon M Hutton and Nigel Leader-Williams (2003) 'Sustainable use and incentive-driven conservation: realigning human and conservation interests', *Oryx* 37: 215–226, and N Leader-Williams (2002) 'Animal conservation, carbon and sustainability', *Philosophical Transactions of the Royal Society of London A* 360: 1781–1806.

105   Steven Broad, Teresa Mulliken and Dilys Roe (2003) 'The nature and extent of legal and illgal trade in wildlife', in Sara Oldfield (ed) *The Trade in Wildlife: regulation for conservation*, Earthscan London, pp3–22.

106   www.fscoax.org/principal.htm.

107   Download from www.fauna-flora.org/around_the_world/global/flower_bulbs.htm.

108   Abigail Entwistle, Sema Atay, Andy Byfield and Sara Oldfield (2002) 'Alternatives for the bulb trade from Turkey: a case study of indigenous bulb propagation', *Oryx* 36: 333–341.

109   www.fauna-flora.org/around_the_world/global/trees.htm.

110   www.sanprota.com/about/about.htm.

CHAPTER 10 SOCIETY WITH NATURE

1   Jonathan Swift (2002) 'Vision is the art of seeing things invisible', in Wildlife Conservation Society (ed) *The Second Century*, Wildlife Conservation Society, New York, pp8–10.

2   Edward O. Wilson (2002) *The Future of Life*, Little Brown, London, p133.

3   Wilson (2002) *The Future of Life*, p156.

4   For a proper discussion of these issues, see David Harvey (1989) *The Condition of Postmodernity: an enquiry into the origins of cultural change*, Blackwell, Oxford, and (1966) *Justice, Nature and the Geography of Difference*, Blackwell, Oxford.

5   Wilson (2002) *The Future of Life* (p112).

6   L Hannah, G F Midgely, T Lovejoy, W J Bond, M Bush, J C Lovett, D Scott, and F I Woodward (2002) 'Conservation of biodiversity in a changing climate', *Conservation Biology* 16: 264–268.

7   Peter D Walsh, Kate A Abernethy, Magdalena Bermejo, Rene Beyers, Pauwel de Wachter, Marc Ella Akou, Bas Huijbregts, Daniel Idiata Mambounga, Andre Kamdem Toham, Annelisa M Kilbourn, Sally A Lahm, Stephanie Latour, Fiona

Maisels, Christian Mbina, Yves Mihindou, Sosthène Ndong Obiang, Ernestine Ntsame Effa, Malcolm P Starkey, Paul Telfer, Marc Thibault, Caroline E G Tutin, Lee J T White and David S Wilkie (2003) 'Catastrophic ape decline in western Equatorial Africa', *Nature* 422, 10 April 2003: 611–614.

8   On extinction see, for example, Richard Leakey and Richard Lewin (1995) *The Sixth Extinction*, Doubleday, New York; on what may be predicted, see Stuart L Pimm, Gareth J Russell, John L Gittleman and Thomas M Brooks (1995) 'The future of Biodiversity', *Science* 269: 347–350.

9   See R Murphy (1994) *Rationality and Nature: a sociological inquiry into a changing relationship*, Westview Press, Boulder, CO and J C Scott (1998) *Seeing Like a State: how certain schemes to improve the human condition have failed*, Yale University Press, New Haven.

10   William J Sutherland (2003) 'Parallel extinction risk and global distribution of languages and species', *Nature* 423, 15 May 2003: 276–279.

11   See www.undp.org/hdr2003/indicator/index_indicators.html.

12   David W Orr (2003) 'Diversity', *Conservation Biology* 17: 948–951 (p949).

13   Wilson (2002) *The Future of Life*, p164.

14   Terborgh (1999) *Requiem for Nature*, p79; see also Chapter 11 'hard choices in the twenty-first century'.

15   Edward Wilson (1992) *The Diversity of Life*, Harvard University Press, Cambridge, MA (p326).

16   David W Orr (2002) 'Four challenges of sustainability', *Conservation Biology* 16: 1457–1460.

17   Michael E Soulé (1995)'The social siege of nature', pp37–170 in Michael E Soulé and Gary Lease (eds) *Reinventing Nature? Responses to postmodern deconstruction*, Island Press, Washington, (pp137, 159).

18   Gary Lease (1995) 'Introduction: nature under fire', in Soulé and Lease *Reinventing Nature?*, pp3–15 (p10).

19   Donald Worster 'Nature and the disorder of history, pp65–85; Gary Paul Nabhan 'Cultural parallax in viewing north American habitats', pp87–101; Stephen R Kellert 'Concepts of nature east and west', pp103–121. All three in Soulé and Lease (eds) *Reinventing Nature?*

20   Michael E Soulé (1995) 'The social siege of nature', in Soulé and Lease (eds) *Reinventing Nature?*, pp37–170 (p162).

21   See the discussion of 'science and the sacred' in Kay Milton's book (2002) *Loving Nature: towards an ecology of emotion*, Routledge, London, especially the issue of the opposition to the superquarry on the island of Harris in the Outer Hebrides, Scotland.

22   See J K Rowling (1997) *Harry Potter and the Philosopher's Stone*, Bloomsbury, London. The power of the imaginary to awaken human awareness of nature should not be underestimated. See for example the work of the Fairyland Trust (www.fairylandtrust.org).

23   C S Holling (1986) 'The resilience of terrestrial ecosystems: local surprise and global change', in W C Clarke and R E Munn (eds) *Sustainable Development of the Biosphere*, Cambridge University Press, Cambridge, pp292–317.

24   Jane Guyer and Paul Richards (1996) 'The invention of biodiversity: social perspectives on the management of biological variety in Africa', *Africa* 66: 1–13, (p3).

25 Katrina Brown (2003) 'Three challenges for a real people-centred conservation', *Global Ecology and Biogeography* 12: 89–92.
26 See, for example, Fikret Berkes, Johan Colding and Carl Folke (2000) 'Rediscovery of traditional ecological knowledge as adaptive management', *Ecological Applications* 10: 1251–1262; Madhav Gadgil, Fikret Berkes and Carl Folke (1993) 'Indigenous knowledge of biodiversity conservation', *Ambio* 22: 151–156; Deep Naryan Pandey (2001) 'Cultural resources for conservation science', *Conservation Biology* 17: 633–635; Fikret Berkes (1999) *Sacred Ecology: traditional ecological knowledge and resource management*, Taylor and Francis, London.
27 See Samantha J Song and R Michael M'Gonigle (2001) 'Science, power and system dynamics: the political economy of conservation biology', *Conservation Biology* 15: 980–989.
28 Katrina Brown (2003) 'Three challenges for a real people-centred conservation'.
29 Sarah A Laird (ed) (2002) *Biodiversity and Traditional Knowledge: equitable partnerships in practice*, Earthscan, London. The People and Plants Initiative website is www.rbgkew.org.uk/peopleplants.
30 On sacred groves, see Madhav Gadgil and V D Vartak (1976) 'The sacred groves of Western Ghats in India', *Economic Botany* 30: 152–160.
31 There is a vast anthropological literature on ideas of nature. See for example Elisabeth Croll and David Parkin (1992) 'Anthropology, the environment and development', in E Croll and D Parkin (eds) *Bush Base: Forest Farm; culture, environment and development*, Routledge, London, pp3–10; Piers Vitebsky (1992) 'Landscape and self-determination aboung the Eveny: the political environment of Siberian reindeer herders today', in Croll and Parkin (eds) *Bush Base*, pp223–246; Tim Ingold (2000) *The Perception of the Environment: essays on livelihood, dwelling and skill*, Routledge, London.
32 James R Miller and Richard J Hobbs (2002) 'Conservation where people live and work', *Conservation Biology* 16: 330–337.
33 See the discussion in Kent H Redford and Brian D Richter (1999) 'Conservation of biodiversity in a world of use', *Conservation Biology* 13: 1246–1256.
34 See, for example, David Western (1989) 'Conservation without parks: wildlife in the rural landscape', in David Western and Mary Pearl (eds) *Conservation for the Twenty-first Century*, Oxford University Press, New York, pp158–165; Reed F Noss (1983) 'A regional landscape diversity approach to maintain diversity', *BioScience* 33: 700–706.
35 Wilson (1992) *The Diversity of Life*, p306.
36 Wilson (1992, p306).
37 Kay Milton (2002) *Loving Nature: towards an ecology of emotion*, Routledge, London, (pp100 and 108).
38 They leave primary school able to name 80 per cent of Pokémon characters but only 50 per cent of common types of wildlife: see Andrew Balmford, Lizzie Clegg, Tim Coulson and Jennie Taylor (2002) 'Why conservationists should heed Pokémon', *Science* 295: 2367.
39 Robert Michael Pyle (2003) 'Nature matrix: reconnecting people and nature', *Oryx* 37: 206–214 (pp206–7, 209).

40   Robert Michael Pyle (1993) *The Thunder Tree: lessons from an urban wildland*, Houghton Mifflin, Boston.

41   Wilson (1992) *The Diversity of Life*, p335.

42   See, for example, Lisa Naughton-Treves, Jose Luis Mena, Adrian Treves, Nora Alvarez and Volker Christian Radeloff (2003) 'Wildlife survival beyond park boundaries: the impact of slash-and-burn agriculture and hunting on mammals in Tambopata, Peru', *Conservation Biology* 17: 1106–1117.

43   William M Adams (2003) *Future Nature: a vision for conservation* (revised edition), Earthscan, London.

44   Robert Michael Pyle (2003) 'Nature matrix: reconnecting people and nature', *Oryx* 37: 206–214. For chapter and verse on restoration ecology, see M R Perrow and A J Davy (eds) (2002) *Handbook of Ecological Restoration*, Cambridge University Press, Cambridge (2 vols). For a divergent view, see William M Adams (2003) 'When nature won't stand still: conservation, equilibrium and control', in W M Adams and M Mulligan (eds) *Decolonizing Nature: strategies for conservation in a post colonial era*, Earthscan, London, pp220–246.

45   James R Miller and Richard J Hobbs (2002) 'Conservation where people live and work', *Conservation Biology* 16: 330–337.

46   Wilson (1992) *The Diversity of Life*, p335.

47   John Rodwell (2003) 'Human relationships with the natural world: an historical perspective', *Ecos: A Review of Conservation* 24 (1): 10–16 (p12).

48   See also Chapter 6; see www.commonground.org.uk.

49   John Cameron (2003) 'Responding to place in a post-colonial era' in Adams and Mulligan *Decolonizing Nature*, pp172–196.

50   Martin Mulligan (2001) 'Re-enchanting conservation work: reflections on the Australian experience', *Environmental Values* 10: 19–33; see also Martin Mulligan (2003) 'Feet to the ground in storied landscapes: disrupting the colonial legacy with a poetic politics', in Adams and Mulligan *Decolonizing Nature*, pp268–289.

51   Sue Clifford (2003) 'Attachment of the ordinary: valuing local distinctiveness', *Ecos: A Review of Conservation* 24 (1): 17–20.

52   C Stoate, R M Morris and J D Wilson (2001) 'Cultural ecology of Whitethroat (*Sylvia communis*) habitat management by farmers: winter farmland trees and shrubs in Senegal', *Journal of Environmental Management* 62: 343–356.

53   Wilson (1992) *The Diversity of Life*, p33.

54   Wilson (1992).

55   Raymond F Dasmann (1976) 'Life-styles and nature conservation', *Oryx* 13: 281–286 (p283). Raymond Dasmann died in 2002, see Radnall Jarrell (2003) 'Raymond F Dasmann: 1919–2002', *Conservation Biology* 17: 636–637.

56   Robert Michael Pyle (2003) 'Nature matrix: reconnecting people and nature', *Oryx* 37: 206–214 (p213).

Index

and Kariba Dam 174–5
and national parks 52, 99, 124
and oil pollution 172, 173
and wildlife trade 195, 196–7, 197–8
see also FFI; FFPS; SPFE; SPWFE
Friends of the Earth (FoE) 61, 207
funding 37–9, 40–1, 46, 50, 56–7, 65, 150, 212–13
fur trade 15, 188–9, 195, 196–7
fynbos biome (South Africa) 119

Gambia 95–6
game 16, 24, 32, 74, 168–9, 221–2
  and agriculture 71–2, 73, 90
  cropping 218–20
  licences 22, 33, 70, 75, 161, 220–1
  preservation 24–5, 28–30, 36–7, 47
  and sleeping sickness 162–7
game farms 221–2
game reserves 4, 24, 29–30, 70–3, 74–6, 89, 112, 136, 235–6
genetic engineering 157, 178
giant panda 25, 54, 128
giraffe 127, 129, 217
global economy 223–4, 240
globalization 229–30
Golden Stream Corridor Preserve (Belize) 123, 151
gorillas 11, 59, 116, 182, 216, 229
  lowland 2, 170
  mountain 1–3, 5–7, 15, 60, 147–50, 196
  tourism (gorilla watching) 6–7, 10, 148, 149, 150, 211
governments 29, 50, 55, 124, 145, 194
grazing 8, 69, 105, 114, 158, 162
great auk 20
Greenpeace 61, 192, 199–200
Grimwood, Ian 113, 139, 141–2
Grinell, George Bird 31, 32, 189
grizzly bear 122–3
Grzimek, Bernhard 67, 69, 95, 124, 138

habitats 17, 53, 123, 237
  loss 3, 57, 150–1, 200, 229
Hingston, Richard 89–91, 108, 148
hippopotami 22, 24, 73, 74, 127, 219, 220

Hobley, C W 46, 82, 84, 91, 111, 148, 221
Hornaday, William 36, 137, 139, 184, 228, 230
Humane Society of the United States, The 200
hunting 14, 20–1, 30–9, 44, 57, 109
  commercial 182–4
  licences 22, 33, 70, 75, 161, 220–1
  revenue from 38, 40–1, 75, 161, 220–3
  see also bushmeat; gorillas; local people; oryx; safaris
Huxley, Julian 54, 55, 60, 105, 137, 152, 228
  and protected areas 48, 52–3, 88, 113
Huxley, Thomas Henry (T H) 186, 187

ICBP (International Committee for Bird Protection) 44–5, 48, 63
ICDPs (integrated conservation and development projects) 121, 213
illegal trade 195–6, 199, 200–1, 201
in situ conservation 4, 15, 195
  species-focused 147–50
incentive-based conservation 224
India 30–1, 46–7, 82, 92, 94, 110, 133, 62, 63
  forest protection 22, 47
  Narmada River dams 174, 175
indigenous people 22, 79, 103–5, 119, 158, 161, 193, 234–5
  land rights 68, 114, 118–19
  see also evictions
industrialization 157, 158
insecticides 167–8
integrated conservation and development projects *see* ICDPs
international action 14, 43–6, 63–5, 186, 187–9, 194–5
International Committee for Bird Protection (ICBP) 44–5, 48, 63
International Office for the Protection of Nature *see* IOPN
International Union for Conservation of Nature and Natural Resources *see* IUCN
International Union for the Preservation of Nature *see* IUPN